INFORM P9-CCA-568 ES

C-4
TC

INFORMATION RESOURCES

ASYNCHRONOUS TRANSFER MODE

ELLIS HORWOOD SERIES IN COMPUTERS AND THEIR APPLICATIONS

Series Editor: IAN CHIVERS, Senior Analyst, The Computer Centre, King's College, London, and formerly Senior Programmer and Analyst, Imperial College of Science and Technology, University of London

Series continued at back of book

ASYNCHRONOUS TRANSFER MODE
Solution for Broadband ISDN

Second Edition

MARTIN de PRYCKER
Alcatel Bell, Antwerp, Belgium

ELLIS HORWOOD
NEW YORK   LONDON   TORONTO   SYDNEY   TOKYO   SINGAPORE

First published 1993 by
Ellis Horwood Limited
Campus 400, Maylands Avenue
Hemel Hempstead
Hertfordshire HP2 7EZ
and
Market Cross House, Cooper Street
Chichester, West Sussex, PO19 1EB
A division of
Simon & Schuster International Group

© Ellis Horwood Limited 1993

All rights reserved. No part of this publication may be reproduced,
stored in a retrieval system, or transmitted, in any form, or by any
means, electronic, mechanical, photocopying, recording or otherwise,
without prior permission, in writing, from the publisher.

Printed and bound in Great Britain
by Bookcraft, Midsomer Norton

British Library Cataloguing in Publication Data

A catalogue record for this book is available from
the British Library

ISBN 0–13–178542–7

Library of Congress Cataloging-in-Publication Data

Prycker, Martin de, 1955–
    Asynchronous transfer mode : solution for broadband ISDN /
Martin de Prycker. — [2nd ed.]
        p.   cm. — (Computer communications and networking)
    Includes bibliographical references and index.
    ISBN 0–13–178542–7
    1. Broadband communication systems. 2. Integrated services
digital networks. 3. Asynchronous transfer mode. 4. Local area
networks (Computer networks) I. Title. II. Series: Ellis Horwood
books in computing science. Series in computer communications
and networking.
TK5103.5.P79 1993
621.382—dc20   93–25395
                                                               CIP

---

1   2   3   4   5   97   96   95   94   93

To my wife Kaat
and my children Liesbeth, Thomas and Stefanie

To my parents

Table of Contents

**CHAPTER 1. EVOLUTION   TOWARDS   AN   INTEGRATED
BROADBAND COMMUNICATION NETWORK**

CHAPTER 2. TRANSFER MODES

CHAPTER 3. ATM STANDARDS

CHAPTER 8. INTRODUCTION STRATEGIES FOR ATM

Preface

The telecommunication networks of today are passing through a rapid evolution. In the early eighties, the first field trials with ISDN took place, with commercial introduction in the late eighties. The breakthrough of ISDN has not yet been achieved, maybe because of the lack of new attractive services and terminals.

This lack of attractive services can possibly be filled by a broadband network. This network can transport telecommunication services, like digital TV, digital HDTV, high quality videophony, high speed data transfer, video on demand, ... which are expected to be more attractive. To gain experience with those new services, researchers have already been experimenting with broadband networks and services since the beginning of the eighties.

The first standards for the broadband network have been defined by CCITT in the transmission domain. These are based on the SDH (Synchronous Digital Hierarchy) concept. This flexible transmission concept is also very interesting and directly applicable to the existing telecommunication networks.

Then the CCITT experts for broadband networks started with the definition of the broadband transfer mode. In 1988 there was only a very reduced recommendation with respect to broadband ISDN. It was already agreed then that ATM (Asynchronous Transfer Mode) would be the transfer mode for the future broadband ISDN (BISDN). Two years later, in 1990, CCITT SGXVIII had already prepared 13 recommendations, using the accelerated procedure. These recommendations define the basics of ATM and determine most of its parameters.

The first ideas on ATM and related techniques were published in 1983 by two research centers (CNET, AT&T Bell Labs). In 1984, the Research Center of Alcatel Bell in Antwerp started working on ATM, and actively contributed to technical and standardization work on this subject.

This book benefited largely of the expertise which has grown since then in the Research Center of Alcatel Bell. The large team of experts on ATM in Alcatel Bell has know-how on all ATM-related domains like the definition of ATM, ATM switching, ATM technology, ATM video coding, ATM traffic studies, etc.

The purpose of this book is to cover all aspects related to ATM. Its intention is to help telecommunication experts, who will start working on broadband ISDN, to acquire the necessary experience on ATM and related issues. Seeing the growing importance of telecommunications in graduate programs at universities, the book can also be used by graduate courses to build the basic ATM know-how and allow the students to start working on projects on more detailed topics such as ATM traffic studies, congestion control, etc.

Second edition

Since the first edition of this book in 1990, several important facts have occurred which have modified the situation with respect to ATM. I mention here the most important :

- CCITT has steadily continued its work with respect to standardization of ATM, filling in further the details related to operations and maintenance, transmission, and traffic characterization parameters. The new recommendations of CCITT are fully taken into account in a completely updated Chapter 3. The traffic parameters defined by CCITT need further clarification. These clarifications are given in a completely new Chapter 7.
- In 1991, the ATM Forum was created by CPE vendors, telecommunication equipment suppliers, public operators and others. The goal of the Forum is to promote ATM in the private environment. In addition, the ATM Forum has issued a number of specifications to guarantee interoperability of ATM equipment. The specifications of the ATM Forum are also described in the updated Chapter 3. In addition, ATM LANs began to appear as alternatives for High Speed LANs. For Chapter 6, a section has been added, explaining ATM in the private environment.
- In several countries, public telecommunication operators and private communication users, are installing or have plans to install ATM to offer various kinds of services. However, for a long time to come most of the existing services will be offered over the existing networks. Careful planning of the introduction of ATM is needed, to ensure an easy evolution to the full BISDN. Introduction strategies are therefore worked out for different parts of the network : private network, access network and switching network. In Chapter 8, some introduction strategies are explained for these 3 parts of the network.

In addition, I received several remarks with respect to the other parts of my book. These remarks have been taken into account in Chapters 1 to 6.

Contents

This book is composed of 8 Chapters, each discussing a particular item related to ATM. Every Chapter contains a detailed bibliography, to guide readers who want to study a particular topic in more detail. This bibliography contains a list of most of the recently published articles on that topic.

Chapter 1 describes the environment in which ATM has been defined. This means the requirements put forward by the market for a broadband network and the technology push, which shows a tremendous increase in performance of the available technologies.

Chapter 2 describes the history and evolution of ATM. Therefore, other possible candidate transfer modes for BISDN are first described. It is shown that ATM has a large number of benefits compared to the other candidate transfer modes. To define ATM in detail, a number of technical options have to be selected, with respect to functions and size of header and information field. These different options are described and compared.

In Chapter 3, a summary is given of the recommendations on ATM, as they are prepared by CCITT and the ATM Forum, based on its status in these bodies as of early 1993. The most important functions and parameters are explained.

Chapter 4 describes an important system to be developed for an ATM network, namely ATM switching systems. First, the key options to be taken by an ATM switching system are explained : queuing and routing. Then a selected number of ATM switching systems, as described in the literature, are explained in detail.

In Chapter 5, it is shown that ATM also has an impact on the edges of the network in the terminals. Different important aspects are discussed : terminal synchronization, the possibility to use variable bit rate video coding, the statistical multiplexing and the requirement to cope with cell loss.

Chapter 6 describes different MAN (Metropolitan Area Network) and ATM LAN topologies. These are FDDI, DQDB, Orwell and ATM LANs. In addition, performance characteristics of these systems are given.

Chapter 7 describes the traffic parameters which can be used to characterize an ATM stream : peak cell rate and sustainable cell rate. In addition, the cell delay variation parameter is explained, as well as usage parameter control and call acceptance control parameters.

Chapter 8 describes introduction strategies for ATM for 3 parts of the network : the private communication network, the public switching network and the public access network.

Acknowledgement

For this second edition, I wish to thank first both of my colleagues who contributed directly to this new edition :

- B. Pauwels who completely adapted Chapter 3 to the current status of the standards as defined by CCITT and the ATM Forum.
- G. Petit who prepared Chapter 7, describing the ATM traffic parameters.

I wish to acknowledge the support of the management of Alcatel Bell, which made it possible to use the know-how of the Research Center of Alcatel Bell on ATM. More specifically I would like to thank the complete staff of the Research Division of Alcatel Bell who contributed directly or indirectly to this book.

I would like to thank J. Boerjan, L. Corveleyn, E. Desmedt, D. Mestdagh, E. Osstyn, R. Peschi, G. Petit, K. Van Assche, T. Van Landegem, W. Verbiest and R. Wulleman for providing technical material or reviewing the manuscript for both editions.

In addition, the secretarial staff who has contributed to the preparation of both editions of this book is acknowledged. More specifically, L. Aerts, L. De Cock, A. De Povere, M. Dumoulin, T. Van Ballegooy, B. Vande Sompele and I. Van de Vyver.

1

Evolution towards an integrated broadband communication network

1.1. INTRODUCTION

In the evolution from the current telecommunication networks towards the Integrated Broadband Communication Network (IBCN) some important directions and guidelines have recently been made. IBCN is often referred to as the Broadband Integrated Services Digital Network (BISDN) since it is considered as a logical extension of the ISDN. The recent directions taken by the BISDN are influenced by a number of parameters, the most important being the emergence of a large number of teleservices with different, sometimes yet unknown requirements. In this information age, customers are requesting an ever-increasing number of new services. The most famous teleservices to appear in the future are HDTV (High Definition TV), video conferencing, high speed data transfer, videophony, video library, home education and video on demand.

Each of these services will generate other requirements for the BISDN. This large span of requirements introduces the need for one universal network which is flexible enough to provide all of these services in the same way.

Two other parameters are influencing the directions taken by the BISDN : they are the fast evolution of the semi-conductor and optical technology, and the evolution in system concept ideas, e.g. the shift of superfluous transport functions to the edge of the network. These system concept ideas are made possible by the technological progress which makes it possible to put more functions on a chip operating at a higher speed and the higher quality and higher speed of transmission systems. Due to these rapid advances in technology, solutions not feasible some years ago, will become economically available in the near future if produced in large quantities.

Both the need for a flexible network and the progress in technology and system concepts led to the definition of the Asynchronous Transfer Mode (ATM) principle. This ATM concept is now accepted as the ultimate solution for the IBCN by CCITT (the International Consultative Committee for Telecommunications and Telegraphy), and plans are being made by different entities to realize experimental

ATM pilots. Examples of these experiments are several RACE (Research for Advanced Communication in Europe) project trials (Tat, 1991), the Belgian broadband experiment (De Prycker, 1988), the US multigigabit project (Giga, 1990), the Japanese trial with ATM nodes, and an Australian experiment transporting ATM over satellite (Burston, 1990). In addition, several operators (in the US, Europe and Japan) have announced ATM pilot and commercial services in the 1993-94 time frame.

This book describes general technical problems related to ATM, independent of the private or public environment. However, seeing the success of ATM in the public domain, it is more oriented towards the public domain.

Indeed in the public telecommunication world, most of the communication services and equipment are under control of the operating companies (USA) or PTTs (Europe, Japan, Australia, ...). These organizations very much require that the delivered equipment is in line with the CCITT Recommendations. So, ATM equipment will in the future easily find its way in the public telecommunication domain.

In the private telecommunication environment, the services and equipment are privately owned. Here, two large groups of players are present : the telecommunications industry, and the computer industry. There is a trend to align the private world to the public world, to guarantee an overall worldwide compatibility, as can be seen by the IEEE 802.6 standard. This standard, worked out by a professional society but with a large impact on computer manufacturers, is as much as possible aligned to the ATM standards of CCITT.

A much more profound step was made by the ATM Forum, which is a non-profit organization, joining all types of industry (computer and telecommunication) with over 100 members worldwide. This Forum has defined ATM specifications based on the international standards, e.g. as defined by CCITT, for ATM systems to be installed in the customer premises network.

1.2. CURRENT SITUATION IN THE TELECOMMUNICATION WORLD

Today's telecommunication networks are characterized by specialization. This means that for every individual telecommunication service at least one network exists that transports this service. A few examples of existing public networks are described below :

- A telex network transports telex information, i.e. messages of characters, transported at very low speed (up to 300 bit/s). The characters are coded based on a specific 5 bit code (Baudot code).
- POTS (plain old telephone service) is transported via the public switched telephone network (PSTN). This ubiquitous network offers the customers classical two-way voice conversation.

- Computer data are transported in the public domain either by a packet switched data network (PSDN) based on X.25 protocols, or in a very limited number of countries by a circuit switched data network (CSDN) based on X.21 protocols.
- Television signals can be transported in three ways : broadcast via radio waves using ground antennae, by the coaxial tree network of the community antenna TV (CATV) network or recently via a satellite, using the so-called direct broadcast system (DBS).
- In the private domain, computer data are mainly transported by LANs (Local Area Networks). The most famous ones are Ethernet, token bus and token ring (IEEE 802 series).

Each of these networks was specially designed for that specific service and is often not at all applicable to transport another service. For instance, the original CATV networks did not allow the transportation of POTS; or the PSTN does not transport TV signals; or the transfer of voice over an X.25 network is very problematic because of a too large end-to-end delay and jitter on this delay.

Only in limited and special cases can service types other than the one the network was originally designed for be transported over it. This is for instance the case for the PSTN which is capable of transporting computer data at a limited speed, if modems are provided at both ends of the network.

An important consequence of this service specialization is the existence of a large number of often worldwide independent networks, each requiring its own design phase, manufacturing and maintenance. In addition, the dimensioning of each network must be done for every individual service type. Even if resources are freely available in one network, they cannot be used by another service type. For instance, the peak hours in the telephone network are between 9 a.m. and 5 p.m., whereas the peak hours in the CATV network are during evening. Since resource pooling is impossible each network must be dimensioned for its worst case traffic conditions which is the peak hour traffic.

A first step, albeit a limited one, towards a single universal network, is the introduction of NISDN (narrowband ISDN) in which voice and data are transported over a single medium. This network cannot transport TV signals due to its limited bandwidth capabilities, so a special TV network is still required. Even in NISDN the integration of narrowband services such as data and voice can be considered as being rather limited : the user access to the network is fully integrated, either by a basic access or primary rate interface. However, inside the network there will still exist for some time a packet switched and a circuit switched network as two overlay networks incapable of transporting other traffic types and each dimensioned either for voice or X.25 data.

Another important consequence of this service specialization is the inability of the network to benefit highly from the progress made in technology and coding algorithms. For instance, current digital NISDN switches are designed for 64 kbit/s voice channels. However, with the current progress in speech coding and chip technology, bit rates of 32 kbit/s (ADPCM : Adaptive Differential PCM), 13 kbit/s (for the mobile network) and even lower will be used in the future. The existing switches and transmission systems are not directly suited and thus need an adaptation, or will not efficiently use their internal resources for these lower speed bit rates.

When designing the future BISDN network, one must take into account all possible existing and future services. Suppose a network is capable of transporting a specific service, e.g. a circuit switched service with a channel rate of 70 Mbit/s. Suppose also that it is specifically designed to transport this bit rate. Some years later a new teleservice of, for example, 40 Mbit/s appears on the scene. This would mean that the network designed for that service (i.e. 70 Mbit/s) will be capable of transporting the new teleservice, but with a large inefficiency : only 40 out of the 70 Mbit/s available will be used. This example is not unrealistic. It is very likely that in the future new services will emerge which have not yet been identified, and of which the requirements are unknown today.

As can be concluded from the above examples, the networks of today are very specialized and suffer from a large number of disadvantages, the most important being :

- Service Dependence.
  Each network is only capable of transporting one specific service (information type) for which it was intentionally designed. Only in a limited number of cases and by using additional equipment (e.g. a modem) and with an inefficient use of its resources can it be adapted to other services.

- Inflexibility.
  Advances in audio, video and speech coding and compression algorithms and progress in Very Large Systems Integration (VLSI) technology influence the bit rate generated by a certain service and thus change the service requirements for the network. In the future, new services with unknown requirements will appear. For the time being it is yet unclear, e.g. what the requirements in terms of bit rate for HDTV (High Definition TV) will be. A specialized network has great difficulties in adapting to changing or new service requirements.

- Inefficiency.
  The internal available resources are used inefficiently. Resources which are available in one network cannot be made available to other networks.

Taking into account all these considerations on flexibility, service dependence and resource usage, it is consequently very important in the future that only a single network exists and that this network of the future (BISDN) is service-independent. This implies a single network capable of transporting all services, sharing all its available resources between the different services.

A single service-independent network will not suffer from the disadvantages described above, but it will have the following main advantages :

- Flexible and future-safe.
  Advances in the state of the art of coding algorithms and VLSI technology may reduce the bandwidth of existing teleservices. A network capable of transporting all types of services will be able to adapt itself to changing or new needs.

- Efficient in the use of its available resources.
  All available resources can be shared between all services, such that an optimal statistical sharing of the resources can be obtained.

- Less expensive.
  Since only one network needs to be designed, manufactured and maintained, the overall costs of the design, manufacturing, operations and maintenance will be smaller.

1.3. PROGRESS IN TECHNOLOGY : TECHNOLOGY PUSH

The definition of a service-independent network has been influenced by an evolution in 2 important factors which are key to a telecommunication system : technology and system concepts. Both factors have passed through an enormous progress, which make it feasible to develop in a cost effective way systems which were some years ago impossible or very expensive to realize. The evolution in these 2 parameters was not happening one independent of the other, but were very related.

1.3.1. Progress in technology

In recent years, large technological progress has occurred both in the field of electronics and in the field of optics. This progress will allow the economical development of new telecommunication networks running at very high speeds.

Semi-conductor technology

Broadband communication systems can be developed based on different technologies, the most promising being CMOS (Complementary Metal Oxide Semiconductor), silicon bipolar (ECL) and GaAs (Gallium Arsenide).

CMOS is at present the most promising technology, since it allows high complexity and reasonably high speeds (up to 200 to 300 Mbit/s) using submicron geometries. The low power dissipation of CMOS is particularly important, and allows the realization of high complexity, high speed systems on a very small chip surface.

In addition the complexity of CMOS chips is ever-growing, as is shown in Fig. 1.1. There we see that when the feature size continues to diminish with the years, the complexity of a single chip continuously increases. The possible chip complexity in gates does of course not only depend on the feature size, but also on the regularity. For instance, memory chips with very regular patterns contain many more transistors than chips with random logic. This difference is seen in the diagram, where 3 different design methods (full custom, standard cell and gate array) are indicated. With this increased complexity per chip, the system cost can easily be reduced, since this large integration will continuously allow the volume of the system to shrink, or to increase the functionality at a constant cost .

There is currently no indication that the trend of increased complexity per chip will be stopped before the year 2000, permitting the functionality to be provided by the future systems.

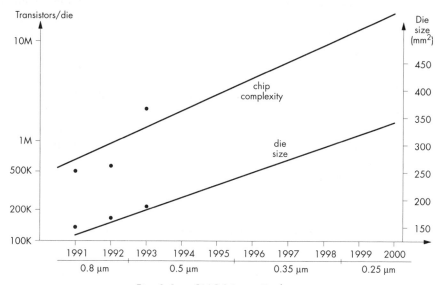

Fig. 1.1. – CMOS Logic Evolution

Silicon bipolar technologies such as ECL (Emitter Coupled Logic) will be used in high speed analog and digital circuits having a low-to-medium complexity. A further improvement in speed and power consumption is expected in the near future (Reiner, 1986). ECL technology currently achieves speeds between 5 and 10 GHz, making it very suitable for high speed transmission systems.

A combination of both CMOS and ECL, the so-called BICMOS (Bipolar CMOS) combines the advantages of both technologies, with high speed drivers and a low power and high complexity CMOS core. This technology is beneficial in places where the combination of high speed and high complexity is required.

At present, speeds even higher than the one described with ECL can be obtained with GaAs technology. However, GaAs technology is not as mature as silicon, and therefore has some cost disadvantages compared to silicon. It is therefore expected that in the near future, the development of high complexity GaAs chips will not be possible at a price comparable to silicon chips.

Optical technology

Optical technology is also evolving quite rapidly. Optical fiber has been installed for interoffice transmission systems for several years. In some limited applications, optical fiber is already applied in the local loop. The type of optical fiber that will be used in the BISDN will probably be a monomode fiber, since its potential for high bandwidth transmission is almost unlimited.

Three parameters of the transmission are constantly being enhanced : the bit rate, the distance, and the quality (Cohen, 1986). Multigigabit systems capable of transporting information over hundreds of kilometers with very low bit error rates have been reported by different sources (Kimura, 1986), (Hanke, 1987).

These high capacity systems still require rather expensive terminal equipment (expensive lasers, optical and electrical receivers, ...). The evolution of these systems is shown in Fig. 1.2. There we see that the product of the bit rate and the distance has been rapidly growing over time, when new optical technologies were used.

In the future, these very high capacity, long distance systems will be used with success in trunk transmission systems, thereby reducing the trunk transmission cost in a broadband network to a value comparable with the trunk transmission cost of today's telephone networks.

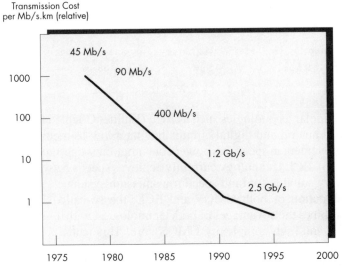

Fig. 1.2. – Lightwave Transmission Cost Trends

With respect to light sources and receivers much progress has occurred, and continuous improvements are being reported (Cheung, 1987). These range from the use of low cost LED (light emitting diodes) for bit rates up to 600 Mbit/s, over the use of cheap CD lasers in the 800 nm window up to low cost lasers in the 1500 nm window.

For the subscriber loop, with a limited distance (a few kilometers) and a smaller bandwidth requirement (a few hundred Mbit/s), these alternative solutions have been applied for the end-user's equipment. These cheap solutions will allow the economic introduction of these systems in the local loop in the mid 1990s, e.g. for a bit rate of about 600 Mbit/s and a transmission span of up to 10 kilometers (De Prycker, 1992), (Shumate, 1991).

1.3.2. System concept progress

As argued above, the ideal network of the future must be flexible. The most flexible network in terms of bandwidth requirements, and the most efficient in terms of resource usage, is a network based on the concepts of packet switching. Indeed, any bandwidth can be transported over a packet switching network, and resources are only used when useful information has to be transported.

However, the X.25 protocol used in today's packet switching networks suffers from high complexity needed because of the low quality transmission links. This high complexity introduces large delays and therefore it does not allow the transport of services with stringent time constraints, and at a very high rate.

Since the first introduction of packet switched networks based on the X.25 concepts, a large evolution in system concepts for those packet-oriented networks has occurred. The basic reasons for these concept changes are the need for greater flexibility, the need to transport services other than pure data services, especially high bit rate services, and the progress in technology which allows the cost effective development of systems of higher speed, quality and larger complexity.

The basic idea behind the concept changes is the fact that functions must not be repeated in the network several times if the required service can still be guaranteed when these functions are only once implemented at the boundary of the network. This basic idea can be applied to two functions offered by the network : semantic transparency, and time transparency.

Semantic transparency

Semantic transparency is the function which guarantees the correct delivery at the destination of the bits which were transmitted by the source. Of course, a network is not ideal, and errors will occur, with a very small probability. This probability is specified, for instance, by CCITT for all sorts of networks (e.g. Q.513 for ISDN).

In the initial packet switched networks the quality of the transmission media was rather poor. In order to guarantee an acceptable end-to-end quality, error control was performed on every link (see Fig. 1.3a.). This error control is supported by a High-Level Data Link Control (HDLC) protocol which includes functions such as frame delimiting, bit transparency, error checking (Cyclic Redundancy Check (CRC)), error recovery (retransmission).

With the advent of ISDN for narrowband services, the quality of the transmission and switching systems increased, thus reducing the errors within the network. In such a high quality network it is proposed to implement only the core functions of the HDLC protocol (frame delimiting, bit transparency and error checking) on a link-by-link basis, and other functions such as error recovery on an end-to-end basis. In Fig. 1.3b. it is shown that layer 2 of the OSI model is divided in two sublayers : layer 2a only supporting the core functions of layer 2, and layer 2b supporting the additional functions. This concept is called frame relaying (Spencer, 1987), and is offered by several telecommunication operators as an upgrade of X.25, to obtain a higher throughput (2 Mbit/s).

Layer 2a operates on a link-by-link basis, layer 2b on an end-to-end basis. This end-to-end operation in layer 2 is in contradiction with the OSI model, where end-to-end operation is only performed at layer 4 and higher. I will not expand on this discussion here.

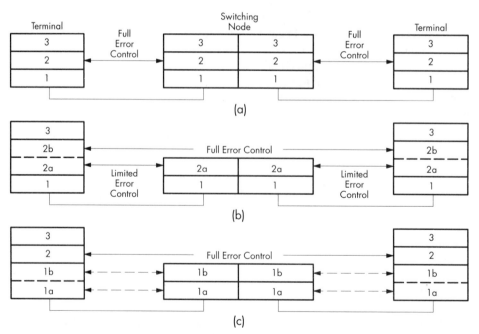

Fig. 1.3. – (a) Full Error Control on Every Link in Packet Switched Networks
          (b) Limited Error Control in Frame Relaying Networks
          (c) Cell Switching in ATM Networks

For broadband ISDN this idea is further extended. In this case, packets (cells) are still used, but the core functions of layer 2a have also been removed to the edges of the network. This concept is called ATM : Asynchronous Transfer Mode (see Fig. 1.3c.). In this case error handling functions are no longer supported in the switching nodes inside the network.

As can be seen in Table 1.1., the functions performed in the network are reduced from full error control in X.25 to a strict minimum in ATM (cell switching). This is also reflected in the complexity of the nodes inside the network : X.25 nodes have large complexity; frame relaying nodes have a smaller complexity, and therefore allow higher speeds; whereas ATM nodes have minimal complexity and thus allow very high speeds (e.g. 600 Mbit/s) (De Prycker, 1987).

	Packet switching	**Frame relaying**	**Cell switching**
Packet retransmission	X	–	–
Frame delimiting	X	X	–
Error checking	X	X	–

Table 1.1. – Functional Evolution Inside the Network

It can therefore be concluded that due to the increased quality of the telecommunication network, semantic transparency can be guaranteed by an error control performed only once on an end-to-end basis.

Time transparency

Time transparency is the function that guarantees the timely delivery of information at the receiver.

Some services require that the bit stream arrives after a short delay at the other end. These services are called real time services and typical examples are voice at 64 kbit/s and video telephony. The requirements for these services are contained in CCITT Recommendations specifying, for example, the delay per exchange (Q.507) and the end-to-end delay (G.161, G.164).

Packet switching and frame relaying systems have difficulties in supporting real time services. Because they require medium-to-large complexity in the switching nodes, they can only operate at medium-to-low speeds. This means that the delay and the jitter on this delay will be quite large, making it unfeasible, or even impossible, to guarantee a small delay. So these networks are unable to guarantee the required time transparency (e.g. G.164).

ATM, on the other hand, needs a minimal functionality in the switching nodes, and therefore allows a very high speed. Because of this high speed, the delay through the network and the jitter on this delay is reduced to very small values (a few hundred microseconds for the jitter on the delay), thus guaranteeing a very small delay at the receiver (De Prycker, 1987). The jitter introduced by the network is only restored at the boundaries of the network. So, the time relation is not reconstructed or maintained inside the network (i.e. in the nodes), as is for instance the case in circuit switched networks.

It can be concluded that due to the high speed of the ATM nodes in the network, it is possible to realize time transparency and thus transport real time services over an ATM network. More details on this time and semantic transparency will be explained in Chapter 2 of this book.

1.4. FUTURE SERVICE REQUIREMENTS : MARKET PULL

With respect to the market expectation one can distinguish mainly 2 classes of subscriber for BISDN : the residential and the business. Both have their own service requirements. The first is more interested in entertainment-like services, the second in services resulting in an increased productivity.

1.4.1. Residential subscriber expectations

An important service to be offered to the residential subscriber is TV in all sorts of quality and accessibility. One can think of video signals with a quality comparable to that of the current CATV networks, or of video signals which have a much better quality thanks to the digital characteristics of the network. This digital TV is sometimes called SDTV (Standard Digital TV). Bit rates required for this service range between 1.5 and 15 Mbit/s. In the future very high quality TV signals, called HDTV (High Definition TV) will also be offered to the residential customer by the BISDN. For HDTV, bit rates between 15 and 150 Mbit/s are envisaged, depending on the complexity of the compression and the picture quality. A major issue in these different video qualities is the compatibility between these different video signals so that for example a SDTV program can be viewed on a HDTV monitor and vice versa.

All these video signals can be offered in different modes. The most straightforward offering is a sort of CATV emulation, in which a set of TV programs is offered on a semi-permanent basis to each customer. One step further is switched access TV in which each customer determines on demand its required TV program. A step further is video on demand using a video library where the customer calls a video vendor and selects a program from a number of available videos.

Another interesting residential service is video telephony. In BISDN, high quality pictures can be transported at an acceptable cost, using bit rates of about 0.5

to 5 Mbit/s. The appearance of video cameras/recorders may help the people to get accustomed to the camera of the video telephone.

Other applications which may gain interest from the residential subscribers are services like video shopping, home education, and transportation of video information like travelling pictures, house-rental information.

It is clear that once the BISDN will become available to every residential subscriber, a large number of new possibilities will emerge which are currently not considered as interesting, or have been unknown.

1.4.2. Business subscriber expectations

The business subscriber has completely different requirements for the BISDN. The only overlapping service with the residential user is the video telephony. But here extensions towards video conferencing have to be provided to allow multiparty video telephony.

Since the ever increasing success of LANs in the business environment, it is expected that a very interesting service to be offered by the BISDN is high speed LAN interconnection.

This LAN interconnectivity will offer the business customer possibilities for distributed database access. Even with the ever increasing capabilities of PCs and workstations in terms of processing speed and disk storage, more and more software applications run on different machines in a distributed environment. Especially for home workers this application might be very interesting.

Also applications like high quality medical image transfer, corporate education, multimedia electronic mail and desktop multimedia teleconferencing in the office environment are expected.

In the manufacturing environment the applications will be more oriented towards remote visual inspections, distribution of visual processing/manufacturing information to the workers in the factory, etc.

Again the list of possible applications for the business subscribers is not exhaustive, and new services will appear when users see the possibilities of the BISDN.

1.5. BIBLIOGRAPHY

Albers R.F., Zachok, Jr. S., Lapides J.D. "Bell Atlantic/QPSX public MAN trial", ISS '92, Yokohama, October 1992

Aoyama T., Tokizawa I., Sato K. "An ATM VP-based broadband network : its technologies and application to multimedia services", ISS '92, Yokohama, October 1992

Berglin J., Petersen L.G. "SMDS in a BISDN environment", ISS '92, Yokohama, October 1992

Bernoux J.P. "SMDS and frame relay : comparing apples and oranges ... and making sense out of it !", ISS '92, Yokohama, October 1992

Borsotto J.L., Delisle D. "LAN interconnection : an early application for ATM", ISS '92, Yokohama, October 1992

Burston K. "An international broadband ATM network", Australian fast packet switching workshop, Melbourne, July 1990

Carbone P., Chhura S., Wernik M., Kwong K. "Evolving ATM service opportunities in public networks", ISS '92, Yokohama, October 1992

Chao J.H. "A general architecture for link-layer congestion control in ATM networks", ISS '92, Yokohama, October 1992

Chipman K., Holzworth P., Loop J., Spears D. "High performance applications development for B-ISDN", ISS '92, Yokohama, October 1992

Cheung J.L. "High speed lightwave technology for future broadband integrated services digital networks", ICC '87, Seattle, June 1987

Cohen L. "Trends in the US broadband fiber optic transmission systems", IEEE Journal on Selected Areas in Communications, Vol. 4, No. 4, July 1986

Crocetti P., Fratta L., Gallasi G., Gerla M., Marsiglia M.A., Romano D. "ATM-based SMDS for LANs/MANs interconnection", ISS '92, Yokohama, October 1992

Damodaram R., Ransom N., Spears D."Evolving Bellsouth's network to B-ISDN", ISS '92, Yokohama, October 1992

De Prycker M., Bauwens J. "A switching exchange for an ATD based network", ICC '87, Seattle, June 1987

De Prycker M., Bauwens J. "The ATD concept : one universal bearer service", CEPT seminar on BISDN, Albufeira (Portugal), January 1987

De Prycker M. "Definition of network options for the Belgian ATM broadband experiment", IEEE Journal on Selected Areas in Communications, Vol. 6, No. 9, December 1988

De Prycker M., Verbiest W., Mestdagh D. "ATM Passive Optical Networks : Preparing the access network for BISDN", ISS '92, Yokohama, October 1992

Dubrovinsky V., Mikhailov V., Artemjev V. "On evolution strategy towards B-ISDN in Ukraine", ISS '92, Yokohama, October 1992

Fastrez M. *et al.* "A broadband ATM network with maximum integration of distribution and interactive services", Telecom Geneve '91, October 1991

Giga "Gigabit Network Testbeds", IEEE Computer, Vol. 23, No. 9, pp. 70-80, September 1990

Hanke G., Hein B. "Monomode transmission system operating with 1300 nm lasers and 1550 nm DFB lasers at a bit rate of 2.23 Gbit/s", ICC '87, Seattle, June 1987

Kimura T. "Fibre optic transmission systems - status and trends in Japan", IEEE Journal on Selected Areas in Communications, Vol. 4, No. 4, July 1986

Moh H.S., Chew M.C., Chok S.Y., Low W.C. "Broadband ISDN trial in Singapore, ISS '92, Yokohama, October 1992

Moondra S.L., Wilkerson J.L., Bangaru B. "Broadband networking strategies – a case study", ISS '92, Yokohama, October 1992

Paone R., Pitt D.A., Schlichthärle D. "An evolutionary customer premises network for business communications", ISS '92, Yokohama, October 1992

Pherson B., Gauffin L., "Multig – distributed multimedia applications and gigabit networks", ISS '92, Yokohama, October 1992

Proietti A., Cataldi F., Ferrero F. "The role of high-speed network field trials for the assessment of early available products", ISS '92, Yokohama, October 1992

Reiner H. "Integrated circuits for broadband communication systems", IEEE Journal on Selected Areas in Communications, Vol. 4, No. 4, July 1986

Roberts L., MacDonald T., Bernstein G. "Fast select virtual circuit routing for B-ISDN networks", ISS '92, Yokohama, October 1992

Sakurai Y., Ohtsuki K., Takase A. "Integrated experimental system for B-ISDN", ISS '92, Yokohama, October 1992

Shumate P. *et al.* "Evolution of fiber in the residential loop plant", IEEE Communications Magazine, March 1991

Spencer D., Dimmick J., Burg F., Kaufeld J. "ISDN packet mode protocol-architectures and services", Forum '87, Geneve, October 1987

Takahashi H. "The impact of the future broadband ISDN is the delivery of television to the home", America telecom '92, Acapulco, April 1992

Tat N., Fox A.L., Verbeeck P. "ATM technology Development in Race" Globecom '91, Phoenix, December 1991

Wachholz G., Grohs K.D. "Concept of Deutsche Bundespost Telekom for a broadband-ISDN pilot project", ISS '92, Yokohama, October 1992

Walters S.M., Ahmed M. "Broadband virtual private networks and their evolution", ISS '92, Yokohama, October 1992

Wong H., Dutkiewicz E., Turner C., Foley C., Follett D. "Developing international B-ISDN : an Australian perspective", ISS '92, Yokohama, October 1992

2

Transfer Modes

2.1. INTRODUCTION

In the future telecommunication world, new services like video telephony, video library, high speed data, ... will be added to the existing services such as voice (POTS : plain old telephone service), TV distribution and low speed data. This arrival of new telecommunication services generates new requirements for the telecommunication network. New telecommunication techniques (called transfer modes) may be required and may offer possible advantages compared to the existing techniques. These techniques are propagated by the ever increasing technological capabilities with respect to speed and complexity. As will be shown in this Chapter, the use of a specific transfer mode at one moment in time is controlled by the available technology of that moment. The selected transfer mode has changed several times during the history.

Due to the forthcoming requirements of the new emerging services, and the available technology, a new transfer mode has been defined for the future broadband ISDN. This Chapter explains in detail all the transfer modes considered for the BISDN with their respective advantages and drawbacks. Then one technique is highlighted in detail, namely ATM (Asynchronous Transfer Mode), since this technique was selected in 1987 by CCITT to be the transfer mode of the future BISDN. In 1990, CCITT issued a first series of Recommendations, specifying the details of ATM for use in BISDN. These Recommendations were further worked out in 1991 and 1992. These Recommendations will be explained in more detail in Chapter 3.

In addition, CPE (Customer's Premises Equipment) suppliers have realized that the increased performance of workstations in terms of processing capabilities, and the emergence of multimedia workstations will create the need for a powerful transfer mode between computers in the office. In this environment, the ATM Forum has recognized the capabilities of ATM and has defined the necessary specifications for interoperability.

2.2. HISTORY

It is interesting to look some years back into history to discover the basic reasons why some transfer modes have been so succesful in the past, and others have never succeeded.

2.2.1. Telegraphy

The first "transfer mode" used in the telecommunication world was some sort of "packet switching". Indeed, in telegraphy a "packet" (i.e. the message in this case) was transported from relay station to relay station. This "packet" also contained the address of source and destination and the content of the message. This "packet switching" type technique was enforced by the limitations of the technology of that period, which were some wires, and a key to generate the pulses. Basically the intelligence of human operators was used to decide what to do with each individual message. It is interesting to note that the way the messages were coded was more or less digital, since only discrete values were possible on the lines (short pulses and long pulses).

2.2.2. Telephony

The next transfer mode introduced at the end of the last century was circuit switching, to be used for POTS, i.e. the classical telephone service. Indeed, in this application, the circuit is established for the duration of the complete conversation.

Two straightforward reasons have enforced the introduction of this transfer mode :

- The use of a relay station as in telegraphy applications (i.e. an operator repeating the whole conversation) is very impractical since it not only inhibits direct contact between speakers, but also reduces the correctness of the information received at the destination.
- The existence of a telephone set no longer required the coding of the signal in a "digital" way, but the signal could be directly transmitted in an analog way. The only requirement was that somewhere in the network one (or more) "switches" were closed so that a circuit was established end-to-end to allow the signal to be conveyed from source to destination.

In an initial stage the closing of this switch was performed manually by an operator. With the advent of automatic switches (crossbar, Strowger,...) the closing or opening of this switch was controlled mechanically. Later on this switch was opened/closed electromechanically and finally electrically. But even this enormous technological progress in the switch devices has not changed the transfer mode of POTS which is still circuit switching. There was and still is no reason to change the transfer mode of a network which must only transfer voice, since the only requirement of POTS is to have a connection closed for the whole duration of the conversation.

For some specific applications, e.g. long distance connections where the circuit is very expensive (like in satellites), circuit switching may not be efficient enough. Indeed some conversations contain 50 % silent periods so that efficiency can be increased by removing the silent periods of a conversation. The silent periods of one conversation can be filled by active periods of another conversation. This specific technique is called TASI (Time Assignment by Speech Interpellation). This technique is not successful for short and medium distance connections in the case of POTS services, because the gain of about 50 % on transmission cost obtained by silence suppression will not be compensated by the additional cost in terminals and switching systems introduced by the higher complexity.

2.2.3. Data

When the requirement to interconnect computers and terminals appeared as an application for telecommunication networks, the existing circuit switched telephone network was used originally. Modems were required to convert the digital computer information into analog signals for the telephone network. Today, a large percentage of the computer and terminal interconnections is using the telephone network.

The fact that the telephone network is ubiquitous is an enormous advantage, which promoted the big success of the telephone network for data applications. However, since data applications are typically very bursty (many more silent periods than the 50 % of POTS), circuit switching is not ideally suited.

Already in the sixties people began to realize that better solutions existed specially adapted for data applications, with their very bursty character. Initially, 2 candidate transfer techniques were considered : circuit switching and packet switching. Both solutions were worked out and standardized by CCITT (X.21 for circuit switching, X.25 for packet switching). The bursty nature of data sources promoted the success of the packet switching solution which is now available in most countries. Indeed, in a packet switching network resources are only occupied when information is really transferred (during the burst), whereas in a circuit switching network resources are occupied during the complete connection (also during "silent" periods).

2.3. PERFORMANCE REQUIREMENTS

In the future broadband network, a large number of services have to be transferred (Fig. 2.1.). These services are low speed, like telemetry, telecontrol, telealarm, voice, telefax, low speed data, ..., medium speed like hifi sound, video telephony, high speed data, ... and very high speed like high quality video distribution, video library, video education, etc. Therefore, the transfer mode for this future network cannot be designed specifically for one service. As is shown in Fig. 2.1., we see a large range of services with an estimated bit rate of a few bit/s up to some hundreds of Mbit/s. Also the holding times are varying of some seconds up to hours. All these services have to be transported over the future broadband network.

It has to be preferred to install a single network capable of transferring all sorts of services, than to install an overlay network per individual service, since such a series of overlay networks will be rather expensive to develop, install and maintain. In addition interworking between all networks has to be provided, which makes the solution with specialized networks even more problematic. Therefore, a single universal broadband network must be defined, capable of fulfilling all the requirements of expected and even unexpected services.

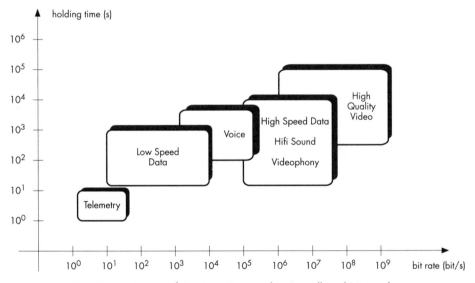

Fig. 2.1. – Range of Services Expected in Broadband Networks

In order to define the transfer mode for this future broadband network, it is important to understand the characteristics of the existing services and their requirements for the transfer mode used in the network. To anticipate future unknown services we must try to characterize as general a service as possible.

Instead of just using the generated bit rate, it is more generic to characterize the services by a <u>natural information rate</u>. This is the rate at which the source is generating information if no limitations in terms of functionality and cost of the telecommunication network are present. The natural information rate of each source (e.g. voice, video,...) is very much dependent on the coding and compression technique used, and thus the state of the art in signal processing and technology with the related economical feasibility.

This natural information rate can be represented by a stochastic process s(t) (Fig. 2.2.). This stochastic process lasts for the duration T of the information transfer : this can be the duration T of the telephone conversation for POTS, the duration of a computer session for computer-to-computer data communication, the duration of a video conference session, etc. Two important values can be obtained from each stochastic process : the peak natural bit rate S and the average natural bit rate E[s(t)], calculated over the duration T. As will be described in Chapter 5 and 7 the duration over which the peak and average is calculated may be an important parameter to characterize a service.

$$S = max \; s(t) \qquad (2.1.)$$

$$E[s(t)] = \frac{1}{T} \int s(t)dt \qquad (2.2.)$$

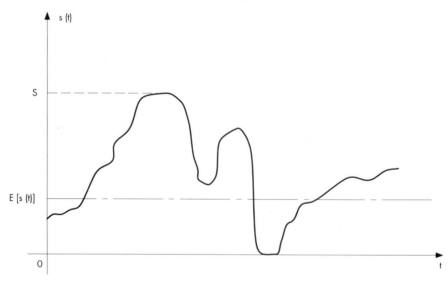

Fig. 2.2. – Natural Bit Rate Fluctuation in Time

Sometimes the ratio between the maximum and the average natural information rate is called the burstiness B.

$$B = \frac{S}{E[s(t)]} \qquad (2.3.)$$

It is clear that per session of a service, the stochastic process s(t) will have a different behavior, but the average and peak values will be typical for a service. In Table 2.1. some typical values are described for a number of services. The burstiness from the voice basically comes from the talkspurts and silence periods, which each typically last about 50 % of the time; for bulk data transfer, the very high burstiness is mainly explained by the fact that some contiguous sectors of a disk are read before the magnetic head of the disk has to be moved and a next set of contiguous sectors is read; for video one can imagine that a coding technique only generates bits if there is non-redundant information available (e.g. some movements on an image).

Service	**E[s(t)]**	**B**
Voice	32 kbit/s	2
Interactive data	1–100 kbit/s	10
Bulk data	1–10 Mbit/s	1–10
Standard quality video	1.5–15 Mbit/s	2–3
High definition TV (HDTV)	15–150 Mbit/s	1–2
High quality video telephony	0.2–2 Mbit/s	5

Table 2.1. – Broadband Services and their Characteristics

Two important conclusions can be drawn from Table 2.1. :

- There exists no such thing like a single "typical" service description : all services have different characteristics both for their average bit rate and burstiness factor.
- None of the services has a burstiness equal to one. By source coding, one can always transform the natural bit rate to one fixed value, but that is either at the expense of lower quality (if the peak bit rate is reduced, Fig. 2.3a.) or at the expense of a lower efficiency (Fig. 2.3b.) because idle information is transported, wasting resources in the network.

Indeed, in Fig. 2.3a. the transfer rate is smaller than the peak of the natural bit rate. This results in a quality reduction, since during the periods that the natural rate is larger than the transfer rate, some bits will have to be discarded to limit the natural rate to the acceptable transfer rate. In Fig. 2.3b. on the contrary, the transfer rate is always larger than or equal to the natural bit rate. Only dummy information can be used to fill up the difference between natural bit rate and transfer rate. So, resources will be wasted in the network.

A transfer mode able to transport all these described services, and other services (not described in Table 2.1.), must be very flexible in the sense that it must transport a wide range of natural bit rates and it should be able to cope with services which have a fluctuating character (i.e. natural bit rate) in time.

So the optimal transfer mode should support the communication of various types of information via an integrated access, especially one which places few or no constraints on the way in which the customer wants to use his access. Ideally, the transfer mode must provide the capability to transport information, whatever type of information is given at the network, very much like the electricity which provides power to its customers, without regarding the way the customer consumes his electricity.

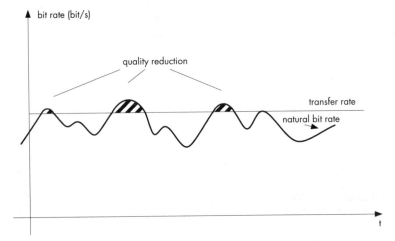

Fig. 2.3a. – Quality Reduction by Peak Bit Rate Reduction

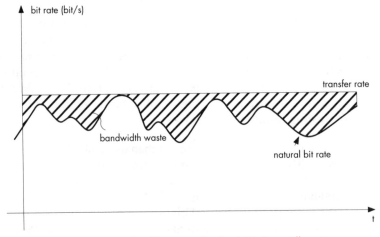

Fig. 2.3b. – Bandwidth Waste by Peak Bit Rate Allocation

As described earlier in this Chapter, different transfer modes exist each with different features. Some of these modes are not directly suited for the requirements described above, others are very suited.

A transfer mode is basically characterized by the switching technique used in the switching nodes of the network. However, the transfer mode is equally visible in the transmission part of the network (between the nodes and between the user and the nodes), and the flexibility or inflexibility of a transfer mode is reflected in both the switching node and the transmission equipment.

Fig. 2.4. describes a spectrum of switching techniques available to transport information in a telecommunication network. In general, the techniques towards the left hand side of the continuum offer only a fixed bit rate and small flexibility, those to the right hand side of the continuum provide increasing flexibility to handle variable bit rate and bursty information. However, as shown later, they also require more processing and complexity, both detrimental to the speed.

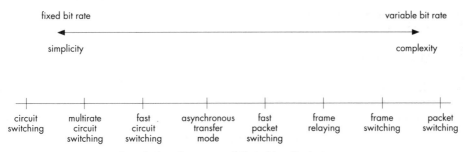

Fig. 2.4. – Spectrum of Switching Techniques

Before going into detail on each of these different transfer modes, some general definitions will be explained. These important definitions characterize the performance and functionality of a network :

- Semantic transparency : this determines the possibility of the network to transport the information error free, i.e. the number of end-to-end errors introduced by the network is acceptable for the service.
- Time transparency : this determines the capability of the network to transport the information through the network from source to destination in a minimal time, i.e. acceptable for the service.

2.3.1. Semantic transparency

Semantic transparency determines the capability of the network to transport information accurately from the source to destination, i.e. with a limited (acceptable) number of errors.

The types of errors (and their value) introduced by the network may differ from one transfer mode to another transfer mode. These types of errors can be specified per system, as shown for 2 examples in Table 2.2. There we see 3 types of errors defined for 2 services : X.25 as specified by CCITT and frequently used in most countries for low-to-medium speed data communication and SMDS (Switched Multimegabit Data Services) as specified by Bellcore for high speed data services (Bellcore, 1989).

The errors identified are : residual error data unit rate, which is the rate of undiscovered errors; misdelivered data unit rate, which indicates the ratio between data units delivered at an incorrect destination and data units transmitted; not delivered data unit rate, which is the ratio between non-delivered data units and transmitted data units.

	X.25	**SMDS**
Residual error data unit rate	10^{-10}	10^{-10}
Misdelivered data unit rate	–	5.10^{-8}
Non-delivered data unit rate	–	10^{-4}

Table 2.2. – Acceptable Error Rate for X.25 and SMDS (Switched Multimegabit Data Services)

No system is perfect. Most of the imperfections of telecommunication systems are caused by noise (white noise, impulse noise,...). However, other factors contribute to a reduced quality. Examples of these other factors are limited resources causing blocking and congestion and imperfect material. Any system (optical or electrical transmission systems and switching systems) will introduce errors of different kinds, since it is designed against a certain cost/performance trade-off. The higher the performance requirement is (i.e. the fewer errors are accepted), the more expensive the system will be. But even the most expensive systems will have errors, albeit with a very low probability. These errors are due to malfunctioning of boards/chips, imperfections of components, alpha particles, etc. For every system (type of system), the probability that a certain error will occur over a certain period of time can be defined and calculated by modeling the system and the probability that imperfections, noise, ... will occur.

One of the most important parameters used to characterize imperfections in digital communication systems is the BER (Bit Error Rate), i.e. the ratio between erroneous bits and transmitted bits.

In the telecommunication networks where the bits are treated as groups, like for instance in packet networks, groups of errors can occur because blocks of information are lost or misrouted. If we call such a group a packet, we can define the

PER (Packet Error Rate) as the ratio between misrouted or lost packets and transmitted packets.

Let us be somewhat more specific and analyze the type of errors that can occur.

Bit error rate

The BER is defined as the number of bits which arrive erroneously, divided by the total number of bits transmitted, and this measured over a representative period of time or

$$BER = \frac{Number\ of\ erroneous\ bits}{Total\ number\ of\ bits\ sent} \qquad (2.4a.)$$

The definition of an erroneous bit is very simple, i.e. when the bit arrives with the value other than that transmitted.

These bit errors can occur isolated (singular errors) or in groups (burst errors). Isolated errors are mainly caused by noise and system imperfections (e.g. bit slip caused by imperfect clocks). Burst errors not caused by packet errors are mainly due to manual handling and impulse noise. These will be described in the next section.

The sentence : "over a representative period of time" is important. Indeed, if we want to measure for instance a BER of 10^{-4}, we must at least have measured 10.000 bits, but in order to have confident values we need to measure at least 2 or 3 orders of magnitude more bits. In the example that means that we have to measure at least 1 million to 10 million bits to be sure of a BER of 10^{-4}. This is mainly because the errors are more or less random.

Packet error rate

In packet oriented networks bits are grouped in packets and treated as such in the network. The PER is defined as the number of erroneous packets over the total number of packets transmitted measured over a representative period of time.

$$PER = \frac{Number\ of\ erroneous\ packets}{Total\ number\ of\ packets\ sent} \qquad (2.4b.)$$

The definition of an erroneous data unit is more complex. Indeed, different types of erroneous packets exist :

(1) Packets which are lost in the network caused by misrouting or congestion. We
     can then define the PLR (Packet Loss Rate) as

$$PLR \; = \; \frac{Number \; of \; lost \; packets}{Total \; number \; of \; packets \; sent} \qquad (2.4c.)$$

(2) Packets which arrive at a destination to which they were not destined and the
     destination accepts this packet as a correct one. We can thus define the PIR
     (Packet Insertion Rate) as

$$PIR \; = \; \frac{Number \; of \; inserted \; packets}{Total \; number \; of \; packets \; sent} \qquad (2.4d.)$$

The nature of these errors and rates may differ from system to system and will
depend on certain assumptions. The characteristics will be explained in more detail
in the next section.
    A network is mainly composed of two sorts of entities each performing a
specific function : transmission and switching/multiplexing. Since transmission
systems   only   know   bits,   only   bit   errors   are   representative;   in
switching/multiplexing systems both bit and packet errors may occur. Let us look at
both systems separately in detail.

2.3.1.1.   Transmission errors

Transmission systems are mainly performing functions at the bit level, and
according to ISO can be categorized as operating in layer 1 of the OSI protocol
stack. Since layer 1 is only concerned with bits, only errors on bits (BER) will
occur. Note that according to CCITT, ATM is also located on layer 1 (see
Chapter 3). However, in this section we will only consider bit errors.
    In transmission systems, different kinds of errors may occur : some are caused
by imperfections of the transmission system itself, others caused by operative
interventions.
    The first sort of imperfections very much depend on the type of transmission
system, and thus on different factors such as :

• What is the transmission medium : coaxial, optical and the related optical devices
  (laser, led, pinfet, ...) ?
• What is the type of line coding, scrambling, etc. ?

Since it may be expected that the broadband network will mainly be equipped with
optical fibers, we describe here some error performance characteristics of an optical
system (ATT, 1989). These results were obtained through measurements performed
by ATT and Bellcore over an optical transmission system (Figs 2.5a. and 2.5b.).

They show the number of bit errors per errored seconds, and thus give an indication on the burstiness of the errors.

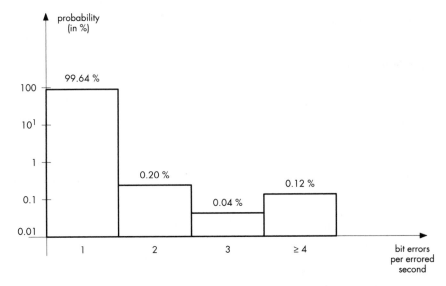

Fig. 2.5a. – Probability Distribution of Errors over an Optical Transmission System Operating in Normal Conditions

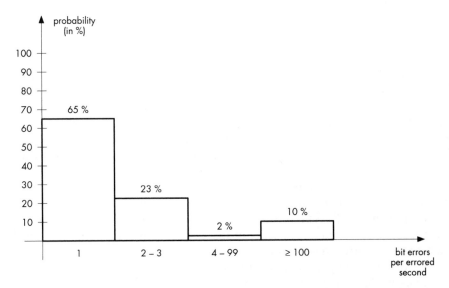

Fig. 2.5b. – Probability Distribution of Errors over an Optical Transmission System during Maintenance Activities

Notice that these results are only obtained via measurements over one system, so that the figures should not be considered as exact for all systems. However, the results and the main trends are representative for all optical transmission systems.

Two remarkable conclusions can be drawn from the experiment :

(1)   In normal operating conditions (Fig. 2.5a.), most of the errors occurring are single bit errors. In the example more than 99.64 % of the errors were single errors. In some minor cases, more than one error occurred during an errored second. Notice, that 2 errors during an errored second is NOT equal to 2 consecutive errors (i.e. a burst of 2 consecutive bits).

(2)   During maintenance conditions, a completely different behavior of the system was measured, as is shown in Fig. 2.5b. Still a large number of single errors occurred but the percentage was reduced to 65 %. It is even more remarkable that 10 % of the errored seconds had more than 100 errors. These errors can be called burst errors.

So, over a transmission system mainly 2 sorts of errors will occur :

(1)   Single bit errors, which are mainly caused by system imperfections.

(2)   Burst errors which are caused by maintenance actions such as protection switching.

2.3.1.2.   *Switching/multiplexing errors*

Switching and multiplexing systems perform functions on a higher level in the OSI protocol stack (levels 2 and 3) than transmission systems (level 1). The levels 2 and 3 of packet switching systems perform processing on a packet level. This means that in a switching system for packet transfer mode (i.e. packet switching, frame switching, frame relaying, fast packet switching, ATM,...) errors on these packets may occur as well as errors on the bits. Note again that according to CCITT, ATM functions can be located at layer 1. However, the errors induced by ATM switching and multiplexing will be considered in this section.

Packet errors are mainly caused by errors of the header. This means that the switching system will discard the packet due to an incorrect value in the header or misinterpret the header. This misinterpretation will cause a misrouting of the packet and consequently a missing packet at the correct destination and an additional packet at an incorrect destination.

Another very important cause for packet errors is an instantaneous lack of resources in the switching/multiplexing system, because too many packets are simultaneously contending for the same resource. This will enforce the switching or multiplexing system to drop packets.

2.3.1.3.   *Error probability distribution model of the network*

In an overall network we must take into account both the errors induced by the transmission systems and the errors occurred in the switching/multiplexing systems.

Instead of trying to model the errors only by BER and PER as in the previous section, we can try to characterize them by a probability distribution function of the number of consecutive bit errors. Indeed, a packet error can be translated as n consecutive bit errors, where n represents the packet size in bits. Therefore, we must model the BER more accurately.

The exact mathematical representation of the Bit Error Rate then becomes a probability distribution function, representing the probability that 1, 2, 3, ... n consecutive errors occur during the measurement period. In general, bit errors are caused by errors on the bit level in transmission and switching systems, and errors on a higher level, such as packet loss (PLR) and packet insertion (PIR).

The probability distribution will then show peaks at multiples of the packet length (in bits) and also a peak at 1 caused by bit errors of the transmission and switching system, as shown in Fig. 2.6. This diagram represents a typical distribution of a packet oriented network. Notice that in this example around 45 % of the errors are single bit errors and 45 % of the errors are caused by packet errors in the switching/multiplexing systems. So, switching and transmission systems have a comparable quality.

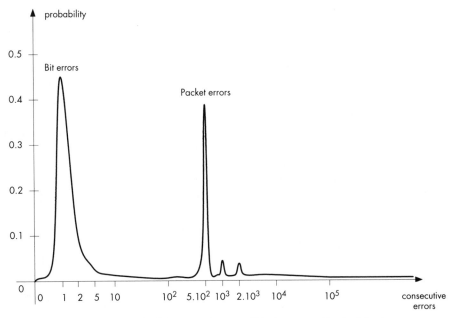

Fig. 2.6. –   Probability Distribution of Errors over a Typical Packet
Network (Packet Size = 512 bits)

Semantic transparency enhancement

If the performance of the network is not acceptable for the quality required by a specific service, it is always possible to increase this quality by using the end-to-end protocols of the transport layer. For instance, electronic fund transfer requires a virtual error free transfer of information to ensure correct transfer of financial information. The enhancement of this end-to-end quality can be achieved either by forward error correction (FEC) techniques or by retransmission if an error is detected using so-called Automatic Repeat Request (ARQ) protocols.

FEC techniques use complex coding schemes to add redundancy on the bit level. Examples are Hamming, Golay, BCH (Bose-Chadhuri-Hocquenghem) codes which can give different error correction capabilities depending on the redundancy added.

ARQ techniques rely on the retransmission of information which was not received correctly. However, in order to detect that the information is not correct at the receiver some bit coding techniques are used, very closely related to FEC techniques. Quite often, these coding techniques (Golay, Hamming, BCH) can be used either with only detection capabilities, only correction capabilities or both.

In today's copper based networks, the intrinsic error performance of the network does not guarantee an adequate level of end-to-end semantic transparency. Already error correction mechanisms have to be provided within the network on a link-by-link basis, e.g. the case in X.25 networks using HDLC (High Level Data Link Control) on every link.

It is clear that if the performance of the network is too low, too many packets will be lost underway, thereby requiring the retransmission of the lost packets, and possibly also of other packets if a sliding window mechanism is used, thus increasing the traffic.

This expected increase in traffic can be calculated for a sliding window protocol with window size W. The real number of packets to be retransmitted depends on the type of ARQ protocol and the number of outstanding not yet acknowledged packets. If we assume a Go-Back-N algorithm, with on the average W/2 packets outstanding, then we can calculate the increase in traffic if P represents the probability that a packet is lost or corrupted.

If a packet is retransmitted once and received correctly (with a probability of P.(1–P)), then the expected number of retransmitted packets is W/2.P.(1–P).

If after its first retransmission, the packet was not received correctly, then it is retransmitted again, and the probability that it arrives correctly is $(1–P).P^2$. The expected number of retransmitted packets becomes $W.P^2.(1–P)$. The process of retransmission continues until the packet finally arrives correctly.

We can then sum all expected retransmissions, resulting in an increase of traffic of :

$$R = \sum_{k=1}^{\infty} k \cdot \frac{W}{2} \cdot P^k \cdot (1 - P) = \frac{W}{2} \cdot \frac{P}{1 - P} \qquad (2.5.)$$

Let us assume that the system has n links in the end-to-end connection, that L represents the number of bits in a packet, and that B represent the BER over the transmission link (so only errors on the bit level are considered here, and all errors are assumed to be randomly distributed) then P can be calculated as follows.

The probability that a packet is delivered correctly over one link is $(1-B)^L$; over n links this probability reduces to $(1-B)^{nL}$; or the probability that a packet arrives with an error after n links is thus

$$P = 1 - (1 - B)^{nL} \qquad (2.6.)$$

So replacing (2.6.) in (2.5.) we get the increase of traffic over n links as

$$R(n) = \frac{W}{2} \cdot \frac{1 - (1 - B)^{nL}}{(1 - B)^{nL}} \qquad (2.7.)$$

Absolute values of this increase in traffic (1 means 100 %) are shown in Figs 2.7a. and Fig. 2.7b. for 2 packet lengths L. In Fig. 2.7a. we assume a long packet of 1000 bytes, in Fig. 2.7b. we assume an ATM packet of 48 bytes. In both cases we assume a window size $W = 7$ and $n = 4$, 2 and 1. The BER B on the links varies between 10^{-6} and 10^{-2}. For BER values smaller than 10^{-6}, the increase in traffic is extremely small and thus negligible.

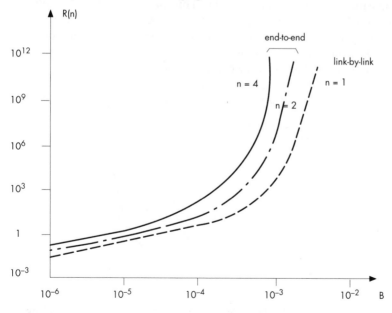

Fig. 2.7a. – Traffic Increase R(n) in Function of BER (B) (L = 1000 bytes)

We see that for small packets, as in ATM, the increase in traffic remains small, even for a BER up to 10^{-4}, and shows an exponential growth for higher BER. However, for very long packets this exponential growth becomes dramatic, already for a BER worse than 10^{-5}.

Relative figures comparing the traffic increase for end-to-end retransmission versus link-by-link retransmission are also interesting to evaluate.

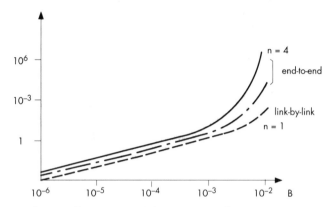

Fig. 2.7b. – Traffic Increase R(n) in Function of BER (B) (L = 48 Bytes)

In Fig. 2.8. we show a comparison of the traffic increase for a system with end-to-end retransmission (n = 4 in the example), versus a system with retransmission on every link (n = 1). This diagram actually shows the ratio R(4)/R(1) for L = 1000 bytes and L = 48 bytes. Again we see that the increase in traffic for very long packets and end-to-end retransmission is dramatic compared to link-by-link retransmission already for a BER of 10^{-4}. For short packets this increase is only important for very bad link quality (BER of 10^{-3}). For links with a quality better than 10^{-5}, the absolute increase in traffic is so small, as shown in Fig. 2.7a., that the small relative increase as shown in Fig. 2.8. can be ignored.

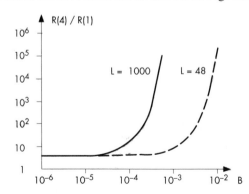

Fig. 2.8. – Error Multiplication Ratio of End-to-End versus Link-by-Link Retransmission in Function of the BER (B)

With the introduction of optical fibers, the transmission medium itself provides a very high quality (B is normally better than 10^{-8}), eliminating the need for link-by-link performance upgrading by retransmissions, especially for short packets. This is very well demonstrated in the previous diagrams (Fig. 2.7. and Fig. 2.8.).

2.3.2. Time transparency

Time transparency can be defined as the absence of delay and delay jitter (i.e. different parts of the information arrive at the destination with a different delay). Two parameters characterize time transparency : delay and delay jitter.

The delay is defined as the time difference between the sending of the information at the source (t_0) and the receiving of this information at the receiver (t_1) (Fig. 2.9.) or :

$$D_f \;=\; t_1 - t_0 \text{ for the first information block}$$

$$D_l \;=\; t_3 - t_2 \text{ for the last information block}$$

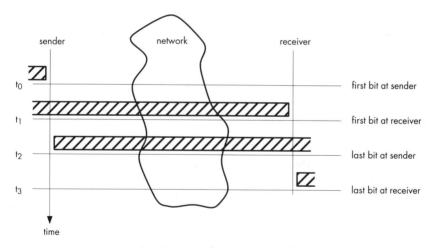

Fig. 2.9. – Delay in a Network

In general, this delay D can be different for every information block (a bit or a packet), and is thus a statistical variable with a minimum value D_m and a maximum value D_M. The difference $D_M - D_m$ is sometimes referred to as the jitter, but more representative is the variation of the delay D in a certain time period. In the context of this book, the probability that a certain delay has occurred will be representative for the delay itself, resulting in a probability density function as shown in (Fig. 2.10.). This diagram shows the probability that each delay has occurred and shows that D is a stochastic variable.

The value of the end-to-end delay is an important parameter for real time services, such as voice and video. Indeed, if the delay becomes too large, echo problems may arise in a voice connection, thereby creating an annoying quality degradation. For instance, CCITT specifies that if the end-to-end delay in POTS becomes larger than 25 ms, echo cancellers should be provided to eliminate the echo.

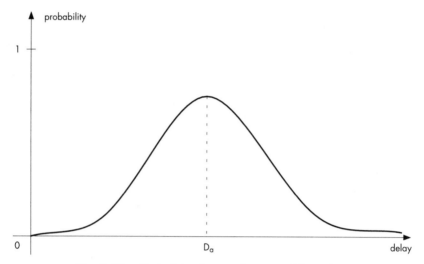

Fig. 2.10. – Probability Density Function of the Delay

Delay contributing parameters

The delay of a network is composed of several components, which can basically be divided in 2 groups : transfer delay D_t (caused by the transmission of the information from source to destination in the network) and processing delay D_p (caused by processing in the switching nodes, multiplexers, ...).

$$D = D_t + D_p \qquad (2.8.)$$

The transfer delay D_t is determined by the physical speed of the medium and the distance to be bridged between sender and receiver. If only one path is available between source and destination, the stochastic variable D_t can be represented by a Dirac function, with only one value; in case several paths exist, D_t has a limited number of discrete values.

The processing delay D_p in the nodes is determined by the physical implementation of each of the nodes on the path between source and destination, but also by the way this information is handled. For instance in early message transfer systems, messages were stored several minutes (hours) before they were sent out again. In current narrowband ISDN systems the processing delay is very short.

For instance, digital switches must have a delay which is on the average smaller than 450 µs (CCITT, Rec. Q.507). In future switching systems for broadband ISDN this processing delay may even become smaller, since the processing speed has increased significantly (150 Mbit/s and up).

The stochastic behavior of D_p is very much influenced by the transfer mode used, e.g. D_p can be different for different information from the same "connection", if information is transferred in packets, and if each packet is suffering a different queuing delay. This point will be explained more in detail for ATM in section 2.4.5.2.

2.3.3. Network conditioning

An important conclusion of this discussion on time and semantic transparency, is that every telecommunication network can mainly be characterized by 2 independent stochastic variables, B (i.e. the probability distribution function of the consecutive bit errors) and D (i.e. the probability density function of the delay).

Or a network can be characterized by a transfer function H, which is function of B and D (Fig. 2.11.).

$$i_l(t) \;=\; H_{B,D} \,(i(t)) \qquad\qquad (2.9.)$$

This means that if the signal is entered at the input of the network (at the source) as i(t), then it will be modified (errors will be added and delay will be introduced) by the network and provided to the destination as $i_1(t)$.

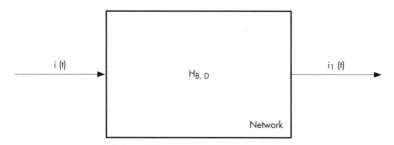

Fig. 2.11. – The Network as a Transfer Function

Ideally, the output signal should be exactly the same as the input signal or $i_1(t) = i(t)$. But, in practice, the network will modify the incoming signal i(t), according to a certain law determined by B and D. This means that the input signal will be modified, i.e. some bits will be changed/lost due to errors and all bits will arrive with a certain delay probability.

However, the difference between input signal and output signal must remain limited. The acceptable difference may vary from service to service.

For instance, certain real time services accept no or very little variability in the delay of the output signal. These services are called CBR (continuous bit rate oriented) or isochronous. They allow no or very small variability in the delay, otherwise the quality becomes unacceptable. For instance, voice still has a good quality with a limited bit jitter and bit slip.

Also the total delay is an important parameter. While the delay is no problem for unidirectional voice and video as such, it becomes disturbing if services are bidirectional. For instance, for telephony this delay may not become larger than about 25 ms (CCITT G.164), otherwise echo cancellers are required. With echo cancellers, it may not become larger than ± 500 ms, otherwise the interactivity of the conversation becomes very difficult.

On the other hand, the bit errors must be kept under control. For instance, for video applications the number of bit errors and the number of consecutive bit errors may not be too large, or the received bit stream will no longer allow the reproduction of a video signal with acceptable quality.

For every service, one can specify the allowable probability density functions of the bit errors and delay. For instance Table 2.3. describes the acceptable delay, bit error ratio, packet loss ratio and packet insertion ratio for some services acceptable over an ATM network, as seen by the RACE (Research on Advanced Communication in Europe) consortium 1022 (Technology for ATM). Note that for data transmission an additional value of 50 ms was added for the delay, because for distributed computing a much smaller delay must also be envisaged.

Service	BER	PLR	PIR	Delay
Telephony	10^{-7}	10^{-3}	10^{-3}	25 ms / 500 ms
Data transmission	10^{-7}	10^{-6}	10^{-6}	1000 ms (50 ms)
Broadcast video	10^{-6}	10^{-8}	10^{-8}	1000 ms
Hifi sound	10^{-5}	10^{-7}	10^{-7}	1000 ms
Remote process control	10^{-5}	10^{-3}	10^{-3}	1000 ms

Table 2.3. – Service Attributes for an ATM Network

However, when some of the parameters (BER, delay) of the network do not fall within the service requirements as shown in Table 2.3., an additional processing can be performed by the receiving terminal, as is shown in Fig. 2.12. The additional transfer function $G_{B,D}$ located in the terminal will convert the signal $i_1(t)$ as it arrives in the terminal into $o(t)$. In the ATM network this additional processing is called the ATM adaptation layer, and will be explained in Chapter 3. This additional processing, which can be considered as a conditioning of the received information can be represented as

$$o(t) = G_{B,D} [H_{B,D}(i(t))] \qquad (2.10.)$$

This additional processing, $G_{B,D}$ which must be installed in the receiving terminal, sometimes with the help of the transmitting terminal (e.g. forward error correction, additional information added to remove delay jitter, ...) , will transform the receiving signal from the network to an acceptable o(t) within the requirements of the service.

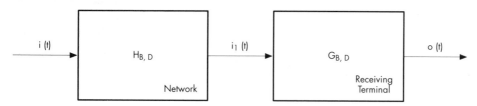

Fig. 2.12. – Network and Terminal as a Transfer Function

For instance, if the jitter on the delay is too large for a specific network (e.g. CBR services), this jitter can be removed by additionally delaying the arriving information to the value d_0 (Fig. 2.13.). This mode of operation is called circuit emulation, since it offers the same service as circuit switching with respect to time jitter (Wu, 1987).

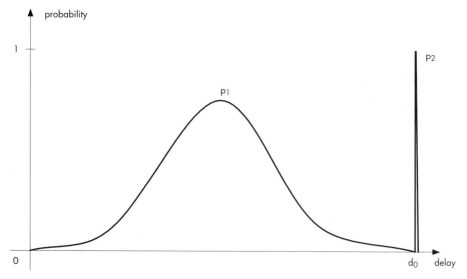

Fig. 2.13. – p1 : Probability Density Function of the Delay of the Network (H)
              p2 : Probability Density Function of the Delay after Conditioning of the
              Terminal (G . H)

Another example of this conditioning in the terminal occurs for EFT over a network where the bit error rate is not acceptable (e.g. too many bit errors). In that case, the quality can be improved by performing error correction at the receiving terminal, or by doing retransmissions.

2.4. DESCRIPTION OF TRANSFER MODES

The words transfer mode are used by CCITT to describe a technique which is used in a telecommunication network, covering aspects related to transmission, multiplexing and switching. As was shown in Fig. 2.4., many different transfer modes exists in the telecommunication world.

I will now explain the most important transfer modes, which have been considered as possible candidates for BISDN and their applicability to the BISDN requirements, mainly with respect to time and semantic transparency.

2.4.1. Circuit switching

This transfer mode has long been used in telephone networks, and is still applied in NISDN. In this classical approach, a circuit is established for the complete duration of the connection. This is based on the TDM (time division multiplexing) principle to transport the information from one node to another. This technique is also referred to as STM (Synchronous Transfer Mode).

The information is transferred with a certain repetition frequency (e.g. 8 bits every 125 μs for 64 kbit/s or 1000 bits every 125 μs for 8 Mbit/s). The basic unit of this repetition frequency is called a time slot. Several connections are time multiplexed over one link by joining together several time slots in a frame, which is again repeated with a certain frequency. A connection (i.e. "circuit") will always use the same time slot in the frame during the complete duration of the session.

The circuit switching can internally in the switching node be performed by space switching, time switching or a combination of both.

The switching of a circuit of an incoming link to an outgoing link is controlled by a translation table which contains the relation of the incoming link and the slot number, to the outgoing link and the associated slot number. As can be seen in Fig. 2.14., connection V on incoming link I_1, occupies time slot 1, and will always be transferred (switched) to outgoing link O_2 and time slot 2. Only when the connection finishes, can time slot 1 of link I_1 be switched to another slot on another link. This relation is unchanged for the complete duration of the connection, i.e. this relation determines the "circuit". The relations between all slots on all incoming links and the outgoing slots on the outgoing links are determined in a translation table. This translation table is only modified when a connection is set up or released.

In pure circuit switching, all connections occupy the same number of bits per time slot, resulting in a single bit rate for all services.

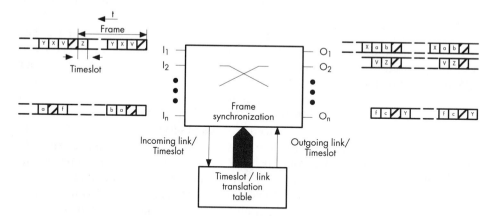

Translation table

Incoming link	Time slot	Outgoing link	Timeslot
I_1	1 2 3 … m	O_2 O_1 O_n … O_2	2 3 m … 1
I_2	1 2 3 … m		
I_n	1 2 … m	O_1 O_1 … $O_{n''}$	2 1 … 2

Fig. 2.14. – Circuit Switching

The BER in circuit switching systems is basically determined by :

- Direct errors on the information bits : single bit errors (caused by transmission or switching malfunctioning) or burst errors (caused by protective switching).
- Indirect errors on the information bits caused by bit slips and loss of frame synchronization. In the case where the frame synchronization is lost, all bits in several consecutive frames will be lost until frame synchronization is recovered.

The delay in circuit switching systems is basically determined by the propagation delay on the transmission links and the processing in the switches. For digital narrowband switches, CCITT specifies that this value must on average be smaller than 450 μs.

In theory, this processing delay is a fixed value for all information of the same connection, and is determined by the time/space switch implementation. A very small jitter on this delay can be introduced because of time slips and wander on the transmission links.

Circuit switching is very inflexible, since once the duration of a time slot has been determined, the related bit rate is fixed. For instance in PCM (Pulse Code Modulation used in G.703 transmission), the basic time slot duration is 8 bits per 125 µs, giving rise to channels of 64 kbit/s.

Since only one basic entity (i.e. the channel defined as the time slot repeated with the frame frequency) for information transfer is available, this solution is very unsuitable for all sorts of services. Indeed broadband services have different bit rate requirements from very low to very high, as was described earlier in this Chapter. In principle, the largest bit rate should be selected as the basic bit rate to be able to support all services, e.g. 140 Mbit/s. But even 1 kbit/s service would then occupy a full 140 Mbit/s channel for the complete duration of the call, which is naturally a large waste of resources. So, simple circuit switching is not at all suitable for a universal broadband network.

2.4.2. Multirate circuit switching

To overcome the inflexibility of only a single bit rate as is the case in pure circuit switching, a more enhanced version was developed, called multirate circuit switching (MRCS).

The transmission system of multirate circuit switching networks uses the same TDM format as in pure circuit switching with a fixed basic channel rate. However, one connection can now allocate n (n ≥ 1) basic channels. So every connection can be built as a multiple of the basic channel rate. This option is currently retained for instance for videophony in NISDN. The video codecs developed for NISDN videophones, and standardized under Recommendation H.261 can operate at bit rates of n times 64 kbit/s (n ≤ 30).

The switching systems based on the multirate circuit transfer mode become more complex than those of pure circuit switching, since the individual channels of one connection must remain synchronized. Indeed, if each channel is switched individually, no correlated synchronization is maintained and the information of one channel may be switched with a smaller delay than that of another channel. This desynchronization is not acceptable from a service point of view, as the terminal considers all the channels as one large entity.

Another difficult problem for multirate circuit switching systems is the selection of the basic rate. Indeed, some services, such as telemetry, require only a very low basic rate, e.g. 1 kbit/s. Others, such as High Definition Television (HDTV) may require around 140 Mbit/s. So, if the basic rate is determined by the minimal required channel rate (1 kbit/s in the example), a very large number of basic rate channels is necessary to construct a high bit rate connection (around 140,000 basic channels of 1 kbit/s for HDTV). The management and correlation of all these channels, for just one connection then becomes very complicated.

If the basic rate is selected much larger to reduce the complexity of the management of the individual channels, then the waste of the bandwidth becomes too large for low bit rate application. If we take, for instance, 2 Mbit/s as the basic channel rate (where still 70 basic channels are required to constitute an HDTV connection), all voice (64 kbit/s) and low speed data will encounter an enormous waste of redundant bandwidth.

In order to overcome this difficult engineering problem of selecting the basic rate, another possible solution was proposed which uses multiple basic rates (Boettle, 1984). In this solution a basic time frame is divided into time slots of different lengths (Fig. 2.15.).

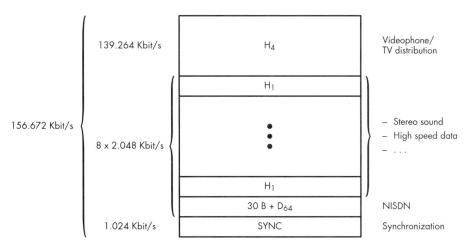

Fig. 2.15. – Multirate Circuit Switching with different Basic Channel Rates

As is shown in this diagram, a channel of 139.264 kbit/s is multiplexed with 7 channels of 2.048 kbit/s, 30 B channels, and a D channel of 64 kbit/s for signalling. In addition, a synchronization channel is defined which allows the receiving side of the link/terminal to determine the frame boundary. The total bit rate capacity is 156.672 kbit/s.

The H4 channel of 139.264 kbit/s was defined to be used for videophone and TV distribution services. The H1 channels (2.048 kbit/s) could be used for HIFI sound, high speed data and other medium speed services. The NISDN channel could be used for voice and other low speed data applications.

We now see already a more efficient mapping of possible services to the available channels, but still with certain limitations very much determined by the choice of the channels.

The switching systems developed for such a solution consist of overlay switches, each switch individually tailored to one specific basic channel rate. A possible switch architecture is shown in Fig. 2.16., where we see that the information coming from (going to) the subscriber access line is demultiplexed/multiplexed into the different channels which are then connected to the different switches. Each individual switch (H4, H1, NISDN) has to be designed and manufactured individually. Control, operation and maintenance can be common to the different switches.

This architecture will inefficiently use its resources. Suppose that all H1 channels are occupied, then no additional H1 connections can be established, even when the H4 switch is completely free.

This solution clearly has some flexibility problems, since once the limited number of basic channel rates are defined, all services must try to fit within one of these channel rates, even sometimes inefficiently, as explained above.

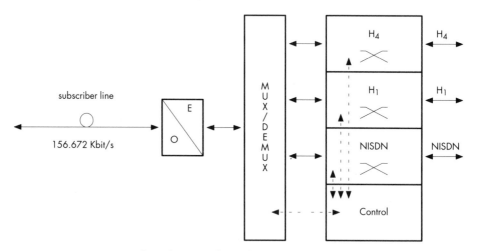

Fig. 2.16. – Switch Architecture for Multirate Circuit Switching with Different Basic Channel Rates

This situation even becomes worse when one considers a number of unknown services and the possible evolution in technology. Take for instance that at the moment the channel rates are defined, the major services are pay TV at 140 Mbit/s, high speed data at 2 Mbit/s and NISDN. At that moment the frame is defined as described in Fig. 2.15. Suppose that some years later, due to the progress in video and audio coding, the pay TV channel now only requires 25 Mbit/s, whereas the high speed data requirements are now around 10 Mbit/s. In addition a new service has emerged, namely videophony at 1 Mbit/s. The channels defined earlier and the switches developed and installed during the first phase can now only be used very inefficiently. And what is even more important, pay TV and high speed data cannot be transported simultaneously, even when they only require in total 35 Mbit/s where 156 Mbit/s is available.

Another important disadvantage of both the pure multirate circuit switching and the enhanced version is its inability to cope efficiently with sources with a fluctuating and bursty character. Indeed, as in a circuit switching solution, the resources are occupied in the network even when the sending terminal is idle. The selected channel rate must be at least equal to or larger than the peak bit rate of the source.

Experiments based on this concept have been built in various countries (Domann, 1990). But because of its inflexibility and inability to treat bursty sources efficiently, it has not been retained by CCITT as the solution for the broadband network of the future.

2.4.3. Fast circuit switching

In order to extend the concepts of circuit switching to sources with fluctuating and bursty nature, fast circuit switching (FCS) has been proposed (O'Reilly, 1987). The resources in the FCS network are only allocated when information is sent, and released when no information is sent.

One can state that FCS relates to circuit switching, as connectionless packet switching (datagram switching) relates to connection-oriented packet switching, in the sense that the resources (i.e. channels) are not permanently allocated, but will only be allocated when needed. This allocation is performed per burst, as is the case in datagram switching, but now under control of fast "associated" signalling, whereas this "signalling" information is present in the header of a datagram for datagram switching.

At call set-up, users request a connection with a bandwidth equal to some integer multiple of the basic rate; the system will not allocate the resources, but store inside the switch information on the required bandwidth and the selected destination, and allocate a header in the signalling channel, identifying that connection. When the source starts sending information, the header will indicate that the source has information, requiring from the switch to allocate the necessary resources immediately.

Since the resources are only allocated on demand, it may happen that the system will not be able to satisfy the simultaneous requests because not enough resources are available.

Clearly, if FCS and MRCS are combined into what may be called multirate fast circuit switching (MRFCS), then one can build a system which allows the use of different information rates. Also, this solution is efficient for bursty services. Still, some drawbacks remain, especially the complexity of designing and controlling such a system. Indeed, the system must be able to set up and tear down connections in a very short time duration.

In some laboratories in the US, prototype systems (Amstutz, 1989) based on FCS-like techniques have been developed. However, especially because of the high requirements for treating signalling at a very high rate, this FCS or MRFCS has not been selected as the solution for the future broadband network.

2.4.4. Packet switching

In packet switching networks, user information is encapsulated in packets which are containing additional information (in the header) used inside the network for routing, error correction, flow control, etc.

These networks, such as X.25, were designed in the sixties, at the time when only poor to medium quality transmission links were available : a BER of 10^{-6} was already considered excellent at that time.

In order to offer an acceptable end-to-end performance on each link of the network, complex protocols were therefore necessary basically performing error and flow control on every link of the connection. This link-by-link error control was required because of the low quality of the links, as explained in section 2.3.1., to ensure that the traffic increase was not too large to guarantee the required semantic transparency.

These packets have a variable length and thus require a rather complex buffer management inside the network. The operating speed was not too high (typically 64 kbit/s), so software buffer control was very well possible. This low speed caused a large delay. However, since real time services did not have to be transmitted over these networks, the lack of time transparency was not a problem.

The higher complexity protocols substantially increase the processing requirements and switching delay inside the network. This makes it very difficult to apply the packet switching technique for real time services (the delay is too long because of retransmissions) and for high speed services at ten/hundreds of Mbit/s (the processing requirements are too high). However, it must be admitted that packet switching is still very efficient and successful for low speed data transfer, as is done in X.25.

An evolution in packet switching can be noticed in CCITT. In a first phase of NISDN, CCITT planned to take the pragmatic approach and support X.25 packet switching over B/D channels.

For the next generation packet switching for NISDN, CCITT envisaged alternative solutions called frame relaying and frame switching. These solutions have less functionality than X.25 and become possible due to the increasing quality of the links. Since less functionality is implemented in the nodes, a higher throughput can be achieved.

In Table 2.4., the functions of these 3 alternative packet switching systems are described. The first is the classical X.25 protocol, which uses at layer 2 the Balanced Link Access Procedure (LAPB) of the HDLC protocol. In LAPB, the links between nodes and terminals and internode links perform all typical layer 2 functions as defined by ISO. These functions are frame boundary recognition using flags (01111110) and the related bit stuffing to guarantee bit transparency.

In addition, it performs CRC generation at the sending side of the link and CRC check at the receiving side, and the related retransmission of missing or erroneous frames by an ARQ (Automatic Repeat Request) protocol. It also performs flow control and multiplexing of logical channels at layer 3.

In the frame relaying solution, retransmissions of user data frames, as needed for error correction, are only performed end-to-end (between users' terminals). Only an error detection function based on the CRC is performed, in order to discard erroneous frames, since it is of no use to continue transporting erroneous frames. No flow control of the frames or a multiplexing at the packet level will be performed.

Functionality	X.25	Frame switching	Frame relaying
Frame boundary recognition (flags)	X	X	X
Bit transparency (bit stuffing)	X	X	X
CRC checking/generation	X	X	X
Error control (ARQ)	X	X	
Flow control	X	X	
Multiplexing of logical channels	X		

Table 2.4. – Functional Difference between Generations of Packet Switching

The frame switching option differs from the frame relaying option in the sense that error and flow control are retained at the frame level, so that frame retransmission and sliding window flow control will continue to be performed on the link level. However, no multiplexing at the packet level is supported, as is the case in X.25.

Feasibility studies have shown that the speed at which these 3 techniques can economically be operated in the early 1990 time frame is limited to around 2 Mbit/s for X.25. A 2 to 4 times speed improvement may be envisaged for frame switching, whereas frame relaying protocols would be capable of operating at around 140 Mbit/s, if proper bit transparency techniques are used.

Frame relaying and frame switching are already drifting away from the original definition of packet switching, and can be placed at the left of packet switching (Fig. 2.4.), quite close to fast packet switching. Currently, CCITT has defined a set of Recommendations for Frame Relay, proposing it as the next generation packet switching, only applicable for data services. Several operators worldwide introduced commercial Frame Relay services in 1992.

2.4.5. Fast packet switching - asynchronous transfer mode

Fast packet switching is a concept that covers several alternatives, all with the same basic characteristic, i.e. packet switching with minimal functionality in the network. Different names were used for alternative solutions as proposed by several organizations. The most famous names are ATM (Asynchronous Transfer Mode) which is the official name used by CCITT, ATD (Asynchronous Time Division) (Coudreuse, 1983) which was the name originally used by CNET and later taken over in Europe, and Fast Packet Switching (Turner, 1983), which was the technique more deeply studied in the United States.

The name fast packet switching is applicable since it allows the systems to operate at a much higher rate than usual packet switching systems thanks to its limited functionalities. In the acronyms ATD and ATM, the word asynchronous has been used since it allows an asynchronous operation between the sender clock and the receiver clock. The difference between both clocks can easily be solved by inserting/removing empty/unassigned "packets" in the information stream, i.e. packets which do not contain useful information.

Since ATM is the name standardized by CCITT, I will continue to use the acronym ATM instead of fast packet switching or ATD. All these alternatives have one common feature which guarantees their success, namely the possibility to transport any service, irrespective of its characteristics such as the bit rate, its quality requirements or its bursty nature. This big advantage was one of the main motivations for CCITT to decide that ATM will be the transfer mode for the future BISDN.

A network based on such a service-independent transfer technique will not suffer from the disadvantages of the other transfer modes described above, like service dependence, not being future-safe, inefficiency in the use of the available resources, not adapted to bursty sources, etc. On the contrary, it will be :

(1) Flexible and future-safe

Advances in the state of the art of coding algorithms and VLSI technology may reduce the bandwidth requirements of existing services. New services may emerge with unknown characteristics. All these changes can be supported with success without modifications of the ATM network and without loss of efficiency. The ATM systems (transmission, switching, multiplexing, ...) do not need to be modified.

(2)   Efficient in the use of its available resources

All available resources in the network can be used by all services, so that an optimal statistical sharing of the resources can be obtained. No resource specialization exists in an ATM network, meaning that every available resource can be used by any service.

(3)   One universal network

Since only one network needs to be designed, controlled, manufactured and maintained, the overall costs of the system may be smaller, due to economies of scale. These advantages will benefit all involved parties in the telecommunication world : customers, operators and manufacturers.

In the rest of this section I will first describe the basic definition of ATM; then will explain the performance of such a system both with respect to time and semantic transparency; finally I will detail the reasons why options have been taken by the CCITT experts with respect to information field size, header functionalities and supportive functions.

2.4.5.1.   Basic definition

ATM, ATD and fast packet switching have the following common characteristics :

(1)   No error protection or flow control on a link-by-link basis

If a link of the connection, either the user-to-network link or the internal links between the network nodes, introduces an error during the transmission, or is temporarily overloaded thereby causing the loss of packets, no special action will be taken on that link to correct this error (e.g. requesting for retransmission on that link as is done in packet switching).

This error protection can be omitted, since the links in the network have a very high quality (i.e. low BER). As was shown in section 2.3.1., no error control is then required on a link-by-link basis. Flow control will also not be supported in an ATM network. Proper resource allocation and queue dimensioning in the network will guarantee a controlled number of queue overflows, causing packet loss. Values of packet loss probability of 10^{-8} up to 10^{-12} are very well achievable.

Different sorts of errors can happen in ATM networks, as described in the previous section on semantic transparency : namely bit errors, packet loss and packet insertion.

First, transmission errors (single bit errors and burst errors) occur in an ATM network. Single bit errors and burst errors occur in any transfer mode, mainly caused by noise, protection switching and loss of synchronization. In circuit switched networks nothing is done against these errors inside the network; in packet switched networks error detection and correction features are provided inside the network (e.g. by CRC and ARQ). ATM thus takes the option of circuit switched networks for this problem and relies on end-to-end protocols.

Loss of packets and insertion of packets caused by errors in the header are typical for packet networks. In classical packet switching networks this problem is solved inside the network by asking retransmission between the nodes (ARQ).

In ATM networks no dynamic actions are defined against packet loss (such as ARQ). Only preventive actions are provided by ATM by allocating resources during connection set-up and checking whether enough resources are available. Loss of packets due to queue overflow is a typical problem for ATM since no flow control is provided in the nodes, and the possibility exist that queues are momentarily overwhelmed by different sources. However, this momentary packet loss is controlled and limited to very small values thanks to the connection-oriented mode.

(2) ATM operates in a connection-oriented mode

Before information is transferred from the terminal to the network, a logical/virtual connection set-up phase must first allow the network to do the reservation of the necessary resources, if these are available. If no sufficient resources are available the connection is refused to the requesting terminal.

When the information transfer phase is finished, the resources are released. This connection-oriented mode of operation allows the network to guarantee in all cases a minimal packet loss ratio, and thus a maximal quality.

Indeed, at call set-up it is checked whether statistically enough resources are available. This means that it can be guaranteed that resources will be available and queue overflow will only occur with a very low probability. The probability of overflow can be dimensioned by queuing theory (see Chapter 4 on switching). Typical values which are considered for ATM systems range between 10^{-8} and 10^{-12} for the probability of losing a packet.

(3) The header functionality is reduced

To guarantee a fast processing in the network, the ATM header has a very limited function. Its main function is the identification of the virtual connection by an identifier which is selected at call set-up and guarantees a proper routing of each packet in the network. In addition, it allows an easy multiplexing of different virtual connections over a single link. As we will see later in the detailed definition of ATM, different sort of connections (paths) can be multiplexed on a single link.

If an error occurs in the header, misrouting can be the consequence. This causes error multiplication : one bit error in the header may result in n consecutive bit errors (if n is the packet size) as a result of the packet loss. To reduce the error multiplication effect caused by misrouting, error detection and/or correction mechanisms on the header bits are proposed to reduce or avoid such a misrouting. The gain of such error detection/correction technique on the performance will be explained later in this Chapter (see section 2.4.5.2.).

In addition to the virtual connection identifier, a very limited number of functions are also supported by the header, mainly related to maintenance (see section 2.4.5.4. in this Chapter). All other header functions of the classical packet switching systems are removed, e.g. sequence number for error and flow control, D-bit, M-bit, etc.

Due to the limited functionality in the header, the implementation of the header processing in the ATM nodes is simple and can be done at very high speeds (150 Mbit/s up to Gbit/s). This results in low processing and queuing delays.

(4)   The information field length is relatively small

In order to reduce the internal buffers in the switching nodes, and to limit the queuing delays in those buffers, the information field length is kept relatively small. Indeed, small buffers guarantee a small delay and delay jitter as required by real time services. More details on these delay values will be given in the next section of this Chapter.

The ATM principle allows the implementation of several kind of ATM switches. In Chapter 4 of this book, a number of alternative switch architectures will be explained with the related performance characteristics. However, all switches can be schematically depicted by the general scheme used in Fig. 2.17. A number of n incoming links $(I_1, ... I_n)$ transport ATM information to the switch, where depending on the value of the header this information is switched to an outgoing link $(O_1, ..., O_q)$.

The incoming header and the incoming link number are used to access a translation table. The result of the access to the translation table is the outgoing link and a new header value. In the example, we see that information with header x on incoming link I_1 will be switched to outgoing link O_1 and will get header k. Information with header y on incoming link I_n will be switched to outgoing link O_2 and will get header j.

Note that this is just a functional diagram and tells nothing about the implementation of the switch, e.g. where the translation table is located.

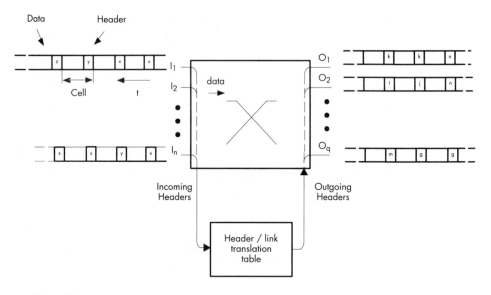

Fig. 2.17. – ATM Switching Principle

Translation table

Incoming link	Time slot	Outgoing link	Timeslot
I_1	x y z	O_1 O_q O_2	k m l
. . .			
I_n	x y s	O_1 O_2 O_q	n i g

2.4.5.2. *Performance characteristics*

The definition of ATM has specific consequences on the performance of an overall ATM based network, especially with respect to time and semantic transparency.

(1) Time transparency

Due to the high speeds used in a broadband network and the small information field of ATM packets, the delay characteristics of an ATM network are very much different from those of classical packet switching networks.

Since delay issues are mainly applicable to real time services such as voice and video, we will focus here on possible problems with respect to these services transported over an ATM network. Packet oriented services (e.g. computer data transfer) are not particularly sensitive to delays caused by information transfer only.

ATM delay characteristics

The delay through an ATM network is determined by different parts of the network, each contributing individually to the total delay. These delays are shown in Fig. 2.18a. for a pure ATM network and in Fig. 2.18b. for a combined ATM/non-ATM network.

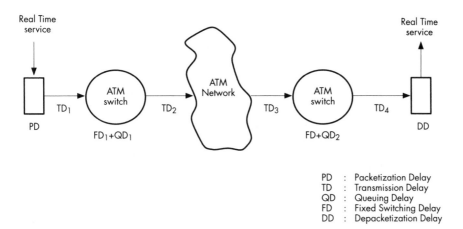

PD	:	Packetization Delay
TD	:	Transmission Delay
QD	:	Queuing Delay
FD	:	Fixed Switching Delay
DD	:	Depacketization Delay

Fig. 2.18a. – Delay in a Pure ATM Network

In a pure ATM network (Fig. 2.18a.), the information is assembled into packets at the source terminal and depacketized at the destination terminal. Internally in the network, packets are used everywhere.

In a combined ATM/non-ATM network (Fig. 2.18b.), parts of the network operate with packets, other parts use synchronous networks (e.g. NISDN). An example is a voice conversation between a user connected to an ATM network and another user connected to the classical telephone network.

The following parameters are contributing to the overall network delay :

(a) Transmission delay (TD)
    This delay depends on the distance between both endpoints. Depending on the transmission medium used, it ranges typically between 4 and 5 μs per km. This delay is independent of the type of transfer mode used.

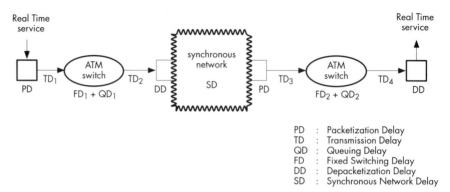

Fig. 2.18b. – Delay in a Combined ATM / Non-ATM Network

(b)   Packetization delay (PD)

This delay is introduced every time a real time service such as voice and video is converted into packets (packetized). In a pure ATM network, packetization is only required at the source. In a network where ATM systems and non-ATM systems coexist, this packetization is required at every boundary between both types of networks.

(c)   Switching delay

In an ATM exchange, the switching delay is composed of a fixed part, called the fixed switching delay (FD) and a variable part, determined by the queues in the exchanges, called the queuing delay (QD).

- Fixed switching delay (FD)

This delay is implementation-dependent, and caused by internal packet transfer through the hardware. It is the delay encountered in the switch at zero load, i.e. if only a single packet passes through the switch. Since the switching is performed in hardware and at very high speeds this fixed switching delay can be kept very low. This low value is obtained by all proposed switching architectures, as will be explained in Chapter 4 on switching.

- Queuing delay (QD)

Since ATM systems are statistically multiplexing and switching ATM packets, queues are necessary in the network to avoid an excessive loss of packets. These queues introduce a delay which is typical for a packet switching network (and also for ATM switches). The delay varies with the load of the network, and is determined by the behavior of the queues. This behavior is characterized by a pdf (probability density function) of the queue length describing the statistical behavior of the queues in the network. Instead of using the complete pdf to describe this queuing delay, we will use only a q quantile. This is the value of the delay which will be surpassed with a probability of 10^{-q}.

(d)   Depacketization delay (DD)

Real time services require at the destination or at the boundaries with synchronous networks an additional delay. This delay must be added to the packets to smooth out the stochastic delay (i.e. delay jitter) introduced by the network in order to guarantee a reconstruction of the original synchronous bit stream. The depacketization delay can be considered as some network conditioning function in the terminal, to remove the jitter on the network delay. This was explained in section 2.3.3., and shown in Fig. 2.13.

This depacketization delay is required at the receiver in a full ATM network. In a mixed ATM/non-ATM network it is required at every boundary between ATM and synchronous networks. This delay will again be determined using the q quantile. Indeed, if the delay of the packet through the network is larger than the depacketization delay, then the packet will arrive too late to be fed into the depacketization process and will be lost. However this will only occur with a probability of 10^{-q}, so that a packet loss probability will be added by the receiver to the overall network packet loss probability. So this 10^{-q} must be kept low enough, at least as good as the network itself.

This additional delay (DD) added to the queuing delay (QD) will be added at the destination, but it is the q quantile value of the queuing delay which will be used for the calculations. Therefore, the depacketization as such will not appear in the formula for the total delay. The sum of the queuing delay and the depacketization delay will result in a delay which has a dirac-like pdf at the q quantile.

These delay parameters can then be combined to calculate the total end-to-end delay in the network in the case where the network is pure ATM (D1) and in the case where ATM will coexist with synchronous networks (D2). These sums add the worst case values for the individual parameters.

$$D1 \;=\; \sum_{i} TD_i \;+\; \sum_{j} FD_j \;+\; maxq \int QD_j + PD \qquad (2.11.)$$

$$D2 \;=\; \sum_{i} TD_i \;+\; \sum_{j} FD_j \;+\; \sum_{k} maxq \int QD_{j_k} + k \,.\, PD \;+\; \sum_{l} SD_l \qquad (2.12.)$$

In these formulae i indicates the number of transmission links, j the number of ATM switches, k the number of paired packetizers/depacketizers between ATM and non-ATM parts of the network including the terminals and l the number of synchronous exchanges. SD_l gives the delay of a synchronous exchange. For instance if we have an ATM - STM - ATM - STM - ATM chain, we have k = 3 (in the example of Fig. 2.18., k = 2). The parameter j_k denotes the number of ATM switches in one of the k ATM sections between a packetizer/depacketizer transmitter/receiver pair. The sum of the queuing delays is not a pure mathematical sum, but rather a statistical convolution of all probability density functions of the delay, and therefore denoted by $\int$. The q quantile value of this convolution denoted as maxq will then be used as the encountered delay, since the depacketizer will ensure that all packets have this maximum delay.

Values in an ATM network

In the example we will further elaborate, we assume a distance between source and destination of 1000 km, resulting in a transmission delay of 4000 μs. We also assume 2 synchronous switches, each with a delay of 450 μs (the average value allowed by CCITT) resulting in a total synchronous switching delay of 900 μs. With respect to the ATM characteristics, we assume 3 lengths of the information field (16, 32 and 64 bytes) and 2 switching and transmission speeds (150 and 600 Mbit/s). We also consider in total 8 ATM exchanges.

The transmission delay (TD) is determined by the distance, and is independent of the ATM concept. The same applies to SD_1, the switching delay of the non-ATM switches.

Packetization delay (PD)
This delay depends on the packet length and on the speed at which the source is generating bits. A typical value for the packet information length is 16 to 64 bytes. Indeed, the packets may not be too long, to limit this delay. On the other hand, the packets may not be too short, in order not to introduce a low transmission efficiency caused by a large overhead from the header, as will be explained later. If the packet is completely filled, then for 64 kbit/s voice this results in a 2 (for 16 bytes) to 8 (for 64 bytes) ms packetization delay. For high speed real time services (2 Mbit/s and higher), this packetization delay becomes very small (125 μs and smaller).

Fixed switching delay (FD)
This delay depends on the implementation (see Chapter 4 on switching), but is in the order of tens of packets per switching exchange. For small sized packets (16–64 bytes) and high switching speeds (150–600 Mbit/s) this results in a value between 2 and 32 μs (see Table 2.5.) per exchange, or between 16 and 256 μs for 8 consecutive exchanges.

Queuing delay (QD)
The queuing delay very much depends on the load of the links inside the networks and on the allowable probability of losing a packet, as can be seen in Fig. 2.19. There we see that at loads around 80 %, the queue size and the

related delay starts to grow exponentially. Therefore, typical load values which are considered for an ATM network are located in the 80 % range. The size of the queues causing this delay depends on the implementation of the ATM switches (see Chapter 4 on switching). Most of the proposed switching architectures need some tens of packets per queue, or less. Only one such queue is required in a small switching architecture (e.g. 16 by 16). For larger configurations (a few thousand inlets and outlets) consecutive queues are required. Therefore, a convolution of the consecutive queuing delays has to be calculated, which will depend on the selected switch architecture. A typical value for this delay can be obtained, for a load around 80 %, a packet loss probability of 10^{-10}, and 50 consecutive queues (e.g. 7 exchanges, each with 6 consecutive queues, and one exchange of 8 consecutive queues). The overall delay is 235 packets for the above assumptions.

Speed	150 Mbit/s			600 Mbit/s		
Packet size (bytes)	16	32	64	16	32	64
TD	4000	4000	4000	4000	4000	4000
FD	64	128	256	16	32	64
QD/DD	200	400	800	50	100	200
PD	2000	4000	8000	200	4000	8000
SD	900	900	900	900	900	900
D1	6264	8528	12256	6166	8132	12364
D2	9365	13828	21956	9016	13132	21364

Link load : 80 %
Packet loss ratio : 10^{-10}

Table 2.5. – Delay (in µs) for Different Speeds and Packet Sizes
and for a 64 Kbit/s Synchronous Connection

For packets between 16 and 64 bytes, and queue processing speeds between 150 and 600 Mbit/s this delay of 235 packets results in a delay between 50 and 800 µs (see Table 2.5.).

Depacketization delay (DD)

The depacketization delay must remove the delay jitter by introducing an additional delay at the receiver. This additional delay is actually determined by the convolution of the queuing delays. If we take the same assumptions as for the queuing delay, then the total jitter to be removed ranges between 50 and 800 μs depending on speed and packet size. This delay will as such not be added, since we have assumed already the maximum value for the queuing delay, so the jitter is already calculated in this value.

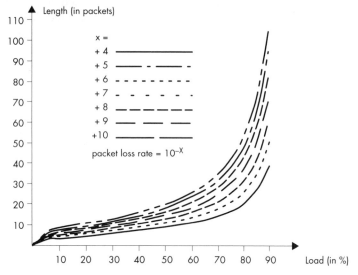

Fig. 2.19. – Queue Length in Function of the Load with an M/D/1 Model

Conclusions on the delay

In Table 2.5. the total delays (D1 and D2) are calculated for the typical example given above for a 64 Kbit/s service (8 ATM exchanges, 2 synchronous exchanges) and a single conversion between ATM and non-ATM (i.e. k = 2). We see that PD is an important contributing factor to the total delay, already for D1, and that for D2 this PD is the major contributing factor, especially for larger packets and low speed services. Note that the QD/DD value for D2 should be somewhat larger than the one shown in the table, since the sum of 2 separate convolutions of for example 25 queues results in a larger value than a single convolution of 50 queues. However, this difference is a few microseconds and thus negligible.

In order to keep the delay small to avoid echo problems for voice, the packets may not be too long. In Table 2.5. we see that all examples still fulfil the requirement of CCITT of an overall delay smaller than 24 ms. But we see that packets larger than 64 bytes or distances more than 1000 km will introduce the need for installing echo cancellers, which is required if the delay is larger than 24 ms. Furthermore, the depacketization delay (and the related buffer) in the receiver will then be large and introduce an expensive buffering at the receiving terminal. Again, this limitation promotes smaller packets.

(2) Semantic transparency

As in any packet switching system, the errors encountered in an ATM network are caused by transmission and switching/multiplexing systems. However, due to the properties of ATM (e.g. no error or flow control) the error behavior is different of that of the classical packet switching systems.

The overall bit error rate of an ATM system is determined by 3 factors :

- The loss and incorrect arrival of bits of the information field due to transmission errors.
- The loss of packets in the switching/multiplexing systems due to queue overflow.
- The loss and incorrect arrival of packets caused by misrouting the packets due to misinterpretation of the header in the switching systems.

The incorrect arrival of bits of the information field caused by transmission errors is independent of the use of ATM and will thus not be discussed here again. I refer to the general section on semantic transparency (3.1.1.) of this Chapter. Only the 2 other errors are affected by the ATM principle and will therefore be discussed in detail in this section.

Packet loss caused by errors in the header

Transmission errors will cause the change of the value of the transmitted bits. If this bit change has occurred on a bit in the information field, this incorrect bit will finally arrive at the destination in ATM, since no error control on a link basis is provided. If the incorrect bit occurs in the header, then the switching/multiplexing equipment will misinterpret the header and may then misroute the packet. This misrouting occurs when the "transformed" header has a value which is that of another connection. In that case 2 connections will suffer from this single bit error. One connection which misses the packet, and another which receives a packet which was not destined for him. If the "transformed" header has a value of a non-existing connection, then the packet will be discarded and only the involved connection will miss a packet. In both cases a multiplication of errors occurs.

Let us calculate this error multiplication effect. In addition I will describe what can be done against it and what gain in performance can be expected.

Suppose that the bit error rate of the transmission system is B. This bit error rate can be either uniformly distributed over all bits (no consecutive errors) or grouped so that very long burst errors occur, longer than one packet, as was explained in section 2.3.1.1.

• In the case where a burst error occurs, the information in the payload (i.e. the information field) of the packet is wrong anyhow, so any error in the header, causing the packet to be lost, has no direct error multiplication effect.
• In the case where a single error occurs, this error in the header will cause a misinterpretation of the header in the switching/multiplexing system resulting in the complete packet to be lost. This results in a multiplication effect, which can be calculated as follows.

We assume that a packet consists of h bits in the header, and i bits in the information field. Let us also assume that all packets have the same length, or that the average length of all packets is H, to simplify the calculations. Thus $H = h + i$. We also assume that the ATM switching node interprets all header bits and uses them to determine the destination.

The transmission system cannot make a distinction between header and information bits, so the errors are uniformly distributed over all H bits. This leads to the following simple observation :

• The probability that an error occurred in the header is

$$\frac{h}{h + i} \cdot B$$

• The probability that an error occurred in the information field is

$$\frac{i}{i + h} \cdot B$$

We take a simple model to calculate the error multiplication effect consisting of a single ATM switching node which receives bits of a transmission system with bit error rate B and is not introducing additional errors in the information field. The overall bit error rate can be calculated as the sum of the bit error rate of the transmission system on the information field, and of the bit error rate caused by misrouting the ATM packets. If a switching system interprets the header then 3 possible cases can arise :

(1) The error(s) in the header is (are) not detected neither corrected : in that case a wrong routing decision will be taken. If we assume the worst case situation, that any misrouting will end at an incorrect destination, then i bits will arrive at an incorrect destination, and at the same time these bits will not arrive at the final destination. Thus 2 . i bits will be incorrect. This will result in an overall bit error rate B_1 of :

$$B_1 = \frac{h}{h+i} B \cdot 2i + \frac{i}{h+i} \cdot B = \frac{i(2h+1)}{h+i} \cdot B \quad (2.13a.)$$

The multiplication effect on the bit error rate is thus $M_1 = B_1/B$, or

$$M_1 = \frac{2h+1}{1+h/i} \quad (2.14a.)$$

(2)   The errors in the header are detected, but not corrected. In that case, i bits will not arrive at the ultimate destination. This will result in an overall bit error rate B_2 of :

$$B_2 = \frac{h}{h+i} B \cdot i + \frac{i}{h+i} \cdot B = \frac{i(h+1)}{h+i} \cdot B \quad (2.13b.)$$

The multiplication effect M_2 is thus

$$M_2 = \frac{h+1}{1+h/i} \quad (2.14b.)$$

(3)   The errors in the header are corrected. All information bits of that packet will arrive at the correct destination. This will result in an overall bit error rate B_3 :

$$B_3 = \frac{h}{h+i} B \cdot O + \frac{i}{h+i} \cdot B = \frac{i}{h+i} \cdot B \quad (2.13c.)$$

The multiplication effect M_3 is then

$$M_3 = \frac{1}{1+h/i} \quad (2.14c.)$$

which is smaller than one, so no error multiplication occurs.

These 3 different multiplication ratios are shown in Fig. 2.20., for different ratios of header to information field length. It is clear that the larger the header field length h, the worse the multiplication effect becomes for a constant information length. Since the probability that an error occurred in the header increases. We also see that multiplication factors around 100 are very possible where no header correction/detection is provided. In case only detection is supported, multiplication factors around 50 are still very possible.

In case 3, full error correction is assumed, i.e. all errors in the header (even multiple errors) can be corrected. However, since such a full error correction using FEC (forward error correction code) requires a large overhead in terms of additional bits and is quite complex to implement, a simpler approach is used.

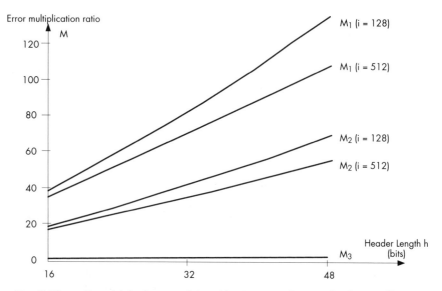

Fig. 2.20. – Error Multiplication Caused by Errors in the Header for 3 Different Error Protection Techniques
(M_1 : No Protection; M_2 : Error Detection; M_3 : Error Correction)

In this simplified approach only limited correction capabilities are used. As explained in section 2.3.1.1. most of the transmission errors are either single errors, or burst errors. Single errors can simply be corrected by cyclic codes such as BCH codes. Burst errors are much more difficult to correct and require more overhead to cope with. On the other hand, these burst errors also corrupt the information bits. So header error correction is useless in this case. Therefore, the option of only single bit error correction solves already most of the severe problems. When a burst error occurs, multiple errors in the header cannot be corrected with these codes. The header will be wrongly corrected, giving also rise to an error multiplication due to misrouting, so that the correction function has a reverse effect.

Therefore, an adaptive error detection/correction mechanism is very attractive (Fig. 2.21.) : in normal mode the header error protection works in correction mode and single bit errors are corrected. When an error is corrected, the protection mechanism switches over to detection mode. This switchover ensures that in case of a burst error, only the first packet will be miscorrected and misrouted, the consecutive incorrect header packets will be discarded, by the detection mechanism, which only discards packets with an incorrect header.

In the case of a single bit header error, the error will be corrected, and in the next packet no error will occur, so that no misrouting will take place.

To complete this adaptive mechanism, when no longer errors are detected in the header, the protection mechanism switches back to correction mode. This already happens in the first packet where a single bit error occurred, and in the case of a burst error only when the burst was followed by a correct header.

This adaptive mechanism is very well suited for single errors in the header and burst errors, and is rather simple to implement.

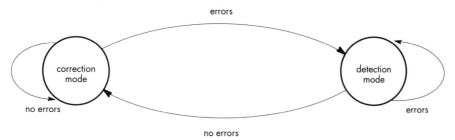

Fig. 2.21. – Adaptive Error Detection / Correction Algorithm in the Header

Transmission systems regularly use line coding techniques (e.g. Manchester, HDB3, 5B/6B, ...) to allow easier bit clock recovery at the receiver and a better distribution of the signal energy over the entire available frequency spectrum. However, some of these line coding techniques may have an impact on this error detection/correction scheme.

Indeed, line coding (e.g. 5B/6B coding) and autonomous scrambling perform a bit error multiplication, in contrast with a reset scrambler where no error multiplication occurs. This means that a single bit error in the transmission system may cause multiple errors after the reverse line coding operation. Note that this is another kind of multiplication as the one described above. In this case of error multiplication, the location of the correlated bit error depends on the type of coding. In line coding techniques, the correlated errored bit will always be located in the same codeword (e.g. 6 bits in a 5B/6B code). In an autonomous scrambler, the correlated error occurs at the position determined by the number of stages in the scrambler. So, if a scrambler is used with more stages than the length of the header, the additional error will arise in the information field. This will cause no multiplication effect if single bit errors can be corrected as explained above. Where the number of stages is smaller than the number of bits in the header, then the described algorithm is no longer valid.

So, when the line coding technique of an ATM system is determined, one must take into account the header error detection/correction capabilities of the

ATM header to avoid large error multiplication effects as described above. Line coding mechanism suited to the adaptive protocol described above are for example reset scrambling and autonomous scrambling with more stages than the length of the header.

Packet loss caused by queue overflow

By proper dimensioning of the queues internally in the network, the packet loss can be reduced to a value which is acceptable by the end-to-end services. In Table 2.3., these values are depicted for some services. It can be seen that there the most stringent requirement lies around a packet loss rate of 10^{-8}. So if the queues in the switches/multiplexers can be dimensioned such that this packet loss ratio can be achieved, no visible/audible degradation of the service will happen. This means that the semantic transparency can be guaranteed, even for the most stringent services, by proper queue dimensioning, call acceptance control and policing functions (see Chapter 7).

This queue dimensioning is very much eased by the connection-oriented characteristic of ATM. This allows the control of the network to accept or refuse new connections if the load is smaller than or larger than the one for which the queues were dimensioned.

As is shown in Fig. 2.19., the packet loss rate can be kept to values of 10^{-10} for loads around 80 % of the maximum link capacity, if queues around 50 packets are implemented, and under certain traffic assumptions (i.e. packet arrival rates).

2.4.5.3.   *Definition of the information field length*

We already mentioned that the information field length of ATM packets has to be rather small. However, it was necessary in the ATM definition to specify whether fixed or variable length packets would be allowed, and in addition what is the size (for fixed) or range (in case variable was selected) of the information field.

As will be shown, several arguments have contributed to the choice of this important parameter.

(1)   Variable versus fixed length packets

An important debate in the definition of the ATM concept was the choice of fixed or variable length packets. In the initial definition of ATD, as proposed by CNET, only very short, fixed length packets were applied. The selected size was 16 bytes. The original FPS option described by Turner contained variable length packets.

Different factors are contributing to the advantages and disadvantages of both solutions. The most important parameters are : the transmission bandwidth efficiency, the achievable switching performance (i.e. the switching speed versus complexity) and the delay.

Transmission bandwidth efficiency

In a packet switching system, overhead appears because of the header. The transmission efficiency is determined as :

$$\eta = \frac{Number\ of\ information\ bytes}{Number\ of\ information\ bytes\ +\ number\ of\ overhead\ bytes} \qquad (2.15.)$$

(a) Fixed length packets
     Where the packets have a fixed length this efficiency can be calculated as

$$\eta_F = \frac{X}{\left| \frac{X}{L} \right| . (L + H)} \qquad (2.16a.)$$

where L = Information size of the packet in bytes
       H = Header size of the packet in bytes
       X = Number of useful information bytes to transmit

if $|z|$ represents the smallest integer larger than or equal to z.

The efficiency is optimal for all information units which are multiples of the packet information size, i.e.

$$\left| \frac{X}{L} \right| . L = X$$

In the optimal case the efficiency becomes

$$\eta_{FOPT} = \frac{L}{L + H} \qquad (2.16b.)$$

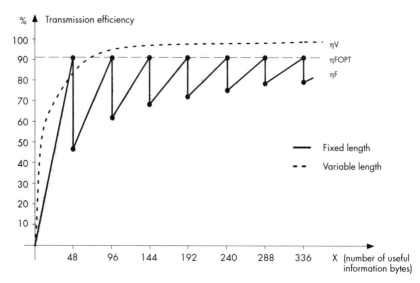

Fig. 2.22. – Transmission Overhead for Fixed and Variable Length Packets

In Fig. 2.22. this efficiency η_{FOPT} is shown for a packet size of 48 bytes and a header of 5 bytes, i.e. L = 48, H = 5. In the same diagram we see that η_F has a sawtooth shape. As we can see, the efficiency very much depends on the useful information bytes to be transmitted. If the number of useful information bytes is large, the optimal achievable efficiency is approached. Only if the number of useful information bytes is small, this efficiency is rather low. So the distribution of the number of useful information bytes to be transmitted largely determines the efficiency. However, when looking at the possible applications which have to be transported over a broadband network, we can see that the following efficiency figures can be obtained :

- Voice : since voice is a CBR (continuous bit rate) service, we can take the option at the sending terminal only to transmit a packet when it is completely filled (thereby introducing a packetization delay). So the efficiency can reach the optimal achievable value, if packets are completely filled, which then puts limitions on the packet size in order to limit the packetization delay (see section 2.4.5.2.).
- Video : Where fixed bit rate video coding techniques are used, this service can be considered as a CBR service, again reaching the optimal efficiency. Where variable bit rate video coding techniques are used, it may occasionally happen that packets are not completely filled. However, a typical video image contains thousands of bytes, so the optimal obtainable efficiency will be very closely approached.

- Data : here we must make a distinction between low speed and high speed applications. For low speed applications (e.g. keyboard input), small information units have to be considered, so the efficiency is rather small (around 10 %); for high speed applications (file transfer, image transfer for CAD, ...) the very long information field (e.g. file, image, ...) can be cut into fixed packets giving rise to an efficiency very close to the optimal (e.g. for 1000 bytes the efficiency is 89 %, instead of an η_{FOPT} of 90.5 % in the example given above).

Since the traffic in a broadband network will largely be composed of video, high speed data and voice, the overall transmission efficiency approaches the optimal, even if fixed length packets are used.

(b) Variable length packets
If the packets have a variable length, then the overhead is determined by the header, and the flags to delimit the packets (e.g. 6 bits as in HDLC) plus in addition some stuffing bits to ensure proper flag recognition. It is also appropriate to add to the header a length indicator, determining the length of the packet. So the overhead becomes

$$\eta_V = \frac{X}{X + H + h_v} \qquad (2.17.)$$

where h_v is the specific packet header overhead determined by its variable length character (flags, length indicator,...). In Fig. 2.22., we assume again a header length of 5 bytes and 2 bytes of specific overhead for variable length (h_v). It can be seen from Fig. 2.22. that the transmission efficiency of variable length packets can be very high (close to 100 %) for very long packets.
      However, for practical reasons such as buffer dimensioning, delay, ..., the maximum length of variable length packets has to be limited to a certain threshold.

(c) Conclusion
With respect to transmission efficiency, it can be concluded that in general, the efficiency of variable length packets is better than that of fixed length packets. However, when we look at the specific case of a broadband network this gain of transmission efficiency is rather limited. Since the main traffic contributing broadband services will consist of a combination of voice, video, and bulk data transfer.

Switching speed and complexity

The complexity of implementing fixed or variable length packet switching, depends on the functions to be performed in both cases, and the related technology requirements for these functions. Two important factors are contributing to the complexity of the implemention of an ATM switching system : the speed of operation and the queue memory size requirements.

(a)   Speed of operation
      This speed depends on the functions to be performed and the available time to perform them.

      Header processing
      One important function in ATM switching systems is the header processing. Let us assume that the header functions are identical in both the fixed and variable length case. In the case of fixed length packets, the available time to perform all functions is fixed (e.g. 2.8 μs in the 48 + 5 byte solution at 150 Mbit/s).
            With variable length packets, the available time depends on the worst case (i.e. the smallest packet), so the speed requirements are much higher (e.g. to perform the same functions for a 5 + 5 byte packet at 150 Mbit/s only 533 ns are available).

      Queue memory management
      In case of fixed length packets, the memory management system can assign memory blocks with always the same size, namely the size of the packet. This operation is rather simple, as well as the management of the free memory list, which is only packet based.
            In case of variable length packets, the memory management system must be able to assign memory blocks in multiples of bytes so that algorithms like Find best fit, Find first fit, ... must be implemented at very high speeds. The free memory management also becomes more complex (Peterson, 1985).

(b)   Queue memory size requirements
      The memory requirements of a system based on fixed length packets depend on the load and the acceptable packet loss rate. This is shown in Fig. 2.19. for an M/D/1 process. The queue dimensioning has to be done in a number of packets. In bytes this means that the larger the packet, the larger the memory requirements are.
            In case variable length packets have to be supported by the queuing system, the queue dimensioning is much more complicated and depends

on the mix of packet lengths. A simple dimensioning rule for variable length packets assumes that the dimensioning is done for the worst case, i.e. the longest packet. With this solution, the memory requirements are much larger for the variable length case than in the case of fixed length packets, since very long packets can occur in the general variable length solution. In case of optimal dimensioning, the traffic mix has to be known in advance, which is quite difficult.

(c) Conclusion
For both parameters, the speed of operation and the queue memory size requirements, the fixed length solution has to be preferred over the variable length solution.

Delay

As shown in section 4.5.2.1., the size of ATM packets has to be rather limited in order not to introduce large delays in the network, thereby causing problems for real time services. An important problem is the delay for voice if the packet size is too large. Therefore, if the ATM packets have to be variable length, they may only fluctuate in a limited range.

Conclusion on fixed or variable length

For a broadband network, where the major envisaged applications are voice, video and bulk data, the gain in transmission efficiency obtained for variable length packets is much smaller than the gain which can be achieved by fixed length packets in terms of switching speed and complexity. In addition, the range of variable length is very limited. Therefore the preferred solution is clearly that with fixed length packets. However, it is important that this conclusion is only valid for the described broadband application, and may be revised for some specific applications.

   In 1988, ATM was already some years under study in SGXVIII of CCITT. At that time, the CCITT experts came to the conclusion that the fixed length solution was to be preferred, based on the arguments described above. It was also decided then to use a name other than "packet" to indicate a fixed length packet. The name cell was adopted. From now on I will therefore use the word "cell" to denote the fixed length ATM packet.

(2)   Size of the ATM cell

Once it is decided to use fixed length packets or cells, the main issue becomes the length of the cell. Several aspects are influenced by the cell length and are determining parameters in the choice of this length. The most important aspects are :

- Transmission efficiency.
- Delay (packetization delay, queuing delay, jitter and related depacketization delay).
- Implementation complexity.

(a)   Transmission efficiency
       This efficiency is determined by the ratio between the header size and the information field size. If we assume that all packets are completely filled then the efficiency becomes

$$\eta_H = \frac{L}{L + H} \tag{2.18.}$$

The longer the information field, the higher the efficiency for the same header size. This can be seen in Fig. 2.23. where we assume H is 4 or 5 bytes and, respectively, show η_4 and η_5. A header of 4 or 5 bytes is a typical value for an ATM cell header, as will be shown in the next section.

(b)   Delay
       Some delay parameters (FD, QD, PD) are impacted by the cell size. However, on some delay parameters, the value of the information field size has a larger impact than on other delay parameters. The following delay parameters have to be considered :

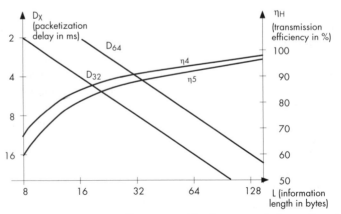

Fig. 2.23. – Transmission Efficiency and Packetization Delay in Function of Information Length

Packetization delay

The packetization delay for constant bit rate services increases with the size of information field size as shown in Fig 2.23. There we show the packetization delay for 32 kbit/s (D_{32}) and 64 kbit/s (D_{64}) voice coding. These curves are only valid if the cells are completely filled. The increase in packetization delay may have an important impact on the overall network performance. This results in larger problems with respect to the time transparency of the network, requiring potentially echo cancellers for voice.

Overall network delay

The overall network delay for voice has to be limited. CCITT Recommendation Q.161 states that a delay of 24 ms is still acceptable without echo cancellers. In case higher delays occur, echo cancellers are required. For typical national connections, the overall end-to-end delay can be kept within limits if the packetization delay remains around 4 ms, (or the cell size around 32 bytes). At 64 bytes, and a few conversions between ATM and non-ATM networks, this 24 ms is rapidly exceeded, requiring even in national connections, the frequent introduction of echo cancellers.

If we take the example used for Table 2.5., with 1000 km transmission, 8 ATM switching nodes and 2 ATM to non-ATM conversions then the total end-to-end delay for 32 bytes cells is around 14 ms, whereas for 64 bytes cells this delay becomes 22 ms.

It is thus shown that in a realistic example, too large a cell size can have an enormous impact on the introduction of ATM and jeopardize the use of ATM networks for voice because of the requirements for echo cancellers. Several options are possible in the choice of the cell length :

- A short cell length (32 bytes or less) so that in almost all situations voice connections can be supported without echo cancellers.
- A longer cell length (64 bytes or more); in this case 2 possible options exist.

  - Install echo cancellers for most of the voice connections
  - Fill the cells only partially for voice, so that the packetization delay is reduced to a level that echo cancellers are no longer required. However, this solution reduces the transmission efficiency

- Intermediate cell length : (between 32 and 64) : in this case echo cancellers can be avoided in a large number of cases where the number of nodes (i), the number of transitions between ATM and non-ATM (k) and the transmission distance are not too large. Also, partially filled cells can be considered here.

Queuing and depacketization delay

The queuing delay is influenced by the ratio between the information field size L and the header size H as is shown in Figure 2.24. The delays are calculated for a switching node operating at 150 Mbit/s. These curves are valid for all values of L and H, but for reference, I have indicated 3 typical values (32 + 4, 64 + 4 and 128 + 4).

Two mechanisms with an opposite influence are playing, especially at higher loads. If the information field size increases, the service time in the queues also increases, thereby increasing the queuing delay. Indeed it will take longer for a cell to leave the queue. On the other hand, if the information field size decreases, so that the service time devoted to a relatively large header will increase, the percentage of the time devoted to serving of the useful data decreases thereby increasing the queuing delay.

However, as can be seen in Fig. 2.24., the absolute impact is negligible even at very high loads for cell sizes up to 64 bytes (e.g. only around 40 µs difference between 32 and 64 bytes).

The depacketization delay is determined by the jitter as the convolution of several queuing delays. As with the queuing delay, this depacketization delay is also affected by the choice of the cell length. As is shown for the queuing delay, the impact is limited for cells up to 64 bytes. However, the absolute delay jitter may not be too high, because the receiving terminal has to dejitter the incoming ATM cells by buffering them. If the absolute delay is too high, a large buffer will be required at the receiving terminal.

(c)   Implementation complexity

Two parameters play in determining the complexity of a system : the speed and the number of required bits, i.e. the number of cells multiplied by the cell size. Again here a trade-off arises between size and speed.

To guarantee a certain limit on the cell loss ratio, a number of cells must be provided per queue. This number is independent of the cell size (Fig. 2.19.). So, the larger the cell size, the larger the queue in bits will be. So for example, a doubling of the cell size will also double the memory requirements.

On the other hand, for every cell, the header has to be processed. This processing must be performed in one cell time; so the longer the cell size, the larger the available time and the lower the speed requirements of the system.

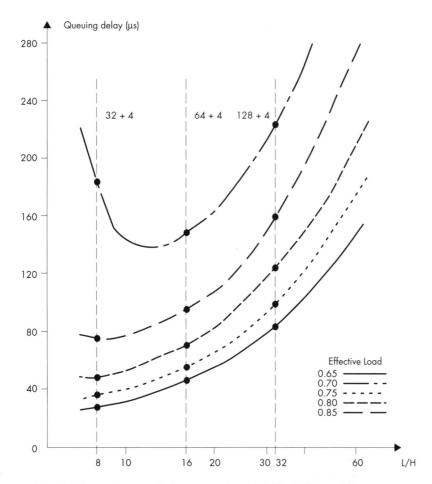

Fig. 2.24. –   Queuing Delay versus Ratio L/H for Different Effective
Load Values

   In Fig. 2.25. we show the speed and memory size in function of the cell size, if the system operates at 150 Mbit/s and if the queue is dimensioned for 50 cells (the header is 4 bytes).

   We see that for a cell of 16 bytes, we need only about 8000 bits for the memory, but the header processing of each cell must be performed in less than 1 μs. For a cell size of 256 bytes, we need already more than 64000 bits for a single queue, but we have about 15 μs for the header processing of a single cell.

   However, as can be seen in the diagram, the speed is not the most critical issue, since in 1 μs (in case of 16 bytes) a lot of processing can be achieved; so the limiting factor is the memory space requirement.

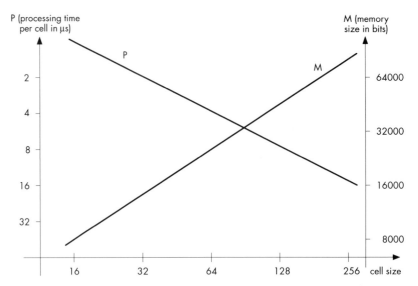

Fig. 2.25. – Processing Time and Memory Requirements in Function of Cell Size

(d)   Conclusion

Contradicting factors are contributing to the choice of the cell size. However, a value between 32 and 64 bytes is preferable. This choice is mainly influenced by the overall network delay, the transmission efficiency and the implementation complexity. Depending on the emphasis which is placed on one of the influencing parameters, a cell size of 32 or 64 can be defended.

In CCITT, before an agreement was finally reached, Europe was more in favor of 32 bytes (because of the requirement for echo cancellers for voice), whereas the US and Japan were more in favor of 64 bytes because of the higher the transmission efficiency. Finally, a compromise of 48 bytes was reached in the CCITT SGXVIII meeting of June 1989 in Geneva.

2.4.5.4.   *Header functionality*

Virtual connections

It was already mentioned that one of the basic characteristics of ATM is a limited functionality in the header. This limited functionality is largely supported by the "connection-oriented" characteristic of ATM. Indeed, functions such as source and destination address and sequence number (for resequencing), which are necessary in connectionless networks, are not required in an ATM network. Every virtual connection will be identified by a number (identifier), which has only local significance per link in the virtual connection.

In addition, error control as present in current X.25 networks on a link per link basis is only present end-to-end if required by the service. This error control function can be removed due to the high quality links as was described earlier in this Chapter. Flow control mechanism, such as ARQ (automatic repeat request), are also not provided link-by-link in ATM because the operating speed (150 Mbit/s or more) has the consequence that huge amounts of bits are being transmitted before a reaction can be given, resulting in a low efficiency. In addition, a good call acceptance control mechanism will guarantee an acceptable number of cells to be lost, as will be described in Chapter 7.

The basic remaining function of the header is the identification of the virtual connection. This function is performed by 2 subfields of the header : VCI (Virtual Channel Identifier) and VPI (Virtual Path Identifier). The VCI field identifies dynamically allocatable connections; the VPI field identifies statically allocatable connections.

Virtual channels

This function is performed by the header subfield, called the VCI. In the future broadband network, optical transmission links will very likely be used. These are capable of transporting hundreds of Mbit/s, whereas on the other hand virtual channels may fill only kbit/s. Thus, a large number of simultaneous channels have to be supported on a transmission link. Typically, in the order of ten thousand simultaneous channels are considered. This requires a VCI field of up to 16 bits.

Since the ATM network is connection oriented, each connection is characterized by a VCI which is assigned at call set-up. A VCI has only local significance on the link between ATM nodes and will be translated in the ATM nodes as was explained in Fig. 2.17. When the connection is released, the VCI values on the involved links will be released, and can be reused by other connections.

An interesting advantage of this VCI principle is the use of multiple VCI values for multicomponent services. Indeed, in the future broadband network, multicomponent services can be envisaged, like video telephony, TV, etc. For instance, video telephony can be composed of 3 components : voice video and data, each of which will be transported over a separate VCI. This allows the network to add or remove components during the connection. For instance, the video telephony service can start with voice only (a single VCI); the video component can later on be added (and removed) over a separate VCI. Also signalling will be transported over a separate VCI.

Virtual paths

In addition, it is envisaged that the future broadband network has to support semi-permanent connections between endpoints. These semi-permanent connections have to transport a large number of simultaneous connections. This concept is also known as a virtual path or virtual network. In this concept, resources of the network are semi-permanently allocated, to allow an efficient and simple management of available network resources (see Fig. 2.26.). To perform this virtual network, another field is defined in the header, namely the Virtual Path Identifier (VPI).

In the example of Fig. 2.26. we see that a virtual path is established between subscriber A and subscriber C, transporting 2 individual connections, each with a separate VCI. Remark that the VCI values used (3 and 4 in the example) are NOT translated in the nodes, which are only switching on the VPI field. In addition, a virtual path between A and B is semi-permanently established, using VCI values 1, 2 and 3. Remark that on the link between A and node 1, twice VCI value 3 is used. This creates no problems, since the different VPI values allow the 2 endpoints (A and node 1) to discriminate between the 2 virtual connections.

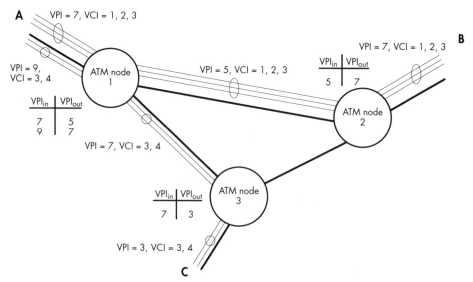

Fig. 2.26. – VPI Use in an ATM Network

However, this example does not depict the general case, in which VPI and VCI switching can be combined together in one single network.

The management of these semi-permanent paths in a network will not typically be performed on a single low bit rate logical connection only, but in most cases on a bundle of logical connections. Therefore this VPI field is 8 to 12 bits long to allow

256 to 4096 virtual paths. Each path can be composed of up to 64 K virtual channels, identified by its VCI.

Priorities

Another possible functionality which can be supported by the header is the differentiation of logical connections by different priorities.

The need for priorities is questioned by some people since it divides the network in different "logical" subnetworks where resource sharing is no longer optimal. However, priorities can be helpful to ensure that in cases of overload only low priority connections are losing information.

Two sorts of priorities exist : time priority and semantic priority. In a time priority system it is assumed that some cells may remain longer in the network than other. This means that some cells of a connection have a better time transparency than other. In a semantic priority system, some cells have a higher probability of being lost, giving rise to a higher cell loss ratio. This means that we may have cells/connections with a different semantic transparency.

Priorities (time or semantic) can either be assigned on a per connection basis (per VPI or per VCI) or on a per cell basis. In the first option, all cells in the virtual channel/path have an identical priority. In the second case, cells within a virtual channel/path may have a different priority.

The provisioning of these priorities can either be done explicitly, by defining a separate field in the header which identifies the priority or implicitly by assigning at call set-up a priority to each virtual connection, negotiated by signalling.

The solution with implicit priorities has the advantage that any VCI value can be used for any priority, and that no firm ideas on the number of priorities has to be defined. The number of priorities can easily be adapted if required since it is negotiated at call set-up by signalling. The solution with an explicit field for priorities has the advantage that the implementation to determine the priority requires a simple verification of the priority bit(s), unlike the implicit solution where a table has to be accessed.

It is clear that no priorities at all guarantee the best sharing of resources, but do not allow a differentiation between services with different quality requirements. Too many priorities divide the network in a number of virtually separated networks. Therefore, a small number of special priority bits is preferred. This number of bits to support priorities may range between 0 (for implicit priorities) and 4 (e.g. 3 explicit bits for semantic priorities and 1 explicit bit for 2 time priorities).

Maintenance

In order to maintain the overall network and to provide performance monitoring of the ATM connections, some additional bits can be useful. An interesting technique makes a distinction between normal data traffic and maintenance traffic. This method is called PTI (Payload Type Identification) since the payload, i.e. the information field, can carry different types of information (data, maintenance, ...). It provides the possibility to insert per virtual connection, special cells which are routed as normal cells, but which contain dedicated maintenance information, such as CRC over the past cells. These special cells can be inserted and extracted in specific places in the network (e.g. end-to-end, per multiplexer, per switching node, ...) to perform quality measurements on the equipment between insertion and extraction of these test cells. Different applications may be envisaged with this method.

In addition a parity bit per cell can be interesting to perform simple and powerful error monitoring. Indeed, a parity bit per cell allows the receiving side to detect with a 50 % probability errors in the information field (all odd number of bit errors, no even number of bit errors).

Depending on the maintenance functions supported by ATM, 0 to 2 maintenance bits are defined in the header.

Multiple access

In addition, to allow multiple terminals (users) to be connected on the same physical link, some point-to-multipoint protocol has to be defined to allow simultaneous use of the same link. To perform these point-to-multipoint functions, some additional bits may be required in the header. However, note that some point-to-multipoint algorithms do not need additional bits such as the register-insertion mechanism (Liu ring) (Stallings, 1988). The number of bits required to perform this function ranges between 0 and 8 bits, depending on the medium access control (MAC) mechanism suppported. This function is also referred to as General Flow Control (GFC).

Header error protection

As was indicated in the section on semantic transparency, misrouting can have a negative impact on the performance since it will cause error multiplication. It was also indicated that, a large gain can be obtained if the header is protected against single bit errors and possibly against burst errors.

As explained in section 2.4.5.2., the most interesting algorithm is adaptive and allows single bit error correction and multiple bit error detection.

To protect the header, a coding principle based on the generalization of the Hamming codes is very suitable, namely the so-called BCH codes (Bose-Chadhuri-Hocquenghem). These are cyclic codes which provide a large selection of lengths and error correcting capabilities as is shown in Table 2.6. for a very limited number of values of n, k and t. There we see that in a code word of n bits, k bits can be corrected thanks to (n – t) redundant bits (n = t + k). So for instance, if we want to correct a single bit error for a useful header of 26 bits we need 5 overhead bits. If we use the values of n, k and t as listed in the table we can only perform a correction of t bits. However, if the number of bits to be protected is not exactly in the list, we will take the value k larger than the one in the table. This will also provide us with an additional error detection capability (which is NOT the one described in the adaptive algorithm). For instance if we need to protect 64 bits with a single bit error correction capability we need 7 code bits (indeed 127 – 120 = 7). But with these 7 bits to be added to the 64 useful bits we cannot only correct a single bit error, but also detect multiple errors. In order to support this function, we must provide at the receiver the following procedure :

(1) Calculate the value of the so called "syndrome", using the incoming bits.
(2) If this syndrome is zero, no error has occurred. If it is non-zero, we can use the syndrome value to calculate which single bit has to be corrected.

     If the number of bits to be corrected is smaller than the one indicated in Table 2.6., then it is possible in the second step to distinguish between single bit and multiple bit errors. For single bit errors, the syndrome will always point to an existing code word and the error will be corrected. For multiple errors, the syndrome may point to a non-existent code word with a certain probability. Then the decoder will notice that multiple errors have occurred, but he will not be able to correct it.

n **Total number of bits**	k **Useful bits**	t **Correctable bits**
31	26	1
	21	2
	16	3
63	57	1
	51	2
	45	3
127	120	1
	113	2
	106	3

Table 2.6. – BCH Codes

In Table 2.7. we show the percentage of multiple errors which can be detected if we assume a single error correction capability. The percentage is calculated as the proportion of all burst lengths. We see from Table 2.6. that for the 3 examples (k = 32, 40, 48) we need at least 6 bits to be able to correct a single bit. If we provide additional coding bits, the detection capabilities increase as we see in Table 2.7. So up to 8 header error coding (HEC) bits might be very appropriate.

It may also be interesting to leave room for future functions which are not yet considered as interesting. Since it is preferable in the ATM systems to work with bytes, it is interesting to fill in the remaining bits of a byte with an unused (reserved) field.

Coding bits Bits to protect	6	7	8
32	48 %	74 %	89 %
40	36 %	68 %	84 %
48	23 %	62 %	81 %

Table 2.7. – Percentage of Error Detection Capabilities for a Single Bit Error Correction

Taking into account all the described functions, the overall header size for an ATM cell ranges between 2 and 7 bytes, depending on the functionalities which will be provided by the network (see Table 2.8.), and standardized by CCITT.

Function	Required bits	CCITT NNI/UNI
Virtual Channel Identifier (VCI)	8–16	16
Virtual Path Identifier (VPI)	8–12	12/8
Priorities	0–4	1
Maintenance / Payload Type	0–2	2
Point-to-multipoint	0–8	0/4
Header Error Control (HEC)	0–8	8
Reserved	0–6	1
Total	16–56	40

Table 2.8. – Header Functionality and Required Size

Table 2.8. also shows the options and number of bits selected by CCITT on the UNI (User Network Interface) and NNI (Network Node Interface). More details on the CCITT selected options will be described in Chapter 3.

2.4.5.5.   *Supportive functions*

In any packet switching system, the receiving terminal node must be able to determine the boundaries of the packets. In HDLC for instance, where variable length packets are allowed, this packet delineation is done by flags, i.e. a special bit pattern not occurring in the packet itself. In order to guarantee full data transparency, the data have to be "bit stuffed" to ensure that the flag does not occur in the packets itself.

In ATM, the same mechanism with flags can be applied, but bit stuffing at high speeds for a broadband network is not optimal to implement. However, since in ATM fixed length packets (cells) are used, also other "cell delineation" mechanisms are possible. We will describe here the ones which were considered as being the most interesting in terms of complexity and performance and of which CCITT finally has selected one. These alternatives are based on :

- The use of empty cells.
- The checking of the header error code (HEC).
- The forcing of a regular framing pattern (or periodic cells).

Each of these solutions (as any synchronization procedure) can be described by a state diagram composed of the following states (Fig. 2.27.) : HUNT, PRESYNC and SYNC.

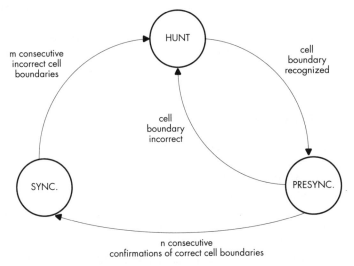

Fig. 2.27. – General Cell Delineation State Diagram

In the HUNT state, the system basically checks by some mechanism (e.g. bit by bit) whether some cell boundary can be found. If yes, the state changes to the PRESYNC state where cell by cell the boundaries are checked. If n consecutive correct cell boundaries are discovered, the system switches to SYNC state. The system only considers itself to have lost the "cell delineation" if m consecutive times a cell boundary was missing. The parameters n and m determine, respectively, the speed at which the system gets in cell synchronization and detects loss of cell synchronization.

The functionality of each state for the 3 mentioned "cell delineation" methods is the following.

Delineation using empty cells

Empty cells are characterized by a specific value of the header. In the HUNT state this specific header value is searched for bit by bit (or byte by byte), in the incoming bit stream. To ensure that this pattern does not occur with too high a probability in the regular bit stream, the length of this header part may not be too short.

Then, in the PRESYNC state, this specific header value is checked cell by cell to confirm the cell boundary. Here already, usage can be made of the known cell boundaries. Since all cells have the same length, an easy extrapolation to all consecutive cells can be made, just by adding the length of a complete cell. However, since empty cells are only present if no information is transmitted, it can take some time before the next empty cell will appear. Therefore, the confidence period over which it is decided that the system is synchronized, must cover a reasonable number of cells (this number is determined by the confidence value which is required). The same applies in the SYNC state. Before the decision is taken that synchronization is no longer available, it can take some time before a confidence level is reached since the probability exists that no empty cells have arrived during that time, because the link was highly loaded. This probability of having long periods without empty cells has to be taken into account.

Header error check cell delineation

This cell delineation method uses the correlation between the header bits to be protected and the relevant control bits introduced in the header by the HEC (Header Error Control) using an associated generating polynomial (cyclic code).

In the HUNT state, the delineation process is performed by checking (bit by bit, byte by byte, ...) whether the HEC coding law is respected for the assumed header field. If this HEC coding is not respected, the same procedure will be performed on the bit/byte stream shifted over one bit/byte position. Once this coding law is respected, the PRESYNC state is entered. Then n confirmations of a correct HEC coding syndrome are required to finally reach the SYNC state.

In the SYNC state m confirmations of an incorrect HEC syndrome are required before out of synchronization is declared and the HUNT procedure is restarted.

Malicious or unintended simulations of the HEC coding in the information field may cause incorrect synchronization and will increase the time to synchronize. Therefore, a scrambler may be provided which randomizes the bits of the information field. This scrambler ensures that the bits of the information field have a pseudo-random sequence, so that the probability that the HEC coding syndrome is matched in the information field is negligible.

Periodic cell synchronization

To avoid malicious or unintended wrong synchronization, which may happen if the confidence period of solution 1 (empty cells) is too short, or when no scrambler on the information field is provided as in solution 2 (HEC delineation), periodic cells may be enforced. In this mechanism, the transmitter forces the regular insertion of periodic (synchronization, recurrent) cells into the information stream, thereby introducing some sort of a frame over a period T with which these periodic cells occur. Such a periodic cell is characterized by a specific header value (or part of it). This mechanism can also be considered as a special case of solution 1, where empty cells (here called periodic cells) are enforced at regular times, to ensure within a certain period T that always at least one "empty" cell arrives. This period T can then be used to detect synchronization.

In this mechanism, the HUNT state searches for the periodic cell header value. Once this value is found, the receiver expects in the PRESYNC state the same header after the period T. Again n consecutive confirmations of this period are required before the SYNC state is reached.

This solution does not suffer from the problem of malicious users inserting the empty cell header in the information field, since here the transmitter system itself forces at regular moments (T) the insertion of these special cells. The selection of this period T is determined by the trade-off between the bandwidth efficiency and the required synchronization time. Indeed the insertion of periodic cells reduces the effective bandwidth since useless cells are inserted. On the other hand, the smaller the period T, the faster the confirmation for (de)synchronization can be obtained.

Conclusion

Alternative solutions than the one described above with slight modifications are also possible, but finally CCITT has selected the second solution, i.e. synchronization based on the HEC, plus scrambling of the information field.

2.5. BIBLIOGRAPHY

Abe S., Hajikano K., Murakami K., "Traffic design for an asynchronous transfer mode switching network", ITC 12, Torino, June 1988

Aboul-Magd O., Gilbert H., "Incorporating congestion feedback in B-ISDN traffic management strategy", ISS '92, Yokohama, October 1992

Albanese A., Limb J.O., Sincoskie W.D., "Multiservice integration with optical fiber networks", Globecom '85, New Orleans, December 1985

Albers R., "Toward broadband network services", ICCC '88, Tel Aviv, October 1988

Amstutz S., "Burst switching - an update", IEEE Communications Magazine, Vol. 27, No. 9, September 1989

Anania L., Solomon R.J., "The ghost in the machine - A natural monopoly in broadband time-sharing", Telecommunications, October 1987

AT&T and Bellcore, "Observations of error characteristics of fiber optic transmission systems", CCITT SGXVIII, San Diego, January 1989

AT&T, "Congestion control in a frame-relaying LAPD based network", CCITT SGVIII, Brasilia, February 1987

Bartel W., Lehmann E., "Bit error bursts in optical-fibre transmission systems", Race 1022, FIDBP-012-0004-CD, September 1989

Batorsky D.V., Spears D.R., Tedesco A.R., "The evolution of broadband network architectures", Globecom '88, Hollywood, November 1988

Bauwens J., "Evolution of IDN towards ISDN in the Belgian network", Forum '87, Geneva, October 1987

Bauwens J., De Prycker M., "Broadband experiment using asynchronous time division techniques", Electrical Communications, Vol. 61, No. 1, 1987

Beckner W., Lee T.T., Minzer S.E., "A protocol and prototype for broadband subscriber access to ISDN", ISS '87, Phoenix, March 1987

Bellcore, "Generic System requirements in support of Switched multimegabit data service", Bellcore, TA-TS4-000772, October 1989

Bermann E.E., Odlyzko A.M., Sangani S.H., "Half weight block codes for optical communications", AT&T Technical Journal, Vol. 65, No. 3, May 1986

Boettle D., "Switching of 140 Mbit/s signals in broadband communication systems", Electrical Communication, Vol. 58, No. 4, 1984

Boyer P.E., Servel M.J., Guillemin F.P., "The spacer-controller : an efficient UPC/NPC for ATM networks", ISS '92, Yokohama, October 1992

Brown L.C., "Statistical switching architectures for future services", Telephony, August 1984

Buchner Jr. M.M., Iwama M., Herr T.J., Staehler R.E., Gitten L.J., "Evolution to a universal information services environment", ISSLS '86, Tokyo, September 1986

Byrne W.R., Kilm T.A., Nelson B.L., Soneru M.D., "Broadband ISDN technologies and architectures", Globecom '88, Hollywood, November 1988

Chen M., "A new principle of statistical multiplexing in multimedia networks", ISS '92, Yokohama, October 1992

Coudreuse J.P., "Les réseaux temporels asynchrones : du transfert de données à l'image animée", L'Echo des Recherches, No. 112, 1983

Coudreuse J.P., Boyer P., "Asynchronous time-division techniques for real time ISDN's", Séminaire international sur les réseaux temps réel, Bandol, April 1986

Cummings J.L., Hickey K.R., Kinney B.D., "AT&T network architecture evolution", AT&T Technical Journal, Vol. 66, No. 3, May 1987

Day A., Dorman D., "Evolution to broadband networks and services", Australian Fast Packet Switching Workshop, Melbourne, July 1990

David R., Bauwens J., "A Belgian broadband experiment based on ATD concepts", ITS '87, Tapei (Taiwan), September 1987

David R., Fastrez M., De Kinder W., Bauwens J., "Integrated broadband communication systems in Belgium", IEEE Journal on Selected Areas in Communications, Vol. 4, No. 4, July 1986

David R., Fastrez M., Bauwens J., De Vleeschouwer A., Van Vyve J., Christians M., "A Belgian Broadband ATM experiment", ISS '90, Stockholm, May 1990

Decina M., "Evolution towards wideband communication networks", ISS '87, Phoenix, March 1987

Decina M., "Evolution towards digital multiservice networks for voice, data and video applications", Second International Conference on new systems and services in telecommunication, Liège, November 1983

De Kinder W., De Prycker M., "ATM : a logical evolution from ISDN" Euroinfo '88, Athens, May 1988

De Kinder W., De Prycker M., "ATM : the basis of the future telecommunication network", ICCT '90, Peking, June 1990

De Kinder W., "The broadband ISDN project in Belgium", ITS '86, Taipei (Taiwan), September 1986

Delli Priscoli F., Listanti M., Roveri A., Vemucci A., "A distributed access protocol for an ATM user-oriented satellite system", ICC '89, Boston, June 1989

De Prycker M., "Reference models for a fast packet based network", Computer Communications, December 1986

De Prycker M., "Data communications in an ATM network", Workshop on fast packet switching, New York, September 1988

De Prycker M., "Definition of network options for the Belgian ATM broadband experiment", IEEE Journal on Selected Areas in Communications, Vol. 6, No. 9, December 1988

De Prycker M., "ATM : Le concept du réseau de télécommunication de l'avenir", Nouvelles de la Science et de Technologies, March 1989

De Prycker M., "Evolution from ISDN to BISDN : a logical step towards ATM", Computer Communications, Vol. 12, No. 3, June 1989

De Prycker M., "Impact of data communication on ATM", ICC '89, Boston, June 1989

De Prycker M., "Architectures and signalling for a B-ISDN offering distributive and interactive services", Australian Fast Packet Switching Workshop, Melbourne, July 1990

De Prycker M., Bauwens J., "The ATD concept : one universal bearer service", GSLB Seminar, Albufeira (Portugal), January 1987

De Prycker M., De Somer M., Pauwels B., Gastaud G., "ATM as a universal transfer medium for user information, signalling and operation and maintenance", ISS '90, Stockholm, May 1990

De Prycker M., De Somer M., Verbiest W., "A service independent broadband network based on the Asynchronous Time Division concept", Revue HF, February 1987

De Somer M., "Considerations on ATM header function characterisation", Workshop on ATM definition, Geneva, June 1988

De Somer M., "Considerations on an ATM transmission system", Workshop on ATM definition, Geneva, June 1988

De Somer M., Pauwels B., "Considerations on a full ATM based UNI interface and usage monitoring", Workshop on ATM definition, Geneva, June 1988

Dobrowski G., Estes G., Spears D., Walters S., "Implications of B-ISDN services on network architecture and switching", ISS '90, Stockholm, June 1990

Dobrowski G., Kemer M., Spears D., Wilson D., "Evolving the network toward B-ISDN", ISS '90, Stockholm, June 1990

Domann G., "Two years of experience with broadband ISDN field trial", ISS '90, Stockholm, June 1990

Eklundh B., Gard I., "Design options for ATM networks", IZS '88, Zurich, March 1988

Eklundh B., Sällberg K., Stavenow B., "Asynchronous transfer modes - options and characteristics", ITC 12, Torino, June 1988

Eklundh B., Stavenow B., "A scenario for broadband communications in the public and private domains", Globecom '88, Hollywood, November 1988

Foster G., Adams J.L., "The ATM zone concept", Globecom '88, Hollywood, November 1988

Filipiak J., "Structure of traffic flow in multiservice networks", Globecom '88, Hollywood, November 1988

Gechter J., O'Reilly P., "Circuit-switched service in broadband ISDN", ICC '89, Boston, June 1989

Gerke P., Huber J.F., "Fast packet switching - a principle for future system generations ?", ISS '87, Phoenix, March 1987

Gilhooly D., "Which way for broadband switching", Telecommunications, June 1987

Gilhooly D., "ISS 87 hails the packetized future", Telecommunications, June 1987

Gilhooly D., "The politics of broadband", Telecommunications, Vol. 22, No. 6, June 1988

Gonet P., Coudreuse J.P., Servel M., "Implementing asynchronous transfer mode concepts : main results of the Prelude experiment", Globecom '87, Tokyo, November 1987

Gonet P., Adam P., Coudreuse J.P., "Asynchronous time-division switching : the way to flexible broadband communication networks", IZS '86, Zurich, March 1986

Gonet P., Coudreuse J.P., "Techniques temporelles asynchrones et réseaux intégrés de videocommunications", Second International Conference on new systems and services in telecommunications, Liège, November 1983

Groen H.B., "Lessons from the DIVAC experiment", ICC '86, Toronto, June 1986

Gruber J.G., Le N.H., "Performance requirements for integrated voice/data networks", IEEE Journal on Selected Areas in Communications, Vol. 1, No. 6, December 1983

Händel R., "Evolution of ISDN towards broadband ISDN", Infocom '88, New Orleans, March 1988

Handler G.J., "A system architecture for the 21st century telecommunications network", Globecom '88, Hollywood, November 1988

Harashima S., Kimura H., "High-speed and broadband communication systems in Japan", IEEE Journal on Selected Areas in Communications, Vol. 4, No. 4, July 1986

Hebuterne G., "STD switching in an ATD environment", Infocom '88, New Orleans, March 1988

Hemrich C.F., Isganitis E.J., Klessig R.W., "A protocol architecture for access to an ISDN offering broadband services", ISS '87, Phoenix, March 1987

Herr T.J., Johnston S.W., "Network systems to support universal information services", ICCC '86, Munich, September 1986

Hoberecht W.L., "Layered network protocols for packet voice and data integration", IEEE Journal on Selected Areas in Communications, Vol. 1, No. 6, December 1983

Hsing D.P., Vakil F., Estes G.H., "On cell size and header error control of asynchronous transfer mode (ATM)", Globecom '88, Hollywood, November 1988

Joos P., Verbiest W., "A statistical bandwidth allocation and usage monitoring algorithm for ATM networks", ICC '89, Boston, June 1989

Kawarazaki M., Inoue Y., "A possible ATM evolution scenario - ATM application to access network ", Workshop on ATM, Geneva, June 1988

Kirton P., Ellershaw J., Littlewood M., "Fast packet switching for integrated network evolution", ISS '87, Phoenix, March 1987

Kulzer J.J., Montgomery W.A., "Statistical switching architecture for future services", ISS '84, Florence, May 1984

Leakey D.M., "Integrated services ditital networks : some possible ongoing evolutionary trends", Computer Networks and ISDN systems, Vol. 15, No. 5, October 1988

Le Bris H., Servel M., "Integrated wideband networks using asynchronous time division techniques", ICC '86, Toronto, June 1986

Luderer G.W.R., Mansell J.J., Messerli E.J., Staehler R.E., Vaidya A.K., "Wideband packet technology for switching systems", ISS '87, Phoenix, March 1987

Matt H.J., "B-ISDN system concepts and technologies", ICC '86, Toronto, June 1986

Matt H.J., "Basic concepts and possibilities for broadband-networks", Third International Conference on new systems and services, Liège, November 1984

Mazzei U., Mazzetti C., Parodi R., "Planning large-size public packet networks with high throughput nodes", ICCC '88. Tel Aviv, October 1988

Mier E.E., "How AT&T plans to conquer voice-data integration", Data Communications, July 1986

Minzer S., "Broadband ISDN and asynchronous transfer mode (ATM)", IEEE Communications Magazine, Vol. 27, No. 9, September 1989

Minzer S.E., Spears D.R., "New directions in signalling for broadband ISDN", IEEE Communications Magazine, Vol. 26, No. 2, February 1989

Mobasser B., "The ISDN packet mode bearer service", ICC '86, Toronto, June 1986

Moth K., Jacobsen S.B., "Consideration on the use of ATD on the subscriber line", EFOC/LAN '87, Basel, June 1987

Muise R.W., Schonfeld T.J., Zimmerman III G.H., "Experiments in wideband packet technology", IZS '86, Zurich, March 1986

Nakamaki K., Kawakatsu M., Notoya A., "Traffic control for ATM networks", ICC '89, Boston, June 1989

Ohnsorge H., "Introduction and overview of broadband communication systems", IEEE Journal on Selected Areas in Communications, Vol. 4, No. 4, July 1986

Ohta S., Sato K., Tokizawa I., "A dynamically controllable ATM transport network based on the virtual path concept", Globecom '88, Hollywood, November 1988

O'Reilly P., "Circuit switching - the switching technology for future broadband networks ?", IEEE Network Magazine, April 1987

O'Reilly P., "The case for circuit switching in future wide bandwidth networks", ICC '88, Philadelphia, June 1988

Pattavina A., "A packet multiplexing scheme for slotted broadband networks", Infocom '88, New Orleans, March 1988

Pauwels B., "Terminal-to-Network communication in an ATM-based ISDN", International Journal of Digital and Analog Cabled Systems, January 1989

Peschi R., De Somer M., "Cell synchronization in ATM", Race 1022 Workshop, Aveiro, November 1988

Peterson J., Silberschatz A., "Operating system concepts", Addison Wesley, 1985

Plehiers P., Fastrez M., Bauwens J., De Prycker M., "Evolution towards a Belgian broadband experiment", ISS '87, Phoenix, March 1987

Popescu-Zeletin R., Butscher B., Egloff P., Kanzow J., "A global architecture for broadband communication systems : the BERKOM approach", ICCC '88, Tel Aviv, October 1988

Price D.J., "A flexible control architecture for B-ISDN", ISS '92, Yokohama, October 1992

Rider M.J., "Protocols for ATM access networks", Globecom '88, Hollywood, November 1988

Roelandt R., "Asynchronous Time Division Multiplexing and Switching as a solution to broadband ISDN", PRC Transmission Symposium, P.R. China, October 1986

RTT Belgium, "Error correction on ATM cell header", CEPT/NA5, Den Haag, March 1988

RTT Belgium, "Asynchronous transfer mode : fixed or variable frame length", CEPT/GSLB, Venice, March 1987

RTT Belgium, "ATD information field size", CCITT SGXVIII, Seoul, January 1988

RTT Belgium, "Asynchronous transfer mode (ATM) : considerations about the cell size", CEPT/NA5, Stuttgart, June 1987

RTT Belgium, "ATD header size", CCITT SGXVIII, Seoul, January 1988

RTT Belgium, "Asynchronous transfer mode (ATM) : network protocol aspects", CEPT/GSLB, Venice, March 1987

RTT Belgium, "New transfer mode based on a single bearer service : a feasible solution", CCITT SGXVIII, Brasilia, February 1987

RTT Belgium, "Architectural reference model for a network using asynchronous time division", CCITT SGXVIII, Geneva, July 1986

RTT Belgium, "New transfer mode : a pure packet oriented concept", CEPT/GSLB, Brasilia, February 1987

RTT Belgium, "Mechanism for cell delineation in ATM", ETSI/NA5, Munchen, March 1989

RTT Belgium, "HEC capabilities for burst error detection", ETSI/NA5, Den Haag, April 1989

Salahi J., "Modeling the performance of a broadband network using various ATM cell formats", ICC '89, Boston, June 1989

Servel M., Thomas A., "Réseaux de transfert en vidéocommunication - La commutation de paquets", L'Echo des Recherches, No. 115, 1984

Sher P., Shantz J., Yum K., "Service concept of the switched multi-megabit data service", Globecom '88, Hollywood, November 1988

Shinohara H., Asatani K., "Evolutionary approach to broadband services and network", Globecom '88, Hollywood, November 1988

Sincoskie W.D., "Part two : broadband packet switching", Bellcore Exchange, November/December 1987

Smith W.L., "Service concepts and plans for broadband network deployment in Bellsouth", Globecom '88, Hollywood, November 1988

Spears D.R., "Broadband ISDN - Service visions and technological realities", International Journal of Digital and Analog Cabled Systems, Vol. 1, January 1988

Spencer D.A., Dimmick J.O., "ISDN packet mode protocol architecture & services", Forum '87, Geneve, October 1987

Stallings W., "Data and computer communications", MacMillan, New York, 1988

Suzuki T., Noguchi O., Yokota K., Shoji Y., "A new speech processing scheme for ATM switching systems", ICC '89, Boston, June 1989

Takahashi K., Yokoi T., Yamamoto Y., "Communications quality analysis for ATM networks", ICC '89, Boston, June 1989

Takami K., Takenaka T., "Architectural and functional aspects of a multi-media packet switched network", ISS '87, Phoenix, March 1987

Terry J.B., "A multi-media network architecture for ISDN and beyond", IZS '88, Zürich, March 1988

Thomas A., Coudreuse J.P., Servel M., "Asynchronous time-division techniques : an experimental network integrating video communication", ISS '84, Florence, May 1984

Tokizawa I., Kanada T., Sato K., "A new transport network architecture based on asynchronous transfer mode techniques", ISSLS '88, Boston, September 1988

Tranchier D.P., Boyer P.E., Rouaud Y.M. *et al.*, "Fast bandwidth allocation in ATM networks", ISS '92, Yokohama, October 1992

Turner J.S., Wyatt L.F., "A packet network architecture for Integrated Services", Globecom '83, San Diego, November 1983

Turner J.S., "New directions in communications (or which way to the information age ?)", IEEE Communications Magazine, October 1986

Turner J.S., "Design of an integrated services packet network", Washington University, Saint Louis, March 1985

T1D1.1 Subworking group on broadband ISDN, "Reasons for new protocol and sample service characteristics", Irving, Texas T1D1 Meeting, January 1987

United States of America, "Load increase under link-by-link and end-to-end error recovery", CCITT SGXVIII, Brasilia, February 1987

Van Landegem T., De Prycker M., "The ATD approach to integrated broadband communication", International Workshop on Future Prospects of Burst/Packetised Multimedia Communications, Osaka, November 1987

Verbiest W., Pinnoo L., Voeten B., "Statistical multiplexing of variable bit rate video sources in Asynchronous Transfer Mode Networks", Globecom '88, Hollywood, December 1988

Vickers R., Wernik M., "Evolution of switch architecture and technology", Telecommunications, Vol. 22, No. 5, May 1988

Walsh A.B., Zima C.H., "Meeting the operations challenges of a multi-megabit data service", ICC '89, Boston, June 1989

Weinstein S.B., "Personalized services on the intelligent, wideband network", IZS '86, Zürich, March 1986

Wernik M., "Architecture and technology considerations for multimedia broadband communications", Globecom '88, Hollywood, November 1988

Wong A.K., "Traffic modelling and buffer dimensioning in a ATM switch with shared-memory end-grids", ISS '92, Yokohama, October 1992

Wu L.T., Lee S.H., Lee T.T., "Dynamic TDM - A packet approach to broadband networking", ICC '87, Seattle, June 1987

Wu L.T., Arthurs E., Sincoskie W.D., "A packet network for BISDN applications", IZS '88, Zürich, March 1988

Yamazaki K., Wada M., Ano S. *et al.* "Flexible QOS communications for integrated video services in B-ISDN", ISS '92, Yokohama, October 1992

3

ATM Standards

3.1. INTRODUCTION

3.1.1. CCITT activities

In the previous Chapter, the basic characteristics of ATM were explained. We started from different alternative root proposals such as ATD and fast packet switching, leading to ATM. We have also shown that different parameters in the definition of ATM could still vary within a certain range. The alternative values within this range each had their respective advantages and disadvantages.

The definition of ATM, filling in all the details, is being finalized by CCITT SGXVIII. Some options taken by CCITT were based on pure technical arguments, others were based on a compromise between technical arguments and preferences of countries. These country preferences were mainly determined by the emphasis put on some influencing parameters. For instance, some countries emphasized the importance of video and voice services, whereas other countries stressed the importance of high speed data services.

It is not the intention of this Chapter to explain why CCITT has selected certain values. This Chapter will describe in detail all selected options taken by CCITT, as decided in the last meetings of SGXVIII, and as described in a series of Recommendations, agreed in June 1992.

Different Recommendations were agreed, filling in a large number of parameters of the ATM definition. However, some issues still are not fully resolved, and will have to be completed in future Recommendations.

In June 1992, CCITT has agreed upon the following Recommendations :

I.113   Vocabulary of Terms for Broadband Aspects of ISDN
I.121   Broadband Aspects of ISDN
I.150   BISDN ATM Functional Characteristics
I.211   BISDN Service Aspects
I.311   BISDN General Network Aspects
I.321   BISDN Protocol Reference Model and its Application

I.327   BISDN Network Functional Architecture
I.361   BISDN ATM Layer Specification
I.362   BISDN ATM Adaptation Layer (AAL) Functional Description
I.363   BISDN ATM Adaptation Layer (AAL) Specification
I.364   Support of broadband connectionless data service on BISDN
I.371   Traffic and congestion control in BISDN
I.413   BISDN User-Network Interface
I.414   Overview of Recommendations on layer 1 for ISDN and BISDN customer
         accesses
I.432   BISDN User-Network Interface – Physical Layer Specification
I.610   OAM Principles of BISDN Access

3.1.2. ATM Forum activities

CCITT primarily concentrates on proper standardization of ATM in the long run, for the future public BISDN network. However, the growing need of users for high bandwidth communication, high bandwidth services and flexibility on long term, made manufacturers of private communication systems aware of the need for speeding up this process. It is expected now that ATM will emerge first in the private, business and corporate environment, because of its increasing need for bandwidth and need for fast introduction of new capabilities.

In October 1991, a group of CPE vendors, public equipment vendors, telecom operators and users formed the ATM Forum, with the goal of accelerating development and deployment of ATM products and services in the private environment. The work of the ATM Forum concentrates on specifying Customer Premises Equipment and private switching. The first specifications released by this body, also in June 1992, treated the Private User-Network Interface, between an ATM user and a private ATM switch, and the Public User-Network Interface, between an ATM user and a public network. It is the intention of the ATM Forum to proceed with specifications in the area of operations, signalling, the Network-to-Network Interface, congestion control, traffic management, additional physical media, new applications and adaptation layers.

Where CCITT mainly reflects the view of the network operators and national administrations, the ATM Forum tends to look more at the objectives of users and CPE manufacturers. Both will be needed, and will have to be brought in line with each other, to make a world-wide BISDN work.

3.1.3. Overview

This Chapter will first describe the basic options retained for the definition of ATM. Then it will explain a general reference configuration which allows an easy functional partitioning between different entities in the network. Next, a layered model will be described, which allows a clear separation and description of functions between different layers and sublayers, as defined by CCITT. Next, the different (sub)layers will be described in more detail as defined by CCITT and the ATM Forum : the physical layer, the ATM layer and the adaptation layer. Finally, the maintenance philosophy adapted for BISDN will be described.

3.2. BASIC PRINCIPLES OF ATM

The basic principles of ATM were already explained in Chapter 2 of this book, with all the reasons for the selection of each option. This section briefly recapitulates the basic principles as put forward by CCITT in Recommendation I.150.

3.2.1. Information transfer

ATM is considered as a specific packet oriented transfer mode based on asynchronous time division multiplexing and the use of fixed length cells. Each cell consists of an information field and a header. The header is primarily used to identify cells belonging to the same virtual channel within the asynchronous time division multiplex, and to perform the appropriate routing. Cell sequence integrity is preserved per virtual channel.

The information field of ATM cells is carried transparently through the network. No processing like error control is performed on it inside the network. All services (voice, video, data, ...) can be transported via ATM, including connectionless services. To accommodate various services, several types of ATM Adaptation Layers (AAL) have been defined, depending on the nature of the service, to fit information into ATM cells, and to provide service specific functions (e.g. clock recovery, cell loss recovery, ...). The AAL specific information is contained in the information field of the ATM cell. Still a 1 bit indication in the header is also at the disposition of the user for this purpose.

3.2.2. Routing

ATM is connection oriented. The header values are assigned to each section of a connection for the complete duration of the connection, and translated when switched from one section to another. Signalling and user information are carried on separate virtual channels.

As was also explained in Chapter 2, 2 sorts of connections are possible : virtual channel connections (VCC) and virtual path connections (VPC). A VPC can be considered as an aggregate of VCCs. When switching/multiplexing on cells is to be performed, it must first be done based on the VPC, then on the VCC. This is shown in Fig. 3.1. There we see an entity which only performs VP switching, and another entity which performs both VP and VC switching. However, the VP switching part may be idle, resulting in a pure VC switch.

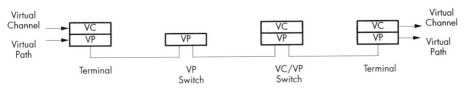

Fig. 3.1. – VC and VP Connections in ATM

3.2.3. Resources

As ATM is connection-oriented, connections are established either semi-permanently, or for the duration of a call, in case of switched services. This establishment includes the allocation of a VCI (Virtual Channel Identifier) and/or VPI (Virtual Path Identifier), but also the allocation of the required resources on the user access and inside the network. These resources are expressed in terms of throughput (bit rate) and Quality of Service. They may be negotiated between user and network for switched connections, during the call set-up phase and possibly during the call.

ATM cell identifiers

ATM cell identifiers, i.e. Virtual Path (VPI) and Virtual Channel (VCI) identifiers, but also Payload Type (PTI) identifiers, support recognition of an ATM cell on a physical transmission medium. Recognition of the cell is the basis for all further operations. VPI and VCI are unique for cells belonging to the same virtual connection on a shared transmission medium. As such, they are a limited resource although CCITT has recommended to make their number quite large ($2^{28} - 16$). Within a particular virtual circuit, cells may be further distinguished by their PTI, which cannot be allocated freely, but depends on the type of payload carried by the cell. This field indicates whether the cell is carrying user information to be delivered transparently through the network, or special network information. In case the field indicates network information, part of the information field indicates the type of network control whereas the remaining part of the information field may be processed inside the network.

A number of pre-assigned ATM cell identifiers have been chosen in the ATM layer for particular cell streams on the user-network interface and the node-network interfaces. They are necessary for enabling communication with the network, and to perform network management. Unassigned cell identifiers mark unused bandwidth. Other pre-assigned values define meta-signalling cells, point-to-point signalling cells, general broadcast signalling cells, physical layer OAM (operations and maintenance) cells and resource management cells.

The physical layer also uses a number of pre-defined identifiers, which will be discussed in section 3.5.

Throughput

Bandwidth has to be reserved in the network for each virtual connection. ATM offers the possibility to realize resource savings in the total bandwidth needed when multiplexing traffic for many Variable Bit Rate connections. However, the amount which can be saved depends heavily on the number of multiplexed connections, on the burstiness of the traffic they carry, on the correlation between them, and on the quality of service they require.

CCITT has only standardized the Peak Cell Rate (PCR) as a throughput parameter up to now. The potential for gain in bandwidth by statistical multiplexing is recognized, yet parameters, and their use in a safe and robust Connection Acceptance Control algorithm that still realizes meaningful savings, are for further study.

The ATM Forum goes further in this respect. It defines a parameter called the Sustainable Cell Rate, which can roughly be described as the maximum for the mean cell rate, measured over a period shorter than the duration of the call, but much longer than the cell interarrival interval. More details on these parameters can be found in Chapter 7.

Quality of service

The quality of service of a connection relates to the cell loss, the delay and the delay variation incurred by the cells belonging to that connection in an ATM network. For ATM, the quality of service of a connection is closely linked to the bandwidth it uses. When providing limited physical resources, using more bandwidth increases the cell loss, the delay and the delay variation incurred, i.e. decreases the QOS, for cells of all connections which share those resources.

It is for further study whether (some of) those specific QOS parameters will be explicitly indicated, or implicitly associated with specific service requests. In the latter case, a standardized service would by definition include the specification of all relevant QOS parameters. For practical reasons, only a limited number of specific QOS classes will be standardized.

Additionally, some services may benefit from an explicit Cell Loss Priority (CLP) indication on a cell by cell basis, carried in a specific bit in the header, as a means of managing cell loss during periods of network congestion. This allows the user to choose between two levels of cell loss ratios in a single virtual connection : high priority for cells which carry basic information, and cells with lower priority which are subject to discarding, depending on the network conditions. However, if this indicator is used it will be necessary during the call set-up phase to indicate the intended incidence of this indicator. This has to facilitate appropriate network resource allocation and usage / network parameter control.

Especially for some variable bit rate services (VBR), which will be described in Chapter 5, it may be of interest that the network guarantees a minimum capacity. In times of network congestion, the network may then discard some ATM cells without impairing the required basic quality and still offering the guaranteed capacity. It is important that cell sequence integrity is respected within each virtual channel, even for cells with a different priority.

Usage parameter control

Unlike in an Synchronous Transfer Mode environment, there is no physical limitation on the user's access rate to the physical transmission medium in ATM, apart from the physical cell rate on the medium itself. On the contrary, multiplexing equipment will do its utmost to avoid cell loss, to offer the highest possible throughput, whatever the user chooses to send.

However, as virtual connections share physical resources, transmission media and buffer space, unforeseen excessive occupation of resources by one user impairs traffic for other users. Therefore, throughput must be monitored (policed) at the user-network interface by a Usage Parameter Control function in the network, to ensure that the negotiated contract per VCC or VPC between network and subscriber is respected by each of the latter. Traffic parameters shall describe the desired throughput and QOS unambiguously in the contract.

In this context it is very important that the traffic parameters which are selected for this purpose, can be monitored in real time at the arrival of each cell. Statistical parameters, e.g. mean cell rate over the duration of the call, are nice for addressing connection acceptance control issues, yet worthless for enforcing the contract and for avoiding abuses, and thus for prevention of network congestion, if they cannot be checked instantaneously.

CCITT currently foresees a check of the PCR of the high priority cell flow (CLP = 0) and a check of the PCR of the aggregate cell flow (CLP = 0 + 1), per virtual connection.

3.2.4. Signalling

The negotiation between the user and network with respect to the resources (VCI/VPI, throughput, QOS) is performed over a separate signalling virtual channel. The signalling protocol to be used over this signalling virtual channel will be an enhancement of those used in NISDN signalling. CCITT is currently working on a Release 1 signalling protocol, allowing call-by-call set-up of point-to-point connecions. This protocol will be specified by the end of 1993. An enhancement of this signalling, in what CCITT calls Release 2/3, will provide functions such as point-to-multipoint and multiconnection calls. Standardization is expected in 1994 – 95.

The ATM Forum on the other hand is finishing a signalling protocol by mid 1993. This signalling protocol is based on an extended subset of CCITT Q.93B Release 1. The ATM Forum signalling protocol already contains limited capabilities for setting up point-to-multipoint connections. It also defines two addressing modes : E.164 (as defined by CCITT) and NSAP (as defined by OSI).

For point-to-point configurations on the UNI, a pre-defined signalling channel exists. For point-to-multipoint configurations, where multiple terminals are connected to a single S_B interface via a shared medium, multiple signalling virtual channels (at least one per terminal) can be established via the meta-signalling channel. This meta-signalling channel is transported over a pre-assigned VCI/VPI defined on the user-network interface. The meta-signalling procedure performs the negotiation of VCI/VPI and required throughput for signalling with a terminal. It is comparable to the TEI (Terminal Endpoint Identifier) assignment procedure for NISDN.

3.2.5. Flow control

In principle, no flow control will be applied to information streams at the ATM layer inside the public BISDN network.

However, in some cases, it will be necessary to be able to control the flow of traffic on ATM connections from a terminal to the network. In order to cope with this, a GFC (general flow control) mechanism is proposed by CCITT at the User Network Interface (UNI). This function is supported by a specific field in the ATM cell header. Two sets of procedures are foreseen for use within the GFC field : Uncontrolled Transmission and Controlled Transmission.

The uncontrolled transmission procedure is for use in point-to-point configurations. The controlled transmission procedure can be used in both point-to-point and shared medium configurations. This procedure is for further study still. However, it must ensure a fair and efficient usage of the available capacity between terminal and network, and it shall be independent of the topology (ring, bus, star, ...) of the user access network. A mechanism exists to distinguish between procedures at a given UNI.

3.2.6. Operations and maintenance

CCITT has defined 5 levels of connectivity in the ATM transport network. The physical layer is composed of the lower 3 : the regenerator section on the lowest level, then the digital section, and the transmission path. The ATM layer consists of the remaining 2 : the virtual path, and above it the virtual channel. Each of these levels has its own operations and maintenance flow, called F1 to F5, starting with F1 on the regenerator section level.

The transfer mode used for the information carried by these flows depends on the nature of the layer. For a physical layer based on SDH, or for the emerging standards for mapping ATM on PDH, flows F1 to F3 are carried in synchronous channels in the overhead of the physical layer. For a cell based physical layer, these flows are carried by Physical Layer OAM (PL-OAM) cells. For the ATM layer itself, the F4 flows are carried in cells distinguished by pre-assigned VCIs in the virtual path, and the F5 flows are carried in cells distinguished by special PTI codes in the virtual circuit.

3.3. BISDN REFERENCE CONFIGURATION

A reference configuration is a practical tool to define clear interfaces between different entities of the network and to define the functions of these different entities. The reference configurations for the user-network interface used for ISDN, defined in CCITT Recommendation I.411 are considered to be general enough to be applicable to all aspects of the BISDN accesses. CCITT has currently only discussed the user-network interface and the related reference configuration for BISDN, in Recommendation I.413.

The reference configuration adopted by CCITT is described in Fig. 3.2. The Reference points R, S, T and U as defined for NISDN are also valid in the BISDN case, as well as the functional groupings B-NT1, B-NT2 (Broadband Network Termination 1 or 2), B-TE1, B-TE2 (Broadband Terminal Equipment 1 or 2) and B-TA (Broadband Terminal Adapter), as is shown in Fig. 3.2. It was decided by CCITT that only the interfaces at reference points S_B and T_B will be standardized.

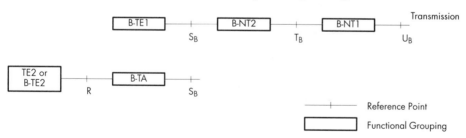

Fig. 3.2. BISDN Reference Configuration

The reference configuration as described can be physically realized in different ways. A few examples for the user-network part are given in Fig. 3.3. where the interfaces shown are now physically implemented, as well as the physical grouping of the functions.

In the first example (Fig. 3.3a.), both the S_B and T_B interface are physically implemented resulting in a physical B-NT2 entity. This is different from the second example where only the S_B is physically present (Fig. 3.3b.). In this example the B-NT2 and B-NT1 are physically co-located in a single entity. In Fig. 3.3c. only T_B

will be physically implemented resulting in a combined B-TE and B-NT2 entity. In Fig. 3.3d., S_B and T_B are coinciding and therefore identical. No physical B-NT2 is present at the customer's premises. In Fig. 3.3e., the physical interfaces between terminals and B-NT2 are both S_B and S (for narrowband ISDN), based on a centralized B-NT2 grouping. The B-NT2 can also be distributed, giving rise to a possible configuration shown in Fig. 3.3f. The Medium Adapter (MA) will provide a medium access mechanism to ensure that all terminals get access to the network. These MA boxes are fully topology dependent and their functions will not be standardized by CCITT. In this example, the W interface may be topology dependent and non-standardized. Other implementations may have a solution in which W is identical to S_B.

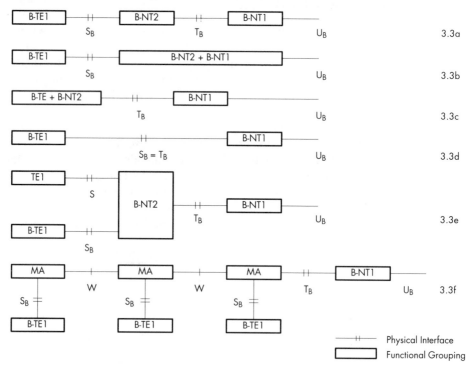

Fig. 3.3. – Examples of Physical Configurations

3.3.1. Reference points

In the currently available CCITT Recommendations, the basic characteristics of the S_B and T_B are described for 155.520 Mbit/s. Characteristics of the S_B and T_B interfaces at 622.080 Mbit/s still need further study.

This 155.520 Mbit/s is the physical bit rate provided at both T_B and S_B. With respect to the structuring of this physical bit/cell stream, CCITT has left 2 options possible : cell based and SDH (Synchronous Digital Hierarchy) based. The ATM Forum specifies three additional ones. These options are explained in the further described TC (Transmission Convergence) sublayers. All options have a common ATM layer.

The T_B and S_B interfaces are physical point-to-point, meaning that receiver and transmitter are always paired (i.e. one receiver receives information from one transmitter). On the higher layers a logical point-to-multipoint functionality may be supported, but this topic is still under study in CCITT.

3.3.2. Functional grouping

CCITT has not yet achieved a full description of all functional groupings. However, some major guidelines can already be described.

The B-NT1 mainly performs low layer functions such as line transmission termination, transmission interface handling and OAM functions.

The B-NT2 functional group performs adaptation functions for different media and topologies, but also higher layer functions such as cell delineation, concentration, buffering, multiplexing/demultiplexing, resource allocation, usage parameter control (policing), signalling adaptation layer functions, signalling protocol handling, switching of local connections and OAM functions. B-NT2 implementations can be concentrated, or physically distributed. It may even consist of physical connections only.

The B-TE1 terminates the user interface (S_B or T_B), and performs the termination of all end protocols from the low layers up to the higher layers. The B-TE2 terminal has an interface not standardized by BISDN Recommendations.

3.4. BISDN LAYERED MODEL

The OSI model of ISO is very famous and used with great success to model all sorts of communication systems. The same logical hierarchical architecture as used in OSI is used for the ATM BISDN network in Recommendation I.321. However, only the lower layers are explained. CCITT has not yet determined the relation between ATM and OSI, and therefore a personal view on this point will be given.

The model will also use the concept of separated planes for the segregation of user, control and management functions. This plane approach was already used in NISDN and is described in CCITT Recommendation I.320, which contains the ISDN Protocol Reference Model (PRM).

The BISDN protocol model for ATM is shown in Fig. 3.4. As the NISDN PRM, it contains 3 planes : a user plane to transport user information, a control plane mainly composed of signalling information and a management plane, used to maintain the network and to perform operational functions. In addition, a third dimension is added to the PRM, called the plane management, which is responsible for the management of the different planes.

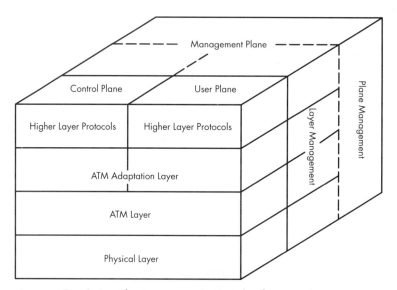

Fig. 3.4. – The BISDN ATM Protocol Reference Model

For each plane, a layered approach as in OSI is used with independence between layers. CCITT has not sorted out the relation between the layers of the BISDN ATM protocol model and those of the OSI model. The following relations can be found : the physical layer is more or less equivalent to the layer 1 (Physical layer) of the OSI model, and mainly performs functions on the bit level. The ATM layer can be located mainly at the lower edge of the layer 2 of the OSI model. The adaptation layer performs the adaptation of higher layer protocols, be it signalling or user information, to the fixed size ATM cells. For control plane information like signalling it is equivalent to the lower part of the data link layer of the OSI model, but for the user plane it is more appropriate to locate it at the lower part of the transport layer (layer 4) of the OSI model, since adaptation layer processing for user information is only performed at the edges of the network, i.e. in the terminals or terminal adapters. These relations are a personal view and by no means the CCITT view.

According to CCITT, the layers can be further divided as described in Fig. 3.5. Three layers are defined : the PHY (physical) layer which mainly transports information (bits/cells); the ATM layer which mainly performs switching/routing and multiplexing and the AAL (ATM adaptation layer) which is mainly responsible for adapting service information to the ATM stream.

These layers can then further be divided into sublayers. Each sublayer performs a number of functions, to be explained in the following sections.

Convergence	CS	AAL
Segmentation and reassembly	SAR	
Generic flow control		ATM
Cell VPI/VCI translation		
Cell multiplex and demultiplex		
Cell rate decoupling		
HEC header sequence generation/verification		
Cell delineation	TC	PHY
Transmission frame adaptation		
Transmission frame generation/recovery		
Bit timing	PM	
Physical medium		

CS : Convergence Sublayer

SAR : Segmentation and Reassembly

TC : Transmission Convergence

PM : Physical Medium

Fig. 3.5. – The Protocol Reference Model Sublayers and Functions

3.4.1. Physical layer

The physical layer of the BISDN is further composed of 2 sublayers : the Physical Medium (PM) sublayer supports pure medium dependent bit functions, the Transmission Convergence (TC) sublayer converts the ATM cell stream into bits to be transported over the physical medium. The physical layer for the User Network Interface (UNI) is described by CCITT in Recommendation I.432, and by the ATM Forum in their ATM User-Network Interface Specification.

Physical medium sublayer

This sublayer is responsible for the correct transmission and reception of bits on the appropriate physical medium. The functions to be performed are shown in Fig. 3.5. At the very lowest level this function is really medium dependent (optical, electrical, ...) and is called physical medium. In addition, this sublayer must guarantee a proper bit timing reconstruction at the receiver. Therefore the transmitting peer entity will be responsible for the insertion of the required bit timing information and line coding. Applicable physical medium sublayers have been specified by CCITT in Recommendations G.703, G.957 and by the ATM Forum.

Transmission convergence sublayer

In this sublayer, bits are already recognized, as they come from the PM sublayer. This sublayer performs basically 5 functions as shown in Fig. 3.5.

The first function after the bit reconstruction is the adaptation to the transmission system used. Possible transmission systems are based on G.709 SDH (Synchronous Digital Hierarchy), G.703 PDH (Plesiochronous Digital Hierarchy), or cell based. The cells are fit within the transmission system according to a standardized mapping. Also here the ATM Forum has added FDDI as an option for the user-network interface.

This sublayer is also responsible for the generation of the HEC (Header Error Check) syndrome of each cell at the transmitter, and its verification at the receiver. For a start, this permits the recognition of the cell boundary, i.e. proper cell delineation at the receiver. The mechanism to perform cell delineation is based on the HEC algorithm of which the general principle was explained in Chapter 2. This means that if a correct HEC syndrome is recognized for a number of consecutive cells, it is assumed that the correct cell boundary is found. To avoid malicious or erroneous cell delineation on user information, the information field of each cell is scrambled at the transmitting side and descrambled at the receiving side. This ensures that the probability of finding a correct HEC syndrome in the information field of an ATM cell (put there on purpose or not) is very low.

Once the cell delineation has been found, an adaptive mechanism uses the HEC syndrome for correction or detection of cell header errors, depending on the situation. Isolated single bit errors are corrected, but as soon as multiple consecutive cells show header errors, correction is given up for higher precision detection and elimination of cells with errors, to avoid slipping through of cells with undetected multiple header errors during periods of bit error bursts. Such errors may not be detected by the correction algorithm. The details of this cell delineation algorithm are found in section 3.5. of this Chapter.

Finally, this sublayer must ensure insertion and suppression of unassigned cells to adapt the useful rate to the available payload of the transmission system. This function is called cell rate uncoupling.

In addition Operations and Maintenance (OAM) information must be exchanged with the Management plane.

3.4.2. ATM layer

The ATM layer is fully independent of the physical medium used to transport the ATM cells and thus of the PHY layer. The following main functions are performed by this layer.

- The multiplexing and demultiplexing of cells of different connections (identified by different VCI and/or VPI values) into a single cell stream on a physical layer.

- A translation of the cell identifier, which is required in most cases when switching a cell from one physical link to another, in an ATM switch or cross connect. This translation can be performed either on the VCI or VPI separately, or on both simultaneously.

- Providing the user of a VCC or VPC with one QOS class, out of a number of classes supported by the network. Some services may require a certain QOS for one part of the cell flow of a connection, and a lower QOS for the remainder. The distinction within the connection is made by means of the CLP bit in the cell header.

- Management functions : the header of user information cells provides for a congestion indication and an ATM user to ATM user indication. Pre-assigned VCI values are defined for F4 segment associated and end-to-end associated flows, and dedicated PTI codes for F5 segment associated, end-to-end associated flows and resource management cells. When the PTI does not indicate user information, further information concerning the type of layer management will be found in the information field of the cell.

- Extraction (addition) of the cell header before (after) the cell is being delivered to (from) the adaptation layer.

- Implementation of a flow control mechanism on the user-network interface. This is supported by the GFC bits in the header.

3.4.3. ATM adaptation layer

The ATM Adaptation Layer enhances the service provided by the ATM layer to a level required by the next higher layer. It performs functions for the user, control and management planes and supports the mapping between the ATM layer and the next higher layer. The functions performed in the AAL depend on the higher layer requirements.

The AAL layer is subdivided in 2 sublayers : the segmentation and reassembly sublayer (SAR) and the convergence sublayer (CS).

The main purpose of the SAR sublayer is segmentation of the higher layer information into a size suitable for the payload of the consecutive ATM cells of a virtual connection, and the inverse operation, reassembly of contents of the cells of a virtual connection, into data units to be delivered to the higher layer.

The convergence sublayer performs functions like message identification, time/clock recovery, etc. For some AAL types, supporting data transport over ATM, the convergence sublayer has been further subdivided in a Common Part Convergence Sublayer (CPCS), and a Service Specific Convergence Sublayer (SSCS).

Some AAL service users may find the ATM service sufficient for their requirements. In that case the AAL protocol may be empty.

AAL Service Data Units (SDU) are transported from one AAL Service Access Point (SAP) to one or more others through the ATM network. The AAL users will have the capability to select a given AAL-SAP associated with the QOS required to transport the AAL-SDU.

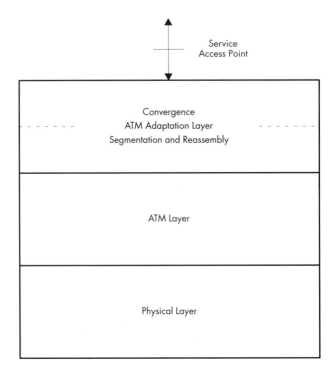

Fig. 3.6. – The Service Access Point

Up to now 4 AALs have been defined by CCITT, one for each class of services. AAL 3 and AAL 4, providing adaptation for connection-oriented and connectionless data services respectively, have been merged up to and including the CPCS layer. The ATM Forum has defined a different AAL for high speed data transfer, called AAL 5. This AAL is also being standardized by CCITT (for instance for Frame Relay).

3.5. THE PHYSICAL LAYER

3.5.1. General

Three kinds of transmission frame adaptation are specified by CCITT : the SDH based option, the PDH based option and the cell based option. The ATM Forum adds a fourth one, the FDDI based option.

3.5.2. Synchronous digital hierarchy based interface

Physical medium characteristics

The preferred physical medium is optical fiber, however, other transmission media such as coaxial cable are also considered.

At the T_B reference point, a bit rate of 155.520 Mbit/s is selected in both directions. Both electrical and optical interfaces are possible, depending on the requirements in terms of distance, reliability, cost, etc. For the electrical interface, electrical parameters are defined in G.703. Maximum range depends on the specific attenuation of the transmission medium used, and lies in the range of 100-200 meters. The optical solution should cover up to at least 800 meters, and possibly up to 2000 meters. The optical media consist of 2 single mode fibers according to G.652. However, national applications may use multimode fibers.

Also a 622.080 Mbit/s interface is recommended, either symmetrical, or asymmetrical with a rate of 155.520 Mbit/s in the upstream direction. Only single mode fiber is applicable.

Transmission convergence characteristics

The bit rate available for user information cells, signalling cells and OAM cells excluding physical layer frame structure octets is 149.760 Mbit/s on a 155.520 Mbit/s transmission system, and 599.040 Mbit/s on a 622.080 Mbit/s transmission system.

In this option, ATM cells are carried in an SDH frame as shown in Fig. 3.7., for an STM-1 signal. The SOH (Section Overhead) and the POH (Path Overhead) comply fully with SDH (G.707, G.708, G.709). The Transmission Convergence Sublayer performs frame generation and recovery, scrambling and descrambling for improving clock extraction, multiplexing of containers, frequency justification of individual containers to the transmission frequency by pointer processing, path signal identification, OAM and 125 µs clock recovery. Especially for ATM cell payloads, cell delineation by using the HEC, cell scrambling and descrambling, and HEC generation and checking are added.

The first Recommendation by CCITT for carrying an ATM cell stream into SDH only considered mapping of cells into the C-4, which is then packed in the VC-4 container along with the POH. ATM cells are octet aligned, and cross the C-4 boundary, since not an integer multiple of cells (N x (48 + 5) bytes) fit into the capacity of a C-4 (260 x 9 bytes). Since then, also mapping of ATM cell streams into lower bit rate containers is being specified.

The OAM implementation is in accordance with the general SDH specifications (G.708 and G.709). This OAM allows frame alignment, error monitoring, error reporting and so on. Transmission performance is monitored and reported per section and per path, using SDH overhead octets. Only the contents of the C2 byte is particular for an SDH frame transporting ATM cells : it contains an indication that the payload consists of ATM cells, an ATM payload construction indication.

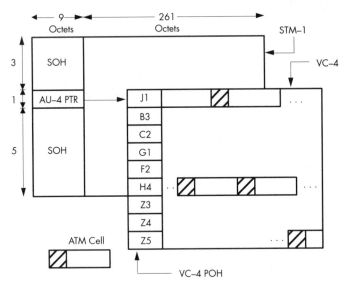

Fig. 3.7. – ATM Cells in an STM-1 or STS-3c Frame

The ATM Forum specifies a SONET STS-3c interface for both public and private UNI interfaces to synchronous networks. SONET is practically compatible with SDH as recommended by CCITT. Particularly the use of the H4 byte in the POH overhead is different. In SONET it will be set by the sending side to point to the next occurrence of a cell boundary in the VC-4. At the receiver this cell boundary indication may optionally be used to help the cell delineation based on the HEC mechanism.

3.5.3. Cell based interface

Physical medium characteristics

For CCITT, the physical medium characteristics of a cell based are identical to the ones for an SDH based interface. The ATM forum also specifies multimode fiber for such an interface.

Transmission convergence characteristics

In this option, cells are transported continuously, without any regular framing related to a time frame. Since no external clock is available at the receiver, this clock may either be derived from the signal received from the local node, or be provided by the clock of the customer equipment.

The Transmission Convergence Sublayer performs cell delineation, HEC generation and checking, cell rate adaptation between the ATM layer and physical layer, and OAM functions. The bit rate available for user information cells, signalling cells and OAM cells is 149.760 Mbit/s on a 155.520 Mbit/s transmission system, and 599.040 Mbit/s on a 622.080 Mbit/s transmission system. These values are identical to the payload of the respective SDH frames.

In order not to exceed the allowed maximum payloads on an interface with a nominally higher physical bit rate, the physical layer carries special Physical Layer (PL) cells, which are neither passed on to, nor received from, the ATM layer. They are generated and interpreted in the physical cell based layer. The maximum spacing between successive PL cells is 26 ATM layer cells. They can either be IDLE cells, or Physical Layer OAM cells (PL-OAM). PL cells are identified by a pre-defined header. IDLE cells merely perform cell rate adaptation, PL-OAM cells convey OAM information concerning the physical layer itself. Table 3.1. shows the pre-assigned header values for PL cell types.

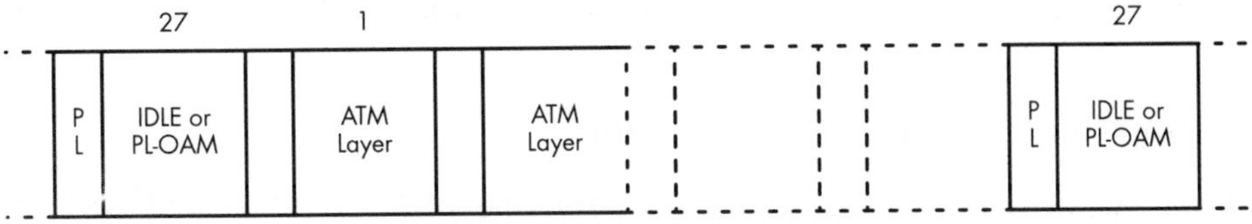

Fig. 3.8. – The Cell Based Interface

PL-OAM cells carry regenerator level (F1) and transmission path (F3) level information. They need to be inserted in the ATM layer cell flow on a recurrent basis. Minimum periodicity for each type is one in 513 cells. The digital section level flow (F2) is not used, as its functions are supported by the F3 flow, by lack of a transmission frame on the cell based UNI.

Cell type	Octet 1	Octet 2	Octet 3	Octet 4
IDLE cells	00000000	00000000	00000000	00000001
Physical Layer OAM	00000000	00000000	00000000	00001001
Reserved for use by PHY	PPPP0000	00000000	00000000	0000PPP1

P : Bit is available for use by the PHY layer

Table 3.1. – Pre-assigned Values of the Cell Header at the Physical Layer

Functions to be supported are the monitoring of the performance, and detection and reporting of transmission errors. Performance checking includes counting, and calculating an error code over the ATM layer and IDLE cells between two subsequent PL-OAM cells. The results are conveyed in the information field of the PL-OAM cell, together with maintenance signalling, and a CRC on the PL-OAM cell information field itself.

The cell based interface specified by the ATM Forum, at the private UNI only, supports additionally 125 μs clock delivery across a transmission link by means of a special symbol.

3.5.4. Plesiochronous digital hierarchy based interface

Physical medium characteristics

Carrying ATM cells in PDH frames as defined in CCITT Recommendation G.703 has the advantage of using on the existing transmission network infrastructure, instead of having to rely on the deployment of new SDH transmission equipment.

Transmission convergence characteristics

Several ways for mapping ATM cells in PDH frames of different bit rates have been proposed. Some early proposals implemented a kind of cell based transmission (see further) on top of the existing PDH frame, using PL-OAM cells for maintenance.

These methods have since been left, in favor of a more SDH-like approach, in which maintenance, performance monitoring and reporting are based on the use of special octets which are added to the frame. The remaining payload of the PDH frame is filled with ATM cells, which are octet aligned to the octet structure of the PDH frame payload area. The ATM cells are delineated by using the HEC, and their payload is scrambled to avoid false frame and cell synchronization. A full description of these mappings for the different bit rates mentioned by Recommendation G.703 will be specified by a new CCITT Recommendation in the G.7xx series.

As an example, Fig. 3.9. shows the frame for a 34.368 Mbit/s PDH interface. The following Path Overhead functions are defined :

FA : Frame Alignment
EM : Bit Interleaved Parity (BIP-8)
TR : Trail Trace
MA : Far End Receive Failure (FERF), Far End Block Error (FEBE), Payload Type
NR : Network Operator byte
GC : General purpose Communications channel (e.g. data or voice for maintenance).

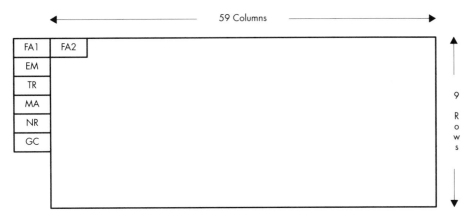

Fig. 3.9. – Frame Structure at 34.368 Mbit/s

The ATM Forum specifies the use of DS3 at the public UNI, and applies a third way for mapping ATM cells into DS3 frames. The method makes use of a Physical Layer Convergence Protocol (PLCP) which is a subset of the one used in DQDB networks (according to IEEE 802.6). A PLCP frame is used, which contains an integer number of ATM cells, and which has no direct relationship with the DS3 frame in which it is carried. In the PLCP frame, each ATM cell is preceded by PLCP framing octets A1 and A2, a path overhead indicator octet (POI), and a path overhead octet (POH) itself. The framing octets allow delineation of the ATM cells without using the HEC, which is only used for cell header checking and correction. The POI octets identify the contents of the succeeding POH octets, i.e. BIP-8, stuffing counter, path status, POH identifier and octets for future use. The trailer of the PLCP frame is stuffed with nibbles. The maximum bit rate available is 40.704 Mbit/s. Fig. 3.10. shows a PLCP frame.

3.5.5. FDDI based interface

Physical medium characteristics

The ATM Forum specifies a 125 Mbaud multimode fiber interface for the private UNI, based on the FDDI physical layer. The Physical Media Dependent sublayer applies a 4B/5B line code, resulting in a bit rate of 100 Mbit/s.

Transmission convergence characteristics

ATM cell delineation is done by using special line codes, not by using the HEC. No OAM support on the physical layer is foreseen. The HEC can be used for error detection, but not for error correction, as the line code causes bit error multiplication.

PLCP Frame 2		POI 1	POH 1	PLCP Payload 53	13 or 14 nibbles
A1	A2	P11	Z6	First ATM cell	
A1	A2	P10	Z5	ATM cell	
A1	A2	P9	Z4	ATM cell	
A1	A2	P8	Z3	ATM cell	
A1	A2	P7	Z2	ATM cell	
A1	A2	P6	Z1	ATM cell	
A1	A2	P5	X	ATM cell	
A1	A2	P4	B1	ATM cell	
A1	A2	P3	G1	ATM cell	
A1	A2	P2	X	ATM cell	
A1	A2	P1	X	ATM cell	
A1	A2	P0	C1	Twelfth ATM cell	Trailer

Fig. 3.10. – The DS3 PLCP Frame

3.5.6. ATM specific transmission convergence sublayer functions

Header error control (HEC)

The header error control covers the entire cell header. The selected code of 8 bits allows us either to correct single bit errors or detect multiple bit errors. An identical solution is used in all transmission convergence sublayers.

In normal (default) mode, the receiving side operates in the single bit error Correction mode (Fig. 3.11.). If a single bit error is detected, the error is corrected, and the state at the receiver switches to Detection mode state. In case a multibit error is detected, the cell is discarded and the state also switches to Detection mode.

In Detection mode state, all cells with a detected header error are discarded. As soon as an header with no error is examined, the receiver switches back to the Correction mode state.

The transmitter therefore calculates the HEC value using the polynomial generated by the header bits (excluding the HEC field) multiplied by 8 and dividing this polynomial by $x^8 + x^2 + x + 1$. The remainder of this division will be transmitted as the 8 bit HEC field.

At the transmitter, the device computing the division is pre-set to all 0s. To the remainder of the division, the following 8 bit pattern 01010101 (called coset value) must be added at the transmitter, to improve the cell delineation performance significantly. The receiver must first subtract this coset value of the 8 HEC bits before calculating the syndrome of the header.

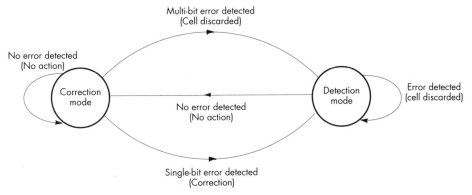

Fig. 3.11. – Dual Mode Operation of the HEC Algorithm

Cell delineation

The Recommendation I.432 states that the cell delineation algorithm has to be self supporting so that it can be transported on every network interface, independent from the used transmission system (cell based, SDH based, plesiochronous, ...).

The proposed cell delineation mechanism is based on the correlation which exists between the header bits and the HEC bits. The state diagram for cell delineation is shown in Fig. 3.12.

- In the HUNT state, the delineation process checks bit by bit the correctness of the HEC bits, for the assumed header field. When octet timing can be obtained in the PHY layer, the cell delineation in the hunt state may be performed octet by octet. This is for instance applicable if SDH transmission is applied.
- When correct, the PRESYNC state is entered. In the PRESYNC state it is assumed that a correct cell delineation has been found. However, a further confirmation is required. Therefore, the correctness of the HEC field is checked. An incorrect HEC before the SYNC state was reached makes the system return to the HUNT state.
- The SYNCH state is attained if this correctness is confirmed DELTA times. The system declares itself to be synchronized.
- The SYNC state is left (loss of cell delineation), when for ALPHA consecutive cells an incorrect HEC syndrome was encountered. Values of ALPHA = 7 and DELTA = 6 are suggested by CCITT for the SDH based physical layer, and ALPHA = 7 and DELTA = 8 for the cell based physical layer.

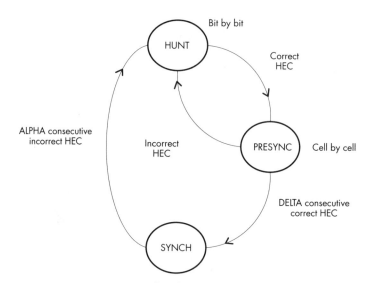

Fig. 3.12. – Cell Delineation State Diagram

Cell payload scrambling

To increase the security and robustness of the delineation process against malicious users or unintended simulations of a correct HEC in the information field, the bits of the information field are randomized.

For the SDH based physical layer, a self-synchronizing scrambler with a polynomial of $x^{43} + 1$ is recommended. This self-synchronizing scrambler has an error multiplication rate of 2. However this multiplication factor has no effect on the quality of the header error correction detection algorithm since the header itself is not scrambled.

For the cell based Physical Layer, a distributed sample scrambler is recommended, in which randomization is achieved by modulo addition of a pseudo-random sequence. Descrambling at the receiver is done by modulo addition of an identical locally generated pseudo-random sequence, having phase synchronization with the first with respect to the transmitted cells. The scrambler has no effect on the quality of the header error correction detection algorithm during steady state operation.

3.6.   THE ASYNCHRONOUS TRANSFER MODE LAYER

In Recommendation I.361 the coding of ATM cells is described in detail. The cell structure which was finally selected by CCITT contains a 48 octet information field and a 5 octet header (Fig. 3.13.). The octets are sent in an increasing order, starting with octet 1 of the header. Within an octet, the bits are sent in a decreasing order, starting with bit 8. For all fields of an ATM cell, the first bit sent is also the Most Significant Bit (MSB).

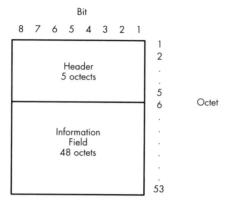

Fig. 3.13. – ATM Cell Structure

At the UNI (User Network Interface), the header structure is shown in Fig. 3.14. The first field contains 4 bits for the Generic Flow Control (GFC). The second field is the routing field, subdivided in a VCI (Virtual Channel Identifier) field of 16 bits and a VPI (Virtual Path Identifier) field of 8 bits. The Payload Type Identifier (PTI) field is coded in 3 bits. The use of the payload type has already been explained. The Cell Loss Priority (CLP) bit indicates whether a cell has a higher priority (CLP = 0) or is subject to discarding in the network (CLP = 1), and has also been explained. Finally, the HEC (Header Error Control) field consists of 8 bits, and its exact operation and coding was explained in section 3.5.

8	7	6	5	4	3	2	1	
GFC				VPI				1
VPI				VCI				2
VCI								3
VCI				PTI			CLP	4
HEC								5

Fig. 3.14. – ATM Header Structure at the UNI

At the NNI (Network-Node Interface) the header format is identical to the format at the UNI (Fig. 3.15.), except for the GFC field of the UNI which is replaced by 4 additional VPI bits. This results in a VPI field of 12 bits at the NNI.

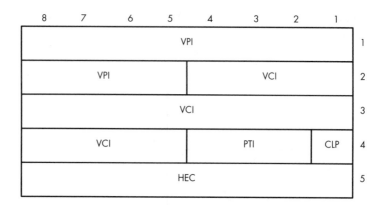

Fig. 3.15. – ATM Header Structure at the NNI

In Chapter 2, the words idle and empty cells were also used for unassigned cells. However, CCITT makes a distinction between IDLE cells and unassigned cells. As discussed already, IDLE cells are only visible at the physical layer (PHY) and not passed to the ATM layer. They are used for stuffing unused bandwidth at the physical layer. Unassigned cells are visible at both the PHY and ATM layer, but at the physical layer they are treated as any ATM layer cell. They characterize available positions, i.e. unused bandwidth, in the cell stream at the ATM layer. Both IDLE and unassigned cells allow a full asynchronous operation of both sender and receiver, at the respective layers (this explains the A of the acronym ATM). The distinction between them is made by bit 1 of octet 4 of the header (CLP bit position), as shown in Tables 3.1. and 3.2. IDLE cells cannot use the GFC field, since Generic Flow Control is not a physical layer function. The unassigned cells may be used for GFC purposes.

The pre-assigned header values for the ATM layer, as recommended by CCITT now, are shown in Table 3.2.

- The meta-signalling cells are used to negotiate on signalling VCI and signalling resources.
- General broadcast signalling cells carry information which has to be broadcast to all terminals at the UNI.
- The point-to-point signalling header is used for signalling on a UNI or NNI featuring a point-to-point configuration at the ATM layer, i.e. the network only sees one signalling entity at the other side.
- The segment and end-to-end F4 flows are coded by VCIs 0003 H and 0004 H within the Virtual Path for which they carry maintenance.
- The segment and end-to-end F5 flows are coded by PTIs 4 H and 5 H within the Virtual Channel for which they carry maintenance.
- Value 6 H of the PTI is reserved for (Fast) Resource Management on the Virtual Channel.

Cell type	VPI	VCI	PTI	CLP
Unassigned cells	00000000	00000000 00000000	–	0
Meta-signalling cells	xxxxxxxx	00000000 00000001	0 A 0	B
General broadcast cells	xxxxxxxx	00000000 00000010	0 A A	B
Point-to-point signalling cells	xxxxxxxx	00000000 00000101	0 A A	B
Segment OAM flow F4 cells	yyyyyyyy	00000000 00000011	0 A 0	A
End-to-end OAM flow F4 cells	yyyyyyyy	00000000 00000100	0 A 0	A
Segment OAM flow F5 cells	yyyyyyyy	zzzzzzzz zzzzzzzz	1 0 0	A
End-to-end OAM flow F5 cells	yyyyyyyy	zzzzzzzz zzzzzzzz	1 0 1	A
Resource management cells	yyyyyyyy	zzzzzzzz zzzzzzzz	1 1 0	A
User information cells	yyyyyyyy	vvvvvvvv vvvvvvvv	0 C U	L

A : Bit is available for use by the ATM layer.
B : Bit to be set to 0 by originating entity, but network may change value.
C : Congestion experienced indication bit.
L : Cell Loss Priority bit.
U : ATM layer user to ATM layer user indication bit.
x : Any VPI value. For VPI = 0, the VCI value is valid for signalling with local exchange.
y : Any VPI value.
z : Any VCI value other than 0.
v : Any VCI value above 0015 H.

Table 3.2. – Pre-assigned Values of the Cell Header at the ATM Layer by CCITT

The ATM Forum deviates slightly from this recommendation, by making all PTI and CLP bits of meta-signalling and general broadcast headers available for use at the ATM layer. Furthermore, the Forum defines an additional pre-assigned header value at the ATM layer, the Interim Local Management Interface (ILMI) VCI (see Table 3.3.). The aim is to provide any ATM user device with status and configuration information concerning the virtual path and channel connections available at its UNI, during the interim period until local network management procedures in the M-plane are available. In addition, more global operations and network management information (e.g. status and operational measurement information for the public and private UNI) may also facilitate diagnostics procedures at the UNI.

Cell type	VPI	VCI	PTI	CLP
ILMI cells	xxxxxxxx	00000000 00010000	0 A A	B

Table 3.3. Pre-assigned Values of the Cell Header at the ATM Layer by the ATM Forum

3.7. THE ATM ADAPTATION LAYER

3.7.1. Functions and types of adaptation layers

The AAL may enhance the service provided by the ATM layer to the requirements of a specific service (I.362). These services can be user services as well as control (e.g. signalling) and management functions. The AAL maps the user/control/ management PDUs (Protocol Data Unit) into the information field of one or more consecutive ATM cells of a virtual connection, and vice versa.

The services which will be transported over the ATM layer are classified in 4 classes, each of which has its own specific requirements towards the AAL.

To obtain these 4 classes, the services are classified according to 3 basic parameters :

(1) *Time relation between source and destination :*
Some services have a time relation between source and destination, for some there is no such time relation. For instance, in 64 kbit/s PCM voice, there is a clear time relation between source and destination. Information transfer between computers has no time relation. Sometimes services with a time relation are also called real time services.

(2) *Bit rate :*
Some services have a constant bit rate, others have a variable bit rate.

(3) *Connection mode :*
Services can be either connectionless or connection oriented.

Only 4 types out of the theoretically 8 combinations of those 3 parameters result in valid existing services. Therefore CCITT, has defined 4 classes, according to these basic parameters as described in Fig. 3.16.

• In Class A, a time relation exists between source and destination. The bit rate is constant and the service is connection oriented. A typical example is voice of 64 kbit/s as in NISDN to be transported over ATM. The offering of this service over an ATM network is also sometimes called circuit emulation. Another example is fixed bit rate video.

- In Class B, again a time relation exists between source and destination, for a connection-oriented service. However, the difference with class A is that Class B sources have a variable bit rate. Typical examples are variable bit rate video and audio.
- In Class C there is no time relation between source and destination and the bit rate is variable. The service is connection oriented. Examples are connection-oriented data transfer and signalling.
- Finally, Class D differs from Class C in being connectionless. An example of such a service is connectionless data transport (e.g. SMDS, i.e. Switched Multimegabit Data Services).

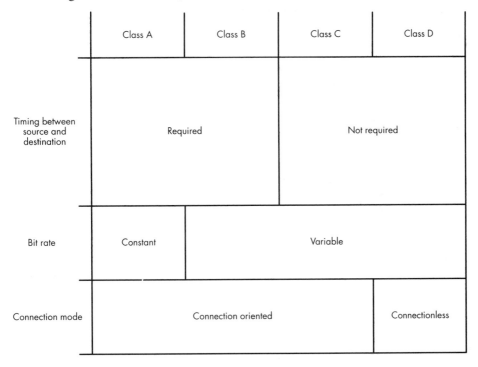

Fig. 3.16. – Service Classes for Adaptation

As discussed above, the AAL is subdivided in 2 sublayers : SAR (Segmentation And Reassembly) Sublayer and CS (Convergence Sublayer). The prime functions of the SAR are the segmentation into ATM cells of PDUs and reassembly of cells into a PDU. The convergence sublayer is service dependent. SAR and/or CS may be empty in some applications.

Recommendation I.363 describes the SAR and CS protocols in a certain combination to be applied to the service classes described above. However, CCITT states that other combinations may also be used, or that even other SARs or CSs may be defined.

Four types of AAL protocols have been recommended up to now by CCITT, named AAL 1, AAL 2, AAL 3/4 and AAL 5. Recommendation I.362 states that CBR services will utilize AAL Type 1, but other AAL protocols for CBR are for further study. Connectionless data services will use the Type 3/4 AAL. Frame Relay services will use AAL 5. The specific association of other services with an AAL type is still for further study. AAL 5 may be recommended for signalling information.

3.7.2. Adaptation for constant bit rate services : AAL 1

Principles

Constant Bit Rate (CBR) services require information to be transferred between source and destination at a constant bit rate, after a virtual connection has been set up. The layer services provided by the AAL type 1 to the AAL user are :

- Transfer of Service Data Units (SDU) with a constant source bit rate, and their delivery with the same bit rate.
- Transfer of timing information between source and destination.
- Transfer of data structure information.
- Indication of lost or errored information which is not recovered by the AAL itself, if needed.

A number of error indications, such as corrupted user information, loss of timing, buffer overflow and underflow, may be passed from the user plane to the management plane. Interactions between the user plane and the control plane are still for further study.

The SAR sublayer functions

The SAR sublayer accepts a 47 octet block of data from the CS, and then adds a one octet SAR-PDU header to each block to form the SAR-PDU. At the receiving end, the SAR sublayer gets a 48 byte block from the ATM layer, and then separates the SAR-PDU header. The 47 octet block of SAR-PDU payload is passed to the CS.

Associated with each 47 octet SAR-PDU, the SAR sublayer receives a sequence number value from the CS. At the receiving end, this number is passed to the peer CS. It may be used to detect loss and misinsertion of SAR payloads, i.e. to lost or inserted cells.

The SAR layer has also the capability to indicate the existence of a CS layer. Associated with each 47 octet SAR-PDU, it receives this indication (CSI) from the CS and conveys it to the peer CS layer. The use of this indication is optional.

Both items of information are protected against bit errors by a 4 bit Sequence Number Protection (SNP) field, capable of single bit error correction and multiple bit error detection. If they are corrupted and cannot be corrected by the SAR sublayer, the CS is informed.

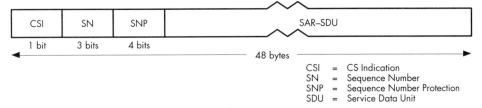

CSI	SN	SNP	SAR–SDU
1 bit	3 bits	4 bits	

48 bytes

CSI = CS Indication
SN = Sequence Number
SNP = Sequence Number Protection
SDU = Service Data Unit

Fig. 3.17. – SAR Structure for AAL 1

The convergence sublayer functions

The convergence sublayer depends on the particular service and may contain different functions :

• Handling of Cell Delay Variation (CDV).

• Handling of cell payload assemby delay.
The SAR-PDU payload may be filled only partially with user data, in order to reduce the payload assembly delay. The number of leading octets utilized for user information in each SAR-PDU is a constant. The remainder consists of dummy octets.

• Source clock recovery at the receiver.
Several methods for source clock recovery at the receiver exist.

CCITT recommends the use of the Synchronous Residual Time Stamp (SRTS) method. It uses a Residual Time Stamp (RTS) to measure and convey information to the receiver about the difference between a common reference clock derived from the network at both the sender and the receiver, and the service clock of the sender. The RTS is transported in the CSI bits of successive SAR-PDUs.

A common reference clock is available if both the sender and receiver communicate via a synchronous network, e.g. an SDH or SONET based network. The method is capable of meeting jitter requirements specified by CCITT for 2.048 and 1.544 Mbit/s hierarchies.

If a common reference clock is unavailable, e.g. on a PDH based network, an adaptive clock recovery method, based on monitoring the buffer filling level at the receiver, may be used.

• Source data structure recovery at the receiver.
A pointer is used for delineation of structure boundaries. The procedure supports any fixed, octet based structure, in particular 8 kHz based structures used in circuit mode services (Recommendation I.231).

- Monitoring of lost and misinserted cells and possible corrective action.

- Monitoring of the AAL Protocol Control Information (PCI) for bit errors and possible corrective action.

- Monitoring of user information field for bit errors and possible corrective action.

- Reporting on the status of end-to-end performance as deduced by the AAL.

For some specific services, special functions can be supported by the CS. Typical examples of these functions are :

(1) *High quality constant bit rate audio and video*
     In this case an error correction in the payload may be required. This may be combined with a method where bits are interleaved before being put in cells (see Chapter 5).

(2) *Voice*
     No specific field in the SAR-SDU has to be provided in the CS. The main function is the clock recovery at the receiving side based on the incoming cell stream. This can be achieved by checking the filling level of a buffer at the receiver. If required, this clock recovery mechanism based on the filling level may take into account the knowledge on cell loss given by the SAR sublayer.

3.7.3. Adaptation for variable bit rate services : AAL 2

The Type 2 AAL offers a transfer of information with a variable bit rate. In addition, timing information is transferred between source and destination. Since the source is generating a variable bit rate, it is possible that cells are not completely filled, and that the filling level varies from cell to cell. Therefore, more functions are required in the SAR. CCITT has not yet reached an agreement on this SAR definition, but has mentioned a possible way the SAR of Type 2 could look like (Fig. 3.18.). The SN (Sequence Number) field contains the sequence number to allow the recovery of lost or misrouted cells. The IT (information type) field indicates the beginning of a message (BOM), continuation of a message (COM), end of a message (EOM), or that the cell transports timing or other information. BOM, COM or EOM indicate that the respective cell is the first; middle or last cell of a message, i.e. an information unit as defined in the CS layer with possibly a variable length. The LI (length indicator) field indicates the number of useful bytes in partially filled cells. The CRC field may allow the SAR to correct bit errors in the SAR-SDU. The coding and length of each field are for further study.

     In the CS sublayer, the following functions have to be performed :

- Clock recovery by means of insertion and extraction of time information (e.g. a time stamp, ...).

- Handling of lost or misdelivered cells.
- Forward error correction (FEC) for audio and video services.

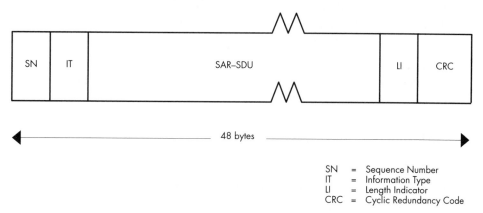

SN = Sequence Number
IT = Information Type
LI = Length Indicator
CRC = Cyclic Redundancy Code

Fig. 3.18. – SAR Structure for AAL 2

The CS functions and protocol are also still for further study.

3.7.4. Adaptation for data services : AAL 3/4

Principles

CCITT recommends the use of AAL 3/4 for transfer of data which is sensitive to loss, but not to delay. The AAL may be used for connection oriented as well as for connectionless data communication. The AAL itself does not perform all functions required by a connectionless service, since functions like routing and network addressing are performed on the network layer.

Two modes of AAL 3/4 are defined : message mode and streaming mode.

- Message mode
  The AAL-SDU is passed across the AAL interface in exactly one AAL Interface Data Unit (IDU). This service provides for transport of fixed or variable length AAL-SDUs.

- Streaming mode
  The AAL-SDU is passed in one or more AAL-IDUs. Transfer of these AAL-IDUs may occur separated in time. The service provides for transport of long variable length AAL-SDUs. It also includes an abort service by which the discarding of a partially transferred AAL-SDU can be requested.

Both modes of service may offer the following peer-to-peer operational procedures :

- Assured operation
  Every SDU is delivered without any content modification caused by errors. Any corrupted or lost CS-PDU is retransmitted. In addition, flow control is supported between the endpoints. The use of this procedure may be restricted to point-to-point AAL connections.

- Non-assured operation
  In this case, an SDU may be delivered incorrectly or not at all. So, lost or errored CS-PDU are not retransmitted. The provision of flow control is optional.

The SAR sublayer functions

The SAR provides the following functions :

- Segmentation and reassembly of variable length CS-PDUs.
  The SAR-PDU contains 2 fields for this purpose :

  – Segment Type (ST) : 2 bits
    The ST indicates which part of a CS-PDU is carried by the SAR-PDU : first, middle, last or single segment. The coding of the ST is as follows : 10 for BOM (Begin Of Message), 00 for COM (Continuation Of Message), 01 for EOM (End Of Message) and 11 for SSM (Single Segment Message).

  – Length Indicator (LI) : 6 bits
    Last segment and single segment SAR-PDUs may contain less payload octets than the maximum of 44, and thus also need an indication of the number of valid octets.

- Error detection.
  To detect bit errors in the SAR-PDU, a CRC field of 10 bits is defined. The coding of the CRC is based on the generating polynomial $G(x) = 1 + x + x^4 + x^5 + x^9 + x^{10}$. In addition, lost or inserted cells must be detected. This function is achieved by means of a sequence number (SN) field of 4 bits.

- Multiplexing of multiple CS-PDUs on a common bearer in the ATM layer (VCI/VPI).
  Multiplexing is supported by a 10 bit Multiplexing Identifier (MID) in the SAR-PDU. The use of the MID allows to multiplex 2^{10} AAL user to AAL user connections on a single user to user ATM layer connection for connection-oriented data communication.
      For connectionless data communication, e.g. SMDS, the MID allows to interleave SAR-PDUs of up to 2^{10} CS-PDUs on the same semi-permanent ATM layer virtual connection. This connection may transport ATM cells from one or more connectionless terminals to a connectionless server at the UNI, or between connectionless service networks at the NNI.

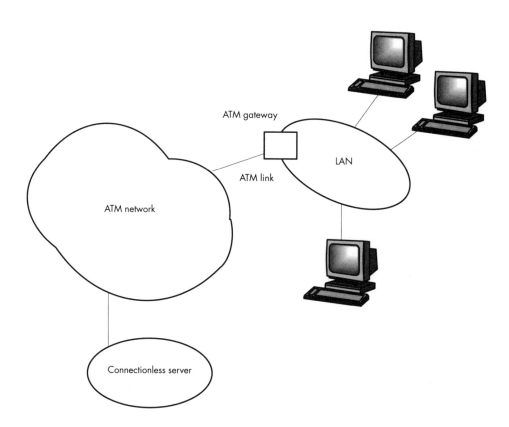

Fig. 3.19. – LAN Connection to an ATM Network

This is for instance the case where a number of terminals are connected to a LAN (connectionless), whereas the LAN is connected via a single ATM gateway (Fig. 3.19.). All terminal information is transported over a single ATM connection to a connectionless server, which will, based on the MID, decide to route the information to the correct destination. However, as described above, the routing information is present in the network layer, and the connectionless server has to establish the link between the MID field and the network layer routing information, which is only transported in the first (BOM) AAL segment of the CS-PDU.

Being multiplexed on a single ATM connection, all CS-PDUs will get the same QOS (Quality Of Service) offered by the network.

These different functions lead to a SAR structured as described in Fig. 3.20. There we see that the SAR payload is 44 bytes, headed by a 2 byte header and followed by a 2 byte trailer.

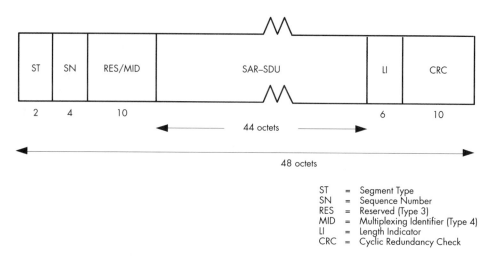

Fig. 3.20. – SAR Structure for AAL 3/4

The convergence sublayer functions

The Common Part Convergence Sublayer (CPCS) of AAL 3/4 provides for non-assured transfer of data frames with any length between 1 and 65535 octets. CPCS connections will be established by management or control plane. One or more CPCS connections may be established between 2 peer CPCS entities, yet no switching of CPCS connections will be supported. The integrity of the CPCS-SDU sequence must be guaranteed on each CPCS connection. The sublayer performs the following functions :

- Preservation of the CPCS-SDU
  This function provides for delineation and transparency of CPCS-SDUs.

- Error detection and handling
  Corrupted CPCS-SDUs are either discarded or optionally delivered to the Service Specific Convergence Sublayer (SSCS). Detected errors include those detected at the CPCS layer as well as those detected at the SAR layer.

- Buffer allocation size
  Each CPCS-PDU carries up front an indication to the receiving peer entity of the maximum buffer requirements to receive this CPCS-PDU.

- Abort
  A partially transmitted CPCS-PDU can be aborted.

The CPCS-PDU of AAL 3/4 uses the format shown in Fig. 3.21.

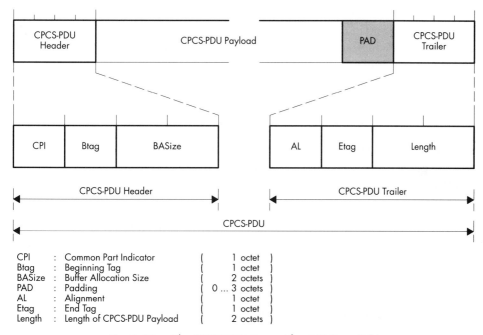

CPI   : Common Part Indicator   (1 octet   )
Btag   : Beginning Tag   (1 octet   )
BASize : Buffer Allocation Size   (2 octets   )
PAD   : Padding   (0 ... 3 octets)
AL   : Alignment   (1 octet   )
Etag   : End Tag   (1 octet   )
Length : Length of CPCS-PDU Payload   (2 octets   )

Fig. 3.21. – The CPCS-PDU Format for AAL Type 3/4

- Common Part Indicator (CPI) field
  This field is used to interpret subsequent fields for the CPCS functions in the CPCS header and trailer. Specifically, it indicates the counting units for the values specified in the BA size and Length fields. Other uses are for further study. In the future, it may be used to identify AAL layer management functions, e.g. performance and fault monitoring, MID allocation and transfer of OAM messages.

- Beginning Tag (Btag) field
  This field allows an association of the CPCS-PDU header and trailer at the receiver. The same value is put by the sender in the Btag and Etag for a given CPCS-PDU, and is changed (e.g. incremented) for each successive CPCS-PDU.
      This mechanism is however redundant with the MID, BOM / EOM and error detection mechanisms used at the SAR sublayer for proper reassembly of a CPCS-PDU.

- Buffer Allocation Size Indication (BASize) field
  This field informs the receiving peer entity of the maximum buffer requirements to receive this CPCS-PDU before the data arrive. In message mode the BASize is encoded equal to the CPCS-PDU payload length. In streaming mode, the BASize is encoded equal to or greater than the CPCS-PDU payload length. It is binary encoded as a number of counting units, the size of which is indicated by the CPI.

- Padding (PAD) field
  Between the end of the CPCS-PDU payload and the 32 bit aligned CPCS-PDU
  trailer, there will be from 0 to 3 unused octets. These are called the Padding field.
  They do not convey any information.

- Alignment (AL) field
  This field only achieves 32 bit alignment of the CPCS-PDU trailer. It does not
  convey any information, and shall be set to "0".

- End Tag (Etag) field
  For a given CPCS-PDU, the sender shall insert the same value as was inserted in
  the Btag.

The CPCS has the basic functionality to support a Connectionless Network Layer
(Class D) as well as a Frame Relaying telecommunication service in Class C. For
the Connectionless Network Layer, there is no need for any Service Specific
Convergence Sublayer. In other cases, the SSCS is still for further study.

3.7.5. Adaptation for data services : AAL 5

Principles

According to end-user equipment manufacturers and high speed, connection-
oriented data service users, the AAL 3/4 as recommended by CCITT is not really
suited to their needs. The AAL 3/4 has a high overhead of 4 bytes per SAR-PDU of
48 bytes. Also, the 10 bit CRC for detecting corrupted segments, and the 4 bit
sequence number for detecting lost and misinserted segments, may not offer enough
protection for conveying very long blocks of data.

Therefore the ATM Forum has specified a new type of AAL, called AAL 5. The
objective is to offer a service with less overhead and better error detection below the
CPCS layer. At this layer, the service of AAL 5 shall be identical to the service
provided by the CPCS of AAL 3/4, except that no multiplexing is supported. If
multiplexing is required at the AAL layer, it will occur in the SSCS layer. CCITT is
also considering to recommend AAL 5 for Class C services.

The SAR sublayer functions

The SAR sublayer accepts variable length SAR-SDUs which are integral multiples
of 48 octets from the CPCS, and generates SAR-PDUs containing 48 octets of SAR
data. Preservation or delineation of the SAR-SDU happens by an end of SAR-SDU
indication, which is carried as a value "1" in the ATM layer user to ATM layer user
indication bit of the PTI for User Information cells, as discussed in section 3.6. A
value "0" means the beginning or continuation of a SAR-SDU.

The convergence sublayer functions

The functions implemented by the AAL 5 CPCS are the same as the ones offered by the AAL 3/4 CPCS, except that the AAL 5 CPCS does not give a buffer allocation size indication to the receiving peer entity. Also, error protection in the AAL 5 is fully handled at the CPCS layer itself, instead of being shared between SAR and CPCS as in AAL 3/4. Fig. 3.22. gives the format of the CPCS-PDU for AAL 5.

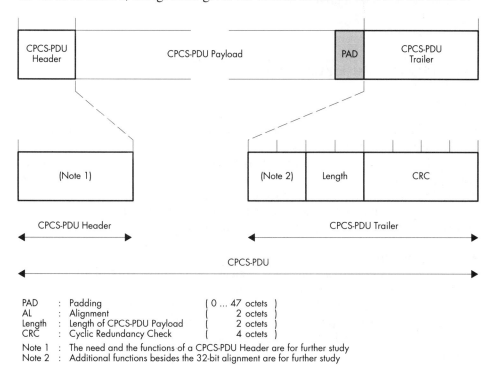

PAD	:	Padding	(0 ... 47 octets)
AL	:	Alignment	(2 octets)
Length	:	Length of CPCS-PDU Payload	(2 octets)
CRC	:	Cyclic Redundancy Check	(4 octets)
Note 1	:	The need and the functions of a CPCS-PDU Header are for further study	
Note 2	:	Additional functions besides the 32-bit alignment are for further study	

Fig. 3.22. – The CPCS-PDU Format for AAL 5

Fields with the same names have the same functions as for the AAL 3/4 CPCS-PDU. Only the CRC field is new. It is filled with the value of a CRC calculation which is performed over the entire contents of the CPCS-PDU, including the CPCS-PDU payload, PAD field, AL field and Length field. The CRC-32 generating polynomial is :

$$G(x) = x^{32} + x^{26} + x^{23} + x^{22} + x^{16} + x^{12} + x^{11} + x^{10} + x^8 + x^7 + x^5 + x^4 + x^2 + x + 1$$

The need for and functions of a CPCS header are still for further study. Any header would also be included in the CRC calculation.

As mentioned in the beginning of this section, AAL 5 will adopt the SSCS specified for AAL 3/4, if any.

3.7.6. Adaptation for signalling

The ATM Adaptation Layer to be used for signalling across the UNI and NNI in the BISDN is still for further study. By the nature of the service required, AAL 3/4 as well as AAL 5 are possible candidates. The ATM Forum also specifies AAL 5 for this purpose, and within CCITT there is a strong tendency to do the same, but no decision has been taken up to now.

3.8. MAINTENANCE FUNCTIONS

3.8.1. Principles

For ISDN, CCITT has already issued a number of Recommendations for operations, and maintenance (OAM) principles (M.20, M.30, M.36, I.600 series, I.430, I.431). The basic OAM principle is based on controlled maintenance which consists of supervision, testing and performance monitoring in order to minimize preventive maintenance and to reduce corrective maintenance.

To obtain an optimal functionality in terms of OAM, CCITT has recommended (I.610) for BISDN to distinguish the following phases :

- Performance monitoring
  In normal operation, a continuous check or periodic control of functions guarantees the provision of maintenance information. The performance information obtained by the relevant performance monitoring mechanisms will be transported to the applicable OAM entities, which will use this information for long-term system evaluation, short-term service quality control or preventive actions.

- Defect and failure detection
  By continuous or periodic checking of the functions, failures can be detected. As a result, maintenance event information or various alarms will be produced.

- System protection
  If a failure is detected, the failed entity will be excluded from operation. The effect of the failure is minimized by blocking or change over to other entities.

- Failure or performance information
  If an entity fails, other management entities will be timely informed. Also status information will be exchanged. This failure information is used by the system protection phase, to enable it to exclude failing entities, but is also used by neighboring entities to ensure that a failure message is spread all over the network.

- Fault localization
  Internal or external test systems will determine the localization of the failed entity. When the faults are localized, the system protection phase ensures that failing entities will be excluded.

3.8.2. OAM network layering

OAM flows

The maintenance and operation of an ATM based network is organized according to a layered approach. Five hierarchical OAM levels are defined with the associated information flows. This is shown in Fig. 3.23., where we see that 2 levels are defined in the ATM layer and 3 levels in the physical layer. In different places of the network, not all levels are necessarily present. In that case the relevant OAM functions will be performed on a higher level. The following levels are identified :

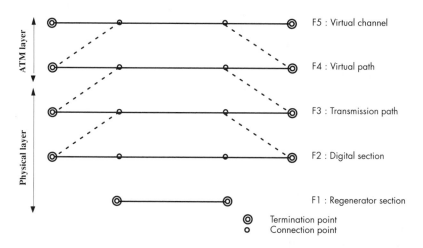

Fig. 3.23. – OAM Hierarchical Levels

- Virtual channel (F5)
  Both endpoints perform VCI termination functions for a BISDN connection. Such a connection is composed of several virtual paths. The OAM functions are performed on a VCI level and may give input to any of the 5 phases described above. For instance, it is possible to do performance monitoring on a VCI level using the PTI bits of the cell header.

- Virtual path (F4)
  Both endpoints perform VPI termination functions for a BISDN connection. Such a connection is composed of several transmission paths. Again, one of the 5 phases described above may be involved in the virtual path maintenance.

- Transmission path (F3)
  Both endpoints perform the assembly / disassembly of the payload and the OAM
  functions of a transmission system. Since cells must be recognized at a
  transmission path to extract OAM cells, cell delineation and HEC functions are
  required at the termination points of each transmission path. A transmission path
  is composed of several digital sections.

- Digital section (F2)
  Both endpoints are section termination points. A digital section comprises a
  maintenance entity. It is capable of transporting OAM information from adjacent
  digital sections.

- Regenerator section (F1)
  This is the smallest recognizable physical entity for OAM, and is located between
  repeaters.

OAM functions are allocated to the Layer Management of the BISDN Protocol
Reference Model. OAM functions related to OAM levels are independent from the
OAM functions of other layers and have to be provided at each layer. Also, each
layer where OAM functions are required, is able to carry out its own processing to
obtain quality and status information. These results may be provided to the Plane
Management or to the adjacent higher layer.

    The mechanism to provide OAM functions and the information flows
associated with it depend on the related layer.

Physical layer mechanisms

At the physical layer, the OAM information flows (F1, F2, F3) depend on the type of
transmission system, as well as on the supervision functions contained in the NT1
and NT2 for the section crossing the T_B reference point.

    In SDH, special bytes in the SOH (Section Overhead) carry the F1 and F2 flows.
Flow F3 is carried by the POH (Path Overhead) of the transmission frame.

    In a cell based transmission system, the F1 and F3 flows are carried by special
OAM cells, called PL-OAM (Physical Layer OAM) cells, and distinguished by a
special pattern in the cell header. The F2 flow is not provided, but the associated
functions are supported by F3. These cells are only valid on the physical layer and
are not passed to the ATM layer.

    PDH transmission systems (G.702, G.703) may only be used on the network
side of the B-NT1. Specific means to monitor section performance exist for these
systems, e.g. the bit error rate per section may be monitored via CRC by counting
the number of code violations. The capability to carry OAM information other than
bit-oriented messages is very limited. CCITT is working on new recommendations
for mapping ATM cells in PDH transmission frames, providing for additional POH
octets similar to SDH-POH.

ATM layer mechanisms

At the ATM layer (F4, F5), dedicated cells are used to perform VC and VP maintenance. These cells are used to transport OAM information within the same layers of the management plane. There exist 2 kinds of both F4 and F5 flows :

- An end-to-end flow, which is used for end-to-end VPC or VCC operations communications
  A segment flow, which is used for VPC or VCC operations communications within the bounds of one link, or multiple interconnected ones, where all of the links are under the control of one administration or organization. F4 and F5 flows must be terminated only at the endpoints of a VPC / VCC, or at the connecting points terminating a VPC / VCC segment.

Adaptation layer mechanisms

The Convergence Sublayer of an AAL contains error performance monitoring, correction and reporting mechanisms, proper to the type of AAL.

3.8.3.   OAM of the physical layer

Different sections of the physical layer have to be maintained. A possible example of a physical configuration is shown in Fig. 3.24. There we see the F1 flow terminated by LTs (Line Termination) and regenerator, whereas F2 is terminated by LTs. The F3 flow requires the recognition of ATM cell streams.

Different errors can be recognized, and be assigned to one of the 3 layers and related flows described in the previous section. The following failures can be detected in an SDH based transmission system.

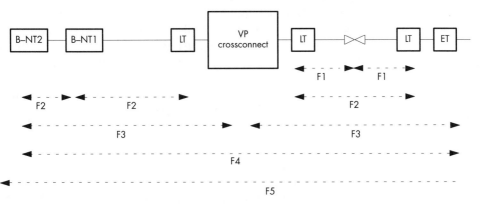

Fig. 3.24. – Example of a Physical Configuration, and OAM Flows at the Physical and the ATM Layer

F1 :   • Loss of signal or loss of frame : the SDH frame synchronization is lost.

F2 :   • Degraded error performance : the quality of the received bit stream is not
         acceptable (e.g. too many bit errors). This may be caused by a too low input
         signal, a bad locking PLL, etc. This can be measured by the BIP in the SOH.

F3 :   • Loss of cell delineation : the cell delineation algorithm is no longer in the
         SYNC state (see Fig.3.12.).
       • Degraded error performance : the quality is no longer acceptable. This can
         be measured by the BIP in the POH.
       • Incorrigible header : the header has more errors than can be corrected (i.e.
         single bit errors). This error is detected using the HEC mechanism.
       • Degraded header error performance : the quality of the header bits is too
         low. This can be detected by the HEC mechanism.
       • Loss of AU4 pointer : the AU4 pointer of the SDH-SOH is not discovered,
         giving rise to an unrecognizable SDH payload.
       • Failure of insertion and suppression of IDLE cells : in case too many IDLE
         cells are arriving, no useful information can be transported.

In case a cell based transmission system is used, the following errors can be
detected :

F1 :   • Loss of signal.
       • Loss of F1 PL-OAM cell recognition.: the receiver no longer
         recognizes PL-OAM cells. Thus, no performance monitoring can be
         provided.
       • Degraded error performance.

F3 :   • Loss of cell delineation.
       • Incorrectable header.
       • Loss of F3 PL-OAM cell recognition.
       • Degraded header error performance : this can be measured by calculating
         the BIP over a block of preceding cells and transporting this BIP in a
         PL-OAM cell, or by use of a special pattern in the information fields of the
         IDLE cells.
       • Failure of insertion and suppression of IDLE cells : where too many IDLE
         cells are arriving, no useful information can be transported.

3.8.4.   OAM of the ATM layer

A possible example of the physical termination points of the OAM flows at the ATM
layer are shown in Fig. 3.18. There we see that a complete virtual path/channel is
maintained with the F4 and F5 flows.

Two possible failures are identified by CCITT :

F4 :   • Path not available : in this case, the virtual path cannot be guaranteed and requires a system protection action.
        • Degraded performance : the ATM cells arriving at the VCI/VPI processing nodes do not have the acceptable performance. This degraded performance can be caused by cell loss, cell insertion, a too high bit error rate in the information field, etc.

F5 :   • Channel not available.
        • Degraded performance.

The CCITT Recommendation I.610 is only a first document on the maintenance principles of an ATM network. Further work on this subject is still ongoing in CCITT.

3.9. BIBLIOGRAPHY

CCITT Recommendations

G.702   Digital Hierarchy Bit Rates
G.703   Physical/electrical Characteristics of Hierarchical Digital Interfaces
G.704   Synchronous Frame Structure used at Primary and Secondary Hierarchical Levels
G.706   Frame Alignment and Cyclic Redundancy Check (CRC) Procedures relating to Basic Frame Structures defined in Recommendation G.704
G.707   Synchronous Digital Hierarchy Bit Rates
G.708   Network Node Interface for the Synchronous Digital Hierarchy
G.709   Synchronous Multiplexing Structure
I.113   Vocabulary of Terms for Broadband Aspects of ISDN
I.121   Broad band Aspects of ISDN
I.150   BISDN ATM Functional Characteristics
I.211   BISDN Service Aspects
I.311   BISDN General Network Aspects
I.321   BISDN Protocol Reference Model and its Application
I.327   BISDN Network Functional Architecture
I.361   BISDN ATM Layer Specification
I.362   BISDN ATM Adaptation Layer (AAL) Functional Description
I.363   BISDN ATM Adaptation Layer (AAL) Specification
I.364   Support of broadband connectionless data service on BISDN
I.371   Traffic and congestion control in BISDN
I.413   BISDN User-Network Interface
I.414   Overview of Recommendations on layer 1 for ISDN and BISDN customer accesses

I.430   Layer 1 Specification at the Basic Rate
I.431   Layer 1 Specification at the Primary Rate User Network Interface
I.432   BISDN User-Network Interface Physical Layer Specification
I.441   ISDN User-Network Interface Data Link Layer Specification
I.600   Application of Maintenance Principles to ISDN Subscriber Access and
         Subscriber Installation
I.610   OAM Principles of BISDN Access
M.20   Maintenance Philosophy for Telecommunications Networks
M.30   Principles for a Telecommunication Management Network
M.36   Principles for the Maintenance of ISDNs

ATM Forum Specifications

ATM User-Network Interface Specification Version 2.0, June 1, 1992
ATM B-Inter Carrier Interface Specification

Other literature

Huber M.N., Frantzen V., Maegerl G., "Proposed evolutionary paths for BISDN
    signalling", ISS '92, Yokohama, October 1992
Peeters H., Van Durme L., De Smedt A., *et al.*, "The UNI protocol architecture in
    the belgian broadband experiment", ISS '92, Yokohama, October 1992

4

Broadband ATM Switching

4.1. INTRODUCTION

In the past, various switching architectures were developed for different applications such as voice and data, based on transfer modes like STM (Synchronous Transfer Mode) and packet switching. These switching architectures have been adapted during history as the available technology allowed other, more cost effective solutions. For instance, for telephone services alone, a large number of different types of switches have already been developed in the past, ranging from mechanical switches (crossbar, Strowger, ...), via semi-electronic to fully electronic (analog and digital) switches, based on the STM principle.

The switching architectures developed for STM are not directly applicable to broadband ATM. Nor are the architectures developed for conventional (e.g. X.25) packet switching. Indeed, two major factors have a large impact on the implementation of broadband ATM switching architectures :

- The high speed at which the switch has to operate (from 150 up to 600 Mbit/s).
- The statistical behavior of the ATM streams passing through the ATM switching systems.

In addition, the definition of ATM with a small fixed cell size and a limited header functionality has an important influence on the definition of optimal ATM switching architectures. A large number of alternative switching architectures have been described in the literature and some of them have been realized, or are in the stage of implementation.

Today, a large number of ATM switches are commercially available from large telecommunication companies and also from small start-up companies. These commercial systems have sizes ranging from very small (4 inputs and outputs) to very large (thousands of inputs and outputs).

These ATM switching products are installed by public operators to offer a public wide area broadband service, and by private users to fulfil internal high speed telecommunication needs. In the first case (public), these systems are sometimes called an ATM Central Office, in the second case (private), they are often called an ATM LAN.

This Chapter describes a number of alternative switching architecture proposals which are particularly designed for switching broadband ATM signals.

In the description of the ATM switching architectures attention will be paid in this Chapter only to the "transport" part of the switch, also called the transport network, and not to the "control" part of the switch, responsible for handling the signalling information.

The transport network is defined as all physical means which are responsible for the correct transportation of the information (i.e. the ATM cells) from an ATM inlet to an ATM outlet, within the quality of service specifications of ATM. This transport network mainly performs functions located in the user plane of the protocol reference model described in Chapter 3. Typical quality of service parameters for the transport network are the cell loss rate, bit error rate, cell delay, cell delay jitter, etc.

The control part of the switch is that which controls the transport network. It for instance decides which inlet to connect to which outlet. This decision is based on incoming signalling information or set by an operator on a semi-permanent basis. The control network mainly performs functions located in the control plane of the protocol reference model described in Chapter 3. Quality of service parameters for the control network are more related to signalling, e.g. the call set-up time, call release time, etc.

In an ATM switch, the ATM cells have to be transported from an inlet (out of N inlets) to one or more outlets (out of M outlets). This switching from inlet to outlet can be combined with concentration, expansion, multiplexing and demultiplexing of ATM traffic. In most switching architectures, all functions described above are available in one combination or another. The meaning of these functions is the following :

- Switching
  The transportation of information from an incoming logical ATM channel to an outgoing logical ATM channel, to be selected between a number of outgoing logical channels. This logical ATM channel is characterized by :

  – A physical inlet/outlet, characterized by a physical port number.
  – A logical channel on the physical port, characterized by a virtual channel identifier (VCI) and/or virtual path identifier (VPI).

To provide the switching function, both the inlet and incoming virtual channel/path identifier have to be related to the outlet and outgoing virtual channel/path identifier. Two functions have to be implemented in an ATM switching system. These 2 functions can be compared to those applied in classical switching systems (for STM systems).

The first function is comparable to a space switching function (S) (Fig. 4.1a.). As can be seen, information from inlet 1 is transported to outlet 3, whereas information from inlet 3 is transported to outlet M. An important aspect in this "space switching" is **routing**. This means how the information is internally routed from the inlet to the outlet.

The second function can be compared to a time slot interchange (T) in a time switch (Fig. 4.1b.). This means that information of time slot i is switched to time slot j, whereas information from time slot k is transported to time slot l. Modern STM switches are often composed of these S and T stages, in different sorts of combinations like STSTS or STSSTS or TSTTST. However, in ATM switching systems, the time identification in a fixed frame is replaced by a logical channel identification. Since the pre-assigned time slot concept disappears in ATM switching systems, contention problems arise if 2 or more logical channels contend for the same time slot. This can be solved by temporarily **queuing** the ATM cells before sending them out. This queuing function is the second important aspect of ATM switching systems.

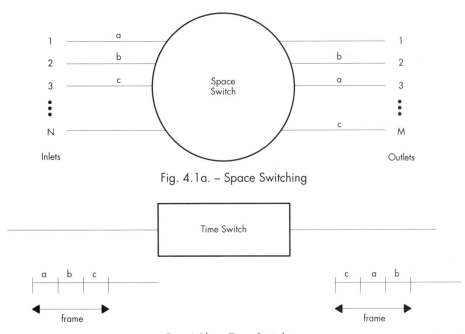

Fig. 4.1a. – Space Switching

Fig. 4.1b. – Time Switching

- Concentration/multiplexing
  Information from N inlets is multiplexed into M outlets, with N > M. In ATM, the distinction between multiplexing and concentration is rather vague. When using the word multiplexing, the emphasis is put on the statistical merging of different ATM virtual channels (cell streams) on a single ATM stream. When using the

word concentration, one wants to stress the reduction of number of inlets to a smaller number of outlets.

- Expansion/demultiplexing is the inverse operation of concentration/ multiplexing.

The basic principle of an ATM switch, seen from the outside, is shown in Fig. 4.2. There it is shown that incoming ATM cells are physically switched from an inlet I_i to an outlet O_j, and that at the same time their header value is translated from an incoming value α to an outgoing value β. On each incoming and outgoing link individually, the values of the header are unique, but identical headers can be found on different links (e.g. x on link I_1 and I_n).

   In the example we see in the translation tables that all cells which have a header equal to x on incoming link I_1 are switched to outlet O_1 and that their header is translated ("switched") to value k. All cells with an header x on link I_n are also switched to outlet O_1, but their header gets value n.

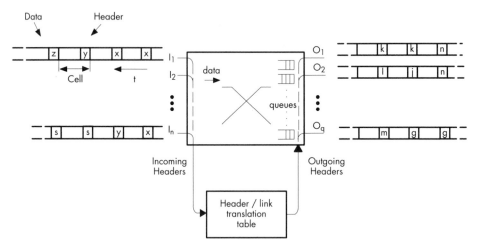

Translation table

Incoming link	Time slot	Outgoing link	Timeslot
I_1	x y z	O_1 O_q O_2	k m l
.			
.			
.			
I_n	x y s	O_1 O_2 O_q	n i g

Fig. 4.2. – ATM Switching Principle

It can thus be seen that the 2 basic functions to be performed by an ATM switch are "space switching" and "header switching". However, as can be seen in Fig. 4.2., it is possible that 2 cells of different inlets (e.g. from I_1 and I_n) arrive simultaneously at the ATM switch and are destined to the same outlet (O_1). Thus, they cannot both be put on the outlet at the same time. So, somewhere in the switch a buffer has to be provided to store the cell(s) which cannot be served. This is typical for an ATM switch, since it statistically multiplexes cells. Therefore, queues must be provided to ensure that ATM cells which are simultaneously destined to the same outlet can be stored and are not to be discarded.

In conclusion, we have demonstrated that an ATM switch performs the following 3 basic functions : routing (space switching), queuing and header translation. The way these functions are implemented and where in the switch these functions are located, will distinguish one switching solution from another.

Definitions

In the publications describing ATM switching architectures, different terminologies are used. To ensure a uniform terminology in this book, the following definitions will be used. They may sometimes be not in line with the one used in some publications.

Switching Fabric :
A switching fabric is composed of identical basic switching building blocks, interconnected in a specific topology. Thus, a switching fabric is defined when its topology is determined and when the basic switching building blocks are defined. Some switching fabrics have some special edge functions.

Basic Switching Building Block :
A basic switching building block is the generic building block to construct an ATM switching fabric. Another name used for basic switching building block is switching element. Identical switching elements will compose a switching fabric.

Switching System :
Any means to switch ATM cells, either by an ATM switching element, or an ATM switching fabric. Also often called an ATM switch.

In this Chapter, I will describe some typical switching systems described in the literature. As mentioned earlier, most of them have been developed either for prototyping or for products. I will not cover all switching fabrics and elements described in the literature or developed but discuss only a rather limited number. The switching systems were selected to cover as much as possible alternative solutions for ATM switching. So most of the switching systems not discussed here are slight modifications of the systems described, or combine features from different described solutions.

To identify these switches in this book, a name will be assigned to each switch. Some of these names have already been used in the literature by the authors, others are only used in the scope of this book. Some solutions have only a typical ATM switching element, others only a typical ATM switching fabric, others both.

The following ATM switching systems will be described under the following names :

- Knockout   : This ATM switching element was described by researchers from ATT in (Eng, 1987). Being extendible for larger systems, it could also be considered as a switching fabric. However, it is here classified as a switching element.

- Roxanne   : This ATM switch proposed by Alcatel researchers in (Henrion, 1990) has special features. It has a typical switching element and switching fabric network architecture.

- Coprin   : This switching element developed within CNET was the first ATM switching system described in the literature (Coudreuse, 1987). It is to be considered as an ATM switching element.

- Athena   : This switching fabric and related switching element were first described by Alcatel Bell researchers in 1987 (De Prycker, 1987).

- St. Louis : This switching fabric was described in (Turner, 1986), and was the first switching fabric in the literature directly applicable to ATM.

- Starlite   : This non-blocking switching fabric was developed by ATT researchers and described in (Huang, 1986).

- Moonshine : This alternative non-blocking switching fabric was described by Bellcore researchers in (Hui, 1987).

4.2. SWITCHING REQUIREMENTS

As already described in the Chapter on transfer modes, the broadband network must be capable of transporting all kinds of information, ranging from telecontrol over voice to high quality video. As we have seen, these services have different requirements in terms of bit rate (from a few kbit/s up to hundreds of Mbit/s), behavior in time (constant bit rate or variable bit rate), semantic transparency (cell loss rate, bit error rate) and time transparency (delay, delay jitter). These different service requirements have to be coped with by the broadband ATM switches.

4.2.1. Information rates

Since the information rates of the different services are very diverse, a large number of information rates must be switched in the future broadband switches. These rates range from a few kbit/s (e.g. for telecontrol), up to values around 150 Mbit/s (e.g. for HDTV : High Definition TeleVision). The maximum bit rate which future ATM switches must be able to switch lies around 150 Mbit/s. This does not mean that ATM switches have to operate internally at 150 Mbit/s. One can imagine that switching is realized over parallel wires, so that a lower speed can be used internally. Or, several 150 Mbit/s can be multiplexed on a single link, so that internally higher speeds than 150 Mbit/s are implemented (potentially Gbit/s).

4.2.2. Broadcast/multicast

In the classical STM and packet switches, only point-to-point connections are available, because information has to be switched from one logical inlet to another logical outlet. However, in the future broadband network an additional requirement arises. Indeed some services have a "copy" nature, and thus require of future ATM switches the capability to provide a multicast and broadcast functionality. Broadcast can be defined as the provision of the information from one source to all destinations, whereas multicast provides the information from one source to many destinations.

These functions are typically required for services such as electronic mail, video library access and TV distribution. Such a multicast/broadcast facility may be required from several trunk circuits to multiple subscriber lines, but also from subscriber lines to multiple subscriber lines. Indeed, one can imagine that a subscriber is sending an electronic mail item to the ATM network and expects the mail to be sent to 5 destinations simultaneously. Another example is a subscriber offering a video library service which is located at its own premises and connected to the network via its ATM subscriber line (local loop).

4.2.3. Performance

The performance of classical STM switches is mainly characterized by the throughput, the connection blocking probability, the bit error rate and the switching delay. However, in an ATM environment, 2 other parameters are important to be characterized, namely the probability that cells get lost or are inserted into other connections and the jitter on the delay.

In ATM switches, as in STM switches, the throughput and the bit error rate are mainly determined by the technology and dimensioning of the system. By using high speed technology, such as high speed CMOS, BICMOS or ECL, bit rates of hundreds of Mbit/s can easily be achieved, with an acceptable bit error rate. A large overall throughput of the switch can be achieved by a proper topology as will be described further in this Chapter.

Three of the above mentioned parameters need some special attention in the case of ATM switches. These are connection blocking, cell loss/cell insertion probability and switching delay.

(1) Connection blocking

ATM is defined as being connection oriented. This means that at connection set-up, a logical connection must be found between a logical inlet and outlet. Note that the fact the ATM is connection oriented does not imply that the ATM switch implementation is internally connection oriented.

The connection blocking is determined as the probability that not enough resources can be found between inlet and outlet in the switch to guarantee the quality of all existing connections and the new connection. We will see that some switch implementations do not have the notion of internal connections. This means that if enough resources (i.e. bandwidth and header values) are available on the inlet and the outlet of the switch, no connection blocking will occur internally. So, a new connection will always be accepted if enough resources are available on the external links, without an explicit check of the internal switch resources.

Other switch implementations have an internal connection blocking, because internally in the switch, resources have to be allocated for every new connection. The blocking probability of those switches is determined by the dimensioning of the switch, such as the number of internal connections and the load on those connections.

(2) Cell loss/cell insertion probability

In ATM switches, it is possible that temporarily too many cells are destined for the same link (this link can be internal in the switch, or external). The consequence is that more cells than a queue in the switch can store will simultaneously compete for this queue. So cells will be lost. The probability of losing a cell must be kept within limits to ensure a high semantic transparency. Typical values for cell loss probability mentioned for ATM switches range between 10^{-8} and 10^{-11}.

However, some switching architectures are designed such that they will not suffer from cells competing for the same resource internally (i.e. queue). So, these architectures will not lose ATM cells internally, but only at their inlets and/or outlets. These switches are sometimes called internally non-blocking in the literature.

Since the cell loss is something special to ATM, the switching fabrics in this Chapter will be classified according to the possible internal cell loss.

In section 4.4.1. I will describe ATM switching fabrics with internal cell loss; in section 4.4.2. ATM switching fabrics without internal cell loss.

It is also possible that ATM cells are internally misrouted in the switch, so that they arrive erroneously on another logical connection. The probability of this cell insertion must be kept within limits, and values of 1000 times or more better than the cell loss rate are typically mentioned in the literature.

(3) Switching delay

The time to switch an ATM cell through the switch is also an important factor, as described in Chapter 2 in the section on time transparency. Typical values mentioned for the delay of ATM switches range between 10 and 1000 µs, with a jitter of a few 100 µs or less. Note that this jitter value is in most cases determined as the probability that the delay of the switch will exceed a certain value. This is called a quantile and typically a value comparable to the acceptable cell loss rate is taken. For instance a jitter of 100 µs at a 10^{-10} quantile means that the probability that the delay in the switch is larger than 100 µs is smaller than 10^{-10}.

4.3. BASIC SWITCHING BUILDING BLOCKS

As defined in section 4.1., an ATM switching fabric is composed of basic ATM switching building blocks, also called switching elements. The interconnection and interworking between those switching elements to compose an ATM switching fabric will be discussed in the next section (4.4.) of this Chapter. Let us now focus on ATM switching elements, which are typically rather small. Values of 2 inlets and 2 outlets at 150 Mbit/s up to 16 inlets and 16 outlets at 2.4 Gbit/s have been reported in the literature. However, these maximum values are not limitations. The size (number of inlets/outlets) and speed depend on the technology used (CMOS, ECL, ...) and the level of integration which one wants to achieve. Since the technology used is not under discussion in this book, I will not expand further on this item, but the impact of the internal architecture on the achievable speed and size will be explained in section 4.3.3.

This section basically discusses the switching functions of such a switching element. These are mainly queuing problems, because actually an ATM switching element acts as a statistical multiplexer. If 2 ATM cells arrive at 2 inlets of the switching element for the same output during the duration of one cell, one of them has to be queued for a later cell time. Depending on the particular architecture of the switching element and on the required internal speed, the possibility exists to queue this cell at the inlet, at the outlet or internally in the switching element. However, it has to be noted, as will be shown in the next section, that some switch architectures are constructed by switching elements which have no internal buffering.

These internal buffers can only be avoided if the switch fabric is fully non-blocking (per cell), i.e. contentionless. This contention-free characteristic guarantees that, if all incoming cells of the switch architecture are destined to a different outlet, no internal contention will arise. However, this point will be discussed later in this Chapter.

It is also important to notice that in this section I will not discuss functions like routing and addressing, because the ATM switching function in a basic switching building block is not influenced by the way routing and addressing are implemented in a switching element. The routing and addressing functions will be discussed in detail in section 4.4. on switching fabrics where the routing function is of prime importance.

4.3.1. Queuing disciplines

As outlined above, the basic function of a switching element is the buffering of cells destined to the same outlet. In a switching element, mainly 3 different buffering strategies are possible. These are determined by the physical location of the buffers : at the inputs, at the outputs, or central in the switching element.

(1) Input queuing

In this solution the approach is taken to solve the possible contention problem at the input (Fig. 4.3a.). Each inlet disposes of a dedicated buffer which allows it to store the incoming cells until the arbitration logic determines that the buffer (queue) may be served. The switching transfer medium will then transfer the ATM cells from the input queues to the outlet without an internal contention. The arbitration logic which decides which inlet to serve, can range from very simple like round-robin, up to quite complex, e.g. taking into account the input buffer filling levels.

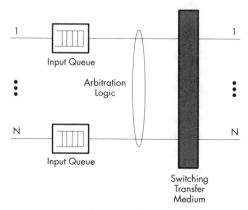

Fig. 4.3a. – Switching Element with Input Queues

Input queuing switching elements suffer from so-called Head of the Line (HOL) blocking. Indeed, suppose that the cell of inlet i is selected to be transferred to outlet p. If inlet j has also a cell destined for outlet p, this cell will be stopped, together with all following cells. Suppose that the second cell in the queue of inlet j is destined to an outlet q for which there is currently no cell waiting in the other queues. This cell cannot be served yet, since the cell in front of it in the queue is blocking the transfer.

The switching transfer medium in the switching element with input queues will, during one cell time, transfer the p (p ≤ N) selected cells from the p inlets to the p selected outlets.

(2) Output queuing

In the output queuing solution (Fig. 4.3b.), the approach is taken that cells of different inlets destined to the same outlet can be transferred (switched) during one cell time. However, only a single cell may be served by an outlet, thus causing possible output contention. The possible output contention is solved by queues which are located at each outlet of the switching element.

Each outlet disposes of a dedicated buffer which allows it to store multiple cells which may arrive during one cell time. In principle, cells can arrive simultaneously at all inlets destined to a single outlet. To ensure that no cell is lost in the switching transfer medium before it arrives at the output queue, the cell transfer must be performed at N times the speed of the inlets. The system must be able to write N cells in the queues during one cell time.

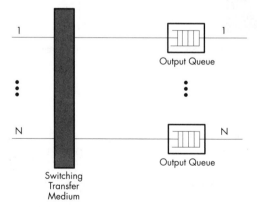

Fig. 4.3b. – Switching Element with Output Queues

In the switching transfer medium, no arbitration logic is required since all cells can go to their respective output queue. The control of the output queues is based on a simple FIFO discipline to ensure that cells will remain in the correct sequence.

(3) Central queuing

In the central queuing approach (Fig. 4.3c.), the queuing buffers are not dedicated to a single inlet or outlet, but shared between all inlets and outlets. In this case each incoming cell will directly be stored in the central queue. Every outlet will select the cells which are destined for him from the central memory in a FIFO discipline.

Internally, the provisions must be made to ensure that the outlets know which cells are destined for them. The read and write discipline of the central queue is not a simple FIFO discipline, since cells for different destinations are all merged in this single queue. This means that the central memory may be addressed in a random way. The logical queues must however apply the first-in-first-out discipline. Since cells may be written and read at random memory locations, a rather complex memory management system has to be provided.

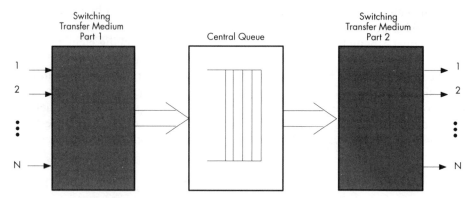

Fig. 4.3c. – Switching Element with Central Queuing

4.3.2. Performance

The 3 queuing solutions described have a different performance in terms of cell loss, delay and required cell buffers for a certain traffic pattern and load at the inlets of the switching element.

It can intuitively be explained that the mean queue length, and hence the mean waiting time will be greater for input queuing switching elements, than for the output queuing or the central queuing solution for the same external load values.

Indeed, with input queuing it is possible that cells are blocked at the input, waiting for another cell in the same queue to be served, even when those cells are destined for different outlets due to Head of the Line (HOL) blocking.

This intuition can easily be explained by the following example. In a post office, 2 officers are serving the waiting clients. One officer is selling postage stamps, the other officer is serving airmail. We suppose that there is only one queue with pure FIFO discipline (Fig. 4.4a.). Then the person who has airmail to send will wait after the one who is waiting to be served by the stamp-selling officer, even when the airmail officer is sitting idle. This example represents an input queuing solution.

In Fig. 4.4b., the selection of one or the other officer is performed in advance, by providing 2 queues. When entering the post office, each person can decide (select, switch) to take the appropriate queue. We see also, that both officers (servers) will have to work harder, so that fewer people will be waiting in the queue. The waiting time of the clients will thus be smaller than in the previous example. This example represents the output queuing principle.

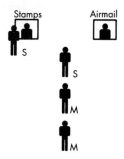

Fig. 4.4a. – Input Queuing in a Post Office

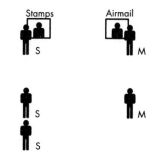

Fig. 4.4b. – Output Queuing in a Post Office

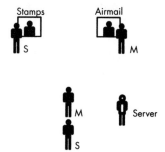

Fig. 4.4c. – Central Queuing in a Post Office

If we consider the number of places to be provided in the queues also an important parameter, then we see that in the output queuing solution more places have to be provided in total, since in principle all people entering the post office may want to buy stamps or send air mail. So, each queue (airmail or stamp queue) has to be dimensioned for the worst case.

This number of places can be reduced by providing one single queue, but with an intelligent server, who is asking the people in the queue what they were waiting for (Fig. 4.4c.). This server will decide that people at the back of the queue may be served before those of the head of the queue, because their respective officer is free. This principle can be called central queuing. The number of locations in the central queuing solution is thus smaller than that of the output queuing.

These intuitive explanations can be backed up by mathematical models and by computer simulations.

4.3.2.1.   *Analytical models*

To obtain analytic formulae which are still not too complicated and result in a good approximation of reality, we assume a simplified model for cell arrivals on the input links (Karol, 1986). The assumption is that the cell arrival process at each inlet is based on independent and identical Bernoulli processes.

This means that in any given time slot, the probability that a cell will arrive on a particular inlet is p $(0 \leq p \leq 1)$. On the average each inlet is utilized at a level p. We also assume that the switching element to be modelled has N inlets and N outlets. Each cell has equal probability 1/N of being addressed to any given output, so the probability of a cell arriving at one inlet for a given outlet is p/N.

(1)   Output queuing

The probability (x_i) that i cells are arriving in a certain output queue during one cell time can be calculated as follows :

$$x_i = Probability\ [i\ cells\ arrived\ in\ a\ certain\ queue]$$

$$= C_N^i \left(\frac{p}{N}\right)^i \left(1 - \frac{p}{N}\right)^{N-i} \tag{4.1.}$$

$$for\ i = 0, 1 .. N$$

The probability generating function $X(z)$ of this random variable x_i is

$$X(z) = \sum_{i=0}^{N} z^i \, x_i = \sum_{i=0}^{N} z^i \, C_N^i \left(\frac{p}{N}\right)^i \left(1 - \frac{p}{N}\right)^{N-i}$$

$$= \left(1 - \frac{p}{N} + z \cdot \frac{p}{N}\right)^N \tag{4.2.}$$

This probability generating function (PGF) can be used to obtain the PGF of the number of cells in the queue $Q(z)$ as was indicated by Kleinrock (Kleinrock, 1975) in

$$Q(z) = \frac{(1-p) \cdot (1-z)}{X(z) - z} \tag{4.3.}$$

The average queue size $\overline{Q}$ can be calculated by differentiating (4.3.) with respect to z and taking the limit for z reaching 1. This average queue size $\overline{Q}$ is then

$$\overline{Q} = \frac{(N-1)}{N} \cdot \frac{p^2}{2 \cdot (1-p)} \tag{4.4.}$$

The average queue size $(\overline{Q_p})$ of the well known M/D/1 queuing system with a Poisson arrival process is known from the basic queuing theory (Kleinrock, 1975) and given by

$$\overline{Q_p} = \frac{p^2}{2 \cdot (1-p)} \tag{4.5.}$$

This allows us to express the average queue size (Q) of the modelled system as a function of that of a Poissonian

$$\overline{Q} = \frac{N-1}{N} \cdot \overline{Q_p} \tag{4.6.}$$

So the average queue size converges to that of a M/D/1 queuing system for N approaching ∞. This statement is not only valid for the average queue size but also for the probability distribution function of the queue size. Indeed if N approaches ∞ then (4.1.) and (4.2.) become

$$\lim_{N \to \infty} x_i = \frac{p^i \, e^{-p}}{i} \tag{4.7.}$$

and

$$\lim_{N\to\infty} X(z) = e^{-p(1-z)}$$

(4.8.)

These formulae show that in the limit the behavior of x_i is exactly represented by that of a Poisson process. By using (4.8.) in (4.3.), we obtain

$$\lim_{N\to\infty} Q(z) = \frac{(1-p) \cdot (1-z)}{e^{-p(1-z)} - z}$$

(4.9.)

which equals the PGF of an M/D/1 queue in a steady state condition. Using Little's theorem we can easily calculate the average waiting time of the system as

$$\overline{W} = \overline{Q} \cdot \frac{1}{p}$$

$$= \frac{(N-1)}{N} \cdot \frac{p}{2 \cdot (1-p)}$$

$$= \frac{(N-1)}{N} \cdot \overline{W}_p$$

(4.10.)

We assume that $\overline{W}_p$ represents the average waiting time of an M/D/1 system.

This mean waiting time ($\overline{W}$) for different values of N is shown in function of the load p in Fig. 4.5. We can see that for low values of the load, the average queue size remains very small (up to a few cells), but above a load of 0.8, the average waiting time increases exponentially. A load of 0.8 (later in this book also referred to as 80 %) means that 80 % of the incoming cells are containing useful data; 20 % of the incoming cells are empty. These empty cells will be discarded and not written in the queue. So, a switching element based on the output queuing principle has a very well controlled behavior up to loads of 80 to 85 %. We also see that the impact of N on the average waiting time is rather limited.

(2) Input queuing

To model the behavior of a switching element with input queues, we take the same assumptions for the arrival process as for the output queuing principle (i.e. a Bernoulli process). The arriving cells are stored in an input queue which acts as a FIFO. The service principle of the different queues is quite simple. If only a single cell of the possible N first cells of the N input queues is destined for one outlet it will obviously be selected. If j cells are addressed to a particular outlet, the selection of the cell is performed at random, each cell to be selected with a probability of 1/j. The other cells must wait for the following selection process in the next cell time.

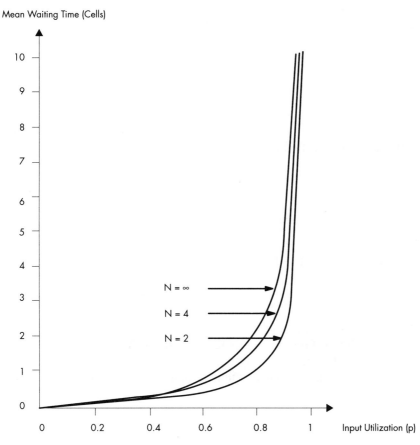

Fig. 4.5. – Mean Waiting Time for Output Queues

To analyze the behavior of the input queues, we assume that all input queues are saturated, i.e. in every input queue always cells are waiting.

Suppose that B_n^i cells are destined to outlet i, but blocked at the head of the line (HOL) during cell time n since they were not selected by the random selection process. During cell time n, a number of cells will be served and transported to their respective outlet, making room for a number of new i head of the line cells. We suppose that A_n^i new cells appear at the head of the line for output i during cell time n. Since only one cell can be served by outlet i during a cell time, it follows that at every new cell time the number of blocked cells at the HOL equals the number of blocked cells during the previous cell time B_{n-1}^i minus 1 (served) plus the new arriving cells A_n^i, i.e.

$$B_n^i \ = \ \max\left(B_{n-1}^i \ - \ 1 \ + \ A_n^i, \ 0\right) \qquad (4.11.)$$

In every input queue, new cells are progressing to the head of the line; their total for all queues at cell time n equals

$$L_n = \sum_{i=1}^{N} A_n^i \qquad (4.12.)$$

This value also represents the total number of cells to be served by the switch during cell time n + 1. If no blocking occurs, N cells will be switched. However, B_{n-1}^i cells were blocked, so L_n can also be written as

$$L_n = N - \sum_{i=1}^{N} B_{n-1}^i \qquad (4.13.)$$

The average of L_n in steady state situation denoted as $\overline{L}$ equals N . p, if p represents the switch throughput per output link, i.e.

$$\overline{L} = N . p \qquad (4.14.)$$

If N → ∞, the number of cells moving to the head of the line in steady state destined for i is Poisson distributed, with rate p. This means that the behavior for N → ∞ of the mean steady state value of B^i is like that of an M/D/1 system explained in the output queuing principle. The results of (4.5.) are thus applicable, or

$$\overline{B}^i = \frac{p^2}{2 . (1 - p)} \qquad (4.15.)$$

If we average (4.13.) then we get, taking (4.14.) into account

$$\overline{L} = N - \sum_{i=1}^{N} \overline{B}^i$$

or

$$\sum_{i=1}^{N} \overline{B}^i = N . (1-p) \qquad (4.16.)$$

Or, for N approaching infinity we get

$$\overline{B}^i = 1-p \qquad (4.17.)$$

If we combine (4.15.) and (4.17.) we see that a saturated switch with $N \to \infty$ reaches a load p equal to

$$p_{max} = 2 - \sqrt{2} = 0.586 \qquad (4.18.)$$

So, switching elements based on the input queuing principle are very limited in performance. The maximal obtainable load is 58.6 %. This low maximal load is showing the poor performance behavior of input queuing systems compared to output queuing systems, where even for loads around 80 %, the average queue size remains very limited.

(3) Central queuing

The central queuing solution behaves exactly as the output queuing solution. This means that the mean waiting time is exactly that of an output queuing system. However, since multiple queues are combined in a single physical memory, the major advantage of the central queuing system is reflected in the number of cells to be stored in the central memory (central queue). A more complicated control logic is required to ensure that the single central memory performs the FIFO discipline to all outlets. The memory size can be calculated as a convolution of N individual output queues.

Indeed, since the buffer memory will be shared, a more effective use of the memory can be made. We can make an estimation of this gain. Therefore we will calculate the cell loss probability by truncating the tail of the probability distribution which is obtained with infinite ouput buffers.

The number of cells Y in the central queue equals the sum of cells X in each output queue. So the probability distribution of the number of cells in the shared buffer is the convolution of the queue distribution of each output port.

We assume that the switch has N outlets, and that $M_x(v)$ is the moment generating function of X. If the process is described by a M/D/1 model then

$$M_x(v) = \frac{(1 - p) \cdot (1 - e^v)}{1 - e^v \cdot e^{(1 - e^v)p}} \qquad (4.19.)$$

or

$$m_x(v) = \log M_x(v)$$

$$= \log(1 - p) + \log(1 - e^v) - \log(1 - e^v \cdot e^{(1 - e^v)p}) \qquad (4.20.)$$

This formula can be used to calculate the Chernoff bound for the shared memory solution as

$$P[Y \geq Nm_x(v)] \leq e^{[N(m_x(v) - v \cdot m_x(v))]} \qquad (4.21.)$$

Using this bound we can calculate the buffer size for a certain cell loss ratio. The relation between the buffer size and cell loss ratio is shown in Fig. 4.6. There it is shown that the central queuing solution can guarantee the same cell loss ratio for a smaller number of cell buffers in the queue per output link. For a cell loss rate of 10^{-8}, the queue size of an output queuing system is around 40 cells; whereas for a central queuing system, only fewer than 10 cells per output link are required.

This figure shows a large gain in memory size for the central queuing solution. This gain depends on the size N of the switch. Indeed, the larger N, the larger the statistical multiplexing of the memory is. The reduction obtained by the central queuing solution compared to the output queuing solution is shown in Fig. 4.7.

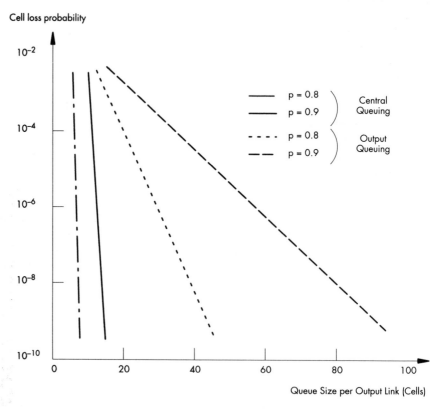

Fig. 4.6. – Cell Loss Probability for Central and Output Queuing (M/D/1 Model)

In this diagram, this relation is drawn in function of the number of outlets N for a load of 0.8 and a cell loss probability of 10^{-9}. There it is shown that the gain factor is about 5 for N = 16, and increases up to 7 for N = 32. For smaller N, the gain in memory reduction becomes less important.

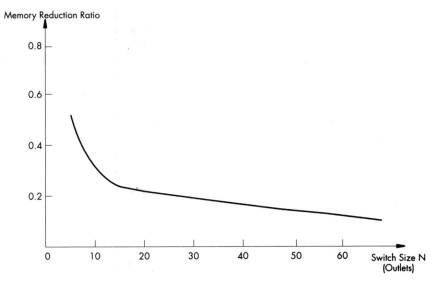

Fig. 4.7. – Memory Reduction by Central Queuing for Cell Loss Probability 10^{-9}
and p = 0.8

4.3.2.2. *Computer simulation*

The analytical models described above are only valid within the assumptions presumed for the models, such as M/D/1 for output queuing and central queuing and $N \rightarrow \infty$ for input queuing. They also only give a limited number of information, such as for instance average values of queue size and delay. More general analytical models exist, and are reported in specialized journals, conferences and books (Bruneel, 1993), but are out of the scope of this book. These models are applicable under more general conditions, and give more information, such as an exact pdf description.

However, these models are often quite cumbersome to develop. Therefore sometimes the more straightforward approach is taken to simulate via computer programs the statistical behavior of queuing systems. These simulations not only give quick results, but allow the easy modification and generalization of assumptions, taken in the analytical models. They are also very useful to validate the results of the analytical queuing models.

On the other hand these simulations have the drawback that they need a large amount of computing power, especially when very low probability values have to be obtained. Indeed, if we want to know that a certain event occurred with a probability of 10^{-8}, we need at least 10^{10} measurement points to have a certain degree of confidence in the simulation results. This results sometimes in extremely large computing power requirements. However, often extrapolations are possible if some properties of the queuing behavior are known, thereby drastically reducing the computer simulation time.

In Fig. 4.8. simulation results are shown for the 3 queuing disciplines, assuming that the cells arrive with a Poisson process. An important parameter is the quantile, which indicates the required queue size for a certain cell loss rate. This is shown in Fig. 4.8. for the 3 queuing disciplines, and a cell loss rate of 10^{-3}. We see the confirmation that the central queuing reduces the required queue size compared to output queuing and that the input queuing discipline has the worst performance as described in the previous section.

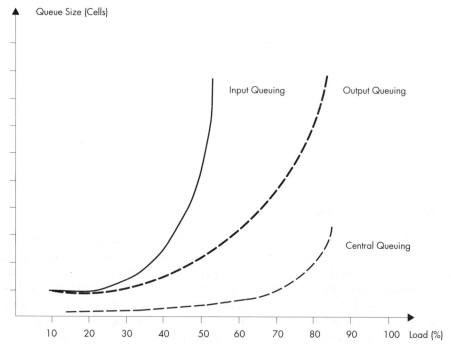

Fig. 4.8. – Queue Size in Function of the Load (Cell Loss Rate = 10^{-3})

4.3.3. Implementation parameters of basic ATM switching building blocks

The physical realization requirements of the 3 alternative queuing systems are very different, not only because of the differences in the queue size as described in the previous section, but also due to speed requirements and additional control logic for the queue memory. Actually, we can say that 3 parameters are influencing the complexity of the different queuing systems :

- *Queue size :* this size depends on the performance requirements of the system (cell loss ratio, load, delay) and the selected queuing principle. It is reflected in the number of cell buffers to be supported by the switching element.

- *Memory speed :* the access time of the queuing memory of the switching element depends on the queuing principle, but also on the size (N) and the speed of the incoming and outgoing links of the switching element.

- *Memory control :* in order to control the queues of a switching element, additional control logic is required. The complexity of this control logic depends on the queuing principle. For instance, the FIFO principle used in input and output queuing requires only simple control logic, whereas the central queuing principle requires a dynamic memory management function.

These 3 different parameters make the choice of one of the 3 queuing systems very much dependent on the available chip technology (CMOS, ECL, ...) and feature size (i.e. line width on the chip), as well as on the speed at which the system has to operate (e.g. 45, 150, 600 Mbit/s) and on the size N of the basic switching building block (2 x 2 up to 32 x 32). To compare the 3 alternatives, we assume that N describes the number of inlets/outlets and F the link speed of each of the inlets/outlets of the basic building block and W the width of memory in bits, since it can be assumed that the queue memory will be accessed in parallel (e.g. byte, word or double word format).

To have some feeling on speed and complexity we will use as an example N = 16, F = 150 Mbit/s and W = 16 for a 16 bit wide memory implementation.

Output queuing

The output queue can receive a cell from all N inputs simultaneously (N write operations), whereas one cell can be sent to the output (1 read operation). All these (N + 1) operations have to be performed during one cell time.

So the memory access time of the output queue system equals W/(N+1).F. In cases where dual ported memory is used (this means that simultaneous read and write operations are possible), only N write operations must be performed during one cell time. The memory access time is then W/N.F. This dual ported memory option only results in a moderate gain for the memory access time. On the other hand, dual ported memory requires typically 1.5 times the chip surface of that of single ported memory. So, dual ported memory is not directly recommended for output queuing systems.

As can be seen in Table 4.1., the access time of the memory in the example is rather small (6.3 nanoseconds, ns), requiring memory on chip. The gain obtained by dual port memory in access time is not worthwile seen the increased complexity.

The control logic of the output queue is quite simple. This logic must only perform a pure FIFO operation and thus requires a single read and write pointer to control the address selection of the queue memory during read and write operations.

	Input queuing	Output queuing	Central queuing
Single ported memory	W/2.F	W/(N+1).F	W/2.N.F
Example (ns)	53.3	6.3	3.8
Dual ported memory	W/F	W/N.F	W/N.F
Example (ns)	106.6	6.7	6.7

Assumption of the example :

Cell size   =   53 bytes
W   =   16 bit
F   =   150 Mbit/s
N   =   16

Table 4.1. – Memory Access Time for the 3 Queuing Disciplines

All inlets and output queues are connected via a transfer medium (Fig. 4.3b.). The most straightforward implementation of connecting all inlets to all output queues is by a TDM bus (Time Division Multiplexing). If no cells must be lost on this TDM bus, it must operate at a speed of N . F to ensure that all N cells are transferred during one cell time. Such high speed requirements, plus the fact that a bus is not ideal for high speeds due to reflections at all bus terminations, make the TDM bus not the ideal choice for the transfer medium of an output queuing system, especially if the switching element has to be implemented by several chips. However, if the bus length can be kept very small (e.g. on chip) these reflection problems disappear, making the TDM bus an ideal solution as a transfer medium due to its low complexity (see section 4.3.5. on the Roxanne switching element).

However, implementations other than the TDM bus are also possible which reduce the physical speed of the transfer medium, but which require somewhat more control logic. They can either be fully non-blocking, i.e. no cells are lost on the transfer medium (see section 4.3.7. on the Athena switching element), or blocking, i.e. cells may be lost but only at a low probability (see section 4.3.4. on the Knockout switching element).

Since all inlets can reach all output queues, broadcast or multicast functionality can easily be supported in the output queuing solution. Indeed, for instance in the TDM bus solution, a single cell put on the TDM bus per inlet can easily be addressed to each individual output queue separately, or to a multiple number of queues. Thus, in principle N . N cells can be put on the N output queues during one cell time if all N cells have to be broadcast to all output queues.

Input queuing

In the input queuing solution, the memory can only be accessed simultaneously by one inlet and one outlet. The memory access time is thus only $W/2.F$ in case of single ported memory or W/F for dual ported memory.

We see in Table 4.1., that the memory access time does not represent a major problem since access times of 50 up to 100 ns are achievable with commercial memory chips. The gain with dual ported memory in this example may be considered as an advantage.

The control logic of the input queue is also as simple as that of the output queue; again a single read and write pointer are required per queue to implement the FIFO discipline.

The transfer medium (Fig. 4.3a.) may operate at a speed lower than $N . F$, since it can rely on the input queues to solve a possible contention situation by buffering the "overflow" cells in those input queues.

But since no queues are provided at the output, the inherent broadcast/multicast capabilities of the transfer medium can only be used if additional control logic is added to avoid possible contention at the outlets.

Central queuing

In case a central memory is used, the access time equals $W/2 . N . F$, since each inlet and outlet can access the memory simultaneously. For dual ported memory the access time is reduced to $W/N.F$.

Again small memory access times are required for the example case, as can be seen in Table 4.1. To achieve such high speeds, memory has to be combined with the control of the queue on a single chip. The advantage of dual ported memory in this case with respect to memory access time has to be evaluated clearly against its larger chip surface requirement.

The transfer media (Fig. 4.3c.) at the input and output of the central memory both operate at $N . F$, if a non-blocking property is required, i.e. if the transfer medium does not want to be the responsible for the cell loss. If cell loss is acceptable at the transfer medium, a lower speed than $N . F$ is allowed.

The control of the central memory is more complicated, since now all cells will be stored and "mixed" in this central memory. Indeed, cells destined for an outlet will not be stored contiguous with other cells destined for the same outlet. So, dynamic memory allocation techniques as developed for operating systems of computers, can be very useful. However, since these mechanisms must be performed in real time at very high speeds, the selection of one of these memory allocation techniques is determined by the hardware implementability. Two memory control mechanisms will be explained in detail in this book : one which uses time and space references (Coprin, see section 4.3.6.), and another which uses linked lists (Roxanne, see section 4.3.5.).

4.3.4. Knockout switching element

The Knockout switching element was first introduced in 1987 by Yeh and colleagues from ATT Bell Laboratories (Yeh, 1987). As we will see in the following description, the Knockout switch can grow to a large size, composed of smaller entities. The switching principle is identical for small and large values of the number of inlets and outlets. So, when the system is described for a small size, it is also known for a large size. It is therefore discussed under the section of ATM switching elements.

It is in principle based on the output queuing solution. However, some of the characteristics of the central queuing are also valid, as will be explained. As shown in Table 4.1., the access time to the output queuing memory has to be very small. In order to decrease this operating speed (to reduce the complexity), the Knockout "transfer medium", uses a concentration stage, thereby introducing a certain cell loss probability. So, the Knockout switch not only requires a dimensioning of the queues, but also of the concentration factor of this transfer medium. Let us look in detail to the switch itself as shown in Fig. 4.9.

The Knockout switch has N inlets and outlets, each operating at an equal speed. Fixed length cells arrive on each inlet in a regular time frame (as ATM cells).

The transfer medium is composed of N broadcast buses, one for each inlet, whereas each outlet has access to cells arriving on all inputs, via a bus interface connected to each individual broadcast bus. In Fig. 4.9. it is shown that each of the N inlets puts its cells on a separate broadcast bus, on which each outlet gets access via a bus interface with N inputs. This means that the transfer medium is non-blocking and that at the input of this bus interface no cells are lost.

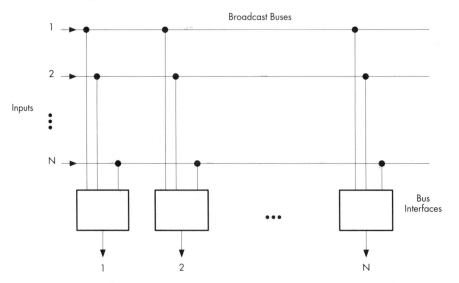

Fig. 4.9. – Knockout Switching Element

Cells will contend for a single outlet in this bus interface, which is very typical for the Knockout switch.

The bus structure has the major advantage that each bus is driven by only one inlet, allowing a simple implementation and high transmission rate compared with a bus which is shared by multiple inlets. Indeed, if the bus has to be shared between inlets, good timing has to be agreed between all involved inputs. However, care has to be taken to signal reflections if the bus interface speed becomes too high.

At one bus interface, several cells may arrive simultaneously all destined to a single outlet. In the worst case, N cells are destined to a single outlet. Thus, the bus interface requires cell buffers somewhere. If zero cell loss has to be guaranteed in the transfer phase to the cell buffer, the memory must operate (write) at N times the speed of each inlet. The Knockout switch has reduced this operating speed, by an intelligent bus interface, which acts as a concentrator, with a non-zero cell loss probability.

This bus interface, associated with each output, is shown in Fig. 4.10. At the top of the diagram, N cell filters are shown each connected to one of the N broadcast buses. These cell filters examine the address of each incoming cell. If destined to that specific outlet, the cell is passed to the concentrator, otherwise the cell is discarded.

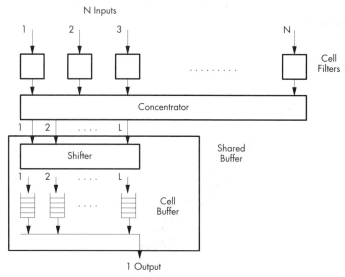

Fig. 4.10. – Knockout Bus Interface

The next part of the bus interface is the concentrator from N inputs to L (intermediate) outputs ($L \leq N$). If k cells arrive simultaneously for the same outlet, then after the concentrator, these k cells will arrive on output 1 to k of the concentrator, if $k \leq L$. If $k > L$, then all L outputs of the concentrator will have cells, and k–L cells will be lost in the concentrator.

The probability of losing cells in the concentrator must not be larger than the probability of losing cells elsewhere in the Knockout switch. This cell loss can easily be calculated as follows. If we assume that all cells arriving at an inlet are independent, with an equal load p, and equally likely destined to each outlet. Then the probability P_k that k cells arrive simultaneously at the concentrator is binomially distributed

$$P_k = C_N^k \left(\frac{p}{N}\right)^k \cdot \left(1 - \frac{p}{N}\right)^{N-k} \quad k = 0, 1, \dots N \quad (4.22.)$$

If only L cells may pass through the concentrator, then the probability of losing cells is

$$P[\ cell\ loss\ ] = \frac{1}{p} \sum_{k=L+1}^{N} (k - L)\ C_N^k \left(\frac{p}{N}\right)^k \left(1 - \frac{p}{N}\right)^{N-k} \quad (4.23.)$$

This formula allows us to calculate the cell loss probability in function of L for different values of N and p = 0.9 (Fig. 4.11a.) and for different values of p and $N \to \infty$ (Fig. 4.11b.). It can be seen that L is not very sensitive to both the load p and the number of inlets N, but is mainly influenced by the required cell loss probability. Hence, if L is selected to be 12, a cell loss probability of 10^{-10} can be achieved for any load and any value of N.

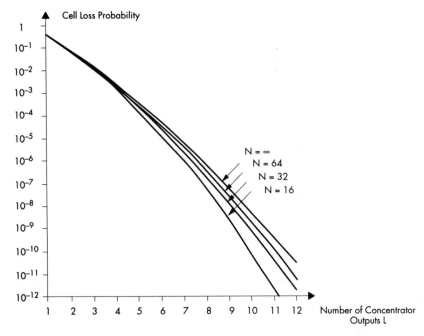

Fig. 4.11a. – Probability of Cell Loss Versus L, for 90 % Load

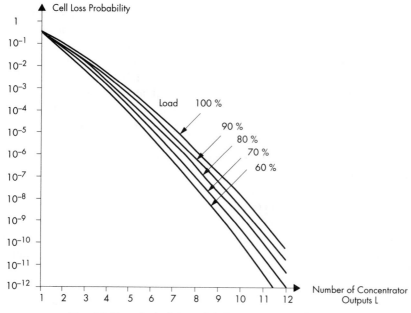

Fig. 4.11b. – Probability of Cell Loss Versus L, for N = ∞

However, we must be very careful with these diagrams, since they only give us the performance of the concentration stage of the Knockout switch. This cell loss probability has then to be combined with the values of the output queuing principle for the queues.

The concentrator itself can be built of very simple building blocks, as shown in Fig. 4.12. These building blocks are basically as switch in which 2 inputs contend for a winner output. If only one ATM cell is present at an inlet then it will logically be selected as the winner; if 2 cells are present then the left cell will be selected as the winner.

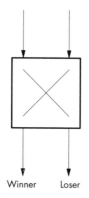

Fig. 4.12. – 2 x 2 Contention Switch

To construct a larger concentrator out of these 2 x 2 contention switches, a "tournament" can be organized. The organization is such that the winners are automatically selected for the next round of the tournament.

Fig. 4.13. shows the architecture of an 8-input, 4-output concentrator composed of these simple 2 x 2 contention switch elements. In addition, single-input/single-output 1-bit delay elements (indicated by "D") are added. At the inputs to the concentrator, the N (8) outputs from the cell filters enter the first stage of N/2 (4) parallel contention switches. The N/2 (4) winners from the first round advance to the second round where they compete with each other using N/4 (2) contention switches. The winners in the second round advance to the third round and this continues until only 2 compete for the championship. Finally, this winner will arrive at the left output of the concentrator. In the example, only 3 rounds (7 games) are necessary to point out the winner of the tournament. This tournament is shown in the left part (left block) of Fig. 4.13.

Instead of selecting L "winners" in one tournament, all losers will again compete in a second tournament. This is required to guarantee a fair access amongst all inputs, however complete faimess is not realized.

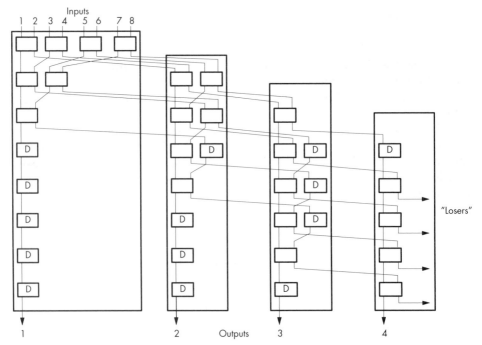

Fig. 4.13. – 8-Input/4-Output Concentrator

This knockout game is thus a tournament with only a single tree-structured competition leading to a single winner. As soon as players lose one match they will be knocked out of the tournament. In a double knockout tournament, the N-1 losers from the first tournament (Section) compete in a second Section, generating the second in rank (silver medal). Applied to the example concentrator, a second output is generated together with $N - 2$ losers. As Fig. 4.13. illustrates, the losers from the first section can begin competing in the second section before the competition is finished in the first.

Whenever there are an odd number of players in a round, one player must wait and compete in a later round. In the concentrator, a simple delay element serves this function of delaying a player. In order to ensure that all cells leave the concentrator at the same time slot, some additional delay elements are added.

For a concentrator with N inputs and L outputs, there are L sections of competition, one for each output. A cell entering the concentrator is given L opportunities to exit successfully through a concentrator output. A cell losing L times is knocked out of the competition and is discarded by the concentrator. However, in all cases, cells are only lost if more than L arrive in a single cell time. As we have seen in Fig. 4.11., for $L \geq 12$, this event has a very low probability.

The next part of the bus interface is the cell buffer responsible for storing the cells which successfully passed the concentrator, but which cannot be served simultaneously by the single outlet as shown in Fig. 4.10.

Since the buffers are located at the output of each bus interface, the option taken in the Knockout switch for the cell buffer is the output queuing principle. As we have seen in the output queuing solution, the number of memory accesses during one cell time equals $N + 1$ for a single ported memory.

In the Knockout switch this number is reduced to $L + 1$, since the concentrator has reduced the number of inputs from N to L. The implementation of this output queue is realized by L separate queues (FIFOs) which need only 2 (i.e. one for reading and one for writing) memory accesses per cell time instead of $L + 1$. However, in order to distribute the load over all queues and to obtain the same cell loss performance as an output queue, the L separate queues must be shared, and operate virtually as one single queue.

To achieve this, a shifter stage is provided which guarantees that all L buffers are equally loaded and optimally used, but also that the cell sequence is guaranteed. This shifter is required since all P "winning" cells will arrive at the left queues (if $P < L$).

This shifter provides a circular shift of the L inputs to the L outputs so that the L buffers are filled in a cyclic way. This operation is shown in Fig. 4.14. In the example, at the first cell time, 5 filled cells arrive at the first 5 inlets of the shifter. During this cell time the 5 cells are directly shifted through to the first 5 outlets. During the next cell time, 4 filled cells arrive, again at the first 4 inlets of the shifter. This is because the concentrator always concentrates to its first outputs. During this cell time, the first cell will be shifted to outlet 6, the second to outlet 7, etc. During the next cell time, the first cell will be shifted to the second buffer. So, we see that all cell buffers will be filled uniformly. Also, cell sequence can be guaranteed by this shifter, by a proper implementation (e.g. by cyclically reading out the buffers).

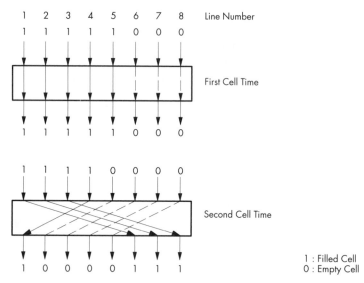

Fig. 4.14. – Shifter Function for 8 Lines

More formally, we can describe the shifter as follows. If S_i describes the number of positions the shifter has to shift to the right during cell time i, then S_{i+1} equals

$$S_{i+1} = (S_i + k_i) \bmod L \qquad (4.24.)$$

if k_i represents the number of filled cells arrived during cell time i. We can take $S_1 = 0$.

The total buffer memory required is already calculated for output queuing (see section 4.3.2.). This total memory must be shared over L inputs. For instance, at 85 % load, and a cell loss rate of 10^{-8}, we need around 40 cell locations. The cell loss rate of the concentrator must be of the same order of magnitude (better than 10^{-8}). This can be achieved with L = 8 as dimensioned in Fig. 4.11. In this case, the shared buffer consists of 8 queues of 5 cells each, resulting in a total of 40 cells.

Expansion

The Knockout switch was described here as a basic building block of size N. However, it was conceived to be easily expandable to a large number of inputs and outputs. This expansion is achieved by providing L additional inputs to each concentrator, so that it becomes an (N + L) to L concentrator. This way of expansion is different of that of other solutions which use multistage interconnection networks as described in section 4.4.

In Fig. 4.15., a Knockout switch for 2N inputs and 2N outputs is shown, built with N x N Knockout basic building blocks. There we see that only 2N buffers and 2N buses are required. On the other hand, the system requires 2 x 2N filters and concentrators. All concentrators have N + L useful inputs and L outputs. Only 2N of these concentrators use these N + L inputs effectively, the other 2N concentrators use only N of these inputs.

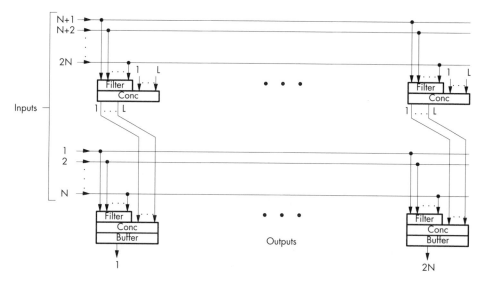

Fig. 4.15. – 2N x 2N Switch Built With N x N Knockout Switches

In principle this expansion method can be applied for large values, but care must be taken that the number of buses and the number of inputs per concentrator do not become too large.

Multicast/broadcast

The broadcast operation is straightforward in the Knockout switch. Since all bus interfaces of the switch are connected to each bus, they can easily all read a broadcast cell. The reception of such a broadcast cell is identical to that of a unicast cell. To allow the packet filter to recognize also broadcast cells, a special routing identification value is given to these broadcast cells.

In order to support the multicast function, the Knockout switch described above has to be upgraded, and special multicast modules have to be added to the system (Fig. 4.16.). We see that the output of the multicast modules is fed back into the bus interface of the unicast switch by adding M additional multicast buses. So, the bus interface now requires N + M inputs. These multicast modules look very similar to the regular bus interfaces as described in Fig. 4.10. The advantage of this solution is that not all cell filters require this complex functionality, but only those equipped for multicast functionality. The number of multicast modules can be increased as the demand for multicast is increased. But, on the other hand, the dimensioning of the system becomes more complex. Indeed, additional multicast buses have to be provided, plus additional inputs to the bus interfaces. If these additional buses and inputs are not planned in advance, a redimensioning and possibly a recabling of the system has to be performed.

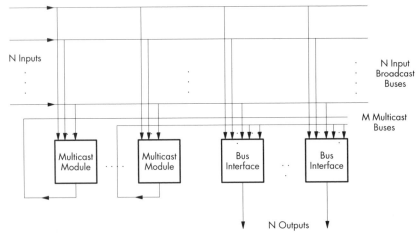

Fig. 4.16. – Knockout Switch with Multicast Modules

To implement those multicast modules a cell duplicator is added to the bus interfaces of the multicast modules (Fig. 4.17.). This cell duplicator generates n copies of the incoming cell each with a different destination address.

During the time the cell duplicator is making copies, the other cells in the multicast module are buffered in the cell buffer.

The number of copies n and the destination addresses of each of those copies are determined using the table of multicast virtual circuits. This table is updated whenever a connection requires an additional multicast destination, or whenever a connection changes from unicast to multicast.

Another implementation of those multicast modules has been reported by Eng in 1988, and consist of a fast packet filter, which is capable of comparing a large number of addresses during a cell time.

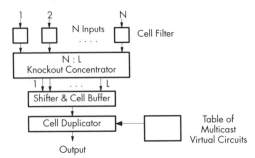

Fig. 4.17. – Multicast Module with a Cell Duplicator

4.3.5. Roxanne switching element

The basic switching building block used in the Roxanne switching fabric, as described under section 4.4.1.1., is based on the central queuing principle. This switching element and the related architecture were described by Alcatel researchers in (Henrion, 1990).

This basic switching element is called ISE in the Roxanne terminology (Integrated Switching Element). The size and speed of this ISE, to be integrated on a single chip depends on the state of the art of the technology and on the applied technology to construct the ISE. In the paper of 1990, Henrion and others describe the ISE as a 32 x 32 basic switching block on a single chip with inlets and outlets operating at 150 Mbit/s. As an interim solution, a 16 x 16 ISE with each inlet and outlet at 150 Mbit/s is also described.

The ISE is capable of routing a cell of any inlet to one or several outlets (in this case multicast/broadcast is performed), according to the routing bits in the routing tag of each cell. The routing information in the routing tag of each cell may indicate a direct routing mode (i.e. a specific outlet of the ISE has to be selected) or a distributed routing mode (i.e. the cell may be routed freely to a group of different outlets), thereby distributing the traffic over this group of outlets.

According to the position in the network, the ISE will interpret different parts of the routing tag to route the cell to the appropriate outputs. In addition, some cells may require a different interpretation of this routing information, depending on the type (routing mode) of the cell. Indeed, normal information cells will be routed to a destination using whatever path is available in the switch; other cells (e.g. maintenance cells) have to follow a specific path. More details on this routing will be described in section 4.4.1.1.

The ISE architecture is based on the central queuing principle described in Fig. 4.18. This central queue (shared buffer memory SBM) is buffering the cells and is connected to all inlets and outlets. In the diagram, an ISE is shown with X inlets and Y outlets.

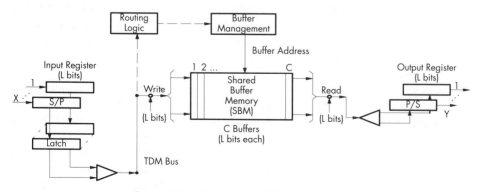

Fig. 4.18. – ISE Functional Block Diagram

When the cells enter the ISE, they are first converted from serial to parallel (L bits wide) to reduce the internal operating speed; then the cells are latched in a register. Simultaneously, a cell synchronization function is performed on each of the X incoming cell streams to recognize the cell boundaries.

The X latched cells are then cyclically transferred via a TDM (time division multiplexing) bus to the shared buffer memory (SBM). For the example of a 32 x 32 ISE, inlets/outlets at 150 Mbit/s and an 8 byte wide TDM bus, the frame period of the bus is 64 bit/150 Mbit/s = 0.43 µs.

During this period, 32 write operations have to be performed into the SBM. The memory access cycle of the SBM, which is implemented as a dual ported memory, is 13 ns. However, before writing the cells into the SBM, some routing tag processing has to be performed in the routing logic. This routing logic is implemented as a pipeline machine, and mainly consists of routing information interpretation. This pipeline machine determines the routing for the 32 incoming cell streams during one cell time.

To reduce the internal routing logic speed, the processing is divided in a sequence of different functions. Different functions of different routing tags can be performed simultaneously.

For each cell, the routing logic analyzes the self-routing tag and, depending on the specific ISE routing mode, will route the cell to a logical queue served by a group of 4, 8, 16 or 32 outlets.

Such a logical queue (a group of 4, 8, 16 or 32 outlets) is served in a multi-service discipline by its respective outlets, but is logically considered as one single queue. This means that for a group of 4 outlets, this logical queue will be served by the 4 serving outlets. If these 4 outlets have exactly the same load, then the queue will consecutively be served by the 4 outlets. The basic principle of the service discipline is that the load will be as much as possible equally distributed on all outlets. Such a multiservice discipline reduces the required memory size of the SBM.

When a cell is selected from the SBM, the corresponding cell location (buffer address) will be released and made available to the buffer management unit. The shared buffer memory (SBM) is controlled by a SBM buffer management function responsible for controlling the free and occupied cells, including the queuing discipline of successive cells contending for the same group of outlets. This is done using a linked list technique.

In case of selective multicast, the routing tag is not sufficient to indicate all required outlets to which copies have to be provided. Therefore, the number of copies and destinations is stored internally in a special memory in the ISE. The routing tag of the multicast cell will then contain an internal reference number which will be used to access this internal ISE memory containing a mask per multicast connection, i.e. per internal reference number. This mask comprises one bit per logical queue, indicating that the cell has to be placed in the logical queue of the group concerned or not.

Each logical queue which is addressed will then read the stored cell from the SBM, and only the last will authorize the release of the corresponding SBM cell location. This function is performed by means of a copy count in the buffer management entity which is stored per cell, and reduced every time a cell is read out by a logical queue.

The Roxanne switch has also an interesting feature that it is compatible with variable cell lengths, so that it can also be used for other applications than only ATM, like packets or synchronous with low delay requirements. Remember in this respect (section 2.4.5.3.) the packetization delay problem caused by the "large" size of an ATM cell (48 bytes).

This flexibility is achieved by working internally in the switch with "multislot cells" (MSC). Each external cell/packet is converted to a number of internally fixed length slots, which are concatenated as one stream of multiple slots. This means that all slots of a single cell/packet follow the same path through the switch as concatenated slots. A single header (including the routing tag) is present per multislot cell/packet, whereas only two bits per slot are required to indicate the cell/packet slot sequence (begin of cell, end of cell) as well as idle slots.

Internally in the ISE, the SBM is fully slot oriented, i.e. all memory accesses are slot based instead of cell based. This means that the SBM management must control slots. Its linked list management entity will therefore be n times larger (if there are n slots in a cell) than if only cells were to be treated.

The dimensioning of the SBM memory has been done by modelling a number G of Geo $(p \times q)/X/Y/K$ queuing systems where

- $p = q = 16$ or 32 (the size of the ISE).
- Y = number of servers (outlets) per group to which cells are routed ($G = Q/Y$ can be 4, 8, 16 or 32).
- K = maximum size of the buffer in cells.

The geometric arrival law is a good model for the Roxanne switch, since the traffic is uniformly distributed due to the randomization process in the network. This means that the internal arrival law is independent of the arrival law of the external sources. This is a very interesting property of the Roxanne switch, which makes its internal dimensioning independent of the external behavior of the network and the sources generating ATM traffic under different kinds of traffic (burst, Poisson, Gaussian, ...).

The worst-case dimensioning of the ISE buffer memory occurs when directed routing to a single group ($Y = 4$) of outlets is required. The simulation/extrapolation results for this worst case are shown in Fig. 4.19. There the memory size (in slots) is shown for various ISE loads and various MSC sizes in number of slots. The diagram shows the required number of slots in function of the load for a cell loss probability of 10^{-11}.

There we see that the required number of cell slot buffers increases with the load and the number of slots per MSC. This is logical since the memory size for fixed length cells grows linearly with the size of the cell. However, in a MSC environment some gain can be expected, since slot locations in the SBM can already be available if not yet a full MSC cell is freely available. So, a new arriving cell can already store its first arriving slot(s).

The load of 0.53 is specially indicated since this gives a worst case load, as will be shown in section 4.4.1.1. The required memory size for ATM cells transported in 8 bytes per slot is 145 slots for a 32 x 32 ISE, or 9280 bits in the SBM.

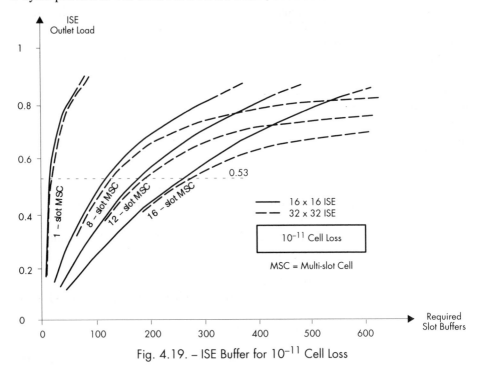

Fig. 4.19. – ISE Buffer for 10^{-11} Cell Loss

4.3.6. Coprin switching element

The Coprin switch was originally designed for an experimental set-up (Prelude), to which data, voice and video sources were connected (Coudreuse, 1987). It was designed and realized by the French CNET. In the prototype realized, the COPRIN switching element operated with links at 280 Mbit/s, cells of 15 bytes information and 1 byte header and consisted of a 16 x 16 square matrix (basic switching element).

The routing in the Coprin switching element is done based on the header of the cell. This header contains a reference number which is pre-set for each connection. This reference number will be used in the Coprin switch to determine the physical outlet; at the same time it will be translated to a new reference number.

The block diagram of the Coprin switch is shown in Fig. 4.20. Besides the standard functions like cell synchronization and header error control to be performed by each inlet, the switch consists mainly of 4 parts, as can be seen in the diagram. These are called : super multiplexing, buffer memory, demultiplexing and control.

The Coprin switch has the special feature that all cells are treated as a parallel stream of information. The headers of all cells are handled sequentially by a central control entity.

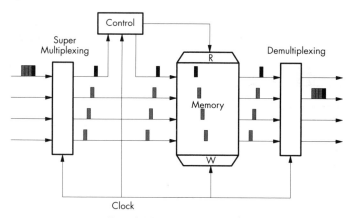

Fig. 4.20. – Coprin Switch

This characteristic explains the 4 basic functions :

- The super multiplexing block is responsible for the transposition of the incoming cell streams to parallel data streams with all headers multiplexed into a special stream.
- The demultiplexing block performs the reverse operation of the super multiplexing and reconstructs the ATM cells.
- The buffer memory stores the ATM cells, but since it receives the cells in the special parallel form, it must take this into account for its internal organization.
- The control block manages the free and occupied locations of the queues of the buffer memory.

The first function is super multiplexing. In the classical time division switching systems, different channels can be put on a TDM (Time Division Multiplexing) bus, which means that successive slots will contain information of different channels. This bus is often implemented via parallel wires, in order to reduce the physical speed of the wires.

A comparable TDM parallel bus multiplexing is performed in this super multiplexing part; however each physical wire of the "bus" has a different meaning : the first wire transports the first information byte of all cells, the second wire transports the second information byte, etc.

The super multiplexing function is shown in Fig. 4.21a., for a 4 by 4 super multiplexing function and assuming a cell of 1 header byte and 3 data bytes (a, b, c). There it can be seen that a space switch of 4 by 4 can implement this function by changing its state every byte. In Fig. 4.21b. we see the 4 states of the space switch. In state 1, inlet i is connected to outlet i; in state 2, inlet i is connected to outlet (i + 1) mod 4; in state 3, inlet i is connected to outlet (i + 2) mod 4 and in state 4, inlet i is connected to outlet (i + 3) mod 4. Or generally speaking, for an n by n space switch in state k, inlet i is connected to outlet (i + k − 1) mod n.

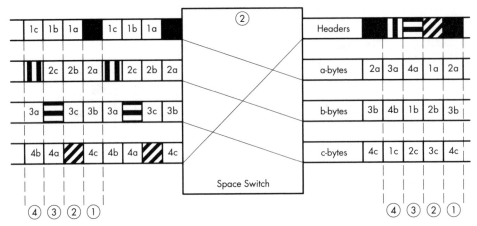

Fig. 4.21a. – Super Multiplexing Function in Coprin

It can already be seen from this part that the size of the switch is strongly related to the ratio between the cell information size and header size. In Fig. 4.21a. we see that all header bytes are transferred to the first outlet, all a-bytes (i.e. the first bytes of the information field) to the second outlet, etc. We also see that a prerequisite for the correct operation of the super multiplexing block is the alignment of the incoming cells at the inlets of the super multiplexing block, such that the headers on different inlets arrive at consecutive time slots.

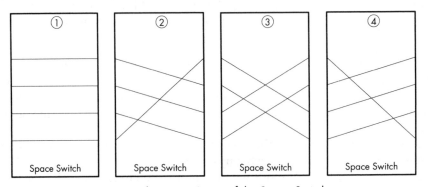

Fig. 4.21b. – Four States of the Space Switch

The information prepared by this super multiplexing function is then forwarded in that form to the second part of the switch. This second part of the Coprin switch is the buffer memory, which can be classified as a central queuing system. The central queue is organized and divided in banks, each bank being dedicated to a byte of the cell. This means that if byte one (i.e. the header) of a cell is stored in memory location A of memory bank 1, byte 2 of the same cell (i.e. the first information byte) will be stored in memory location A + 1 of memory bank 2, etc. This is shown in Fig. 4.22., where 4 memory banks are shown.

The third part of the Coprin switch is the demultiplexing. Suppose that we received from the control part of the switch the command that address A has to be read; this actually means that from bank 1 address A has to be read, address A + 1 from bank 2, etc. These actions have to be performed in consecutive order to guarantee that byte 1 of the cell is available on the physical outlet one byte time before byte 2 of the same cell, which will become available on physical outlet 2, etc. (see Fig. 4.22.).

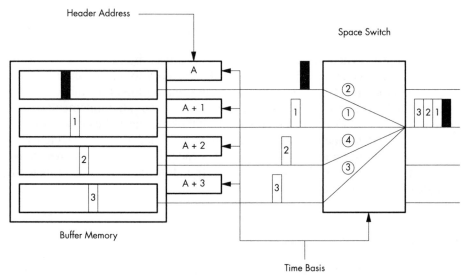

Fig. 4.22. – Buffer Memory and Demultiplexing in Coprin

The reconstruction of the cells will again be performed by a space switch which changes its state every other byte as was explained in Fig. 4.21. for the super multiplexing, but now in the reverse order (first state 4, then state 3, ...).

The fourth part of the Coprin switch is the control (Fig. 4.23.) of the memory buffers and the translation tables. The translation tables are addressed based on the time basis and the value of the incoming header. Indeed, the time basis indicates the incoming link, as the headers of the cells on link 1 (the header link) are placed in the order of the incoming links, as shown in Fig. 4.21a. For every incoming link, the header then unambiguously determines the location in the translation memory which contains the translated header (to be used on the outgoing link) and the number of the outgoing link(s) to which the cell has to be sent to.

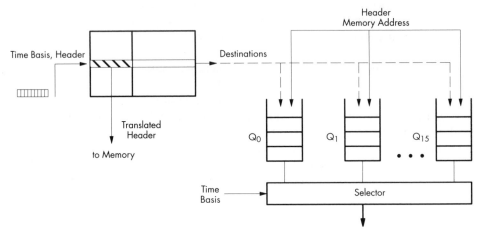

Fig. 4.23. – Control of the Coprin Switch

In the Coprin switch, the translation table contains 3 bytes, i.e. 1 byte for the translated header which is written to the buffer memory to replace the incoming reference number and 16 bits to indicate the destinating link(s) of this cell. This non-coded information of the outgoing links allows a simple implementation of multicast/broadcast. A value of 1 on position i of those 16 bits indicates that the cell has to be copied in queue i (Q_i). If an outgoing link has been selected as a destination, the buffer memory address of the header is then put in the respective queue(s). In the example of Fig. 4.22. this corresponds to the value A pointing to the first byte of the buffer memory.

4.3.7. Athena switching element

The Athena switch principle was first described in (De Prycker, 1987) as a switching fabric composed of basic switching elements based on the output queuing principle. A description of the implementation of this Athena switch was given in (De Prycker, 1990). In this paper, the Athena switch and its basic switching block are described, designed with the technology available in the years 1988-89. The ATM switching element is realized on a single printed circuit board with 16 ATM inlets and 16 ATM outlets, each operating at 600 Mbit/s.

The Athena basic switching building block is part of a connection-oriented switching fabric with header translation in each stage, as will be described in section 4.4.1.2. The basic switching block is based on the output queuing principle : the transfer of the information from the inlets to the output queues is performed by a transfer medium which is fully non-blocking. This means that this transfer medium must be capable of transporting 9.6 Gbit/s (16 x 600 Mbit/s). The implementation of this transfer medium is very typical for this Athena switch. The straightforward solution for it is a simple TDM bus at 9.6 Gbit/s. Even a parallel implementation of such a TDM bus on a board between chips causes great technological difficulties due to electrical signal reflections.

Therefore, a cell slice architecture with an internal (i.e. in chip) TDM bus is selected. This means that the output queues are implemented in different identical chips as is shown in Fig. 4.24. These chips are called CMCs (Central Memory Chips) of which 8 contain all the 16 output queues, i.e. a queue per outlet. The CMCs are somewhat like a bit slice processor; each CMC operates on one eighth of an ATM cell stream. These 8 CMC chips are connected to 16 RTP (Receive and Transmit Port) chips which perform mainly cell reception, header processing (header error detection/correction, ...), label translation, maintenance and cell transmission to the next stage of the switching fabric.

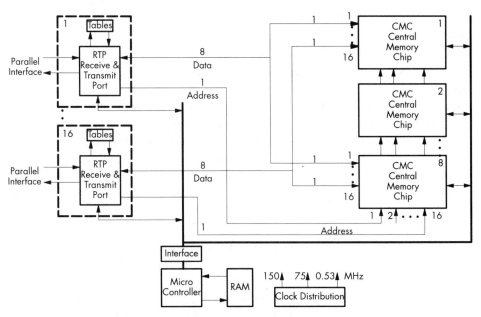

Fig. 4.24. – The Athena Basic Switching Block

The interconnection of the 8 CMCs and 16 RTPs to form the Athena basic switching element is shown in Fig. 4.24. Each RTP has 8 outlets at 75 Mbit/s (8 x 75 = 600 Mbit/s), each line connected to a CMC. This results in total 8 x 16 = 128 wires from RTP to CMC. Each CMC handles one eighth of the data of each inlet, and transfers one eighth of the data again to each outlet. Again 128 wires are required from CMC to RTP, to transfer the information from the output queues, distributed over the 8 CMCs to the 16 RTPs.

Since each CMC has to handle one-eighth of the information of each inlet, each CMC has to receive identical routing information from each RTP. The distribution of this routing information is provided by a physical address bus from each RTP to the 8 CMCs, requiring one address routing outlet per RTP and 16 address routing inlets per CMC. This address routing information identifies to which outlet the current cell has to be sent. Since multicast is implemented in this switching element, 16 routing bits are required, each bit identifying whether a copy to a specific outlet has to be made.

A microcontroller is also connected to the RTPs and CMCs to receive control information. This control information is required to fill in the routing tables of all switching elements in the switching fabric. This control information is transmitted internally in the switching fabric by ATM cells, characterized by a special ATM header value. In addition, a priority bit is added to indicate whether the cell has to be handled with high priority in the queue or that it may be discarded in case of temporary overload. This way a semantic priority is implemented, as specified by the CLP bit in the ATM header.

The internal architecture of the CMC is shown in Fig. 4.25. As described above, each CMC is responsible of queuing one-eighth of the data stream as a bit slice processor. Each CMC has 16 data input lines and 16 address routing input lines (one from each RTP), each being buffered at the input of the CMC. An internal bus transfers the 53 bits (one-eighth of 53 bytes) of one cell to the FIFO(s) selected by the routing information in the routing buffer. The FIFO(s) then receive one-eighth of the cell to be buffered. The FIFOs are controlled by a simple write pointer and a read pointer pointing to the first free and first cell to be read, respectively. Each queue contains 47 cell places (actually 47 places of one-eighth of a cell) for normal traffic, plus additionally 5 locations for cells with high priority. So, a total of 52 cell portions have to be provided per queue.

At 80 % load of normal cells, this queue size guarantees a cell loss rate better than 10^{-10} for normal cells, and better than 10^{-15} for the high priority cells, if not more than 10 % of the cells have a high priority.

As can also be seen in Fig. 4.25., a seventeenth queue (FIFO 16) is provided, to transfer incoming control information cells to the microcontroller on board. In addition, the microcontroller can itself send control information cells to other switch elements' microcontrollers or other controllers in the switching fabric.

As can be seen from the previous description, the Athena switch is mainly characterized by its large number of wiring interconnections on the board between CMC and RTP. It is also characterized by a simple memory control mechanism for the output queuing principle, requiring little control logic to design, but a rather large memory buffer (no pooling of resources as in central queuing). However, memory is very simple to design due to its inherent repetitiveness.

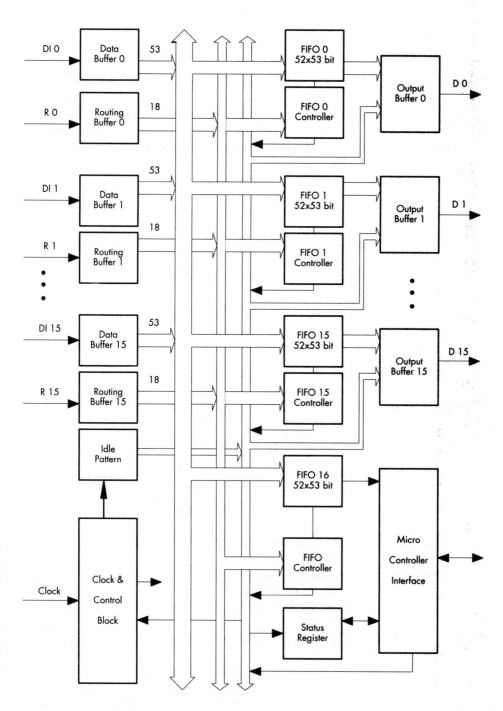

Fig. 4.25. – The CMC of the Athena Switch

4.4. ATM SWITCHING FABRICS

When several basic switching building blocks, as described in the previous sections, are interconnected together in a network, we obtain a switching fabric as shown in Fig. 4.26. These switching fabrics typically have a large number of inlets and outlets (up to some hundred or tens of thousands). Very often such a switching fabric is composed of a large number of identical basic switching building blocks, as the one described in section 4.3. of this book. These fabrics are referred to as Multistage Interconnection Networks (MIN).

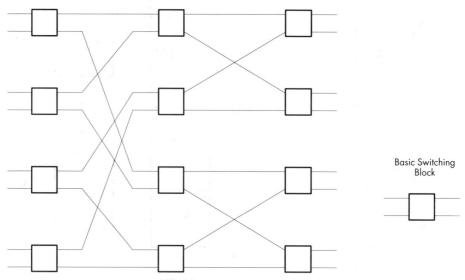

Fig. 4.26. – Multistage Interconnection Network

This section will explain some typical examples, but again it is not meant to be exhaustive. The bibliography in this Chapter contains a list of most papers published in this domain. We see in the example of Fig. 4.26., that the basic switching blocks of 2 by 2 are organized in 3 stages, each stage having 4 elements. The interconnection of the stages is such that all 8 inlets of the fabric can reach all 8 outlets, which is of course required to obtain a full interconnectivity of all inlets and outlets. As will be described later, the interconnection patterns may introduce other interesting features of these MINs. Note that it is not mandatory that the basic switching block is a 2 x 2 element, but it can as well be a 32 x 32 element. Obviously larger switching fabrics can be constructed with fewer stages and elements of a 32 x 32 version than of a 2 x 2 version.

It must be noted that the Knockout switch described in section 4.3.4., can also be considered as a switching fabric, since it can easily be expanded to a large number of inlets and outlets. However, since it is not a MIN, its expansion capabilities will not be explained here, but are explained in section 4.3.4.

Initially, MINs were used in circuit switched networks. Here, C.Clos was one of the most famous researchers in the 1950s with his work on non-blocking networks. The word non-blocking in this context means that all external calls (i.e. connections) can be connected internally without blocking, for the duration of the call.

The study on the use of the MINs for packet-like applications was only initiated in the 1970s, mainly to be used in parallel computer systems. One of the most famous MIN is a Banyan network, originally introduced by Goke and Lipovski (1972). The major property of a Banyan network is that there exists exactly one path from any input to any output. Different subclasses of Banyan networks have been defined, of which the Delta networks are the most famous. These Delta networks have the self-routing property, i.e. independent of the inlet at which the cell (packet) enters the Delta network, it will always arrive at the correct outlet.

The route to be followed can be described by a single string of digits called the routing tag containing the address of the outlet. This is shown in Fig. 4.27.

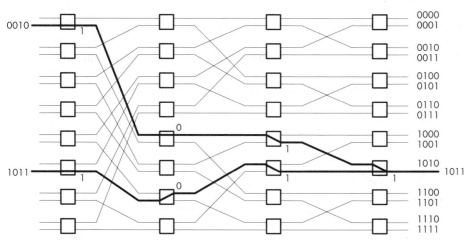

Fig. 4.27. – Self-Routing Properties of a Delta Network

The consecutive bits of the destination address, called the routing tag, are interpreted stage by stage. If the bit is a 0, the upper outlet of the 2 x 2 switching element has to be selected; if the bit is a 1, the lower outlet has to be selected, independent of the inlet at which the cell arrived. In Fig. 4.27. it is shown that 2 cells both arrive at destination 1011, the first cell originating from inlet 0010, the second cell from inlet 1011. At every stage the same decision (selection of upper or lower outlet) is taken in both cases, independent of the basic switching element's position in that stage. To make the routing function in the switching element independent of the stage, the routing tag can be shifted internally over one bit or digit position, to allow each switching element always to interpret the first bit (digit).

Note that self-routing networks can be built using larger switching elements than the 2 x 2, shown in the example. However, in that case, the routing function will require more bits. For instance, with 16 x 16 switching elements, 4 bits of the routing tag are interpreted per stage.

These self-routing networks are very suitable for packet switching applications. Since the routing functions to be performed are minimal, high speeds can be obtained by implementing the routing functions in hardware. In addition, the MINs allow cells to pass parallel through it.

These Delta networks all have the same major characteristics, to build an NxN switching fabric :

(1) They are constructed of identical bxb switching elements.
(2) Their regularity and interconnection pattern makes them very suitable for very large scale chip integration.
(3) They have the self-routing property, requiring $\log_b N$ digits to route a cell from input to output.
(4) They consist of $\log_b N$ stages, each stage having N/b basic switching elements.

As can be seen in Fig. 4.27., simultaneous cells can be switched through the network. However, these networks are internally blocking, since it may happen that cells contend internally with each other for the same resource (queue, link, ...) and thus may get lost if no special provisions are taken. In Fig. 4.28. we see that even cells which have a different destination can easily contend.

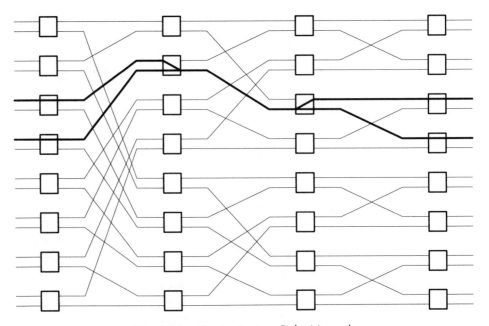

Fig. 4.28. – Contention in a Delta Network

Note that also a collision can occur at the outlet of the switching fabric, since several cells can be destined to the same outlet. However, this outlet collision is not considered as a blocking of the switching fabric itself.

There are several ways to reduce the internal blocking to a level which is acceptable for ATM :

(1)   Provide buffers (queues) in every basic switching element within the switching fabric.
(2)   Increase the internal link speed relative to the external speed, so that the internal link load is reduced to arrive to a virtual zero contention probability.
(3)   Use a backpressure mechanism between the switching nodes, to delay the transfer of blocked cells.
(4)   Use multiple networks in parallel (multiple planes) to provide multiple paths between inlet and outlet.
(5)   Provide multiple links internally between the switching nodes. This option may cause out-of-sequence arrival at the output of the switching fabric, introducing the need for resequencing means at the output of the switching fabric.

As will be demonstrated in the following examples, these different methods can be combined, depending on the options taken for reducing the cell loss.

Those MINs can be categorized in 2 main categories : internally blocking and non-blocking. Internally blocking means that internal cell loss may occur; internally non-blocking MINs do not have an internal cell loss in the switching fabric, but only at the edges.

4.4.1.   Multistage interconnection networks with internal cell loss

We define a MIN which is internally blocking as an interconnection network of basic switching elements, in which cells can get lost because they are contending internally for the same resource (link, queue, ...) of which there are not enough available internally. However, by a proper dimensioning of the basic switching elements and a good interconnection strategy, the cell loss can be limited to values acceptable for ATM. Values of a cell loss rate around 10^{-10} are readily achievable with the proposed MINs.

The routing of cells in MINs which allow an internal cell loss can be implemented in different ways. I will classify it according to 2 parameters : the time/instant when the routing decision is performed and the place where the routing information is present. As shown in Table 4.2., this gives rise to 4 different classes of routing in a MIN.

With respect to the routing decision time, this decision can be performed once for the complete duration of the connection, or it can be performed for every cell separately. In the first case, we say that the MIN is internally connection oriented or uses pre-set path routing; in the second case the MIN operates internally connectionless. In the first case, all the cells of the virtual connection follow the same route/path through the MIN, in the second case not.

With respect to the routing information place, the routing information can either be transported by each cell itself via a so-called routing tag, or it can be stored in routing tables in the basic switching blocks which are composing the MIN. In case a routing table is used, this table must be accessed via an entry. This entry can either have only local significance for the basic switching block, or significance over the complete MIN.

Routing information place Routing decision time	Cell based (Routing tag)	Network based (Routing table)
Connection based	I	III
Cell based	II	IV

Table 4.2. – Routing in a Multistage Interconnection Network

Routing time

In type I and III, the path in the MIN of an ATM logical connection is determined once for the duration of the connection. This means that all cells of the ATM connection will always follow the same path through the MIN switching fabric. So, full cell sequence integrity is guaranteed. Since some resources have to be allocated internally for each connection, it may happen that a new connection is refused. Indeed, a new connection will only be accepted if internally in the MIN a path can be determined with enough internal resources. This means that the internal links may only be loaded to a value for which the internal queues of the basic switching elements were dimensioned.

The path can be determined in different ways : some parts may be randomly selected to ensure that the traffic of different connections is evenly distributed over the MIN. Other parts will be selected to arrive at the correct destination. This results in a switching fabric composed of a randomization/distribution network and a routing network . The distribution of the traffic of different connections over the MIN ensures that the internal connection blocking probability is reduced, since this internal blocking is caused by a lack of internal resources. The path can be determined in a central computer (centralized path search), or it can be determined step by step by checking the resources in the basic switching blocks in the MIN (distributed path search).

Once this path is determined, it can then be transported in every cell individually by the routing tag (type I), or this path can be stored in routing tables in the basic switching blocks (type III). In case of a routing tag, this tag contains an address (routing information) which is interpreted step by step through the MIN. No routing tables are required. In the case of a routing table, the entry to the routing table has only local significance, per basic switching block, if internal routing label translation is provided. This label translation guarantees that the label identifying a virtual connection, has a unique value on the link between 2 adjacent switching elements.

In type II and IV the routing decision is taken cell by cell. This means that different paths through the MIN can be taken by different cells of the same ATM connection. Depending on the implementation of the MIN, cells can arrive out of sequence, and may thus require resequencing, or arrive in sequence. In type II, every cell carries enough information in the routing tag to find its way through the MIN. This routing tag contains then routing information to be interpreted step by step through the switching fabric. In type IV, the routing information is present in routing tables in the basic switching blocks. However, since the routing decision can differ for every cell, so that cells of a single connection can arrive in different places of the MIN, this information must be present in the routing tables of all basic switching blocks, i.e. the entry to the routing table must have global significance over the complete MIN (or at least over an entire stage of a MIN).

An important difference between the connection based and cell based routing decision is that in type I and III, the resources in the MIN are only shared between different connections on every link individually, whereas in type II and IV, the resources are shared between all cells of different connections on all links. To be more precise, in type I and III the resources are shared per (individual) link, in type II and IV the resources are shared between all links.

So, if m_i connections are present on link i, only the m_i connections are statistically multiplexed in type I and III. In type II and IV all cells of all m_i connections over all N internal links between stages share the internal resources. So a much larger statistical multiplexing gain can be achieved. The sharing of the resources is thus better in type II and IV than in type I and III, which may, for example, lead to a smaller memory requirement in type II and IV than in type I and III for an identical external load. In addition, the internal traffic characteristics of type II and IV are independent of the external traffic characteristics. On the contrary, in type I and III, the internal and external traffic characteristics are identical.

In type I and III, the path is determined once for the complete connection, so that cells will never arrive out of sequence (which is a prerequisite of ATM). In type II and IV precautions must be taken to ensure that cells do not arrive out of sequence, or in case they arrive out of sequence, resequencing means must be provided.

Routing information place

In type I and II, the routing information is stored in a routing tag, which is added to each cell. This routing tag must contain the routing information for each stage in the MIN. For instance, a MIN composed of 5 routing stages, built of 16 x 16 basic switching blocks, requires a routing tag of 5 x 4 = 20 routing bits. If distribution/randomization stages are also present, then by proper coding, some routing bits can be used to indicate whether routing or randomization has to be performed or the stages itself may know whether they have to route or randomize. In type I, the full routing information of all stages (including that of randomization stages) must be present in the routing tag, since the randomization stages only perform randomization at connection set-up. This means that once the path of the connection is determined, the complete routing tag (of all stages) can be calculated. In type II, only routing information of the routing stages will be stored in the routing tag. The randomization stages may select freely an outlet for every cell, so no routing tag bits are interpreted here.

In type III and IV a routing table in each basic switching block provides the necessary routing information. In type III, two subtypes can be distinguished : the routing table can or cannot perform a routing label translation. In case no translation is provided, the routing table must have an overall MIN significance. If a translation is provided, the entry used to access the routing table only has local significance (i.e. only for that routing table of that basic building block).

In type IV, cells of the same connection can follow different paths. So, the routing information of the routing tables of the different basic switching blocks must contain identical or at least related information, to guarantee that all cells of the same connection arrive at the correct destination.

With respect to implementation, in type I and II, a routing tag must be added to each cell. This means additional overhead to each cell, and results in an increase of internal operating speed compared to the external speed, if the same load has to be supported. Or if the same internal and external speed is preferred, a lower internal load can be transported. At the edges of the switching fabric, memory must be provided to add the routing tag to each cell. In type III and IV, no increase of speed is required, but in all the basic switching blocks routing table memory is required, which contains the routing information.

With respect to functionality, routing tables (type III and IV) are more straightforward to implement multicast. In each routing table, it is easy to indicate to which outlet a copy has to be sent. Thus, in a MIN with routing tables a multicast tree can easily be constructed. With routing tags (type I and II) multicast trees are more difficult to construct. Either a routing tag per copy is required, resulting in a very high overhead, or a special coding of the routing tag is required.

It must be noted that most switching fabrics opted for a single solution (i.e. type I, II, III or IV) for all connection types (unicast, multicast, broadcast). However, some switching fabrics selected a combination of 2 types, one for unicast and another for multicast/broadcast, and combine the advantages of both techniques.

Two different MINs will be described in this section. We use the code names given in the previous section to describe those MINs :

- Roxanne switching fabric : this fabric uses type II routing for its point-to-point connections and type IV routing for its point-to-multipoint (multicast/broadcast) connections. It was first described in (Henrion, 1990).
- Athena switching fabric : this fabric is of the type III with routing tables filled in for the duration of a connection. It was first described in (De Prycker, 1987), using distributed path search.

4.4.1.1.   *Roxanne switching fabric*

The Roxanne switching fabric can be classified as a MIN which is internally blocking, i.e. the cell loss is non-zero in the fabric. The cells in the switching fabric are routed according to a routing tag which is added to the cells at the entrance of the switching fabric, but no internal connection will be set-up between the 2 endpoints in the fabric. This means that the routing in the switching network is type II as described in Table 4.2., but only for the point-to-point connections. As described above, type II MINS perform routing decisions individually per cell, with no routing information present in the fabric, but in the cell. No routing decision per connection is required. Since no internal connection is set-up, no internal resources (links, queues) have to be reserved, resulting in very fast connection set-up and in an optimal sharing of all internal resources.

To ensure that the incoming traffic is fully distributed over all links and queues, the cells are in the first stages randomly spread over all links. Therefore, the routing tag will not contain the complete path to be followed by the cell. In certain places in the network a random route may be selected, in other places, the direct route is determined by parts of the routing tag.

The reduction of the blocking to a value which is acceptable for ATM (e.g. better than 10^{-10} cell loss rate), has guided a number of key options. These key options are

(1)   Internal queuing in the basic switching blocks. As explained in section 4.3.5. on Roxanne's basic switching block the central queuing has been selected for which a dimensioning in terms of cell loss rate and load has been calculated.
(2)   Multiple networks (planes) are provided to ensure reliable operation of the switching fabric, and to guarantee multiple paths in the network. This also allows the network to grow gradually with increasing external loads, for an identical number of connections.

(3)   Multiple paths are provided in the network to distribute the traffic as much as possible. This distribution ensures maximum statistical multiplexing gain independent of the external source type. Therefore, the Roxanne fabric is often called a "multipath self-routing switch", as opposed to traditional self-routing switches with no multipath capabilities.

Since the basic switching block of Roxanne has internal queues, these multiple paths cause the out-of-sequence arrival of different cells of a single connection. Therefore, a resequencing function must be provided at the edge of the switching fabric.

On the other hand, this multiple path solution ensures that cells of a single connection are randomly distributed over the switching fabric, thereby introducing the interesting property that the cell arrival rate of the basic switching blocks is fully memoryless (geometrically distributed). This ensures that the queues in the switching blocks can be dimensioned independently of any external service mix. In addition, the queue dimensioning is optimal (i.e. minimal memory requirements) in the case of a full memoryless arrival process.

This multiple path solution also guarantees that a failure internally in the switching fabric will have a minimal impact on the connections. By providing a proper self-isolating mechanism, a highly fault-tolerant switching fabric is constructed.

The resulting switching fabric in its maximum configuration is a folded 3-stage multiplane network, as shown in Fig. 4.29. This switching fabric is easily extendable in terms of number of lines, (by adding new stages), as well as in throughput (by adding more planes) as shown in Table 4.3. We see that for a fabric of 16,000 lines at 150 Mbit/s we need 3 stages, and depending on the average external link load, a different number of planes is required. For instance if the average load is 0.6 E we need a maximum of 12 planes. For a small configuration of maximum 256 links at 150 Mbit/s we need only a single stage (namely that of the so-called access switch). No planes are required and a maximum external load of 0.8 can be supported.

Type of extension	Expandability
Capacity (150 Mbit/s links)	16K links max. with 3 stages 1024 links max. with 2 stages 256 links max. with 1 stage (no plane)
Throughput, i.e. external link load	0.8 max. with 16 planes 0.6 max. with 12 planes 0.4 max. with 8 planes

Table 4.3. – Roxanne Expandability

The switching fabric is composed of standard switch module boards of 128x128 inlets/outlets at 150 Mbit/s. Physically 4 links of 150 Mbit/s are multiplexed to 600 Mbit/s, resulting in 32 physical inlets/outlets per switch module board (Fig. 4.30.). This standard switch module is identical for all stages, i.e. AS (access switch) and PS_i (plane switch stage i).

In addition a terminal module (TS) is defined which multiplexes 8 incoming external links of 150 Mbit/s, and then distributes the traffic over 4 groups of 4 links. This multiplexing/distribution is performed by the Roxanne basic switching element (ISE) described in section 4.3.5.

Sixteen of those TS modules, together with 4 AS boards, construct a TSU (terminal subscriber unit), capable of concentrating the traffic of 128 terminals. In its maximum configuration, the switch fabric can be composed of 128 of those TSUs.

The switch fabric has a folded characteristic. This means that some parts of the fabric will transport information in one direction, and the same parts will transport other information in the other direction. As we see in Fig. 4.29., an AS (Access Switch) or PS_1 (Plane Switch 1) is annotated with a value of 64×64, where we know that the basic block is a 128 x 128 switch, but half of it operates logically as a 64 x 64 in one direction towards the reflection stage (called AS_i or PS_{1i}), the other half operates as a 64 x 64 switch in the other direction (called AS_o or PS_{1o}). So AS_i and AS_o together form a single AS board.

Each external link (e.g. A in Fig. 4.29.) is via its TS_i connected to a first stage of 4 Access Switches (AS), to realize an expansion of 2. This expansion results in an average internal load of 0.4, if the average external link load is 0.8.

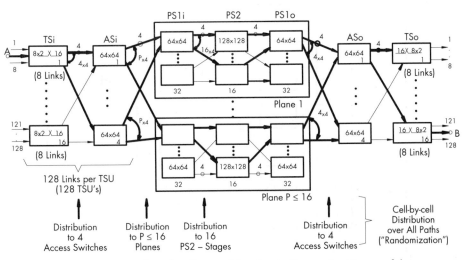

Fig. 4.29. – Distributed or Directed Routing in Successive Stages of the Roxanne Switching Fabric

From the AS_i to the P planes the traffic is again distributed, with a factor which is depending on the number of planes equipped. In each plane, a distribution again occurs between PS_{1i} and PS_2, and finally the last distribution is performed when the planes are left from the PS_{1o} to 4 possible AS. So we see that a maximum utilization of the cell distribution principle (randomization) is performed.

Since directed routing is only performed in PS_2, AS_o and PS_{1o}, real cell congestion can occur there. The buffer dimensioning for the Roxanne basic switching element is thus determined by these 3 cases. In the other cases, a random selection of an outlet can be made, in which the congestion will be minimal.

By construction of the switching network configuration, as shown in Fig. 4.29., the internal link load is half the average load on the external links. This value is 0.4, for typical external loads of 0.8. However, in case an AS fails, the other 3 access switches must be capable of taking over the traffic of the failing one without an increase of cell loss. The resulting internal load is then $0.4 \times 4/3 = 0.53$. This value of 0.53 is used for internal buffer dimensioning. In section 4.3.5., we have indicated that we need around 145 slots for a cell loss of 10^{-11} and a multislot cell of 8 slots.

The standard switch module of 128 x 128 at 150 Mbit/s is itself composed of 2 substages, interconnected via regular trunking. Each substage is composed of 4 identical basic switching building blocks, called ISE (Integrated Switching Element) as shown in Fig. 4.30. These ISEs are explained in section 4.3.5. as the basic switching elements of Roxanne. The cell loss rate on the standard switch module of 128 x 128 is better than 10^{-11}. Each substage of ISE performs a specific routing mode (randomization, routing or a combination of both, e.g. select any of the outlets 1, 2, 3, 4).

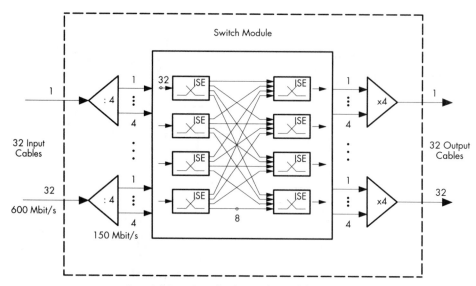

Fig. 4.30. – Standard Switch Module Board

In order to monitor the correct operation of the standard switch module and their interconnections permanently, each ISE has an additional inlet/outlet to the on-board test routiner which performs a continuous check of the correct operation of the standard switch module. This permanent monitoring allows to immediately take out of service malfunctioning parts of the switch, or informs correct functioning parts to direct their cells such that they avoid the malfunctioning subentities.

As all traffic is randomly distributed over all planes, when somewhere in the switching fabric a switching module is faulty, all connections of the switching fabric are affected. So a very quick isolation of the faulty module is required.

The error detection is done by a set of fast continuous tests, checking the correct operation of each switch module, by means of an on-board test routiner. Where the module works correctly, the previous stages are informed by a "Backward Availability Signal", which is transmitted upstream to the previous stage. In case of failure, this signal is not propagated upstream, allowing the switch modules connected upstream of the faulty module to avoid routing to the faulty module.

Due to the multipath principles cells may arrive out of sequence at the outlet of the switching fabric. Therefore, a resequencing function is performed at each outlet of the switching fabric, located on the TS boards. This resequencing is based on the principle of delay equalization, where any variable transfer delay is compensated at the outlet so that every cell is delivered with constant total maximum delay. To achieve this, each cell entering the switch is given a time stamp (at the TS_i), and at the output (at the TS_o) the cell is buffered until its total delay becomes equal to this maximum delay. The buffer required for this resequencing is combined with the output queue of the switch fabric. Calculations have shown that only an additional buffer size of 20 % is needed for this resequencing function. The dimensioning of this buffer is such that a cell loss rate equal to that of the internal switch elements is allowed. The maximum delay of a cell in the resequencing buffer is thus determined by the 10^{-11} quantile of the delay of the switching fabric in its maximum configuration. An advantage of this concept is that any information (ATM, synchronous traffic) leaves the fabric fully jitter-free.

Multicast

For multicast, Roxanne has opted for type IV routing mode as described in Table 4.2. In each ISE, a multicast routing table is implemented with per stage network wide significance (Schrodi, 1992). This routing table contains the number of copies to be made per stage per virtual connection. This allows the network to make as many copies as necessary.

The routing tables of all ISEs of one stage contain identical information since the cells of one connection can arrive in all switching elements of that stage, due to the multipath principle. Per stage, the routing tables contain the number of copies to be made in that stage. The routing tables of all ISEs have to be filled in at connection set-up time. Different control cells have to be launched from the edge to the respective ISEs to fill in those routing tables.

Since all routing tables at a certain stage must contain identical information, identical copies of these control cells can be used to fill in those tables. To make those copies, the multicast capabilities of the switching fabric can be used efficiently, e.g. by launching those control cells as multicast cells with a semi-permanent multicast reference number. This reduces to a minimum the number of control cells to be launched.

For each multicast cell, the routing tag is replaced by an internal reference number, which is added at the entry of the switch fabric to each cell and removed when leaving the switch fabric. The internal reference number used to access the routing tables is unique over the complete switch for one multicast connection. This puts a limitation on the maximum number of simultaneous multicast connections which can exist in the switching fabric. However, this limitation is only determined by the technology, i.e. the number of entries in the routing table.

4.4.1.2.　Athena switching fabric

The Athena switching fabric is a MIN, which can be classified according to Table 4.2. as a type III switching fabric. This means that the path finding is performed once for the complete duration of a connection, and that the information with respect to this path is stored in routing tables in the switching elements of the switching fabric.

These characterics have two important consequences :

- Since a path has to be found in the switching fabric, the connection blocking probability is non-zero, as will be explained in this section.
- Since routing tables are available inside the switching fabric, multicast functionality can easily be implemented.

The switching fabric is composed of basic switching blocks, as described under section 4.3.7.

A sample configuration of the switching fabric is shown in Fig. 4.31. This diagram show that the fabric is composed of an ASN (ATM Switching Network), and several ASCs (ATM Subscriber Concentrator). In the Fig. 4.31., the ASN is composed of 3 folded stages.

Two main building blocks are used to construct both the ASN and the ASC (De Prycker, 1990). These building blocks are a switching element (SE) and a subscriber terminal unit (STU). The SE is the Athena switching element of 16 inlets and 16 outlets described in section 4.3.7. The STU performs the LT (Line Termination) and ET (Exchange Termination) functions of the switch. It therefore terminates the external links (e.g. optical fibers) connecting the subscribers/trunks with ATM streams as well as the external protocol. A set of STUs with an SE together form a concentrator called an ASC.

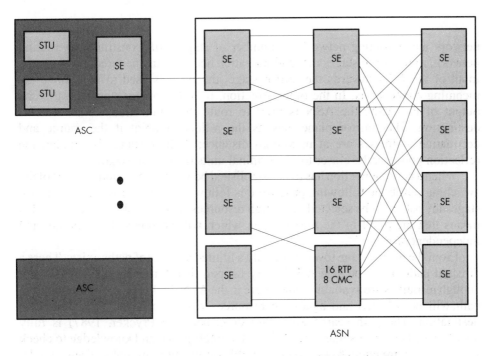

SE	:	Switching Element	ASC	:	ATM Subscriber Concentrator
STU	:	Subscriber Terminal Unit	ASN	:	ATM Switching Network
RTP	:	Receive & Transmit Port	CMC	:	Central Memory Chip

Fig. 4.31. – Configuration of Athena Switching Fabric

Here, the SE is not connected as a 16 x 16 switch, but rather as a concentrator of for example 14 to 2, or 12 to 4 bidirectional links depending on the concentration factor which can be achieved with the external traffic. This ASC can be connected via 1, 2 or 4 links to the ASN.

The ASN is a bidirectional network. Therefore, the switching elements are bidirectional, meaning that with any inlet of a switching element, a fixed outlet is associated in the reverse direction and vice versa. So, a switching element of 16 inlets and 16 outlets may act as an 8 by 8 switching element with bidirectional links, a 12 by 4 or any other combination.

Internally, the resources in the SE and on the links between the SEs, have to be allocated for the duration of a connection. When a new connection requires some resources of that specific link, it will be checked whether there are still enough available resources. If no resources are available, the connection is blocked and cannot be accepted. To reduce this connection blocking probability, multiple paths have to be provided between the inlets and outlets of the Athena switching fabric. At call set-up, one of those multiple paths will be selected. These multiple paths can be provided by the multistage network (ASN) shown in Fig. 4.31. When a path has to be searched, the ASN can functionally be divided in two parts : a randomization network and a routing network. A number of stages will constitute the routing network, a number of stages the randomization network. In one direction, from the input of the ASN towards the mirror stage, the ASN is used to randomize the incoming connections. In the other direction, from the mirror stage towards the output of the ASN, the ASN is used to route the connections to the correct destination. This mirror plane acts as the reflection point if the source and destination addresses are at maximum distance; if the distance is smaller, the reflection point can be closer to the terminal units (reflection stage).

When a new connection has to be established between inlet A and outlet B of the switching fabric the following procedure is followed. From A towards the mirror stage, any path may be selected, if enough resources are available on that path. This means that the point in the mirror stage which will be selected is random, and independent of B.

From the mirror stage towards B, only a limited number of paths exists. There a directed path has to be selected. It may happen that during the path search not enough resources are available somewhere in the ASN. In that case, another random path will be selected and again the resources will be checked from source to destination. The path search algorithm described (De Prycker, 1987) is fully distributed. This means that every SE has the intelligence and knowledge to check whether there are enough resources available on its outgoing links. Then, step by step, the path through the switching fabric will be checked against the required resources. If no resources are available on a certain link, another path will be searched for. Depending on the place where the blocking (i.e. not enough resources) occurs, different actions will be taken. In a SE in the randomization network, another link of that SE will be checked. In the routing network, the randomization is redone, so that another point at the mirror stage will be selected.

So we see that this randomization network is required to reduce the blocking probability of finding a path inside the switching fabric.

The blocking probability of the ASN depends on the internal load on the links and on the externally requested bit rate. On the internal links, physically 600 Mbit/s is available. If all connections are requesting for example 30 Mbit/s, and suppose a maximum load of 0.8 E then only 16 connections can be supported on a single link. (16 x 30 Mbit/s = 0.8 E x 600 Mbit/s). The number of possible virtual paths between 2 endpoints of the switching fabric is then the product of 16 and the number of physical paths between those 2 endpoints. Where the requested bit rate is only 2 Mbit/s, the number of virtual paths is the product of 240 and the number of physical paths. This value is much larger than for the 30 Mbit/s service. This is reflected in the blocking probability of both cases for the ASN as shown in Fig. 4.32.

This diagram shows the probability that no path can be found from inlet to outlet of the switching fabric in function of the load of the internal links between the SE. The smaller the acceptable average load on an internal link, the larger the chance that a path will be found. We see that for the 2 Mbit/s services the internal blocking can be neglected even at an average load around 0.8 E.

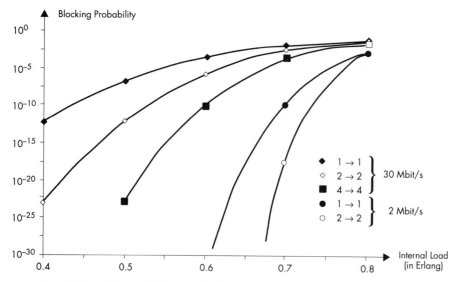

Fig. 4.32. – Network Blocking for Connections of 30 Mbit/s and 2 Mbit/s

In case the virtual connections require 30 Mbit/s, the internal links can on the average be loaded up to around 0.6 E and still have an acceptable blocking probability better than 10^{-4}. So, there is one chance in 10,000 that a call set-up with 30 Mbit/s will be refused due to lack of internal resources, if all other connections are 30 Mbit/s. However, in reality, the network will be loaded with connections at different bit rates (from very low to very high), in which the blocking probability will be determined by the mix of bit rates of the different connections. To improve further this performance, it is possible that for an ASC more than one outlet may be selected, since most ASCs are connected to the ASN via multiple links. This gives rise to the curves indicated as "$2 \rightarrow 2$" or "$4 \rightarrow 4$", meaning, e.g. that any of 2 specific inlets has to be connected to any of 2 specific outlets.

The routing tables in the basic switching elements allow an easy implementation of multicast trees. Each routing table is accessed, based on a reference number which has only local significance on that incoming link and contains a new reference number to be used on the outgoing link(s), as well as the identification of the outgoing links of that switching element which need to get a copy. The reference number can easily make use of the VCI/VPI field of the ATM cells (as described in Chapter 3). So, no additional overhead for routing tags is required, nor a speed-up at the edge of the switch.

The process of translation can be repeated in every stage of the switching fabric, so that very easily a large number of multicast trees can be constructed, as shown in Fig. 4.33. In this diagram only 2 x 2 switching elements are shown, whereas the

Athena switch is built of 16 x 16 elements, but the principle remains the same. It is shown that multicast trees and point-to-point connections can easily be mixed together in a single network.

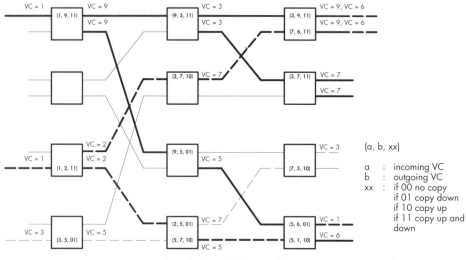

Fig. 4.33. – Multicast Trees

The Virtual Connections (VC) on a link are identified by a VC value, which may be the VCI/VPI field (or part) of the ATM header. The routing tables and the relations defined in it are shown as a triple (a, b, xx), in which "a" means the incoming VC, "b" the outgoing VC and xx the selected output port(s). 00 means no copy at all, 01 a copy at the lower output, 10 a copy at the upper output and 11 a copy at both outputs. In the diagram, 2 multicast connections and a single point-to-point connection are shown.

For the point-to-point connection (with VC = 3 as incoming value on link 7), the VC is simply translated and the selected outlet is indicated by the xx bits. For the multicast connections (with incoming VC = 1 on link 0, and the same VC on link 5), different copies are made at multiple stages. This results in a total of 3 copies for one connection and 5 of the other, on different outlets. The only limitation with the multicast trees exists in the selection of the outgoing reference number. The outgoing reference number (VC) of one multicast tree must be identical for all copies on different outgoing links of a single basic switching element. This limitation is imposed by the translation table implementation. A different outgoing reference number would require a large translation table with very fast access times (16 times faster than the selected option). The Athena switching fabric is implemented with the solution as shown in Fig. 4.33., i.e. for a multicast connection identical VCs will be selected for different outlets of a single basic switching element.

4.4.2.   Multistage interconnection networks without internal cell loss

MINs without internal cell loss are designed such that no cells will be lost inside the fabric. However, cells will be lost at the entrance and/or exit of the fabric, since there a collision of cells will occur.

MINs without internal cell loss are further divided in 2 subcategories : those with internal buffering (i.e. internal queues), and those without internal buffering.

The switching networks with internal buffering require an internal backpressure mechanism to ensure that the internal queues are not overloaded and thus cause cell loss. The most famous switching network of this kind is the St. Louis, as described in (Turner, 1986).

Switching fabrics without internal cell loss and without internal buffering require that different cells do not contend at any place in the fabric for the same resource. Such a condition can be met by a special sort of MINs, called Batcher-Banyan networks, under the condition that no cells are destined to the same outlet. To solve this destination contention problem, different variants, based on the Batcher-Banyan topology, are described in the literature.

Two alternative solutions to solve this contention will be discussed here :

- Starlite, as proposed by Huang in 1984, initially for electronic switching, but upgradable to optical switching.
- Moonshine, as proposed by Hui in 1987 with a special 3 phase algorithm.

4.4.2.1.   *St. Louis switching fabric*

This switching fabric was not specifically designed for fixed length ATM cells, but was proposed by Turner (Turner, 1986) for switching variable length packets. Its basic functional blocks are described in Fig. 4.34. The packet processor (PP) terminates the external protocol and adds the routing tag to the incoming packets, so that the packets can find their way through the switching fabric. The switching fabric (SF) provides multiple paths between inlet and outlet, and allows multicast functionality. The connection processor (CP) establishes both point-to-point and multicast connections. As is shown in the diagram, the different functions are duplicated to ensure highly reliable functionality. This is achieved by multiple planes, each containing a CP, SF and PP. In normal operational mode, one plane is active, the other acts as a hot stand-by.

The switching fabric itself is composed of 4 major functional entities (Fig. 4.35.) : a copy network (CN), a distribution network (DN), a routing network (RN) and a number of broadcast and group translators (BGT). The routing mode selected is that of type II as described in Table 4.2. This means that routing decision time and routing place are both cell based. All networks are self-routing networks.

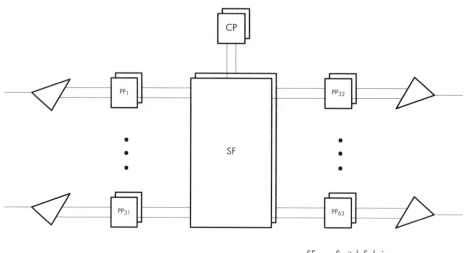

SF : Switch Fabric
PP : Packet Processor
CP : Connection Processor

Fig. 4.34. – St. Louis Switching Fabric

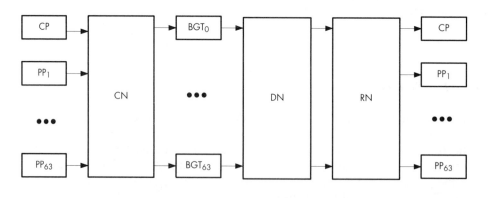

CP : Connection Processor
CN : Copy Network
DN : Distribution Network
RN : Routing Network
BGT : Broadcast & Group Translator
PP : Packet Processor

Fig. 4.35. – St. Louis Switching Fabric Building Blocks

The CN is responsible for making the required copies of the incoming packets. If required, up to 64 copies (in the example of Fig. 4.35.) can be made by this network. In a point-to-point connection, this CN does not perform any function.

The BGTs are responsible for the translation and filling in of the routing tags, especially for multicast connections. Indeed, all copies made by the CN of a single packet will have an identical "routing tag". The BGT will translate this "routing tag", which is more to be considered as an identification of the virtual connection, to a real routing tag containing the identification of the destination address to be used by the RN.

The DN is distributing the incoming traffic randomly over all its outlets, so that on its outlets (the inlets of the RN) the traffic is as much as possible uniformly distributed over all links. The routing tag generated by the BGTs is not used in the DN, since random routing is performed.

Finally the RN will ensure that the packets will arrive at the correct destination, using the routing tag of the packet.

All networks (CN, DN, RN) are built of identical 2x2 basic switching blocks, shown in Fig. 4.36.

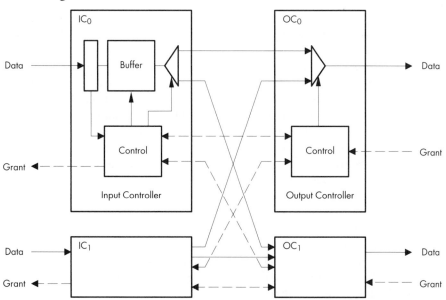

Fig. 4.36. – St. Louis Basic Switching Block

The Input Controller (IC) of this switching block determines the selected output, using the routing tag of the incoming packet. It also provides buffers to store the packet if necessary in case the addressed Output Controller (OC) is occupied. If the buffer of the IC is filled, it applies upstream flow control (backpressure) to prevent buffer overflow by sending a negative grant signal to the previous basic switching block. If the OC receives a positive grant signal from the next switching block, it will select one of the packets temporarily stored in one of the buffers of the IC, and send it out. The decision which packet to take is made by the control logic in both IC and OC.

If the OC receives a negative grant signal, it will not select a packet from an IC, but wait a packet time until the grant signal switches to a positive state.

If the desired output port is free when the packet arrives, it will pass through the node without being buffered (virtual cut through).

The internal link speed between the basic switching blocks is twice the external link speed. This means that an external occupancy of 80 %, results in an internal 40 % load. As we have seen in the section 4.3.2., at a load of 40 %, the buffer requirements are very limited (only a few packets, depending on the queuing discipline) for a small packet loss rate. Since no packet loss is allowed, a backpressure mechanism will ensure that no cell arrives if the queue is full. If the probability that a queue overflows is limited, the backpressure mechanism will not be used too often. Thus, the low load guarantees low internal backpressure and low transfer delay through the switching fabric.

Each switching block has in its IC a buffer of two packets long. The larger the buffer size, the smaller the backpressure through the switch will be, as demonstrated in (Bubenik, 1987).

As was shown in Fig. 4.28., congestion may occur in a self-routing network. To reduce the congestion (in this case the use of backpressure) in the routing network (RN), a distribution network (DN) is placed in front of it. This DN will evenly distribute the packets across all its outputs. The DN has the same internal topology as the RN, but its switching blocks ignore the destination address information in the routing tag, and route the packets alternately to each of their output ports. Only if one of the output ports is occupied, the first port which becomes free is selected. The DN is also built with the elements used to construct the RN.

The Copy Network (CN) is responsible for making copies where a multicast or broadcast function has to be performed. The structure of the CN is identical to that of the DN and RN. The copy function is shown in Fig. 4.37. In the example given, the packets entering the CN belong to multicast virtual connection 23, and must be sent to 7 different destinations. This is indicated in a field (fanout) of the header of each packet. The CN shown is capable of making a maximum of 16 copies. In the example, 7 copies are less than half of 16, so the copy function must only be activated in stage 2 of the CN; in stage 1 of the CN a random output port is selected. In stage 2, two copies will be made, and the fanout-field of the two copies will be modified by splitting 7 into 4 and 3, requiring 4 copies in the upper branch of the tree and 3 copies in the lower branch of the tree. To distribute the traffic more evenly, multicast connections with an even virtual connection number will send more copies in the upper part, those with an odd virtual connection number will do the reverse. For instance, multicast virtual connection 16, with a fanout field of 7 will generate 3 copies at its upper branch and 4 copies at its lower branch.

The update of the fanout field according to the copies made, can very simply be formalized as follows, if we denote s as the stage number (numbered from right to left), starting from 0 :

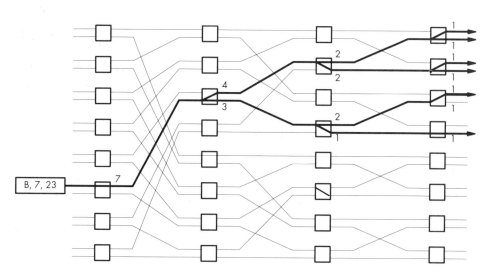

Fig. 4.37. – A Copy Network Making 7 Copies

if FANOUT > 2^s then

    begin duplicate

        if multicast-connection is even then

            upper : FANOUT = $\lfloor (FANOUT+1)/2 \rfloor$
            lower : FANOUT = $\lfloor FANOUT/2 \rfloor$

        else

            upper : FANOUT = $\lfloor (FANOUT/2 \rfloor$
            lower : FANOUT = $\lfloor FANOUT+1)/2 \rfloor$

    end

else distribute traffic as in DN.

Here $\lfloor z \rfloor$ denotes the largest integer smaller than z.

    This algorithm keeps the load in the CN to the absolute minimum, by delaying the copy process as long as possible. When the copied packets leave the CN, we do not yet know their final destinations. The filling of this address is performed by the Broadcast and Group Translator (BGT) located between CN and DN. This BGT will assign a new routing field to each copy of the multicast connection. The translation information stored in each BGT will be different for packets of the same multicast connection. The translation tables in the BGT are controlled by the CP to ensure their consistency.

4.4.2.2. *Batcher-Banyan based MINs*

A special class of MINs consists of switching fabrics which do not have internal contention of cells passing through the switch. Since no contention exists in the switch, there is no need to provide internal buffering or backpressure in the switching fabric.

Such switching fabrics are called non-blocking. They can be constructed by a proper fabric topology, but in addition one condition must be fulfilled : the cells may not be destined to the same outlet.

However, since there exists a possibility of output contention, i.e. 2 or more cells are destined to the same output of the switching fabric, this output contention has to be solved by additional arbitration logic and information storage at the entrance of the switch fabric.

The most famous non-blocking switching fabrics are based on the Batcher-Banyan network topology. This topology is shown in Fig. 4.38., where we see a Batcher network preceding a Banyan network, interconnected in a special way (called Shuffle-Exchange).

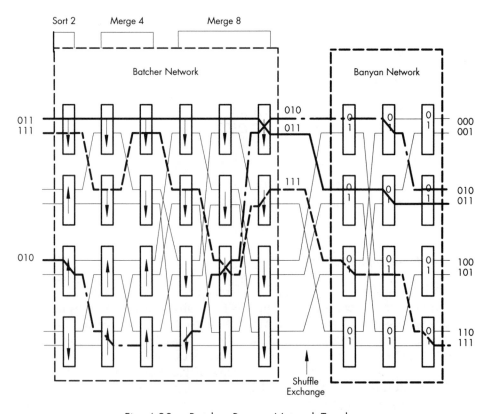

Fig. 4.38. – Batcher–Banyan Network Topology

Batcher network

The Batcher network of this switching fabric sorts the cells according to their destination address. The result of this sorting operation puts the cells with the lower address at the upper outlet of the Batcher network. As we see in Fig. 4.38., the 3 cells passing through the switch are sorted from low-to-high at the outlet of the sorting Batcher network.

The Batcher sorting network is constructed of sorting elements (of 2 inlets) which compare the bits of the destination address and switch to either "pass" or "exchange". The sorting option selected in every stage is indicated by the arrow. This arrow points to the outlet at which the largest number is to be routed. If only a single cell is present at one of the 2 inlets, it will be considered as the lowest value, so it will be routed to the outlet not indicated by the arrow. For instance the 010 cell will be destined to the lower outlet in the first 3 stages, and to the upper outlet in the next 3 stages. Cells 011 and 111 are sorted in the first stage, with the lowest value on top. The comparison is only enabled during the destination address. After setting, the switch stays set for the duration of the cell. The figure gives an example of 3 numbers being sorted by the network.

The full sorter is built from a succession of "bitonic sorters" which accept a sequence that ascends, then descends and outputs a sorted (monotonic) sequence. Fig. 4.38. shows how the outputs of two times two elements (sorters) with opposite sorting direction are merged by two elements of 4 lines to sort (again with opposite sorting mode), and how those in turn feed an 8 line bitonic sorter that merges 8 lines into a sorted output. At the output of the Batcher network all cells are sorted but do not yet arrive at the correct destination.

Banyan network

The Banyan network is a simple self-routing network which guarantees that all cells will arrive at the destination indicated by a routing tag, equal to the address of the destination.

Since no multiple cells are destined to a single outlet, maximum one cell will be present at each outlet of the Batcher network, i.e. at each inlet of the Banyan network. So there is no head of the line (HOL) collision at the entrance of the Banyan network (note that this HOL blocking however, could be present at the entrance of the Batcher network). Also internally in the Banyan network no blocking will arise, since all cells are already sorted at the inlet of the Banyan network, and the Banyan only operates as an expander network.

Starlite

The first switch described in the literature which is based on the Batcher-Banyan concept, was the Starlite switch, proposed by Huang and Knauer in 1984. The switch is designed with constant latency. Its construction makes use of a sequence of regularly structured routing networks, i.e. a Batcher and Banyan network, plus in addition a trap and concentrator network. In the Starlite switch, the Banyan part of the Batcher-Banyan system is called the Expander network.

It allows a growth in the number of external ports, and the amount of bandwidth per user. The switch handles fixed length cells, to which at the entrance of the switch a routing tag is added.

To overcome the output port contention problem of the Batcher-Banyan network, the Starlite approach adds a Trap network between the Batcher and Banyan network (Fig. 4.39.). This trap network detects cells with equal destination address at the output of the Banyan network (i.e. contending cells). The procedure consists of separating cells which are simultaneously arriving at the output of the Batcher network with the same destination. These "conflicting" cells are fed back to the entrance of the Batcher network to try again in the next cycle. The trap network is a hardware solution which discovers cells with an identical destination and routes them to the rightmost outputs of the trap network. It consist of a single stage of comparators followed by a routing (Banyan) network. Since the Batcher sorting network ensures that duplicated addresses will arrive at adjacent inputs of the trap network, only a single stage of comparators is required. These comparators indicate duplicated destination, but let pass the first instance of the cells with duplicated addresses. The address applied for routing in the Banyan part of this trap network is calculated via the running sum (i.e. the sum of all flags above it) of the flags of the cells of the non-duplicated addresses or of the empty cells.

This procedure will guarantee that cells with unrepeated addresses are forwarded to the left, those with repeated addresses to the right of the trap network.

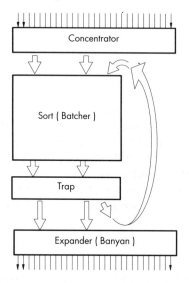

Fig. 4.39. – Starlite Switch Architecture

Since there exists a large probability that all entries of the switch will not have active cells present simultaneously, an additional concentration stage is added to the Starlite structure via a concentrator network. This concentrator allows a reduction of the size of the sorting network. The concentrator must perform the inverse operation of the expander network, and is thus implemented as an inverse routing (Banyan) network. The routing in this concentrator network is based on the running sum of the activity bit (ACT). This bit indicates which cell is empty or "active". This means that the empty cells will be directed to non-connected outlets, and can thus easily be dropped. Non-empty cells will arrive with a very high probability at a connected input to the sorting network. Active cells arriving at a non-connected output of the concentrator will be dropped. This will however happen with a very low probability (see also the Knockout switch).

The recycled cells of the trap network are fed in again at the sorting network inputs which are idle. Since it may occur that more cells will be recycled than there are free input ports, it is required to provide a buffering stage before the recycled inputs. Recycled cells may be recycled again if another cell is destined for the same address. To avoid out-of-sequence problems, "aged" cells (i.e. recirculated cells) get priority in the sorting network over the non-recirculated cells.

The Starlite switch also allows a multicast functionality by adding 2 additional networks, as is shown in Fig. 4.40. The sort-to-copy network gets at its inputs original source cells and empty copy cells generated by a special entity.

These empty copy cells may be used internally to produce copies of the cells requesting multicast. A special bit in the header is defined to differentiate normal cells from "copy" cells. Normal filled cells have a source and destination address in the header.

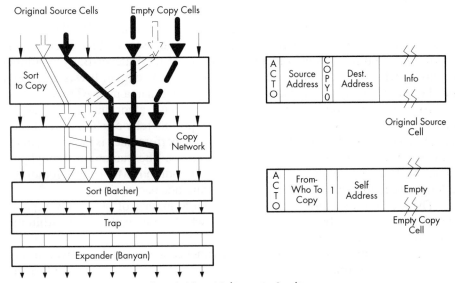

Fig. 4.40. – Multicast in Starlite

Empty cells have a format very comparable to the original filled cells (Fig. 4.40.). Empty copy cells can be produced at the inlets of the fabric, where they receive a destination address (Self-Address) for each intended recipient. The source address field of the empty copy cell contains the address of the source generating the cells which have to be copied (From Who To Copy).

Both the empty cells and source cells are input to the modified switch. The "sort-to-copy" network uses the source address of each incoming cell, together with its copy bit, as the least significant bit, to order the cells such that their source addresses increase from left to right. This operation groups "copy cells" together with their appropriate broadcast source cell on physically adjacent lines. Moving left to right at this sorter's output, each source cell will be followed by the number of copy cells that share the same source address.

The next stage in the broadcast switch is a "copy network" which takes the information in the data field of each broadcast source cell and copies it into the empty data field of all blank cells to the right until another source cell is encountered. This routing is accomplished using the "copy bit" in each header. The final stages of the modified network are the sort and expander stages of the original network. These route both original source cells and filled copy cells to their destination addresses.

The approach of the Starlite switch lends itself very well to VLSI implementation, because of its regular structure. A Starlite prototype has been built by ATT. Later on, the Starlite approach was also applied to an optical implementation (Huang, 1986).

Moonshine

This switching fabric architecture, also based on the sort-routing (Batcher-Banyan) concept, was initially proposed by Hui in 1987. It uses another principle than Starlite to avoid the output contention problem of the Batcher-Banyan solution, occurring when multiple cells are destined to the same output. It was designed to handle variable length packets, so it is more general than a pure ATM switch.

To resolve the output port conflict, a 3-phase algorithm is proposed in combination with input queuing at each input port thereby causing HOL (head of line) blocking. The effect of HOL blocking on the performance is rather negative as was shown in the section on performance (4.3.2.). The maximum throughput is about 58 % as for input queuing systems. In addition, Moonshine requires an internal speedup to perform the 3 phases during one packet time.

The problem of conflicting requests from a number of physically separated input ports is resolved by 3 phases which are called the arbitration, acknowledgement and sending phase.

In the arbitration phase, it is checked whether contending cells are waiting at the input. This is performed by sending special "messages" called requests. Once these contending requests are sorted out and the winning requests selected, the waiting cells must be informed. This function is performed in the acknowledgement phase. Finally, the winning input ports will send their cells in the sending phase.

To arrange the arbitration of the conflicts, an interconnection network on its own is required. The sorting network can bring the conflicting requests adjacent to each other by sorting the requests (Fig. 4.41a.). A request can then decide that it can continue (no contention at the output), if the request above it in the sorted order is not making the same request. This means that in Phase I (arbitration phase) of the algorithm, each input port i will send a trial, i.e. a short request packet, which only contains the source-destination address pair (i, j_i).

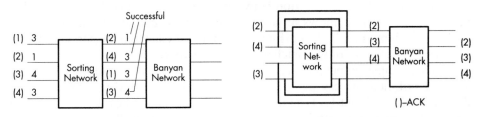

Phase I : Send and Resolve Request
- Send source-destination pair through sorting network
- Sort destination in non-decreasing order
- Purge adjacent requests with same destination

Phase II : Acknowledge Winning Port
- Send ACK with destination to port winning contention
- Route ACK through Batchers-Banyan Network

(a)   (b)

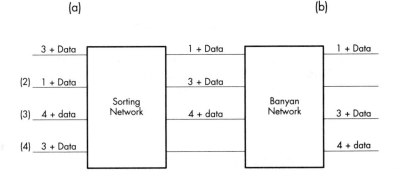

Phase III : Send Packet
- Acknowledged Ports Send Packet through Batcher-Banyan Network
- Buffers at Port Controller

(c)

Fig. 4.41. – Moonshine 3-Phase Algorithm

The sorting (Batcher) network sorts the request in a non-decreasing order according to the destination address j_i of the packet. The request can only be granted if j_i is different from the destination value above it in the sorted list of destination addresses. In the example shown, packets with source address 2, 4 and 3 are successful, i.e. arrive at output 1, 2 and 4 of the Batcher network. The packet from input 1 destined to output 3 is unsuccessful, since another packet (from input 4) is also destined to output port 3. After the sorting network, those 2 conflicting packets are on an adjacent outlet of the Batcher network.

Now, the input ports must be informed about the positive or negative result of the arbitration. This is achieved during Phase II (acknowledgement phase). The request packets (i, j_i) which won the arbitration phase must send an acknowledgement to input port i via an interconnection network.

Therefore, a fixed connection between output k and input k of the Batcher network (Fig. 4.41b.) allows an accepted packet to send an acknowledgement packet from input port k, the position of the request packet in the sorted order, to output (= input) port i of the Batcher-Banyan network.

In the example, output ports 1, 2 and 4 of the Batcher network inform input ports 1, 2 and 4 of their success and allow these input ports to send an ack packet with destination (2) on input 1, (4) on input 2 and (3) on input 4. These destinations 2, 3 and 4 will receive an ack packet, so that input 2, 3 and 4 know that they can proceed successfully.

During Phase III, the acknowledged input ports will send their information packets through the Batcher-Banyan network, without conflicts at the output. Input ports which were unsuccessful during the first phases, will store their information packet in a buffer at the input. During the next arbitration phase, the buffered packet will again try its chances.

Since Phase I and II do not perform real data transfer, but merely constitute overhead processing of the switch fabric, a speed-up is required. This speed-up depends on the number of stages of the switch fabric, and on the packet length but values around 14 % have been described by Hui. This means that for output speeds of 150 Mbit/s, the switch has to operate at around 170 Mbit/s.

4.5. CONCLUDING REMARKS

This Chapter has explained some basic principles of ATM switching systems. Since ATM is a typically statistical technique, queues must somewhere be provided in the switch, resulting in 3 large classes of switching systems : input queuing, output queuing and central queuing. Of each of those classes, some typical examples were described, with their respective possible implementation proposals and problems.

To build larger switches, interconnection networks (fabrics) are needed, with then some typical routing problems. Again, different classes were identified and some examples were explained in more detail.

Currently, different ATM switching systems are commercially available on the market, both for the private domain (ATM LAN) and for the public operators. These commercial systems are almost all based on the basic switching concepts described in this Chapter, often combining features of different described architectures.

However, when looking at these architectures, one can conclude that they all try to achieve one main characteristic as much as possible : share the internal resources to its maximum to achieve a minimal cost (queues and links).

On switching element level, the most important resources are the internal queues. Thus, sharing means opting for central queuing, as is done by most commercial ATM switching elements.

On switching fabric level, the most important resources are the internal links. So, on switching fabric level, sharing means selecting a solution where the internal links can be shared either by using multiple paths, or by using an internal link rate much higher than the external link rate, thereby multiplexing traffic from multiple external links to less internal links.

However, neither for the basic switching element, nor the switching fabric, all existing systems described in the literature were discussed in this Chapter. I therefore refer to the attached bibliography.

4.6. BIBLIOGRAPHY

Agrawal D., "Graph theoretical analysis and design of multistage interconnection networks", IEEE Transactions on Computers, Vol. 32, No. 7, July 1983

Ahmadi H., Denzel W., "A survey of modern high-performance switching techniques", IEEE Journal on Selected Areas in Communications, Vol. 7, No. 7, September 1989

Ahmadi H., Denzel W., Murphy C., Port E., "A high-performance switch fabric for integrated circuit and packet switching", Infocom '88, New Orleans, March 1988

Anido G.J., Seeto A.W., "Multi-path routing techniques for a class of multistage fast packet switches", IZS '88, Zurich, March 1988

Arakawa N., Noiri A., Inoue H., "ATM switch for multi-media switching system", ISS '90, Stockholm, June 1990

Arango M., Badr H., Gelernter D., "Staged circuit switching", IEEE Transactions on Computers, Vol. 34, No. 2, February 1985

Balboni G., Bellman A., Collivignarelli M., "Key issues in designing a flexible ATM switch", ISS '92, Yokohama, October 1992

Banniza T.R., Eilenberger G.J., Pauwels B., Therasse Y., "Design and Technology aspects of VLSI's for ATM switches", IEEE JSAC, Vol. 9, No. 8, October 1991, pp. 1255

Banwell T.C., Estes R.C., Habiby S.F., Hayward G.A., Helstern T.K., Lalk G.R., Mahoney D.D., Wilson D.K., Yound K.C. Jr., "Physical design issues for very large ATM switching systems", IEEE JSAC, Vol. 9, No. 8, October 1991, pp. 1227

Barnaby C., Richards N., "A generic architecture for private ATM systems", ISS '92, Yokohama, October 1992

Barri P., "A switching element for Asynchronous Transfer Mode", Fifth International Workshop on Integrated Electronics and Photonics in Communications, North Carolina, October 1987

Barri P., Boettle D., "Implementation aspects of ATM switching element topologies", ITS '88, Taipei (Taiwan), September 1988

Bauwens J., Van Landegem Th., "Architecture of the Local Exchange in the Belgian Broadband Experiment", Revue HF, Vol. 5+6, November 1989

Bernabei F., Listanti M., "A hybrid switching exchange for broadband communications", ICCC '88, Tel Aviv, October 1988

Bhuyan L.N., Agrawal D.P., "Design and performance of generalized interconnection networks", IEEE Transactions on Computers, Vol. 32, No. 12, December 1983

Bhuyan L.N., Yang Q., Agrawal D.P., "Performance of multiprocessor interconnection networks", IEEE Computer, Vol. 22, No. 2, February 1989

Birdsall T.G., Ristenbatt M.P., Weinstein S.B., "Analysis of Asynchronous Time Multiplexing of Speech Sources", IRE Transactions on Communications Systems, December 1962

Bonatti M., Fratta L., Tomasi C., "A call set-up architecture for very large switching systems", Globecom '86, Houston, December 1986

Bruneel H., Kun G., "Discrete Time modelling for communication systems including ATM", Kluwer Academie Publishers, Boston, 1993

Bubenik R., Turner J., "Performance of a broadcast packet switch", IEEE Transactions on Communications, Vol. 37, No. 1, January 1989

Bussey H.E., Porter F.D., "A second generation prototype for broadband integrated access and packet switching", Globecom '88, Hollywood, November 1988

Chao H.J., "A recursive modular terabit/second ATM switch", IEEE JSAC, Vol. 9, No. 8, October 1991, pp. 1161

Chas Alonso P.L., Herrera Galvez J., Alonso Hernan A., "On the use of priorities in ATM switching structures", ICC '89, Boston, June 1989

Chen P., Lawrie D.H., Yew P.C., Padua D.A., "Interconnection networks using shuffles", IEEE Computer, Vol. 14, No. 12, December 1981

Chin C., Hwang K., "Packet switching networks for multiprocessors and data flow computers", IEEE Transactions on Computers, Vol. 33, No. 11, November 1984

Chu W.W., "Buffer behaviour for poisson arrivals and multiple synchronous constant outputs", IEEE Transaction on Computers, Vol. 19, No. 6, June 1970

Cidon I., Gopal I., Grover G., "Memory requirements for a fast packet switching node", ICCC '88, Tel Aviv, October 1988

Cisneros A., Brackett C.A., "A large ATM switch based on memory switches and optical star couplers", IEEE JSAC, Vol. 9, No. 8, October 1991, pp. 1348

Coudreuse J.P., "Les réseaux temporels asynchrones : du transfert de données à l'image animée", L'Echo des Recherches, No. 112, 2e trimestre 1983

Coudreuse J.P., Servel M., "Prelude : an asynchronous time-division switched network", ICC '87, Seattle, June 1987

Daddis G.E., Torng H.C., "A Taxonomy of Broadband Integrated Switching Architectures", IEEE Communications Magazine, May 1989

Decina M., Masetti F., Pattavina A. *et al.*, "Shuffleout architectures for ATM switching", ISS '92, Yokohama, October 1992

Denissen F., Desmet E., Petit G.H., "The Policing Function in an ATM Network", IZS '90, Zurich, March 1990

Denzel W.E., Engbersen A.P.J., Iliadis I., "A highly modular packet switch for GB/S rates", ISS '92, Yokohama, October 1992

De Prycker M., Bauwens J., "A Switching Exchange for an Asynchronous Time Division based Network", ICC '87, Seattle, June 1987

De Prycker M., Bauwens J., "A Broadband Central Office for ATM", International Journal of Digital and Analog Cabled System, May 1988

De Prycker M., De Somer M., "Performance of a service independent switching network with distributed control", IEEE Journal on Selected Areas in Communications, Vol. 5, No. 8, October 1987

De Prycker M., De Somer M., "An ATD broadband switching exchange with distributed control", CEPT Seminar on BISDN, Albufeira (Portugal), January 1987

De Prycker M., De Somer M., Watteyne M., Vandedrinck J., Van Vyve J. Van Laethem M., "An ATM Switching Architecture with Intrinsic Multicast Capabilities for the Belgian Broadband Experiment", ISS '90, Stockholm, May 1990

De Somer M., "Building a mathematical model describing the behaviour of a variable bitrate switching network", ITC Seminar, Brussels, May 1986

Dias D.M., Jump J.R., "Packet switching interconnection networks for modular systems", IEEE Computer, Vol. 14, No. 12, December 1981

Dias D.M., Kumar M., "Packet Switching in N log N multistage networks", Globecom '84, Atlanta, November 1984

Dieudonne M., Quinquis M., "Switching techniques for asynchronous time division multiplexing (or fast packet switching)", ISS '87, Phoenix, March 1987

Doi Y., Endo K., Yamada H., "A very high-speed ATM switch with input and output buffers", ISS '92, Yokohama, October 1992

Dor N.M., "Guide to the length of Buffer Storage Required for Random (Poisson) Input and Constant Output rates", IEEE Transactions on Electronic Computers, October 1967

Doty K.W., "New designs for dense processor interconnection networks", IEEE Transactions on Computers, Vol. 33, No. 5, May 1984

Eng K., Hluchyj M., Yeh Y., "Multicast and broadcast services in a Knockout packet switch", Infocom '88, New Orleans, March 1988

Eng K., Hluchyj M., Yeh Y., "A Knockout switch for variable-length packets", IEEE Journal on Selected Areas in Communications, Vol. 5, No. 9, December 1987

Eng K., Hluchyj M.G., Yeh Y.S., "A Knockout switch for variable-length packets", ICC '87, Seattle, June 1987

Eng K., Karol M., Yeh Y., "A growable packet (ATM) switch architecture : design principles and applications", Globecom '89, Dallas, November 1989

Eng K., Karol M., Chih-lin I., "A modular broadband (ATM) switch architecture with optimum performance", ISS '90, Stockholm, June 1990

Feng T., "A survey of interconnection networks", IEEE Computer, Vol. 14, No. 12, December 1981

Fischer W., Fundneider O., Goeldner E.H., Lutz K.A., "A scalable ATM switching system architecture", IEEE JSAC, Vol. 9, No. 8, October 1991, pp. 1299

Forcina A., Di Stefano T., Taormina E., "A multicast broadband switching module in a hybrid ATM environment", ICC '89, Boston, June 1989

Fundneider O., Skaperda N., "Universal ATM communication node – a realistic proposition ?", ISS '92, Yokohama, October 1992

Gabrielli L., Lotito N., Sposini M., "Performance analysis and system design of a variable bit rate hybrid switch", Forum Telecom '83, Geneva, October 1983

Gard I., Rooth J., "An ATM switching implementation - Technique and technology", ISS '90, Stockholm, June 1990

Garetti E., Melen R., Arnold J., Scozzari G., Gallassi G., Fox A., Fundneider G., Idner E., "An experimental ATM switching architecture for the evolving B-ISDN scenario", ISS '90, Stockholm, June 1990

Giacopelli J.N., Hickey J.J., Marcus W.S., Sincoskie W.D., Littewood M., "Sunshine : a high-performance self-routing broadband packet switch architecture", IEEE JSAC, Vol. 9, No. 8, October 1991, pp. 1289

Giorcelli S., Demichelis C., Giandonato G., Melen R., "Experimenting with fast packet switching techniques in first generation ISDN environment", ISS '87, Phoenix, March 1987

Glon J.P., Debuysscher P., Paul J.L., "An ATM switching unit architecture for B-ISDN", ISS '90, Stockholm, June 1990

Goke L., Lipovski G., "Banyan Networks for partitioning multiprocessor systems", 1st Internal Symposium on Computer Architectures, December 1972

Henrion M., Schrodi K., Boettle D., De Somer M., Dieudonne M., "Switching network architecture for ATM based broadband communications", ISS '90, Stockholm, June 1990

Henrion M.A., Eilenberger G.J., Petit G.H. *et al.*, "Technology, distributed control and performance of a multipath self-routing switch", ISS '92, Yokohama, October 1992

Hickey J.J., Bogovic T.J., Davie B.S. *et al.*, "The architecture of the sunshine broadband testbed", ISS '92, Yokohama, October 1992

Hirano M., Watanabe N., "Characteristics of a cell multiplexer for bursty ATM traffic", ICC '89, Boston, June 1989

Hluchyi M.G., Karol M.J., "Queuing in space division packet switching", Infocom '88, New Orleans, March 1988

Huang A., "The relationship between STARLITE, a wideband digital switch and optics", ICC '86, Toronto, June 1986

Huang A., Knauer S., "Starlite : a wideband digital switch", Globecom '84, Atlanta, November 1984

Huang N., "An integrated voice/data network architecture using virtual circuit switching", Globecom '85, New Orleans, December 1985

Huang N., Lea C., "Architecture of a time multiplexed switch", Globecom '86, Houston, November 1986

Huber M.N., Rathgeb E.P., Theimer T.H., "Self routing banyan networks in an ATM-environment", ICCC '88, Tel Aviv, October 1988

Hui J., "A broadband packet switch for multi-rate services", ICC '87, Seattle, June 1987

Hurley B.R., Seidl C.J.R., Sewell W.F., "A survey of dynamic routing methods for circuit-switched traffic", IEEE Communications Magazine, Vol. 25, No. 9, September 1987

Hwang F.K., "Control algorithms for rearrangeable Clos networks", IEEE Transactions on Communications, Vol. 31, No. 8, August 1983

Imagawa H., Urushidani S., Hagishima K., "A new self-routing switch driven with input-to-output address difference", Globecom '88, Hollywood, November 1988

Itoh A., "A fault-tolerant switching network for B-ISDN", IEEE JSAC, Vol. 9, No. 8, October 1991, pp. 1218

Itoh A., Takahashi W., Nagano H., Kurisaka M., Iwasaki S., "Practical implementation and packaging technologies for a large-scale ATM switching system", IEEE JSAC, Vol. 9, No. 8, October 1991, pp. 1280

Jajszczyk A., "A dynamic programming approach to optimization of switching networks composed of digital switching matrices", IEEE Transactions on Communications, Vol. 35, No. 12, December 1987

Jeno Y., "Performance analysis of a packet switch based on single-buffered banyan network", IEEE Journal on Selected Areas in Communications, Vol. 1, No. 6, December 1983

Joos P., Verbiest W., "A statistical bandwidth allocation and usage monitoring algorithm for ATM networks", ICC '89, Boston, June 1989

Kalmanek C.R., Morgan S.P., Restrick III R.C., "A high-performance queuing engine for ATM networks", ISS '92, Yokohama, October 1992

Karol M.J., Eng K.Y., Pashan R.A. *et al.*, "Hierarchical gigabit ATM switching : applications and performance", ISS '92, Yokohama, October 1992

Karol M.J., Hluchyj M.G., Morgan S.P., "Input versus output queuing in a space-division packet switch", IEEE Transactions on Communications, Vol. 35, No. 12, December 1987

Karol M., I Ching-Li, "Performance analysis of a growable architecture for broadband packet (ATM) switching", Globecom '89, Dallas, November 1989

Katevenis M., Sidiropoulos S., Courcoubetis C., "Weighted round-Robin cell multiplexing in a general-purpose ATM switch chip", IEEE JSAC, Vol. 9, No. 8, October 1991, pp. 1265

Kato Y., Shimoe T., Hajikano K., Murakami K., "Experimental broadband ATM switching system", Globecom '88, Hollywood, November 1988

Kermani P., Kleinrock L., "Virtual cut-through : a new computer communication switching technique", Computer Networks, Vol. 3, No. 4, September 1979

Killat U., "Asynchrone Zeitvielfachübermittlung fur Breitbandnetze", NTZ Bd.40 (Heft 8), 1987

Killat U., Kowalk W., Noll J., Keller H., Reumerman H., Ziegler U., "A versatile ATM switch concept", ISS '90, Stockholm, May 1990

Kim H.S., Bianchini R.P. Jr., "Omega network based modular multicast ATM switch", ISS '92, Yokohama, October 1992

Kim H.S., Leon-Garcia A., "Performance of buffered banyan networks under nonuniform traffic patterns", Infocom '88, New Orleans, March 1988

Kleinrock L., "queuing systems", John Wiley & Sons Publication, New York, 1975, Vol. 1

Koinuma T., Takahashi T., Yamada H., Hino S., Hirano M., "An ATM switching system based on a distributed control architecture", ISS '90, Stockholm, June 1990

Kozaki T., Endo N., Sakurai Y., Matsubara O., Mizukami M., Asano K.I., "32 x 32 shared buffer type ATM switch VLSI's for B-ISDN's", IEEE JSAC, Vol. 9, No. 8, October 1991, pp. 1239

Kraimeche B., Schwartz M., "Analysis of traffic access control strategies in integrated service networks", IEEE Transactions on Communications, Vol. 33, No. 10, October 1985

Kruskal C.P., Snir M., "The performance of multistage interconnection networks for multiprocessors", IEEE Transactions on Computers, Vol. 32, No. 12, December 1983

Kulzer J.J., Montgomery W.A., "Statistical Switching Architectures for Future Services", ISS '84, Florence, May 1984

Kuwahara H., Endo N., Ogino M., Kozaki T., "A shared buffer memory switch for an ATM exchange", ICC '89, Boston, June 1989

Lampe D., "Transfer delay deviation of packets in ATD switching matrices and its effect on dimensioning a depacketizer buffer", ICCC '88, Tel Aviv, October 1988

Lea C, "A high performance LAN internetwork design", Globecom '86 Houston, December 1986

Lea C.T., "A new broadcast switching network", IEEE Transactions on Communications, Vol. 36, No. 10, October 1988

Lee T.T., "Non-blocking copy networks for multicast packet switching", IZS '88, Zurich, March 1988

Lee T.T., Boorstyn R., Arthurs E., "The architecture of a multicast broadband packet switch", Infocom '88, New Orleans, March 1988

Liao K., Mason L.G., "An approximate performance model for a multislot integrated services system", IEEE Transactions on Communications, Vol. 37, No. 3, March 1989

Listanti M., Roveri A., "Switching structures for ATM", Computer Communications, Vol. 12, No. 6, December 1989

Ma J., Rahko K., "Architecture and implementation of a connectionless server for B-ISDN", ISS '92, Yokohama, October 1992

Masetti F., Raffaelli C., "System design and evaluation of ATM replicated banyan switches", ISS '92, Yokohama, October 1992

Matsunaga H., Uematsu H., "A 1.5 Gb/s 8 x 8 cross-connect switch using a time reservation algorithm", IEEE JSAC, Vol. 9, No. 8, October 1991, pp. 1308

McMillen R.J., "A survey of interconnection networks", Globecom '84, Atlanta, November 1984

Melen R., Garetti E., Perardi F., "Advanced switching techniques for future telecommunication services", ICC '86, Toronto, June 1986

Melen R., Turner J.S., "Non-blocking multirate networks", SIAM Journal on Computing, Vol. 18, No. 2, April 1989

Miyaho N., Hirano M., Takagi Y., *et al.*, "An ATM switching system architecture for first generation of broadband services", ISS '92, Yokohama, October 1992

Morita S., Katsuyama T., Ito K., Hayami H., "Elastic basket switching", International Journal of Digital and Analog Cabled Systems, Vol. 2, August 1988

Moth K., Pedersen L.A., "Time switching of gigabit/s Highways", ISS '87, Phoenix, March 1987

Newman P., "A Broad-band packet switch for multi-service communications", Infocom '88, New Orleans, March 1988

Nillson G., Westin T., "Integrated BISDN access connection", International Journal of Digital and Analog Cabled Systems, Vol. 2, January 1989

O'Reilly P., "Burst and fast packet switching : performance comparisons", Computer Networks and ISDN Systems, Vol. 13, No. 1, 1987

Ohnishi H., Morita N., Suzuki S., "ATM Ring Protocol and Performance", ICC '89, Boston, June 1989

Oie Y., Murata M., Kubota K., Miyahara H., "Effect of speedup in nonblocking packet switch", ICC '89, Boston, June 1989

Oshima K., Yamanaka H., Saito H., *et al.*, "A new ATM switch architecture based on STS-type shared buffering and its LSI implementation", ISS '92, Yokohama, October 1992

Padmanabhan K., Lawrie D.H., "A class of redundant path multistage interconnection networks", IEEE Transactions on Computers, Vol. 32, No. 12, December 1983

Padmanabhan K., Netravali A.N., "Dilated networks for photonic switching", IEEE Transactions on Communications, Vol. 35, No. 12, December 1987

Parker D.S., Raghavendra C.S., "The gamma network : a multiprocessor interconnection network with redundant paths", 9th Annual Symposium on Computer Architecture, Austin, April 1982

Patel J.H., "Performance of processor-memory interconnections for multiprocessors", IEEE Transactions on Computers, Vol. 30, No. 10, October 1981

Pattavina A., "Fairness in a broadband packet switch", ICC '89, Boston, June 1989

Pauwels B., Desmet E., Orlamünder H., "Application of the multipath self-routing switch in a combined STM/ATM crossconnect system", ISS '92, Yokohama, October 1992

Perruca G., Garetti E., Melen R., "Modular ATM switching for the evolution to broadband ISDN", ICC '89, Boston, June 1989

Perucca G., Belforte P., Garetti E., Perardi F., "Research on advanced switching techniques for the evolution to ISDN and broadband ISDN", IEEE Journal on Selected Areas in Communications, Vol. 5, No. 8, October 1987

Pradhan D.K., Kodandapani K.L., "A uniform representation of single and multistage interconnection networks used in SIMD machines", IEEE Transactions on Computers, Vol. 29, No. 9, September 1980

Rathgeb E., Theimer T., Huber M., "Buffering concepts for ATM switching networks", Globecom '88, Hollywood, November 1988

Richards G.W., Hwang F., "A two-stage rearrangeable broadcast switching network", IEEE Transactions on Communications, Vol. 33, No. 10, October 1985

Rothermel K., Seeger D., "Traffic studies of switching networks for asynchronous transfer mode (ATM)", ITC 12, Torino, June 1988

Sakita Y., Miyahara N., Saito K., Ohama M., "A study on exchange functions and cross-connect functions on communication network", ICC '89, Boston, June 1989

Sakurai Y., Ido N., Gohara S., Endo N., "Large scale ATM multi-stage switching network with shared buffer memory switches", ISS '90, Stockholm, June 1990

Salahi J., "Modeling the Performance of a Broadband Network using Various ATM Cell Formats", ICC '89, Boston, June 1989

Sato S., Aramaki T., Suzuki H., *et al.*, "Cell-distribution-routing architecture for ATM switching network – high-performance switching for bursty and/or multicast traffic, ISS '92, Yokohama, October 1992

Schrodi K.J., Pfeifer B., Delmas J.M., De Somer M., "Multicast handling in a self-routing switch architecture", ISS '92, Yokohama, October 1992

Schroeder M.D., Birrell A.D., Burrows M., Murray H., Needham R.M., Rodeheffer T.L., Satterthwaite E.H., Thacker C.P., "Autonet : a high-speed, self-reconfiguring Local Area Network using point-to-point links", IEEE JSAC, Vol. 9, No. 8, October 1991, pp. 1318

Servel M., Thomas A., "Réseaux de transfert en videocommunication - La commutation de paquets", L'Echo des Recherches, No. 115, 1984

Shimizu H., "A synchronously triggered packet loop for wideband and multiple services communications", Globecom '83, San Diego, November 1983

Shobotake Y., Motoyama M., Shobotake E., Kamitake T., Shimizu S., Noda M., Sakaue K., "A one-chip scalable 8 x 8 ATM switch LSI employing shared buffer architecture, IEEE JSAC, Vol. 9, No. 8, October 1991, pp. 1248

Shumate P.W., Berthold J.E., "Progress in switching technology for the emerging broadband network", ICCC '88, Tel Aviv, October 1988

Siegel H.J., "Interconnection networks for SIMD machines", IEEE Computer, Vol. 12, No. 6, June 1979

Siegel H.J., McMillen R.J., "The multistage cube : a versatile interconnection network", IEEE Computer, Vol. 14, No. 12, December 1981

Siegel H.J., Smith S.D., "Study of multistage SIMD interconnection networks", 5th Annual Symposium on Computer Architecture, Palo Alto, April 1978

Silberschatz A., Peterson J.L., "Operating system concepts", Addison-Wesley, 1988

Skillicorn D.B., "A taxonomy for computer architectures", IEEE Computer, Vol. 21, No. 11, November 1988

Stavrakakis I., "Efficient modeling of merging and splitting processes in large networking structures", IEEE JSAC, Vol. 9, No. 8, October 1991, pp. 1336

Stephens W.E., De Prycker M., Tobagi F.A., Yamaguchi T., "Large-scale ATM switching systems for B-ISDN, IEEE JSAC, Vol. 9, No. 8, October 1991, pp. 1157

Strauss P., Borrus A., "New fruit of hybrid circuit/packet switches promises network efficiency", Data Communications, October 1986

Suzuki H., Takeuchi T., Yamaguchi T., "Very high speed and high capacity packet switching for broadband ISDN", ICC '86, Toronto, June 1986

Takahashi A., Nishino T., Murakami K., Dunning S., "A broadband switching system for public network", ISS '90, Stockholm, June 1990

Takeuchi T., Yamaguchi T., "Synchronous composite packet switching for ISDN switching system architecture", ISS '84, Florence, May 1984

Takeuchi T., Yamaguchi T., "A new switching system architecture for ISDN environment - Synchronous, Composite Packet Switching", ICC '84, Amsterdam, May 1984

Tobagi F.A., Kwok T., Chiussi F.M., "Architecture, Performance, and Implementation of the Tandem Banyan Fast Packet Switch", IEEE JSAC, Vol. 9, No. 8, October 1991, pp. 1173

Turner J., "Design of a broadcast packet network", Infocom '86, Miami, April 1986

Turner J., "Design of a broadcast packet switching network", IEEE Transactions on Communications, Vol 36, No. 6, June 1988

Turner J.S., "Fluid flow loading analysis of packet switching networks" ITC 12, Torino, June 1988

Turner J.S., "New directions in communications (or which way to the information age ?)", IZS '86, Zurich, March 1986

Urushidani S., "Rerouting network : a high-performance self-routing switch for B-ISDN", IEEE JSAC, Vol. 9, No. 8, October 1991, pp. 1194

Urushidani S., Hino S., Yamasaki K. *et al.*, "A high-performance multicast switch for Broadband ISDN", ISS '92, Yokohama, October 1992

Vaidya A.K., Pashan M.A., "Technology advances in wideband packet switching", Globecom '88, Hollywood, November 1988

Varma A., "Rearrangeability of multistage shuffle/exchange networks", IEEE Transactions on Communications, Vol. 36, No. 10, October 1988

Verbiest W., De Somer M., Voeten B., "VBR Video Coding and ATM Switching : A Bell-RC lab experiment", Second International Workshop on Packet Video, Torino, September 1988

Wah B.W., "A comparative study of distributed resource sharing on multiprocessors", IEEE Transactions on Computers, Vol. 33, No. 8, August 1984

Wei S.X., Kumar V.P., "Performance analysis of a multiple shared memory module ATM switch", ISS '92, Yokohama, October 1992

Widjaja I., Leon-Garcia A., "Starburst : a flexible output-buffered ATM switch with $Nlog^2N$ complexity", ISS '92, Yokohama, October 1992

White P.E., Holcomb J.E., "Towards a next generation switching system", ISS '87, Phoenix, March 1987

Wilson D.K., "A new architecture for packaging wideband communication equipment using a 3-D, orthogonal edge-to-edge topology", Globecom '88, Hollywood, November 1988

Wu C., Feng T., "Routing techniques for a class of multistage interconnection networks", International Conference on Parallel Processing, Bellavie, August 1978

Wu L.T., Huang N.C., "Synchronous wideband network - an interoffice facility hubbing network", IZS '86, Zurich, March 1986

Wu L.T., Kerner M., "Emulating circuits in a broadband packet network", Globecom '88, Hollywood, November 1988

Wulleman R., Van Landegem T., "Comparison of ATM switching architectures", International Journal of Digital and Analog Cabled Systems, January 1990

Yamada H., Kataoka H., Sampei T., "High-speed digital switching technology using space-division-switch LSI's", IEEE Journal on Selected Areas in Communications, Vol. 4, No. 4, July 1986

Yang S.C., Silvester J.A., "A reconfigurable ATM switch fabric for fault tolerance and traffic balancing", IEEE JSAC, Vol. 9, No. 8, October 1991, pp. 1205

Yeh Y.S., Hluchyj M., Acampora A., "The Knockout switch : a simple, modular architecture for high-performance packet switching", IEEE Journal on Selected Areas in Communications, Vol. 5, No. 8, October 1987

Yeh Y.S., Hluchyj M.G., Acampora A., "The Knockout switch : a simple, modular architecture for high-performance packet switching", ISS '87, Phoenix, March 1987

Zhong W.D., Shimamoto S., Onozato Y., Kaniyil J., "A recursive copy network for a large multicast ATM switch", ISS '92, Yokohama, October 1992

5

Impact of ATM on Terminals and Services

5.1. INTRODUCTION

As was already described in the previous Chapters, ATM offers a maximal flexibility for an acceptable complexity. This flexibility is reflected in the network, with an optimal use of available resources and applicability to all kind of services. However, this flexibility is also visible to the services itself. For the services, and the terminals which offer these services, this flexibility is translated into an unlimited freedom with respect to the generated bit rate. Such a vast flexibility is applicable both in terms of the value of the bit rate (from a few bit/s up to 150 or 600 Mbit/s with any value in between) as in terms of the behavior in time (from constant to very fluctuating). In addition, the ATM network offers the possibility for the services and terminals to operate with a clock, which is independent of the network clock.

On the other hand, ATM networks introduce some problems which have to be solved in the terminals. These problems are the cell loss and the cell delay jitter. They must be taken into account in the terminals.

This Chapter will describe the opportunities offered by ATM networks to the terminals, such as variable bit rate (VBR) video coding and layered video coding, as well as the facility to work with network-independent clocks. I will also describe how problems caused by cell loss and cell delay jitter can be solved in the terminals. A very particular problem which may have impact on the network and the terminal is the source policing, i.e. the controlling of the bit rate behavior of the terminal according to the agreements made between terminal and network at call set-up. This source policing is required to guarantee the quality of service of the other connections. This police function must be provided as close as possible to the terminals. This function will be described in Chapter 7.

5.2. VARIABLE BIT RATE VIDEO CODING

When video signals are encoded in digital format using a simple PCM (Pulse Code Modulation) method, the resulting bit rate is fixed and simply the product of the sampling rate (preferably close to the Nyquist frequency) and the number of bits per sample. However, as soon as a compression algorithm is used, the resulting bit rate varies in time. This fluctuation in time is caused by 2 phenomena, namely the varying visual irrelevancy present in the video image and the variable amount of redundancy present in the PCM coded source signal. The video coding techniques used in today's video codecs or under study for future video coding methods are based on a combination of both phenomena.

The varying irrelevancy is caused by the imperfections of the human eye (visual perception), which is not able to perceive all details of an image. The most famous example which is using the reduced perception characteristics of an eye, is that of the normal TV. Here only 25 (in Europe) or 30 (in USA and Japan) pictures are transmitted and displayed per second, even when most of the pictures are changing more than 25/30 times per second. No annoying degradation in quality is perceived, because the eye is not capable of perceiving more rapid changes.

The varying redundancy is caused by the video compression techniques used to compress the required digital bit stream, without losing any information. The following coding techniques contribute to these fluctuations of the bit rate in time :

- The spatial correlation within a picture, between adjacent pixels is normally relatively high. This means that there exists a large probability that the adjacent pixel has the same or almost the same chrominance and luminance levels. The intrafield video coding technique makes with large benefit use of this spatial redundancy.
- The temporal relation between consecutive fields of a picture is also quite high. The probability that a pixel in a frame is the same or almost the same as the corresponding pixel in the previous frame is very high. The interframe coding technique relies on this time relation to reduce the bit rate of the coded signal.
- If a part of a picture is moving, consecutive fields contain redundant information, however at different places in the fields. This redundancy can successfully be exploited by a coding technique based on motion compensation, where one tries to predict the movement of the object. Wrong predictions are corrected by compensating for the errors.
- Also other coding techniques such as transform coding (e.g. FFT : Fast Fourier Transform or DCT Discrete Cosine Transform) may result in a fluctuating bit rate in time.
- To finally encode the obtained picture information, a sort of Huffman coding (variable length coding) can be used by using a minimal number of bits for signals with the highest probability versus a large number of bits for very unlikely signals.

The coding techniques which are under investigation for the future ATM based BISDN are the ones previously described. It is very likely that the adopted solution for the future codecs will be based on a combination of some of these described techniques. The bit rate generated by the future video codec will thus fluctuate in time or will be different for different qualities of video images like in MPEG (Moving Pictures Expert Group) I, II, III.

In 1987, Verbiest (Verbiest, 1987) measured these fluctuations on an experimental video codec. These results are shown in Fig. 5.1., where we see the bit rate (in Mbit/s) of a typical video sequence. The bit rate in Mbit/s is averaged over a complete frame, with a repetition frequency of 25 per second. The coding is based on interframe/intrafield video coding. We see that during time, peaks as high as 28 Mbit/s and as low as 8 Mbit/s were measured.

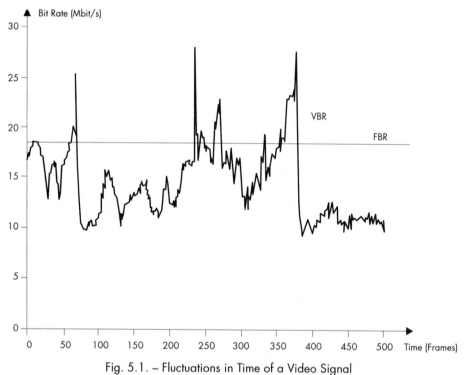

Fig. 5.1. – Fluctuations in Time of a Video Signal

In the classical STM networks, this fluctuating information rate must be converted into a fixed bit rate (FBR) namely the rate at which this STM network is operating. For instance, 64 kbit/s or 2 Mbit/s in NISDN, or 139.264 kbit/s in the STM broadband experiment described in section 2.4.2. This bit rate equalization can be realized by an output buffer between the encoder and the network and a feedback signal between encoder and buffer (Fig. 5.2a.). The buffer produces at its output the fixed bit rate as is required by the network, by smoothing the variable bit rate generated by the encoder. To ensure that the output buffer is not overflowing or underflowing, a feedback signal is required to the encoder. If the output buffer is reaching an "almost full" threshold, the encoder is informed and urged to produce less information (e.g. by reducing the number of bits per pixel). The visible result will be a reduction in quality. If the output buffer is reaching an "almost empty" threshold, the encoder is urged to generate more information. If no useful information is present, redundant (dummy) information is transferred. In the "almost full" case the quality is reduced, which is at the detriment of the acceptance of the service quality. In the "almost empty" case, there are more bits generated than needed for the specified quality. So the cost of transferring the information is more than what is actually required.

In ATM networks, the limitation of working at a constant bit rate disappears, so the output buffer is basically no longer required at the output of the encoder. (Fig. 5.2b.). The output of the encoder can directly be fed into the ATM network, resulting in a variable bit rate (VBR) video encoder.

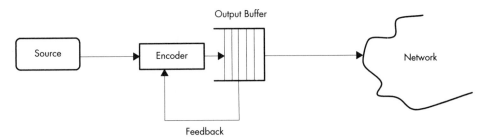

Fig. 5.2a. – Fixed Bit Rate Coding (FBR)

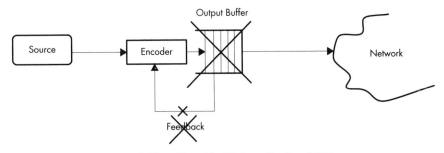

Fig. 5.2b. – Variable Bit Rate Coding (VBR)

The 2 main parameters to be compared between VBR and FBR coding are the bit rate and the quality of the image (or the inverse of the quality, namely the distortion). For every video coding algorithm, a trade-off must be made between the bit rate and the quality/distortion. The higher the bit rate, the better the quality, i.e. the smaller the distortion. This is shown in Fig. 5.3. If the complexity of the picture is increasing (because of larger temporal or spatial detail), the bit rate is increasing for the same value of the distortion.

In a FBR coding scheme, the bit rate is determined by the rate allowed by the network (e.g. 2 Mbit/s). It is thus very well possible that for some scenes the distortion is too high, resulting in a reduced or unacceptable quality, whereas for other scenes the distortion is smaller than required so the transmitted bit rate and the related cost is too high.

For a VBR coding scheme (Fig. 5.3.), the distortion can be determined by the quality requirements of that specific service. This means that the selected quality can be better for HDTV than for standard quality TV, and better than video telephony. The bit rate of this VBR codec will thus vary depending on the image complexity, thereby resulting in a constant quality at the minimal required bit rate. This will then be reflected in a minimal information transfer cost.

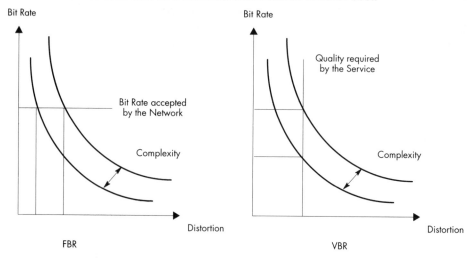

Fig. 5.3. – Bit Rate versus Distortion for VBR and FBR

The quality required and the images to be transmitted differ from service to service. For instance, standard TV images require more resolution than videophony and video conference, and also often contain much more movements (e.g. a rodeo on TV versus a person sitting still in front of the camera of a video conference). If we use the same video encoder/decoder to code pictures of these different services, we will have an identical rate distortion function (Fig. 5.3.) for all services. But for one service (e.g. HDTV) we will require a higher quality than for other services. This may result in different quality levels and different bit rates for different services.

Since the bit rate is fluctuating in time, we need a pdf (probability density function) to describe the behavior of a VBR video codec. Fig. 5.4. represents the pdf of the bit rate for 3 different services as described by Verbiest in 1989. Here, an identical codec was used for different service classes, but the quality and the coded images were adapted according to the specific service. With the applied coding algorithm, an average bit rate around 16 Mbit/s was required for Standard TV, whereas only about 5 Mbit/s on the average was required for video telephony and video conferencing. We see that the maximum bit rate required for video conference is around 14 Mbit/s. However, these values should only be considered as an example, since they depend very much on the coding algorithm used. Note that the experiment not only used different service quality levels but also different images to obtain its results.

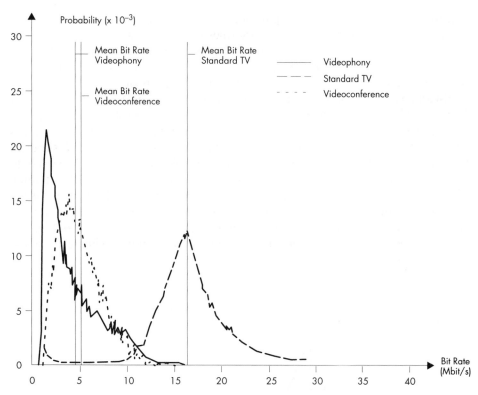

Fig. 5.4. – Bit Rate Probability Distribution Function for Various Sources

We may thus conclude this section with the following statement : ATM networks in cooperation with VBR codecs only transport useful (i.e. non-redundant) information and they offer inherently a selectable quality level.

5.3. STATISTICAL MULTIPLEXING

In an ATM network, several sources will be combined on a single link, e.g. a trunk line which may carry hundreds of videophone calls. In an STM network, or a network with FBR coding, the required bandwidth on that trunk will simply be the mathematical sum of all individual fixed bit rates. However, in an ATM network, we can gain on the efficiency by relying on the statistical multiplexing effect of sources, on the condition that enough sources are multiplexed and that they are not correlated.

This can be demonstrated with the following example where we assume that the video conference source generates a pdf as described in Fig. 5.4. This same pdf can also be expressed as a negative pdf as is shown in Fig. 5.5. In this diagram we show an n-fold convolution of the same pdf for n = 16, 32 and 64, assuming uncorrelated sources. Such an n-fold convolution describes the probability that n uncorrelated sources multiplexed on a single link surpass a certain bit rate. For each video connection the network will only allocate a certain bandwidth, determined by the acceptable cell loss rate. In Fig. 5.5. we see that the probability that the required bandwidth per source of the 16 uncorrelated sources is larger than 7 Mbit/s is lower than 10^{-9}. The network can thus accept 16 video connections (of virtually 7 Mbit/s) instead of 8 (of physically 14 Mbit/s), and still stay within the acceptable cell loss rate on that multiplexing link. So, if the network is dimensioned for a cell loss rate of 10^{-9}, and if the multiplexing factor is larger than 16, the network will be able to accept about double the number of connections compared to an FBR situation without the quality caused by excessive cell loss deteriorating. Indeed, in the case of an FBR codec the maximum bit rate must be allocated. In case of a larger link bit rate than in the example, an even higher multiplexing gain can be achieved. In Fig. 5.5. we see that less than 5 Mbit/s per source is required for a multiplexing factor of 64.

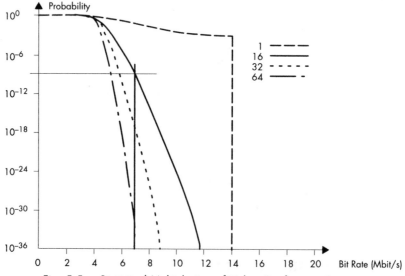

Fig. 5.5. – Statistical Multiplexing of Video Conference Sources

This statistical multiplexing gain can only be achieved if the network knows the pdf of the individual sources. This assumption is not always fulfilled, nor is it an easy job to calculate the convolution at every link where different sources are multiplexed.

So, therefore, a simpler method must be preferred, which allows the network to check at every new call request, by a call acceptance algorithm, whether enough resources are available on the paths in the network. This check is required to guarantee an acceptable quality of service for the new connection and also for all virtual connections already using that link(s).

A simpler method is based on the parameterization of the pdf. A good representation of the pdf is based on the first-order moments (to be calculated by the moment generating functions) of the pdf, such as average, variance, etc. The more moments used, the more accurate the representation of the pdf will be. However, in order not to complicate the call acceptance algorithm too much, not too many moments may be selected.

If we only take the first 2 order moments, i.e. the average and the variance, of the bit rate the moments of the convolution pdf can easily be calculated as follows :

$$Average\ (sum\ pdf)\quad = \quad \Sigma\ average\ (pdf) \tag{5.1.}$$

$$Variance\ (sum\ pdf)\quad = \quad \Sigma\ variance\ (pdf) \tag{5.2.}$$

It is interesting to have an idea of the complete pdf, and not only of the first order moments in the example of video sources. If the number of sources to be multiplexed is high enough, then the sum pdf will very closely resemble the Gaussian. However, an exact match will only be achieved if the number of simultaneous multiplexed connections becomes high (above 100 in the example). This is achievable if the trunk rates are operating at 622 Mbit/s or higher in the example, so that the allocated bit rate is around 5 Mbit/s per video connection, with a video conference quality. In Table 5.1. the resemblance between the Gaussian distribution and the measured convolution of video conference scenes is shown. It shows the difference of the distribution at a probability of 10^{-7}, for an identical average and variance for both distributions. We can see that the difference is still 8 % at 16 multiplexed video connections, but becomes very small (less than 1 %) at 128 connections. So, a very good approximation for the sum pdf is the Gaussian distribution, if only video sources are to be multiplexed. However, in case of other sources (bursty data, CBR services, ...) this approximation is not completely valid, and other methods have to be used.

Number of connections	16	32	64	128
μ (Mbit/s)	4.13	4.13	4.12	4.12
σ ((Mbit/s) **2)	0.130	0.067	0.034	0.017
Measured distribution (Mbit/s)	6.50	5.65	5.15	4.81
Gaussian distribution (Mbit/s)	5.93	5.42	5.04	4.77
Difference (%)	8.73	4.00	2.10	0.79

Table 5.1. – Comparison between Gaussian and Measured Distributions for a 10^{-7} Probability

The subject of statistical multiplexing and bandwidth allocation algorithms is still a research topic. Alternative solutions to the one described above are the use of higher moments which will result in an increased complexity, or the use of only a single parameter resulting in a smaller statistical multiplexing gain. More details on this subject can be found in Chapter 7.

5.4. SERVICE MULTIPLEXING

In the future BISDN network, the new services to be transported will almost all have more than one service component, each component transporting a specific type of information. They are called multimedia services. Table 5.2. represents a number of possible broadband services with the respective components as described in (David, 1990). There we see that simple telephony is composed of a single audio component (2 in each direction), whereas an High Definition TV (HDTV) is composed of 5 different service components. These components are :

- *Audio :* This component transports the audio signal. Different audio quality codings are possible with different bit rates, from the classical PCM (64 kbit/s) to the high quality HIFI sound generated by a CD player.

- *Standard video :* This component transfers the so-called standard video image. It can be a variable bit rate signal with an average value between 1.5 and 15 Mbit/s and a very high quality in case a distribution service is considered. For a video conference video telephony, the quality and image resolution may be lower, resulting in a lower bit rate (e.g. around 1 to 5 Mbit/s or even lower as in H.261 of CCITT).

- *High definition video overhead :* This component contains the additional information required by the HDTV set to compose, together with the standard video component, the HDTV signal. It contains both the higher quality information and the additional information for the different aspect ratio of an HDTV set.

- *Teletext :* This component transfers the teletext information related to a specific TV channel.

- *Data :* This component transports data information. In the case of video services (TV distribution) it is related to the program itself. Applications envisaged are subtitling, and transfer of information related to the type of program, etc. In the case of high speed data, it may be LAN-to-LAN data, or in case of video telephony it may be low speed user-to-user data.

Component / Service	Data	Teletext	Audio	Standard video	High definition video overhead
Telephony			X		
Video telephony	X		X	X	
Standard definition TV	X	X	X	X	
High definition TV (HDTV)	X	X	X	X	X
Video library	X		X	X	
High quality ratio	X		X		
High speed data	X				

Table 5.2. – Services and Components

In an ATM network all these individual components can be transported over individually separate virtual channels, identified by a different VCI/VPI in the header of the respective ATM cells. However, some restrictions must be taken into account between those different virtual channels, mainly with respect to the relative delay through the network. For instance, in order to guarantee good lip synchronization between the voice sound and the video image, for video telephony and video distribution the delay difference between audio and video components may not be larger than 100 ms. If no different transmission lines are taken over long distance, then ATM networks do not create any problems, as was demonstrated in section 2.4.5.2.

One can go even one step further in separating service components by possibly dividing a single information type (e.g. video) into several components, also called layers. These layers can then be adapted to the service quality and required error sensitivity.

Such a layered model is shown in Fig. 5.6., where we see some already described non-hierarchical components, such as HIFI sound, subtitling (i.e. data) ..., but also some hierarchical pure video components. The lowest layer in the hierarchy contains a very low resolution video image, possibly useful for security services. This layer also contains synchronization information required to synchronize the receiving TV set. A second layer is a medium resolution layer to be used by communication services like video telephony and video conference. A third layer is a high resolution layer required for broadcast TV quality. The upper layer is used for very high resolution and applicable for HDTV.

Every higher layer will use the information of the lower layers to construct the image of that layer with the required quality. For instance, the communication service requires both the medium and low resolution layer to construct the required image quality.

An important advantage of this layered approach is the compatibility between the different services and terminals. With this principle, it is for instance possible to watch a program which is transmitted as an HDTV signal (with 4 hierarchical components) on a standard quality digital TV set, by only considering the 3 lowest hierarchical layers. Or, it is possible to receive a TV program on a videophone set, of course only with the quality of the low and medium layer.

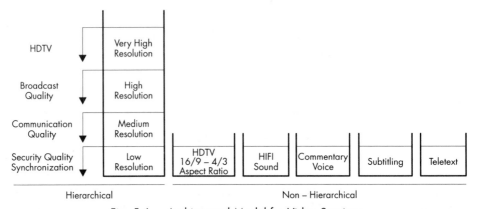

Fig. 5.6. – Architectural Model for Video Services

An additional advantage of this layered coding principle is its possibility to cope efficiently with cell loss caused by the ATM network. Table 5.3. describes the average time between consecutive bit errors/cell losses for different service bit rates. We see that for instance for a cell loss rate of 10^{-8}, the interval between 2 consecutive cell losses is 6.9 days for a 64 kbit/s service, but only 4.7 minutes for a 135 Mbit/s. If no special actions are taken in the terminals for a service of 135 Mbit/s (e.g. HDTV), the receiver will have on the average every 4.7 minutes a cell loss. This cell loss may cause parts of the image to be shown incorrectly or complete loss of picture synchronization. The layered approach offers an efficient answer to the problem of cell loss and bit error, based on the following 3 principles :

- If a cell is lost/corrupted of the high quality layer, the receiving terminal may still rely on information available in the lower layer(s), and thereby reduce the visible effects of the cell loss or bit error. On the higher layers, no forward error correction (FEC) scheme is thus required. This has 2 interesting consequences : any overhead relative to a high bit rate generates on itself a high bit rate so that the elimination of the FEC overhead eliminates the bit rate of the overhead; the implementation complexity of a FEC scheme is rather large, especially at high bit rates, and can thus be avoided.

* Since the lower layers operate at a lower bit rate, the average time interval between cell loss / bit errors is larger. This principle increases the quality by reducing the interval time between consecutive errors.
* The lower layers can more easily be protected by a FEC method against cell loss, because their bit rate is lower. So the implementation of this cell loss / bit error protection scheme requires less complex technology. In addition, the generated overhead bits to protect against errors are only required for this lower layer(s). So the overhead introduced by this error protection scheme is very limited.

Average bit rate		64 kbit/s	256kbit/s	1.5 Mbit/s	10 Mbit/s	45 Mbit/s	135 Mbit/s
Bit Error Rate	10^{-6}	16.0 sec	3.9 sec	0.7 sec	0.1 sec	22.0 ms	7.4 ms
	10^{-9}	4.3 hour	65.0 min	11.0 min	1.7 min	22.0 sec	7.4 sec
	10^{-12}	6.0 month	1.5 month	7.7 day	1.2 day	6.2 hour	2.1 hour
Cell Loss Rate	10^{-6}	1.7 hour	25.0 min	4.3 min	38.0 sec	8.5 sec	2.8 sec
	10^{-8}	6.9 day	1.7 day	7.1 hour	1.1 hour	14.0 min	4.7 min
	10^{-10}	1.9 year	5.8 month	1.0 month	4.4 day	1.0 day	7.9 hour

Table 5.3. – Average Time Interval between Consecutive Bit Errors and Cell Losses

The division of a video signal into several layers can be based on several techniques. One technique uses DCT (discrete cosine transform) coefficients. In this solution, the spatial domain of the image is DCT transformed into a frequency domain resulting in a 2 dimensional set of frequency components. The low frequency components can be used by the lower layers, since they contain less resolution, the high frequency components can be used by the higher layers.

Another approach is based on sub-band coding, where the original signal is passed via a series of 2 low pass and high pass filters : a low and high pass filter for the horizontal resolution, and a second set of low and high pass filters for the vertical resolution. This results in 4 different signals which can be considered as 4 layers of the video signal.

VBR video coding for the ATM network has already gained large interest throughout the world. However, there is not yet a world consensus on the coding algorithms neither on the concept to be taken (layered or not, fully compatible between all services or not, ...). CCITT SGXV has started in 1990 an expert group on this subject to resolve all the pending issues and come to a worldwide agreement on this subject. Coding algorithms defined by the MPEG (Motion Pictures Experts Group) of ISO are considered as very valuable candidates by this expert group.

bit rates considered are around 1.5 Mbit/s for VHS picture quality (MPEG I) and between 4 and 9 Mbit/s for distribution quality (MPEG II).

5.5. CELL LOSS PROTECTION

An important characteristic of an ATM network is the cell loss rate. A cell loss rate around 10^{-8} and 10^{-9} for an end-to-end virtual connection is feasible by using the switching systems described in Chapter 4. This value is acceptable for most services, but some services may have to take special actions because even this very low cell loss rate may degrade the quality offered to the specific application. For instance, the transfer of information (e.g. EFT electronic fund transfer) of banks requires a 100 % accuracy. Therefore, an end-to-end protection has to be provided in the transport layer of the OSI model, to guarantee a 100 % semantic transparency.

With respect to this semantic transparency 2 sorts of services can be defined. For each service a different approach can be taken with respect to the protection against cell loss.

- Services which have no real time contraints.
  These services are not bound by real time transmission of information and can accept a limited delay (e.g. a few hundred ms up to a second). Examples of these services are data transmission for some specific applications, such as transfer of CAD information to the screen where the user can accept a delay of some hundred ms. However, other data applications, such as distributed processing in computers are much more demanding on delay.

  These non-real time services can rely on the retransmission of missing or incorrect information. They can thus rely on the classical protocols of the type ARQ (automatic repeat request). However, for high speed data, the classical ARQ protocols may be too complicated to operate at high speed. Therefore, a reduced complexity protocol may be recommended, such as XTP (eXpress Transport Protocol) or a variant of it (Chesson, 1988).

- Services with real time contraints.
  These services, e.g. video, cannot rely on the retransmission of information because of a too high delay, but need some sort of forward error detection and/or forward error correction (FEC) method. Typical forward error detection methods are based on cell sequence numbering. By using a sequence number modulo N, this method is capable of detecting the loss of N–1 consecutive cells. Such a sequence numbering scheme is quite simple to implement, and for some services (e.g. voice) already enough to avoid any unacceptable (audible) errors caused by cell loss.

  Forward error correction techniques can be based on several principles. A BCH code per cell does not detect cell loss. So, the BCH code must be implemented over more than one cell. A straightforward implementation of a

BCH code over consecutive cells will require a large number of overhead bits, and a rather complex implementation. A simpler method can be based on a combination of bit/cell interleaving and BCH coding. The interleaving guarantees that the number of bits covered by a simple BCH code word is very limited, so that the BCH code itself must not cover too many bits and is thus not too complicated. An example is shown in Fig. 5.7., where we see that the information bits and the code for correction are transmitted in different cells. A disadvantage of this solution is the memory required to perform this two-dimensional conversion, especially for high bit rate services.

As already mentioned in the previous section, the layered video coding is also a valid tool to perform cell loss correction, by substituting the incorrect/missing bits by those of a lower resolution layer.

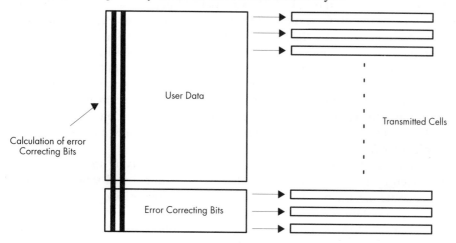

Fig. 5.7. – Two-Dimensional Error Correction Technique

5.6. SERVICE SYNCHRONIZATION

In ATM networks there is in general no need to synchronize the terminals/services to the network, thanks to the asynchronous nature of ATM. There is only a need to synchronize the receiving terminal to the sending terminal. The local clock at the terminal can be reconstructed using the incoming information stream. This allows the terminals to operate at a frequency/bit rate which is independent of the network clock. Different methods can be applied to reconstruct the clock at the receiver and to synchronize it to the transmitting source clock. This synchronization is required for certain so-called synchronous services, such as voice, video, NISDN, etc.

One method to reconstruct this local clock is by measuring the filling level of a cell buffer at the receiver (De Prycker, 1987). This method is shown in Fig. 5.8a., where we see a FIFO buffer which stores the incoming cells of the network, at the rate they arrive from the network.

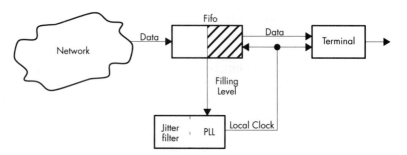

Fig. 5.8a. – Service Synchronization based on Buffer Filling Level

The data are delivered to the terminal at a rate generated by a local clock. This local clock is generated by a PLL (Phase Locked Loop), which is controlled by the filling level of the FIFO. If the FIFO tends to underflow, the PLL is slowed down, when it tends to overflow, the PLL is speeded up. To assure that when the first cells arrive, the FIFO is not underflowing, the FIFO must first be filled to a certain level before the terminal may start operating and receive date from the FIFO.

A problem which must be taken into account in this clock reconstruction method is the jitter on the network delay. This jitter causes a permanent probabilistic fluctuation in the filling level of the FIFO. This will cause a constant fluctuation in the clock generated by the PLL. This jitter on the PLL must be filtered out by a specific jitter filter.

Another method to reconstruct the local clock is by using special information transmitted by the source terminal. The source terminal will send a time stamp (sequence number), at regular times generated by its local clock. At the receiver, the incoming time stamps are detected (Fig. 5.8b.) and fed into a PLL which generates the local clock. The same problem as in the first solution with respect to the network delay jitter arises, with an identical solution.

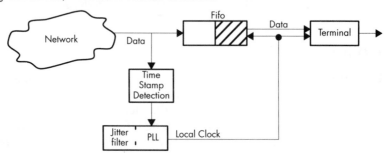

Fig. 5.8b. – Service Synchronization using Time Stamps

Since cells may be lost in the network, the clock may be start drifting due to this cell loss. Depending on the quality requirements of the local clock and on the cell loss rate, the cell losses may be acceptable. If not acceptable, then special precautions must be taken to ensure that cell loss is discovered at the receiver. In the solution with a time stamp, this cell loss is already inherently discovered at the time stamp detection block, so that the PLL can remain hidden of this problem. In the solution based on the filling level, cell loss detection must be provided.

This can simply be achieved by inserting a sequence number in the cells. If cell loss only happens in isolation (i.e. no consecutive cells are lost), only a single bit sequence number is required. If more consecutive cells may be lost, then the generated jitter on the clock will cause an effect which is less important than the effect caused by the loss of information of the cells itself. So, a single bit seems enough for the sequence number.

5.7. BIBLIOGRAPHY

Barberis G., "Buffer sizing of a packet-voice receiver", IEEE Transactions on Communication, Vol. 29, No. 2, February 1981

Barberis G., Calabrese M., Lambarelli L., Roffinella D., "Coding speech in packet switched networks : models and experiments", Globecom '83, San Diego, November 1983

Barberis G., Pazzaglia D., "Analysis and optimal design of a packet-voice receiver", IEEE Transactions on Communications, Vol. 28, No. 2, February 1980

Bhargava A., Hluchyj M.G., Humblet P., "Queueing analysis of continuous bit stream transport in packet networks", Globecom '89, Dallas, November 1989

Brainard R.C., Othmer J.H., "Television compression algorithms and transmission on packet networks", Visual Communication and Image Processing, Cambridge (USA), 1988

Buenning H., Kreutzer H.W., Schmidt F., "Subscriber stations in service integrated optical broadband communications systems", IEEE Transactions on Communications, Vol. 30, No. 9, September 1982

Chaillet B., Cabanel J.P., Sazbon D., "Towards a formal approach for baseband local area networks carrying integrated real time voice and data traffic", Proceedings of the IFIP W.G.6.4, University of Kent Workshop, September 1983, Canterbury

Chesson G., "XTP/PE overview", 13th Conference on Local Computer Networks, Minneapolis, October 1988

Chiariglione L., Guglielmo M., van Veen W.M.D., "A family of frame structures for local digital video distribution", Globecom '85, New Orleans, December 1985

Cho D.H., Un C.K., "Variable-rate ADM with efficient residual coding for packet voice transmission", ICC '86, Toronto, June 1986

Cochennec J.-Y., Adam P., Houdoin T., "Asynchronous time-division networks : terminal synchronization for video and sound signals", Globecom '85, New Orleans, December, 1985

Cole R., "Packet voice : when it makes sense", Speech Technology, Vol. 1, No. 3, September 1982

Darragh J.C., Baker R.L., "Fixed distortion, variable rate subband coding images", Visual Communication and Image Processing, Cambridge (USA), 1988 de Boiso A., Melindo F., Moncalvo A., Ricaldone P.G., "Wide-band interactive services experiment (WISE) : a first test of future video services", IEEE Journal on Selected Areas in Communications, Vol. 3, No. 6, November 1985

De Prycker M., "Functional description and analysis of a packet video transceiver", Second Esprit Technical Week, Brussels, September 1985

De Prycker M., "Functional description and analysis of a video transceiver for a broad site local wideband communication system", Esprit '85 : Status Report of Continuing Work, 1986, North-Holland

De Prycker M., Ryckebusch M., Barri P., "Terminal synchronization in asynchronous networks", ICC '87, Seattle, June 1987

De Prycker M., De Somer M., Verbiest W., "A service independent broadband network based on the Asynchronous Time Division", Revue HF, Vol.13, No. 8, 1986

De Prycker M., "Impact of data communication on ATM", ICC'89, Boston, June 1989

Douglas P., Karlsson G., Vetterli M., "Statistical analysis of the output rate of a subband video coder", Visual Communication and Image Processing, Cambridge (USA), November 1988

Gersho A., Ho Y., "A variable rate image coding scheme with vector quantization and clustering interpolation", Globecom '89, Dallas, November 1989

Goodman D.J., Sundberg C.-E., "Combined source and channel coding for variable-bit-rate speech transmission", The Bell System Technical Journal, Vol. 62, No. 7, September 1983

Gruber J.G., Le N.H., "Performance requirements for integrated voice/data networks", Globecom '83, San Diego, November 1983

Holtzman J.M., "The interaction between queueing and voice quality in variable bit rate packet voice systems", ITC 11, Kyoto, September 1985

Huang S., "Modelling and analysis for packet video", Globecom '89, Dallas, November 1989

Hughes D., Anido G., Bradlow H., "Characterising leaky bucket performance for small bucket depths", Australian Fast Packet Switching Workshop, Melbourne, July 1990

Iversen W.R., "Picture phones get a new image", Electronics, August 1985

Janakiraman N., Pagurek B., Neilson J.E., "Performance analysis of an integrated switch with fixed or variable frame rate and movable voice/data boundary", IEEE Transactions on Communications, Vol. 32, No. 1, January 1984

Joos P., Verbiest W., "A statistical bandwidth allocation and usage monitoring algorithm for ATM networks", ICC '89, Boston, June 1989

Judice C.N., Addeo E.J., Eiger M.I., Lemberg H.L., "Video on demand : a wideband service or myth ?", ICC '86, Toronto, June 1986

Judice C.N., LeGall D., "Telematic services and terminals : are we ready ?", IEEE Communications Magazine, Vol. 25, No. 7, July 1987

Kapauan A.A., Leung W.-H.F., Luderer G.W.R., Morgan M.J., Vaidya A.K., "Wideband packet access for workstations : integrated voice/data/image services on the Unix PC", Globecom '86, Houston, December 1986

Kishino F., Ohta N., Yasuda Y., "Packet video transmission through ATM networks", Globecom '89, Dallas, November 1989

Lee S.H., Wu L.T., "Variable rate video transport in broadband packet networks", Visual Communications and Image Processing, Cambridge (USA), 1988

Linnell J.S., Lehman H.R., "Customer-controlled DS3 video switch application", Globecom '85, New Orleans, December 1985

Lippman A., Bender W., "News and movies in the 50 Megabit living room", Globecom '87, Tokyo, November 1987

Listanti M., Villani F., "An X.25-compatible protocol for packet voice communications", Computer Communications, Vol. 6, No. 1, February 1983

Listanti M., Villani F., "Voice communication handling in X.25 packet switching networks", Globecom '83, San Diego, November 1983

Lundgren C.W., Venkatesan P.S., "Applications of video on fiber cable", IEEE Communications Magazine, Vol. 24, No. 5, May 1986

Maglaris B., Anastassiou D., Sen P., Karlsson G., Robbins J., "Performance analysis of statistical multiplexing for packet video sources", Globecom '87, Tokyo, November 1987

Maglaris B., Anastassiou D., Sen P., Karlsson G., Robbins G., "Performance models of statistical multiplexing in packet video communications", IEEE Transactions on Communications, Vol. 36, No. 7, July 1988

Majithia J.C., Li Sang-gi, "Buffer analysis of an integrated voice and data terminal", Computer Communications, Vol. 6, No. 4, August 1983

Manikopoulos C.N., Sun H., Hsu H., "Investigation of threshold dependence in adaptive vector quantization for image transmission in packet switched networks", Visual Communication and Image Processing, Cambridge (USA), November 1988

Maxemchuk N.F., Netravali A.N., "Voice and data on a CATV network" IEEE Journal on Selected Areas in Communications, Vol. 3, No. 2, March 1985

Mehmet-Ali M.K., Woodside C.M., "Optimal choice of packet size and reconstruction delay for a packet voice system", Globecom '83, San Diego, November 1983

Montgomery W.A., "Techniques for packet voice synchronization", IEEE Journal on Selected Areas in Communications, Vol. 1, No. 6, December 1983

Musser J.M., Liu T.T., Tredeau F.P., "Packet-voice performance on a CSMA-CD local area network", ISSLS '82, Toronto, September 1982

Nomura M., Suzuki J., Ohta N., Ono S., "Implementation of video codec with programmable parallel DSP", Globecom '89, Dallas, November 1989

Pauwels B., "A flexible customer premises network concept based on ATM principles", ISSLS '88, Boston, September 1988

Pauwels B., Bauwens J., "Customer Premises Network Topologies based on ATM principles", SPN Seminar CEPT-NA5, Nürnberg, November 1987

Pauwels B., De Prycker M., De Somer M., "Some aspects of network functions in an ATM based broadband CPN", SPN Seminar CEPT-NA5, Nürnberg, November 1987

Pearlman W.A., "Variable rate, adaptive transform tree coding of images", Visual Communication and Image Processing, Cambridge (USA), November 1988

Rathgeb E., Theimer T., "The policing function in ATM networks", ISS '90, Stockholm, June 1990

Rayala S.A., Lee W.M., "Segmentation-based image coding in a packet-switched network environment", Visual Communication and Image Processing, Cambridge (USA), November 1988

Sällberg K., Andersen I., Stavenow B., "A resource allocation framework in B-ISDN", ISS '90, Stockholm, June 1990

Sen P., Maglaris B., Riki N.E., Anastassiou D., "Models for packet switching of variable-bit-rate video sources", IEEE Journal on Selected Areas in Communications, Vol. 7, No.5, June 1989

Shimamura K., Hayashi Y., Kishino F., "Variable bit rate coding capable of compensating for packet loss", SPIE Visual Communication and Image Processing, Cambridge (USA), 1988

Stenger L., "Digital coding of TV signals for ISDN-B applications", IEEE Journal on Selected Areas in Communications, Vol. 4, No. 4, July 1986

Stern T.E., "A queueing analysis of packet voice", Globecom '83, San Diego, November 1983

Stuck B.W., "Imaging technologies : the next decade", IEEE Communications Magazine, Vol. 25, No. 7, July 1987

Suzuki T., Noguchi O., "Development of a standard TV video codec for ATM networks", ISS '92, Yokohama, October 1992

Van den Dool F., "Synchronization aspects of ATD-IBC networks", ISS '87, Phoenix, March 1987

Verbiest W., "Video coding in an ATD environment", Third International Conference on New Systems and Services in Telecommunications, Liege, November 1986

Verbiest W., "A Variable Bit Rate Video Codec", First International Packet Video Workshop, New York, May 1987

Verbiest W., "Variable Bit Rate Video Coding in an ATD Network", PCS '87, Stockholm, June 1987

Verbiest W., "The influence of Packetisation Defects on video coding", PCS '88, Torino, September 1988

Verbiest W., "The Impact of ATM networks on Video Coding", IEEE Colloquium on Packet Video, London, May 1989

Verbiest W., De Somer M., Voeten B., "VBR video coding and ATM switching : A Bell-RC lab experiment", Second International workshop on Packet video, Torino, September. 1988

Verbiest W., Duponcheel M., "Video Coding in an ATD environment", CEPT Seminar on BISDN, Albufeira (Portugal), January 1987

Verbiest W., Pinnoo L., "A Variable Bit Rate Video Codec for Asynchronous Transfer Mode Networks", IEEE Journal on Selected Areas in Communication, Vol. 7, No. 5, June 1989

Verbiest W., Pinnoo L., Voeten B., "Variable bit rate video coding in ATM networks", Visual Communications and Image Processing '88, Cambridge (USA), November 1988

Verbiest W., Pinnoo L., Voeten B., "Statistical multiplexing of variable bit rate video sources in Asynchronous Transfer Mode networks", Globecom '88, Hollywood, November 1988

Verbiest W., Pinnoo L., Voeten B., "The impact of the ATM concept on video coding", IEEE Journal on Selected Areas in Communications, Vol. 6, No. 9, December 1988

Verbiest W., Rousseau A., Heiss R., "Video Coding Family for STM and ATM networks", Electrical Communications, December 1988

Verbiest W., Voeten B., Elewaut L., "Definition of a universal ATM video coding architecture", Third International Workshop on Packet Video, Morristown, March 1990

Voeten B., Van der Putten F., Verbiest W., "Implementation of a full ATM video codec", Third International Workshop on Packet Video, Morristown, March 1990

Voeten B., Verbiest W., David J., "Integrating video codecs in ATM networks", ISS '90, Stockholm, June 1990

Wallmeier E., Worster T., "The spacing policer, an algorithm for efficient peak bit rate control in ATM networks", ISS '92, Yokohama, October 1992

Wu C.T., Dhadesugoor V.R., "An adaptive multiple access protocol for integrated voice/data local area networks", Globecom '83, San Diego, November 1983

Yamashita M., "Bandwidth reduction technology for video transmission – Intraframe and interframe codecs", JTR, January 1985

Yasuda H., Talami K., "Routing functional arrangements for a distributed switching system in B-ISDN", Globecom '89, Dallas, November 1989

Zdepski J., Joseph K., Raychaudhui D., "Packet transport of VBR interframe DCT compressed digital video on a CSMA/CD LAN", Globecom '89, Dallas, November 1989

6

ATM LAN, High Speed Local and Metropolitan Area Networks

6.1. INTRODUCTION

Local Area Networks (LANs) were introduced in the mid seventies for business environments to interconnect computers, terminals, printers, etc. Ethernet was one of the earliest introduced and standardized by the IEEE 802 committee (IEEE 802.3), and it still is the most successful, especially if success is expressed in number of LANs deployed. In the eighties, a number of alternative solutions also became available on the market, such as token bus (IEEE 802.4) and token ring (IEEE 802.5). The success and acceptance of these alternatives is largely determined by their standardization by IEEE 802. LANs are successful both in an office and also in a manufacturing environment, insofar that today more than one million LANs have been installed.

The capabilities of all these LANs are limited in distance and bit rate because a LAN is basically designed to interconnect data processing equipment (host computers, personal computers, plotters, servers, printers, ...) in one building, or on one floor. Its physical span is therefore limited to a few kilometers, and the data rate reaches up to typically 10 Mbit/s.

With this large base of installed LANs a new requirement is emerging : the need to interconnect these LANs in a limited regional area like a university campus or a large factory. Since multiple LANs will generate an interLAN traffic larger than that of a single LAN, the traffic requirement also goes up to tens and even hundreds of Mbit/s. Such a system, capable of connecting LANs over a limited distance with a large data rate is called a High Speed Local Area Network (HSLAN). In addition, high performance computers (e.g. powerful workstations, servers) may be linked directly to these HSLANs.

In another case, different large companies may require interconnectivity for information transfer at high speed amongst their LANs or supercomputers, again over a limited regional area (some tens of km) or a metropolitan area. Such a system, capable of connecting a number of LANs of different companies, often under control of a public operator, is called a MAN (Metropolitan Area Network). Typically the physical span of a MAN is larger than that of a HSLAN.

Contributing to the success of MANs is the dramatic improvement in the price and performance capabilities of silicon technology, optical components and optical fibers. In addition many other optical fiber advantages appear, such as high bandwidth, security, safety, immunity to electromagnetic interference and reduced weight and size.

On the other hand, the performance of the workstations and PCs is continuously increasing, and will continue to increase the coming years. More than 100 MIPS (Million Instructions Per Second) will be available on every workstation. In addition, workstations will not only be used to process and display data, but will become multimedia terminals integrating data, voice and video. The amount of information to be transported between these multimedia terminals and multimedia servers will require LANs with bit rates between 10 and 100 Mbit/s, with possibly hundreds of Mbit/s to the multimedia servers. The type of information is a combination of voice, video and data, thus needing a transfer mode capable of transporting and switching these different types of information. This need has resulted in the creation of the ATM Forum, which is specifying the interfaces for ATM LANs. These ATM LANs will initially be used to interconnect multiple LANs and to connect directly to powerful workstations and servers. More details on the introduction of ATM LANs can be found in section 8.2.

In this Chapter, I will first explain the definition and interfaces of an ATM LAN according to the work done in the ATM Forum. These ATM LANs are very suitable to transport all kinds of information, thanks to ATM. I will also explain existing systems, developed as HSLANs and MANs. These are an FDDI (Fiber Distributed Data Interface) ring, a DQDB bus and an Orwell ring. FDDI has been initially developed as a backbone of LANs, transporting only data. In order to answer the increasing demand for multimedia transport, the FDDI solution had to be updated to an FDDI-II. The DQDB bus has been defined as a MAN, with the requirements from the start to transport multimedia information. It is using ATM-like cells to transfer all information over the bus. Another cell/slotted solution is also described, called the Orwell ring.

6.2. ATM LAN

As was described earlier, the ATM Forum was founded in 1991 and has over 170 members from different types of industries : CPE (Customer Premises Equipment) vendors, computer vendors, public telecommunication operators, vendors of public telecommunication equipment, and others. The ATM Forum is a non-profit organization, with very active members meetings every month. The main objective of the ATM Forum is the definition of an ATM LAN, to be used as an High Speed LAN or backbone. It is expected that the Forum will speed up the eventual deployment of a worldwide BISDN network. Since the Forum joins users and product developers, it is expected to create better market awareness through user participation and interactions.

Such an ATM LAN will connect on one side directly to ATM multimedia terminals, i.e. workstations or servers with an ATM interface, through a private UNI (User Network Interface) and to the public ATM network through a public UNI, as shown in Fig. 6.1.

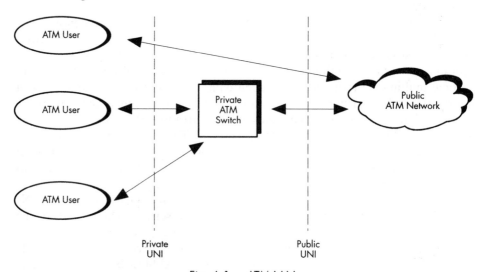

Fig. 6.1. – ATM LAN

As can be seen from Fig. 6.1., a simple star configuration has been selected, so that no MAC (Medium Access Control) protocol has to be defined, as was done in other HSLAN systems (FDDI, DQDB, Orwell). Multiplexing functions are performed inside the ATM system (black box), and need not be specified in a specification yet to be agreed by different equipment vendors. Every LAN vendor can select its own internal multiplexing/switching solution without affecting the external interfaces as specified by the ATM Forum. For more information on ATM switches, I refer to Chapter 4.

With this star architecture, only a point-to-point interface has to be defined, which helped the ATM Forum to align to the recommendations from CCITT (also point-to-point) as much as possible.

An ATM LAN can be used to cover a small geographical area or a large one, with a small number of terminals or a large number of terminals, just by dimensioning the size of the ATM LAN switch (in number of interfaces), and by using interfaces with short or long distances. As can be seen in Fig. 6.2., a larger campus network can also be built by interconnecting multiple smaller ATM switches (ATM LANs) together in a distributed manner.

Multimedia workstations will be connected directly to the ATM switches, as well as existing LANs (Ethernet, FDDI, ...). These LANs will provide connectivity to installed terminals and PCs. More details on a possible introduction scenario of ATM into the private environment will be given in Chapter 8.

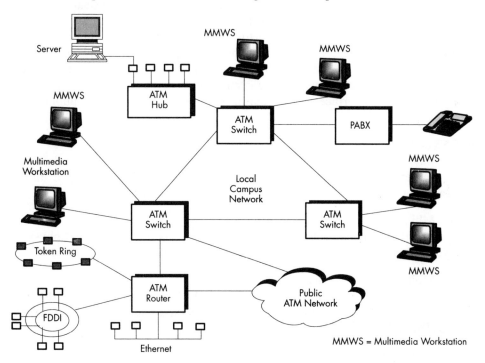

Fig. 6.2. – ATM Campus Network

Since beginning 1993, several ATM LAN products are already available and a large number of companies have announced the availability of ATM LANs during 1993 and 1994. These ATM LANs all have internally a proprietary switching and multiplexing solution, but are able to transfer ATM cells from inlet to outlet using a standardized interface (UNI). Interoperability is thus guaranteed between these ATM LANs, using a standardized UNI.

In addition, workstation and terminal vendors have developed plug-in boards, which provide their powerful workstations with a direct ATM UNI interface. Most of them even have plans to put the functionality, to offer an external ATM interface, directly on the motherboard of their workstations.

Finally, also router vendors have products (routers, hubs, bridges) with an ATM interface, providing connectivity amongst installed LANs, high speed ATM terminals and the ATM public network.

As was described in Chapter 3, the ATM Forum aims as much as possible at an alignment with worldwide standards agreed by CCITT and other standard bodies. The standards selected by the ATM Forum will briefly be recapitulated here. For more details, I refer to Chapter 3.

6.2.1. Physical layer

Currently, 4 physical layers are specified on the UNI. These physical layers are based on existing solutions (SDH, DS3). On the private UNI, multimode fiber has been selected, as well as monomode. However, a copper based solution using an unshielded twisted pair, is expected to become an important physical layer, since it can be used over existing installed wires and does not require optical devices which are still more expensive than copper transmission systems.

The following interfaces are standardized, either for the private or public UNI or both :

- DS3 at 44.736 Mbit/s
  The mapping in this interface is according to the PLCP (Physical Layer Convergence Protocol), protocol in which 12 ATM cells are mapped into a 125 µs frame. This interface is specified for the public UNI only.

- 100 Mbit/s using multimode fiber
  This interface, specified for the private UNI only, is using the FDDI physical layer with a 4B/5B line code. This results in a 125 Mbaud physical rate.

- 155 Mbit/s block coded using multimode fiber.
  This interface is again limited to the private UNI. It is using an 8B/10B line coding (194 Mbaud) with a special frame structure, using 1 OAM cell every 26 ATM cells.

- 155 Mbit/s SDH framing.
  This interface is used for both the private and public UNI. Currently, only an optical physical interface is specified. For the private UNI, a standard is also envisaged with 155 Mbit/s SDH framing, over twisted pair copper, (UTP : unshielded twisted pair) but with a very limited distance, e.g. up to 100 m. It has been shown in (Banwell, 1992) that 155 Mbit/s can be transported over copper pairs using multilevel coding.

6.2.2. AAL and signalling

For the AAL, it is proposed to use the AAL5, for the transportation of signalling. For user information, the AAL will depend on the type of information. AAL1/2 for voice/video services, AAL5 for the other services.

For the signalling, the Q.93B protocol, to be specified by end 1993 by CCITT, has been used as a starting point. This Q.93B protocol is a derivative of Q.931 which was standardized by CCITT for NISDN signalling. The modifications by CCITT take into account the fact that instead of negotiating on a B channel (as in Q.931), the negotiations now take place on a VCI/VPI and the related performance parameters. This is the major modification built into the Q.93B protocol compared with Q.931.

No features as mentioned in previous chapters, like multicast, or multicomponents are provided into this Q.93B protocol. To provide these features, CCITT is planning, what is called a Release 2/3 protocol in a later phase (by 1995 and later).

The ATM Forum has taken a somewhat different approach for the private UNI signalling, but has based its starting point on Q.93B. However, the point-to-multipoint option has been built into a modified Q.93B protocol. Also other traffic parameters are included in the protocol messages. It must be remarked that this solution is not the utmost point-to-multipoint capability, since only a new connection can be added to an already established connection. A more powerful signalling protocol with multicast capabilities can be found in (De Prycker, 1991), (Minzer, 1991).

Further enhancements to this private UNI protocol are envisaged in the 1993-1994 time frame. The following features will be provided by the signalling protocol in different releases.

- Connection types
  It is envisaged to support permanent connections via provisioning, as well as reserved and on demand connections.

- Connection topologies
  All potential topologies will be supported such as point-to-point, point-to-multipoint and multipoint-to-multipoint.

- Bandwidth symmetry
  In the point-to-point topology, unidirectional and bidirectional symmetric and asymmetric bandwidth is planned (Fig. 6.3a.). In the point-to-multipoint topology, the bandwidth will be unidirectionally asymmetric (Fig. 6.3b.). In the multipoint-to-point solution, the asymmetric solution described in Fig. 6.3c. is possible.

- Dynamic multipoint connections
  During the call, endpoints can dynamically be added or dropped from a connection in a multipoint call. In addition, the bandwidth of a call can be modified dynamically.

- Call/connection establishment
  A simple sequential call set-up, as well as a solution where a parallel set-up is performed, can be provided. In a simple sequential set-up, an endpoint is added later, after the initial establishment of a point-to-point connection. In the parallel solution, multiple endpoints can be connected simultaneously. It is also possible to execute the set-up function towards multiple destination as an atomic set-up, which is only successful if all destinations reply positively. It is also possible for a leaf to join an established connection.

  It is clear that a maximum commonality between the public and private UNI will guarantee terminal portability from public to private UNI and will reduce the interworking problems.

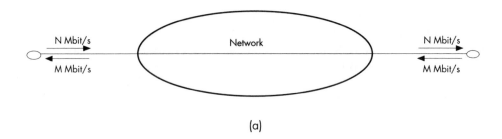

(a)

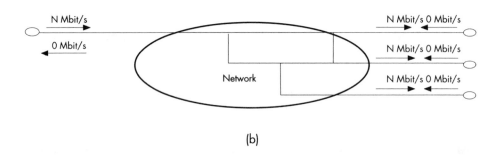

(b)

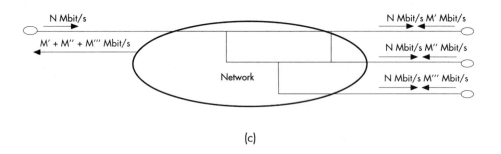

(c)

Fig. 6.3. –   Connection Types
(a) Point-to-Point
(b) Point-to Multipoint
(c) Multipoint-to-Point

6.2.3. Network management

For the network management, the major option taken is to use the SNMP (Simple Network Management Protocol) solution, coming from the TCP/IP protocol suite.

This solution, called the ILMI (Interim Local Management Interface) provides access to management data via the UNI. This management information is related to the connection status, and the configuration information. In addition, performance statistics can be provided by this protocol.

6.2.4. Quality of service parameters

The ATM Forum, again has taken over the parameters as defined by CCITT. These parameters will be explained more in detail in Chapter 7.

6.3. DEFINITION OF A MAN

A MAN is a network capable of providing high speed (more than 1 Mbit/s) switched end-to-end connectivity across distances typically ranging between 5 and 50 km (i.e. a metropolitan area). This allows a MAN to span an entire university campus, an entire city or an office park. In addition, a MAN allows the simultaneous carrying of different types of traffic such as data, voice and video. These characteristics make the MAN complementary to the definition of BISDN. It was described in the previous Chapters of this book that ATM is accepted as the solution for the future BISDN. So, it may be considered as a large advantage for a MAN of being compatible with ATM as defined by CCITT.

The two basic characteristics of a MAN (medium distance and large service range) make it different from currently used and installed LANs. These LANs are designed to span a few km (typically inside buildings) unlike the 50 km of MANs. A LAN interconnects hosts, file servers, workstation, personal computers, terminals and printers in an office or manufacturing environment, and therefore only transports computer data, whereas a MAN must be able to transport all kinds of services, including voice and video. In addition, the MAN will be able to interconnect LANs, but also directly high performance workstations, hosts, file servers, etc.

To interconnect all these different devices, one can use different topologies, such as a star, multistar, bus, ring, etc. The option chosen for the MAN is to use a shared medium with distributed switching and medium access control (MAC). This is different from the ATM LAN solution, where a star solution is preferred, since this requires only the standardization of transmission intelligence in a single box with centralized operations. A generic shared medium network, interconnecting different LANs and other devices, shown in Fig. 6.4. This depicts data devices as well as telephone sets connected to the network. In the figure a bus architecture is depicted for the MAN, but a MAN may take other topologies such as a ring, dual bus, dual ring, ... or a combination of these simple topologies.

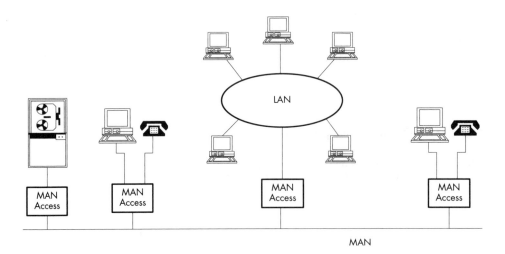

Fig. 6.4. – Generic MAN Shared Medium Network

The following alternative MAN solutions will be explained in this Chapter : DQDB, FDDI and Orwell.

MAN service capabilities

As mentioned earlier, the initial and main purpose of the MAN system is the LAN interconnection, but other services have been identified as well, the most important being host-to-host computer networking and voice and video communication.

For the LAN interconnection, a gateway/bridge has to be provided to connect the LAN to the MAN. Such a LAN gateway/bridge performs functions such as protocol conversion, address mapping, access control, ..., depending on the compatibility of the interconnected LANs. Since most LANs operate in a connectionless mode, it is appropriate that the MAN will also interconnect these LANs in a connectionless way. This means that no resources are allocated on the MAN. Resources will only be occupied if there is information to transmit. Another possible service capability of the MAN is host-to-host networking.

This networking may be supported by :

- Providing a semi-permanent point-to-point connection with high throughput and high reliability. This service is equivalent to a high speed private/leased line. In this case a connection is established at installation, and ensures that enough resources are available on the MAN. The mode of operation is thus connection oriented, with a semi-permanent assignment of resources.
- Offering a number of isochronous slots, requested on demand by signalling. This solution is more comparable to a circuit switched solution, where a TDM (Time Division Multiplexing) approach is taken. The time slots are allocated on

demand by a signalling procedure. This functionality may not be available on all MANs.

- Offering a number of non-isochronous slots. In this case, resources of the MAN are only occupied when information has to be transported, and information is transported in a connectionless way.

Voice and video communication may als be offered on the MAN. For these services, the 3 alternatives described above can be used, depending on the quality requirements. In case voice and video are offered either via solution 1 or 3, the jitter introduced by the MAN has to be removed at the receiving terminal, as was described in Chapter 2 on ATM.

In addition to these services, additional functionalities may be offered by the MAN, including broadcast and multicast, X.25 access, connection-oriented and connectionless bearer service, etc.

The need for such a MAN has been recognized, initially mainly in the United States and Australia. The interest in the US in MANs is largely influenced by a much larger installed base of LANs than in Europe. Due to the large success and interest in MANs in the US, different organizations in the US started working on it. Two important standardization organizations have worked on MAN standardization : ANSI, with the FDDI (Fiber Distributed Data Interface) proposal and IEEE 802.6 with the DQDB (Distributed Queue Dual Bus) proposal.

The FDDI was initially proposed as a high speed LAN, running at 100 Mbit/s, but with a span of up to 100 km. The initial requirements for FDDI were data services, but later other service requirements for isochronous services were taken into account, giving rise to a second generation called FDDI-II.

In IEEE 802, a special group was created to study and standardize a MAN for a wide variety of services, including data, voice and video. This group, IEEE 802.6, proposed a MAN mechanism based on the DQDB principle.

The basic principles of both the FDDI and the DQDB will be explained in detail in this Chapter. Enhancements for FDDI and DQDB will also briefly be explained. In Europe, an additional MAN mechanism called Orwell has been considered and developed by researchers of British Telecom. However, it has not been retained by a standards body. This proposal will also be explained in this Chapter.

6.4. MAN RELATION WITH BISDN AND ATM

The MANs which will be described in this Chapter are based upon a shared medium using distributed switching. This shared medium approach efficiently utilizes the available bandwidth, provides a mechanism for distributed access and supports broadcast and multicast services. However, due to its distributed approach, the functionality of a MAN is inferior to a centralized connection-oriented approach using ATM. For instance, since shared access is provided, special precautions have to be made to provide a high level of security and privacy to the different users.

In addition, flexibility is also somewhat more limited than a star topology, since the extension of bandwidth requirements of a single user may require the upgrade of the complete MAN system.

The physical limitations of a MAN prevent it from being used as a wide-area solution, so BISDN ATM systems must provide connectivity between different MANs. In addition, the capacity of a MAN is limited.

In an initial period the shared medium MAN solution will be able to support the traffic offered by the connected subscribers. However, on a longer term, limitations in the amount of supported traffic of the shared medium architecture will appear. In addition, islands of MANs, for instance located in different cities or countries, need to be interconnected. This will introduce the need of the MANs to interwork with the BISDN. In this case the ATM BISDN will act on a higher hierarchical level than the MAN.

The MAN limitations are shown in the following example. We use a traffic model of a powerful workstation, and extrapolate this into a 5 year time frame from now. We may expect the following workstation traffic characteristics (Clapp, 1988) :

- An average of 28 messages per second.
- 70 % of the messages are less than 1 kbit.
- 25 % of the messages are between 1 and 16 kbit.
- 5 % of the messages are between 10 kbit and 1 Mbit.

This model results in an average traffic of approximately 1.5 Mbit/s per workstation. Even a MAN operating at 100 Mbit/s and an acceptable occupancy level of 60 % only allows 80 workstations to be attached to the MAN, assuming that around 50 % of the workstations are simultaneously active.

In the future, it may be expected that in large offices, far more than 80 workstations will be connected to the MAN, resulting in too low a capacity of the MAN. So several MANs have to be provided, but again these MANs have to interwork. Here, the ATM BISDN comes into play. The BISDN can function as a higher hierarchical level of switching, interconnecting different MANs.

In Fig. 6.5. such a MAN interconnection is shown, where the BISDN performs all the functions expected from a network such as routing, call processing, network management, etc. Traffic destined to devices not attached to the MAN of the originating device, enters the BISDN and is routed to an outgoing link, connected to another MAN. Traffic between devices directly attached to the MAN normally does not enter the BISDN, although it may be seen by the BISDN for purposes of billing and network management.

The interconnection of these MANs over the ATM BISDN can be done on a semi-permanent basis, using Virtual Paths (VPI), transporting different Virtual Channels (VCI) between all MANs to be interconnected. This may result in a virtually meshed network (Tirtaatmadja, 1990). However, for connectionless data, instead of virtually linking all the MANs, one can also think of linking them to one or more servers, capable of serving connectionless data. A connectionless server based on SMDS (Switched Multimegabit Data Service) or CBDS (Connectionless Broadband Data Services) might be very appropriate (Hemrick, 1990), (Verbeeck, 1992).

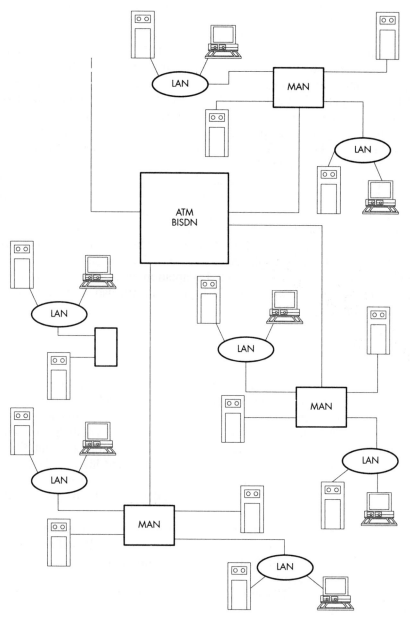

Fig. 6.5. – MAN to BISDN Connection

The traffic increase may continue until each device within the user's premises has its own direct connection to the BISDN via an ATM LAN. This then results in a full star topology with every subscriber directly connected to the ATM network, with the maximum functionalities in terms of traffic of a full BISDN. Moreover, the evolution described above has happened in a smooth way without rendering installed equipment obsolete.

Depending on the MAN technology used (DQDB, Orwell, FDDI, ...), the interworking between the MAN and the ATM BISDN will require more or less functionality. The specifications of the FDDI system by ANSI were already completed some years before the ATM standards were finished by CCITT. So, there is a large incompatibility between ATM and FDDI, requiring additional adaptation functions. For instance, the cell size of ATM and the FDDI packet size is completely incompatible, requiring a permanent segmentation and reassembly at the interworking unit. This can for instance be achieved by a Type 4 ATM adaptation layer as described in Chapter 3.

The specification work of DQDB and of Orwell ran more or less in parallel with the CCITT work on ATM. This parallelism allowed those MANs to be as much as possible in line with the ATM specifications of CCITT. However, for connectionless operation, some special precautions have to be taken due to the connection-oriented nature of the ATM principle. This may include functions such as the installation of semi-permanent connections, the provision of special message identification (MID) values in the ATM adaptation layer (see Chapter 3), or even the provision of very fast call set-up (De Prycker, 1989), also called fast reservation protocol in (Tranchier, 1992).

6.5. FDDI

In the early 1980s, the need was recognized to interconnect host computers at a very high speed. This high speed interconnection could not be achieved with the existing LANs, mainly due to their speed limitations. This gave rise to the development of FDDI, based on an original proposal of Sperry. In the process of its specification and development new demands and requirements were put forward, initially in the computer data world, such as LAN interconnection, and high performance data applications. Later on, other than data services were added; such as voice and video. These services were added in order to allow FDDI to satisfy the needs of diverse environments.

The first version of FDDI, currently available on the market, is only intended for data applications. An enhancement of FDDI, called FDDI-II will offer increased services by integrating isochronous services to the (as in FDDI) original pure packet oriented service approach.

FDDI is based on a double ring topology. This topology offers a number of advantages as mentioned by the FDDI promotors. These advantages are the following :

- Ring topologies impose no restrictive limitations on the length of the links, the number of stations or the total span of the MAN.
- Very high performance values can be obtained with ring topologies. Other performance advantages are the fair allocation possibility and the relative insensitivity to load unbalance.

In addition, a double ring can be designed such that even in case of failures, it continues operation, by proper reconfiguration. An example is given in Fig. 6.6., where 2 counter-rotating rings are shown. In case of a failure of the link, the 2 stations at the edge of the break have been reconfigured and allow the operation of the rings as a single ring. A comparable reconfiguration allows correct operation in case a node of the network fails. Another advantage of a ring is the fact that the links between the stations are point-to-point. This allows possible optimization of individual links of the same ring.

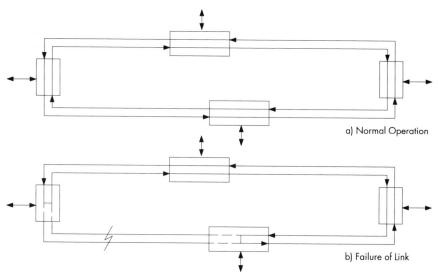

a) Normal Operation

b) Failure of Link

Fig. 6.6. – Reconfiguration of Counter Rotating Rings

6.5.1. Layered structure

Within the layered structure of OSI, IEEE 802 has defined a layered structure for the 2 lowest layers (physical and data link layer) of the OSI model. This relation is applicable for all LAN and MAN standards of IEEE 802. The relation between the 2 approaches is shown in Fig. 6.7. There we see that the OSI data link layer is divided in 2 sublayers : the logical link control protocol, which is independent of the topology, and the medium access mechanism. Different logical link control protocols are standardized by IEEE, in order to support connectionless or connection-oriented services (IEEE 802.2). The medium access control protocols are defined for different LANs, such as token ring (IEEE 802.5), token bus (IEEE 802.4) and Ethernet (IEEE 802.3). We also see that the physical layer is divided in 2 sublayers : the Physical (PHY) and Physical Medium Dependent (PMD) sublayer. In addition, a station management plane has been added.

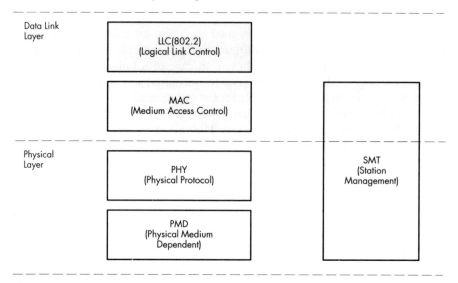

Fig. 6.7. – Relation Between IEEE 802 and OSI Model

Two alternative versions of the PMD are defined for FDDI depending on the medium : the basic PMD (multimode fiber) and the SMF-PMD (Single Mode Fiber). The physical layer specifies the bit rate and possible framing. The Medium Access Control (MAC) sublayer specifies the lower sublayer of the data link layer, and includes the access to the medium using the token passing principle and provides addressing, data checking and data framing. The LLC (Logical Link Control), as specified in IEEE 802.2, is independent of the LAN technology used. So, the different LLC protocols can be applied on the FDDI.

Physical medium dependent sublayer (PMD)

Two versions of the PMD are defined for FDDI. The first uses multimode fiber in the 1325 nm optical window, whereas light is generated by cheap LEDs. This solution has some limitations in terms of the distance, due to the selected options (LED, multimode) but allows the realization of a cheap solution. Connections between stations are realized with a dual fiber cable, one for each direction in normal operation.

The second version (SMF-PMD) uses single mode fiber and laser diode transmitters. This will allow the extension of the links between stations up to 100 km, but at a higher cost.

In principle, a combination of the 2 PMD solutions is possible between different nodes on a single FDDI ring. For instance, short distance links between nodes will be connected through the multimode solution, whereas long distance links may use the SMF-PMD.

Physical sublayer (PHY)

The physical layer specifies a data transmission rate of 100 Mbit/s, but since a 4B/5B code is used, a 125 Mbaud transmission rate is used over the PMD. Frames (this is the name used for packets at the MAC layer) are limited up to 4500 octets. This limitation is imposed by the possible accumulated jitter which in case of longer frames would cause clocking problems at the receiver. In case of errors, the network is capable of reconfiguring itself. Recovery timers are defined in the PHY layer and calculated for a maximum of 500 stations and 100 km (duplex) optical fiber. No periodic time frame is defined in the FDDI solution.

The FDDI-II solution uses a time frame of 125 μs, allowing the allocation of maximum 16 isochronous channels of 6.144 Mbit/s each. Each of these channels offers a full duplex data highway of 4 subchannels of 1.536 Mbit/s (US standard) or 3 subchannels of 2.048 Mbit/s (European standard). Even in case all 16 isochronous channels are used, a residual token channel of 768 kbit/s remains available. Isochronous channels may be dynamically assigned and released on a real time basis. The unassigned bandwidth for isochronous services remains available to the token channel for packet-like applications, as described in the next section on the MAC. So, at least 768 kbit/s is available for the packet-like applications.

Medium access control (MAC)

The MAC sublayer is defined for a ring topology, using the token ring principle, i.e. only the station which has the token is allowed to transmit. The basic entity known to the MAC layer is a called a frame (Fig. 6.8.), composed of control fields (address, preamble, ...) and an information field to be transported for the LLC layer.

Note here that the word frame has not the same meaning as in TDM, since a frame in FDDI will have different time durations, depending on its length.

In a ring, each station repeats the frame it receives from the upstream neighbor to the downstream neighbor. If the destination address of the frame equals its own local address, the frame is read by the station via copying into a buffer. The frame continues its way on the ring until it arrives at the originating station, which will remove (strip) the frame of the ring. This recognition is performed using the source address in the frame and comparing it with its local address. During stripping, the station will put IDLE symbols on the ring. A token is also transmitted via a frame and is identified by a special control field. Only one token is available using on the ring.

If a station wants to transmit a frame, it may only do so when it has captured the token. When finished transmitting frames, the token is released again and makes its tour on the ring to be captured by the next station waiting to transmit a frame.

At the instant when a station, having captured the token, initiates transmission, a long and active ring contains a number of frames in transit that were placed on the ring earlier by other stations. These frames will all be removed from the ring by the respective stations that originally transmitted them before they arrive at the current transmitting station's receiver again. Thus, input to this station's receiver will consist of IDLE symbols and the remnants of stripped frames. No useful frames will arrive at the station holding the token. In any case, because the station is transmitting, it will be removing from the ring anything that arrives at its receiver.

Remnants of stripped frames may occur, because a station's decision to strip a frame is based upon recognition of its own address in the source address field. However, this recognition can only be performed after the initial part of the frame has already been repeated.

Upon the completion of transmission, the transmitting station issues a new token on the ring to be captured by the next active waiting station. Finally, it continues to generate IDLE symbols until the starting delimiter of a new frame is received. At this time the MAC mechanism initiates the examination of all arriving frames, stripping those that it has originated and repeating the others.

To ensure that no station will keep the token forever, a timed token rotation (TTR) protocol is applied. The main objectives of this TTR protocol are twofold to :

- Give a higher priority to real time services (voice, video) than to data, thereby ensuring that the delay is limited to an upper bound.
- Allow that the remaining bandwidth is used by pure packet applications with no real time requirements.

The mechanism to support this TTR protocol is based on a measurement by each station sending non real time data, of the time that has elapsed since a token was last received. If the time exceeds a specified limit, the token is passed and no data can be transmitted.

A Target Token Rotation Time (TTRT) is defined, identical for all stations on the ring. In addition, each station holds a Token Rotation Timer (TRT) and a Token Hold Timer (THT). The TRT contains the time since the token was last received at that station, while THT contains the allowed time a token can be held by that terminal.

The protocol is different for packet (non-real time) applications and real time applications. Real time applications may always transmit, when the token is captured, of course within the allocated bandwidth.

Packet services may only capture the token when the time since a token was last received has not exceeded the defined target token rotation time (TTRT). This ensures that free time is filled with packet-like traffic. During transmission of this packet like information, the THT is decremented.

This TTRT mechanism guarantees that the utilization of the ring is always better than :

$$\eta \;\; = \frac{TTRT \;-\; RL}{TTRT} \tag{6.1.}$$

In this formula RL is the physical ring latency, mainly determined by the propagation time over a ring at zero load conditions. The response time of the ring is guaranteed to be less than twice the TTRT.

For optimal ring efficiency ($\eta = 1$), the TTRT should be as high as possible, but this introduces very high response times. For time-critical applications, the TTRT should be kept rather small. This means that the token is almost permanently rotating. This reduces the ring efficiency.

The MAC frame format used for FDDI is described in Fig. 6.8. The preamble field (PA) precedes every frame and contains IDLE symbols, i.e. it is composed of a maximum number of transitions to maintain easy clock synchronization at each receiver. The Starting Delimiter (SD) field guarantees uniquely recognizable frame boundaries.

The frame control field (FC) defines the type of the frame, such as real-time or packet like, token, etc. The Destination Address (DA) and Source Address (SA) fields are either 16 or 48 bits, indicating the respective addresses. A multicast addressing facility is possible. The Frame Check Sequence (FCS) of 32 bit calculates a 32 bit CRC over the previous frame. The Ending Delimiter (ED) ends the information field (including FCS). The Frame Status (FS) field indicates whether the addressed station has recognized its address, whether the frame was copied by the destination, or whether a frame error was detected by a station. This FS field is mainly used for maintenance purposes.

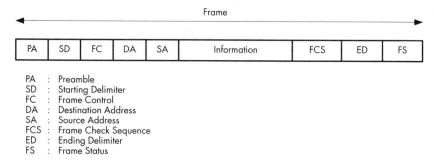

Fig. 6.8. – FDDI Frame Format

6.5.2. FDDI-II

As was described under the requirements of the MANs, the need to transport isochronous services was also recognized. In principle this synchronous operation could also be offered by so-called circuit-emulation as is done in the ATM solution (see Chapter 2). This circuit emulation means that the continuous bit rate information, as generated by the CBR (Continuous Bit Rate) source is transmitted in frames. At the receiver all induced network jitter is removed and the CBR is restored. However, this requires special equipment at the receiver to restore the continuous bit rate. Since the jitter in FDDI can be rather large (typically ten to hundreds of ms), thereby requiring large dejittering buffers, for FDDI-II the option was taken not to operate in circuit-emulation mode, but to add to the FDDI packet mode operation an additional isochronous mode of operation. In this case, no local clock extraction is required, but the local clock is deduced from the transmission clock.

However, the enhancements added to the FDDI concept are such that an upwardly compatible operation is guaranteed, between FDDI and FDDI-II. The isochronous mode of FDDI-II does not use the addressing capabilities of the frames of FDDI, but on the contrary relies on a connection established based upon some prior agreement. In fact, FDDI-II combines a connection-oriented and connectionless approach in a single solution. The establishment of the connection may be negotiated using the frames or by a pre-assignment (semi-permanently) in the stations.

The basic time reference used is 125 μs, as is used in all PCM systems. Each 125 μs cycle is composed of a preamble (to synchronize the 8 kHz clock), a cycle header and 16 wideband channels (WBC) of 6.144 Mbit/s each (Fig. 6.9.). This leaves room for a residual 768 kbit/s for packet traffic, composed of 12 bytes every 125 μs. This packet channel is called PDG (Packet Data Group) and is interleaved with the 16 WBCs.

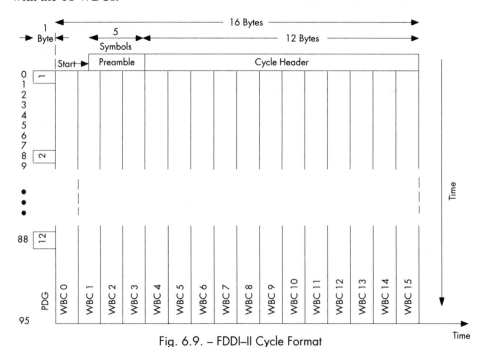

Fig. 6.9. – FDDI–II Cycle Format

Each WBC can operate either in isochronous (circuit switched) mode or in packet mode. A WBC will be allocated to a specific station for some time (semi-permanent or switched). Within each WBC, the bandwidth can be allocated by the station in terms of any multiple of 8 kbit/s, including 64, 384, 1536 and 2048 kbit/s subchannels.

The cycle header contains information on each WBC, to indicate whether the WBC is allocated to packet or circuit switched traffic.

In FDDI-II, 4 types of service quality are offered, using different priority levels. These 4 levels are achieved by working either in isochronous or in packet mode, and by using 2 sorts of tokens : restricted and unrestricted.

- The highest priority level is the isochronously associated WBC for the circuit mode operation, typically for CBR services. No token is used in this case, but a WBC is allocated for the duration of the connection, or semi-permanently.
- The second highest priority is given to the so-called synchronous packet traffic. Delivery in this case is guaranteed with a delay which will not be larger than twice the TTRT. Data of this priority level may be transmitted whenever a token is captured at the terminal, irrelevant of the token type (restricted or non-restricted) and regardless of the TTRT.
- The third highest priority is given to packet mode traffic without restrictions to the delay. Again, such information may be transmitted when a token of any type is captured. Stations may only issue and use restricted mode tokens after negotiation, to ensure that the available bandwidth is not exceeded.
- The lowest priority is given to packet traffic only when a unrestricted token is captured. This lowest priority will fill all the remaining available bandwidth.

6.5.3. Performance of FDDI

Various performance figures can be obtained for FDDI, depending on the traffic (i.e. various packet sizes) and configuration such as number of nodes and distance. In Wainwright (1988), results are shown for an FDDI with small packets (40 bytes) as input and very long packets (4472 bytes, i.e. the maximum size of FDDI), for various configurations. The target TTRT used in the model is 4 ms. Both rings carry 100 Mbit/s information and are operating fully in packet mode and no real time services are transported.

We see that for short packets the maximum obtainable load is around 58 %, mainly caused by the overhead of the frame and the token rotation time (Fig. 6.10a.). For very long packets, very high loads can be achieved, especially for short rings (Fig. 6.10b.). However, the delay on the ring is also much larger for long packets than for short packets.

It can also be noted from Fig. 6.10. that the distance is a very important parameter in achievable load and delay, far more important than the number of stations. We see that in both cases (short and long packets), the 1 km FDDI ring performs much better than the 100 km ring. A difference of 20 % in achievable load is shown. This effect is caused by the ring latency, requiring the token to circulate to the next active station. The impact of the number of stations on the performance is negligible.

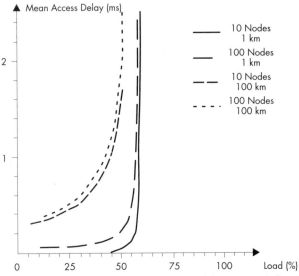

Fig. 6.10a. – FDDI Access Delay for Various Sizes of the Network for Short Packets (40 Bytes)

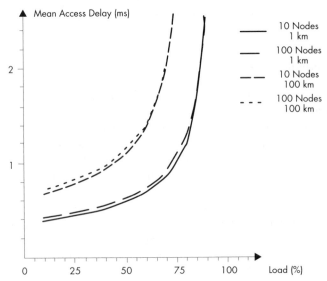

Fig. 6.10b. – FDDI Access Delay for Various Sizes of the Network for Long Packets (4472 Bytes)

6.6. DQDB

In the mid eighties, IEEE 802 recognized the need to start working on the definition of a metropolitan area network. In the subcommittee 802.6, different shared media topologies and access mechanisms were discussed and compared, of which one was selected. The selected and standardized solution is based on the principle of a physical dual bus with a distributed queueing access mechanism. This resulted in the name DQDB (Distributed Queue Dual Bus). This DQDB mechanism is based on a proposal which got initially the name of QPSX (Queued Packet and Synchronous Switch). The original work was done at the University of Western Australia (Newman, 1988).

Several draft versions of the DQDB principle have been discussed with different parameters for the cell size, different solutions for fairness regulation, etc. The standard adopted by IEEE 802 is defined as much as possible in line with the ATM standard. This compatibility was readily achievable since the standardization process of IEEE on DQDB and of CCITT on ATM was performed almost in parallel with inputs and influences in both directions. This allowed the DQDB standard to adopt it to CCITT standards wherever possible.

As FDDI-II, the DQDB provides both isochronous (circuit switched) and packet like (non-isochronous) services. The way this is implemented is based on a hybrid mode, i.e. by using a framed transmission structure and not by circuit emulation as in the pure ATM solution.

6.6.1. DQDB topology

The DQDB MAN is composed of 2 unidirectional buses, to which the access units (nodes) are connected. In addition, a head-end station is provided. This head-end station, also called a frame generator, is generating DQDB frames (segments). The 2 unidirectional buses operate in the opposite direction, as is shown in Fig. 6.11. The nodes are connected to both buses, using a read and write connection to each bus. The reading of the bus is not affecting the incoming data so that information can pass transparently through the nodes.

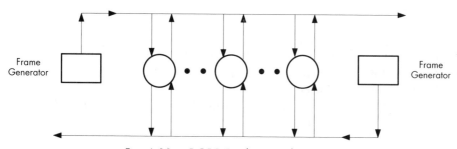

Fig. 6.11. – DQDB Dual Bus Architecture

The writing on each bus is performed by a logical OR function of the data which were already on the bus and data from the node (if available). This logical OR function guarantees a high reliability since the data are not passing through the nodes. The consequence is that nodes can fail, or be removed from the bus without disturbing its correct operation.

In case of failure of the bus, a reconfiguration procedure must be initiated. The reconfiguration is possible when the bus is installed as a looped bus as shown in Fig. 6.12. Since it is now physically a double open "ring", a reconfiguration procedure as for rings is possible. The buses will be closed at the head-end by removing the frame generator function. The place where the break or line fault occurred will be considered as the "natural" endpoint of the bus. The nodes at the failure will become frame generators. This closing of the head-end is only possible since both buses are looped back to a single location.

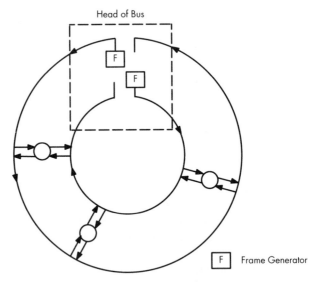

Fig. 6.12. – DQDB as a Looped Bus

6.6.2. The DQDB protocol

In IEEE 802.6, 2 sorts of accesses are defined towards the dual bus : Queued Arbitrated (QA) and Pre-Arbitrated (PA). QA accesses use the MAC mechanism described below to transport the connectionless data. PA accesses offer an isochronous service to the connected stations.

The medium access control (MAC) mechanism is based on a distributed queueing principle : this means that the system (i.e. one bus) has logically one queue for transfer of information in one direction, but this queue is physically distributed over the nodes. The service discipline of the queue is FIFO

(First-In-First-Out). On a DQDB system, 2 logical queues are available, one for traffic in each direction (i.e. one per bus). One bus is used to coordinate the queueing discipline for information to be transferred over the other bus, and vice versa. This coordination is achieved by collecting the requests of the nodes when these nodes have information to transmit.

Fixed length segments (cells) are transported, with a format compatible to that of ATM. The MAC mechanism is fundamentally different from most other LAN/MAN protocols with shared access where no continuous record of the state of the network is kept in the nodes. This information must in those networks first be derived from the medium before accessing it. This makes these systems' performance very sensitive to the size of the network.

For instance, in Ethernet a maximum distance is determined by the minimum frame size. In FDDI, it was shown in the previous section that the performance is negatively influenced by the length of the ring. In the distributed queuing principle, the current state of the network is stored in each node; namely every node knows the exact number of segments still waiting to be put on the bus. When a node has a segment to transmit, it uses this local information (stored in a counter) to determine the position of the segment in the queue.

So whenever a segment is waiting for transmission and an empty slot is passing by, it will never wait "in vain", i.e. empty slots which traverse the complete medium are only possible when all queues are empty.

The protocol itself is very simple and principly uses only 2 control bits : a busy bit and a request bit; also two identical bits are required for the bus with the opposite direction.

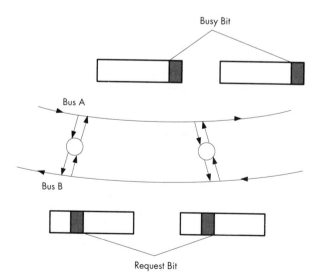

Fig. 6.13. – Control Bits Required to Transmit Information on Bus A

The procedure described here, as shown in Fig. 6.13. applies to the transfer of information on bus A, but an identical procedure applies to bus B. The busy bit marks each segment, whether it is full, i.e. it may not be used further on the bus to put information in, or empty. When a node has a segment ready for transmission on bus A it will issue a single request bit on bus B. So, in a segment passing over bus B the request bit will be set. This bit will pass all nodes on the upstream direction of the data direction (i.e. bus A). This bit will be used in every upstream node to keep track of the number of downstream queued segments. This can easily be achieved by providing a counter in each node, which counts the request bits as they pass by, as is shown in Fig. 6.14. For every request bit the RC (Request Counter) is incremented by one; for every empty segment passing by on the data bus the RC is decremented by one. This decrement function is performed since an empty segment passing by, will in one of the downstream nodes be filled with one of the waiting segments, for which a request bit has passed by.

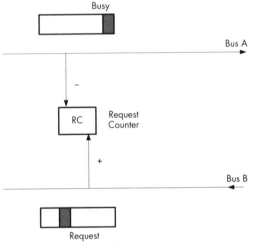

Fig. 6.14. – Node Collecting the Status of the Bus with no Information Queued

When a node has a segment to transmit over the bus, it will place this segment in the distributed queue, and inform all other nodes of the upstream direction by setting a request bit to ensure that an empty segment will be passing by.

To ensure that waiting segments will be transferred at the right time, the value of the request counter will be copied to another counter, the countdown counter (CD) (Fig. 6.15.). At the same time the RC is reset to zero. To ensure that the queued segment will take its correct position in the distributed queue, i.e. that at the correct time an empty segment is passing by, the request bit of a passing segment on bus B will be set. The CD counter knows the number of segments queued before it in the downstream direction of bus A. When all segments waiting in the queue before him are served, the node will put its segment on the bus. The node keeps track of the served segments waiting before it by decrementing by one the CD counter for every empty segment passing by. When the number of empty segments passed by equals the actual RC value (i.e. when the CD has reached a value of 0), the segment may be put on bus A (Fig. 6.15.).

All new requests coming in on bus B after the segment was queued, will be registered by incrementing the RC counter whenever a request bit is passing by on bus B. So, the exact status of the distributed queue can be stored in each node by those 2 counters (RC and CD). Together with 2 bits (busy and request) every node knows exactly when it can transmit, without a waste of segments. When there is somewhere in a node a segment waiting, there will never be an empty segment passing from the frame generator to the other end of the bus.

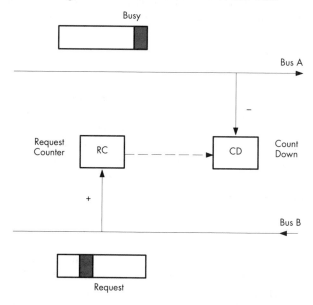

Fig. 6.15. – Node with a Segment Queued for Bus A

Priorities can also be implemented in this MAC principle by introducing separate distributed queues, one for each level of priority required. This can easily be achieved by installing a RC counter per priority level, and a request (RQ) bit per level. The RC of a particular level will have to count all RQ bits of its or of a higher priority level. So the RC records all requests of its level and of all higher priority levels.

The countdown operation must also take into account these priority levels. This can be implemented by modifying the CD counter by 2 actions : decrementing if an empty segment passes by and incrementing if a RQ bit of a higher priority passes by. This action ensures that higher priority segments can get access to the bus before already queued segments of a lower priority.

To enhance the performance of the DQDB, the destination deletion principle was added to the shared access protocol. A special bit in the header is defined to support this function, called the PSR bit (previous segment received). If a segment arrives at its destination, it will in the previously described DQDB mechanism be transported until the end of the bus. By releasing this segment at the destination, the remaining part of the bus can reuse the released segment. However, since the busy bit has already passed the node when the destination recognizes its own address, the segment itself cannot be released. Therefore, the next segment's PSR bit is set, to indicate that the previous segment should be considered as an empty segment. Since normal nodes cannot reuse the segments preceding a segment with a PSR bit set, special nodes (Eraser Nodes) are defined which alter cleared segments followed by a PSR bit to empty segments. These eraser nodes must store more than one segment to be able to modify the busy bit, if the PSR bit of the next segment is set. The performance gain of this PSR principle is described by Zukerman in (Zukerman, 1990).

Isochronous services are transported in PA segments. The framing period is not provided by an explicit framing method, but by an implicit repetition of DQDB segments. PA segments are characterized by a specific header (VCI) value. The assignment of the PA segments is based on a connection acceptance procedure, checking the available segments on the bus. QA and PA segments can be fully mixed. However, in case PA segments are used, they will not pass via the MAC mechanism described above, but the nodes will fill in their pre-assigned segments as they pass by on the bus. In PA segments, the bytes of a segment can be assigned to different virtual connections. By using multiple bytes per segment, a higher channel rate can be constructed.

The DQDB segment is made as much as possible compatible with the ATM standard as is shown in Fig. 6.16. There an ATM cell using an AAL4 and a DQDB segment is shown. We see a large commonality between both the ATM cells and the DQDB segments. Both the header and information field size are identical for DQDB and ATM. Only the first octet of the header is specific for DQDB. It contains a busy bit to indicate an empty or used segment. The Slot-Type bit (SL-TY) indicates whether the slot is an isochronous (PA) or a packet type (QA) service. Four levels of priorities are foreseen, each representing a request bit for a certain priority level (PRIO1 up to PRIO4). One bit (RES) is still under study. The PSR bit (Previous Segment Received) bit is defined to upgrade the performance by applying the destination deletion principle. The SPR (Segment Priority bits) are reserved for further use. The HEC calculates the CRC over the header, not taking into account the first 8 bits (ACF : Access Control Field). This is different from the ATM approach, where the HEC is calculated over the complete header. Thus the HEC has always to be recalculated when passing from a DQDB to ATM or vice versa.

Also, the first 2 octets of the payload are not exactly the same. The AAL4 provides 10 bits for the MID and 4 bits for a sequence number. The DQDB uses 14 bits for the MID and no sequence number bits. So, a mapping between both MID fields has to be provided at the interworking between ATM and DQDB.

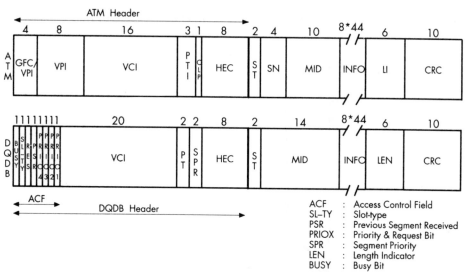

Fig. 6.16. – ATM Cells with a Type 4 AAL and DQDB Segments

6.6.3. Performance of DQDB

When discussing the performance of a DQDB system, 2 important parameters have to be considered : the mean access delay and the fairness of the system. The first, i.e. the mean access delay was also described for FDDI, but the second, i.e. the fairness is only valid for DQDB and not for a ring topology. Indeed, in the DQDB system the performance of each node depends on its location on the bus, whereas on a ring there is no "first" or "last" node. This fairness will also be expressed as a mean access delay, but in function of the position of the node on the bus.

The average access delay (averaged over all nodes on the DQDB bus) depends first of all on the size of the packets to be transmitted, as can be seen in Fig. 6.17a. and Fig. 6.17b. In Fig. 6.17a., the performance of a system transporting only short packets is shown. A very poor performance figure is achieved (only up to 25 % of the maximum achievable load) caused by the very bad filling level of the DQDB segments. A packet of 40 bytes requires 2 segments, since the useful information length of 44 bytes of one segment is not enough to transport the 40 bytes plus the overhead of the MAC PDU (packet data unit) such as source and destination address. The very low performance (around 25 %) is mainly caused by the large overhead of the higher layer protocols.

For large packets, the performance becomes much better, since the problem of overhead disappears because most DQDB segments can be filled completely (Fig. 6.17b.). However, the maximal obtainable performance is limited to 75 % of the maximal link capacity. This limitation is mainly caused by the overhead of the DQDB segment header (5 bytes) and the overhead in the payload of the segment

(4 bytes). We also see that the impact of the number of nodes or the length of the bus is minimal on the average performance of the bus.

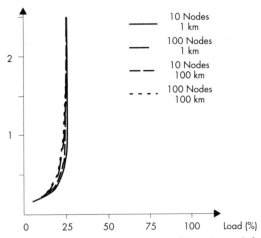

Fig. 6.17a. – DQDB Access Delay for Various Sizes of the Network for Short Packets (40 Bytes)

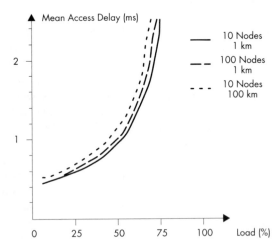

Fig. 6.17b. – DQDB Access Delay for Various Sizes of the Network for Long Packets (4472 Bytes)

With respect to the fairness of the DQDB system, for high loads the position of the station is a determining factor for the packet delay. The reason is that stations in the middle of the DQDB bus will very likely distribute their traffic over both buses, since part of the traffic is destined for stations reachable by bus A, the other part of the traffic for stations reachable by bus B.

A station at one end of the bus will have to send all its traffic over one bus, thereby limiting the available traffic on the bus of its neighbors. This fairness problem is most visible at high loads since then the bus occupation will be much more important at the end of the buses.

The impact on the delay is shown in Fig. 6.18., for a bus speed of 140 Mbit/s, a bus length of 100 km and a total bus load of 84 % of which 40 % is packet switched data. The performance (packet delay) of each node is shown for 25 nodes on the bus. The waiting time is defined as the time a segment has to wait in the node before it can be served. The transmission delay is the time it takes for a segment to be transferred from source to destination, not taking into account the waiting time. The transfer delay is the sum of the waiting time and the transmission delay. In Fig. 6.18. we see clearly that the delay of the middle nodes is lower than that of nodes at the extremes of the buses.

Note that the sum of the CS load (24 %) and the PS load (40 %) is smaller than the bus load (84 %). The remaining part (20 %) is caused by the overhead, such as the header, framing bits and the 8B/9B line coding (11 %). To relate Fig. 6.18. to Fig. 6.17., we see that the absolute figures of the segment delay in Fig. 6.18. is rather small. This is because the assumption was taken here that the information to be transmitted from the higher layer plus the MAC overhead fits completely in a single DQDB segment.

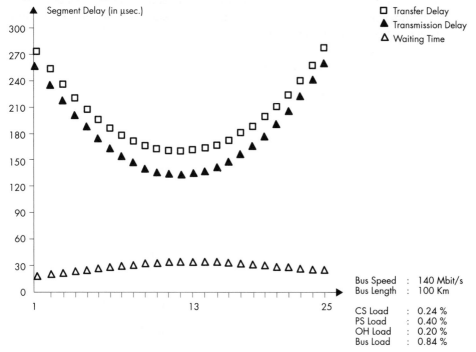

Fig. 6.18. – Fairness in DQDB

6.7. ORWELL

6.7.1. Orwell description

Another interesting medium access protocol for MANs is based on the slotted ring approach. This approach was originally used in the Cambridge ring (Hopper, 1980). The use of fixed slots allows an easy synchronization mechanism (as in ATM), whereas high performance is achievable at very high rates. This scheme allows the integration of asynchronous (packet-like) and isochronous traffic. The basic principle of the slotted ring is shown in Fig. 6.19. The ring is partitioned into equal length slots. Every slot has bits on the transmission lines and in the node(s). To ensure that an integer number of slots is present on the ring, a latency register, located in a monitor node is introduced to virtually lengthen the ring to a multiple number of slots. Slots are also sometimes called "minipackets".

These slots circulate around the ring and are either empty or full, indicated by a single bit. Nodes are actively coupled to the ring, i.e. they repeat or modify a slot. If the slot is destined to the node it will be read; writing of information can be performed by a node if an empty slot is passing by.

The deletion of a filled slot, i.e. the changing of a full slot into an empty one, can be done either in the source or destination node, giving rise to 2 different access methods. Within the source releasing approach, different variants exist depending on the number of slots which may be occupied by a station at any instant in time. When the slot is emptied one can decide to reuse the slot already in the releasing station, or the approach can instead be to pass it to next station downstream on the bus. The latter is the selected principle in the Cambridge ring.

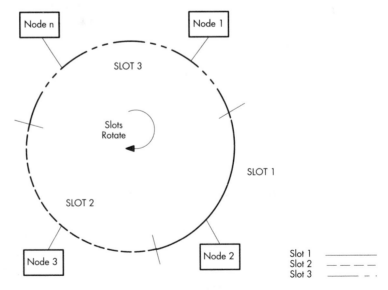

Fig. 6.19. – Slotted Ring Principle

In Orwell, the approach is to release the filled slot at the destination. This results in a better performance for Orwell, since the released slot can already be used by another node which is located between destination and source node. However, when a slot is emptied, the node has to pass it to the next node on the ring. In order to ensure fairness on the ring and to prevent a node from hogging the ring, the access is organized in cycles, also called reset intervals. Each node on the ring has a counter i indicating how many slots may be occupied by that node during a cycle.

Two classes of services are defined in Orwell : class 1 for isochronous, delay sensitive services; class 2 for asynchronous, delay tolerant services.

During a cycle, each node i can send up to $D_i - D_{min}$ packets of class 1. D_{min} guarantees a minimal bandwidth for class 2 services. Each node can regulate its throughput using this D_i counter. When the node has sent D_i slots it must wait until the cycle is finished, so that its D_i counter is reset to its maximum value. The counter is decremented every time a slot is sent. This counter in principle prevents a station from hogging the ring. After some time all nodes' counters will have reached the zero value.

In order to reset the D_i counters, a special procedure is applied : whenever a node empties a slot, it is marked as a "trial" slot, destined to itself by filling in its own address as the destination address. A trial slot is considered as an empty slot by all nodes, so whenever a node has something to send, the trial slot will not arrive at its destination, but will be filled.

Only when all nodes have nothing to transmit, the trial slot will arrive at its destination successfully. The originator of this trial slot will modify it into a reset slot, which will travel around the ring to reset all the D_i counters to their original value.

The rate at which reset slots are rotating on the ring gives a measure for the occupancy of the ring. When the reset rate becomes too small, the occupancy is too high.

This information can be used by every node to decide whether a new call will be accepted or not. Indeed, when the call would be accepted the new virtual reset rate can be calculated and checked against the allowable. If the reset rate is still acceptable, the call will be accepted and the counter D_i of that station will be incremented with a value depending on the service, i.e. the required bandwidth.

Four priority levels are provided in Orwell, implemented by four independent queues in each node. This is also reflected in the Orwell slot header.

In order to increase the bandwidth of the Orwell ring, several rings can be put in parallel, thereby creating a torus (see Fig. 6.20.). Each ring acts as an independent Orwell ring. This solution allows a flexible means of increasing network capacity, by adding new rings as required, as well as providing for higher network reliability.

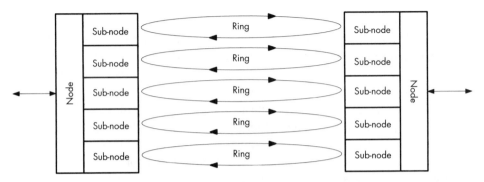

Fig. 6.20. – Orwell Torus Ring Configuration

6.7.2. Slot structure

The principle of the Orwell ring (slotted ring) does not impose any information field length. This means that the slot length can have any size, but once determined for an Orwell ring, it is fixed for the complete ring and all nodes connected to it. However, for practical reasons it may not be too long, otherwise not many slots may circulate on the ring.

The option taken by the Orwell designers is to line it up as much as possible with the ATM structure. Therefore, ATM cells can be completely transported by the Orwell ring. As is shown in Fig. 6.21., an ATM cell fits completely in an Orwell slot. In addition some special Orwell bits (2 bytes) are added to perform the slotted ring access mechanism.

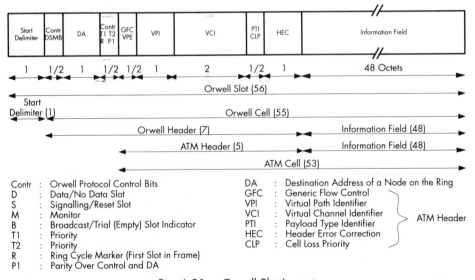

Fig. 6.21. – Orwell Slot Layout

The following Orwell header bits are defined. The Destination Address (DA) is composed of 8 bits to allow 256 destinations on the ring. It is clear that address bits have only local significance, i.e. on one Orwell ring. Eight control bits are defined. They consist of 2 priority bits (T1, T2) for 4 priorities; the D bit which indicates whether the slot is full or empty; the S bit which indicates that the counters of the different nodes on the ring may be reset; the R bit which indicates the first slot in a frame; the P1 bit which calculates the parity over the Orwell header (the destination address and the control bits) to ensure proper routing and control interpretation; the M bit which can be used to monitor the ring quality and the B bit which indicates whether it is a normal slot, or a trial (empty) slot to check whether there is still a station with valid data waiting to be put on the ring.

6.7.3. Performance of Orwell

The performance of the Orwell ring is very good, mainly thanks to the destination deletion principle. Since the slots are already released at the destination, it is possible that more than the physical bit rate on the ring can effectively be used. This can easily be seen in Fig. 6.22., where the delay versus the load is shown for the Cambridge (source deletion) and Orwell ring.

We see that for a physical rate of 140 Mbit/s, the maximum useful bit rate for Cambridge is around 120 Mbit/s, due to the source deletion principle. Thanks to the destination deletion principle, an Orwell ring can be loaded up to 240 Mbit/s under certain assumptions. This double capacity can be explained, since on the average all slots will make a half tour around the ring, so that the other half of the ring may be reused by consecutive stations on the ring. However, we see that at these high loads, the delay on the ring becomes rather large (around 1 ms).

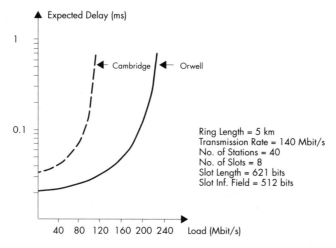

Fig. 6.22. – Packet Delay versus Load for the Cambridge and Orwell Ring

6.8. BIBLIOGRAPHY

Banwell T.C. Stephens W.E., Lalk G.R., "Transmission of 155 Mbit/s (SONET STS-3) signals over unshielded and shielded twisted pair copper wire", Electronics Letters, June 1992, Vol. 28, No. 12

Biocca A., Freschi G., Forcina A., Melen R., "Architectural issues in the interoperability between MAN and the ATM network", ISS '90, Stockholm, June 1990

Byrne W., Kafka H., Luderer G., Nelson B., Clapp G., "Evolution of metropolitan area networks to broadband ISDN", ISS '90, Stockholm, June 1990

Caves K., "FDDI-II : A new standard for integrated services high speed LANs", Telecommunications, September 1987

Clapp G., Singh M., Karr S., "Metropolitan area network architecture and services", Globecom '88, Hollywood, November 1988

Deloddere D., Gastaud G., Peschi R., "DQDB MAN, a step towards B-ISDN", EFOC/LAN '90, Munich, June 1990

Deloddere D., Reynders P., Verbeeck P., "Architecture and implementation of a connectionless server for B-ISDN", ISS '92, Yokohama, October 1992

Denissen F., Desmet E., Petit G.H., "The policing function in an ATM network", IZS '90, Zurich, March 1990

De Prycker M., "Impact of data communication on ATM", ICC '89, Boston, June 1989

De Prycker M., Verhoeyen M., Decuypere H., "Integration of interactive and distribution services : impact on the network architecture and signalling", IJDACS, Vol. 4, 1991

Falconer R., Adams J., "Orwell : a protocol for an integrated services local network", BT Technology Journal, October 1985

Flatman A., Caves K., "Progress with FDDI", EFOC/LAN '86, Amsterdam, June 1986

Frontini M., Watson J., "An investigation of packetised voice on the FDDI token ring", IZS '88, Zurich, March 1988

Gallagher I., "A multiservice network based on the Orwell protocol", ISS '87, Phoenix, March 1987

Hemrick C., Lang L., "Introduction to switched multi-megabit data services (SMDS), an early broadband service", ISS '90, Stockholm, June 1990

Henry P., "High-capacity lightwave local area networks", IEEE Communications Magazine, Vol. 27, No. 10, October 1989,

Heywood P., "The rise of metropolitan area networks", Data Communications International, December 1989

Hopper A., "The Cambridge ring : A local network", Advanced techniques for microprocessor systems, Hanna F.K., Ed. Stevenage UK, Peter Pergrinus Ltd, 1980

Hullett J.L., Evans P., "New proposal extends the reach of metro area nets", Data Communications, Vol. 17, No. 2, February 1988

Ibe O., Howe R., "Architectures for metropolitan area networks", Computer Communications, December 1989

Klessig R., "Overview of Metropolitan Area Networks", IEEE Communications Magazine, January 1986

Lin Y., Spears D., Yin M., "Fiber-based local access network architectures", IEEE Communications Magazine, Vol. 24, No. 5, May 1986

Lombardo A., Palazzo Z., "An architecture for a pure ATM metropolitan area network", Globecom '89, Dallas, November 1989

Martini P., "The DQDB protocol - What about fairness ?", Globecom '89, Dallas, November 1989

Materna B., Vaughan B., Britney C., "Evolution from LAN and MAN access networks towards the integrated ATM network", Globecom '89, Dallas, November 1989

Mc Cool J., "FDDI : Getting to know the inside of the ring", Telecommunications, March 1988

Mc Cool J., "The emerging FDDI standard", Telecommunications, Vol. 21, No 5, May 1987

Michnowicz S., "Interworking IEEE 802.6 (DQDB) MANs with the Broadband ISDN", Australian Fast Packet Switching Workshop, Melbourne, July 1990

Minzer S., "A signalling Protocol for Complex Mutimedia Services", IEEE JSAC, Vol. 9, No. 9, December 1991

Mitrani I., Adams J., Falconer R., "A modelling study of the Orwell ring protocol", Teletraffic analysis and computer performance evaluation, 1986

Mollenauer J., "Metropolitan area network update : The global LAN is getting closer", Data Communications International, December 1989

Mollenauer J., "Metropolitan area networks and ATM technology", International Journal of Digital and Analog Cabled Systems, Vol.1, No 4, October 1988

Mollenauer J., "Standards for metropolitan area networks", IEEE Communications Magazine, April 1988

Newman R.M., Budrikis Z.L., Hullett J.L., "The QPSX MAN", IEEE Communications Magazine, Vol. 26, No. 4, April 1988

Pohlit R., "ATM transmission in FDDI 2", EFOC/LAN '89, Amsterdam, June 1989

Potter P., Zukerman M., "Cyclic request control for provision of guaranteed bandwidth within the DQDB framework", ISS '90, Stockholm, June 1990

Quinquis J.P., Lespagnol A., François J., Gastaud G., "Data services and LANs interconnection using ATM technique", ISS '90, Stockholm, June 1990

Rao S., "Optical MANs in the public network", Telecommunications, Vol. 23, No 11, November 1989

Ross F., "An overview of FDDI : the fiber distributed data interface", IEEE Journal on Selected Areas in Communications, Vol. 7, No. 7, September 1989

Ross F., "FDDI - a tutorial", IEEE Communications Magazine, Vol. 24, No. 5, May 1986

Shandle J., "A firm FDDI standard has vendors scrambling for a piece of the action", Electronics, September 1989

Skov M., "Implementation of physical and media access protocols for high speed networks", IEEE Communication Magazine, June 1989

Tirtaatmadja E., Palmer R., "The application of virtual paths to the interconnection of IEEE 802.6 Metropolitan Area Network", ISS '90, Stockholm, June 1990

Tranchier D.P., Boyer P.E., Rowand Y.M., *et al.*, "Fast bandwidth allocation in ATM networks", ISS '92, Yokohama, October 1992

Wainwright N., Myles A., "A comparison of the FDDI Fibre Optic Network with the Emerging IEEE 802.6 Metropolitan Area Network", IEE Colloquium on Fibre Optic LANs and Techniques for the Local Loop, No. 4, London, March 1989

Yamazaki K., Ikeda Y., "Connectionless cell switching schemes for broadband ISDN", ISS '90, Stockholm, June 1990

Zafirovic-Vukotic M., Niemegeers I., "Analytical modelling and performance analyses of the Orwell access mechanism", ITC 12, Torino, June 1988

Zafirovic-Vukotic M., Niemegeers I, Valk D., "Performance analysis of slotted ring protocols in HSLANs", IEEE Journal on Selected Areas in Communication, Vol. 6, No. 6, July 1988

Zukerman M., Potter P., "A proposed scheme for implementing eraser nodes within the framework of the IEEE 802.6 MAN standard", Australian Fast Packet Switching Workshop, Melbourne, July 1990

7

Traffic Control in ATM Networks

7.1. INTRODUCTION

Traffic control in ATM based BISDN has been the subject of vigorous research over the past several years. The design of a suitable ATM traffic control is considered as a fundamental challenge for the success of BISDN.

According to CCITT Recommendation I.371, the primary role of traffic control in BISDN is to protect the network and the user in order to achieve predefined network performance objectives e.g. in terms of cell loss probability or cell transfer delays. Basically, traffic control refers to the set of actions taken by the network to avoid congestion. The latter can be caused by unpredictable statistical fluctuations of traffic flows or by fault conditions within the ATM network possibly leading to excessive cell losses or unacceptable end-to-end cell transfer delays. An additional role of traffic control is to optimize the use of network resources for the purpose of achieving realistic network efficiency.

The objectives of ATM layer traffic control for BISDN can be summarized as follows :

- Flexibility : it should support a set of ATM layer Quality of Service (QoS) classes sufficient for all existing and foreseeable services.
- Simplicity : the challenge is to design a simple ATM layer traffic control which minimizes network equipment complexity while maximizing network utilization.
- Robustness : the requirement of achieving high resource efficiency under any traffic circumstance while maintaining simple control functions.

7.2. BASIC ATM TRAFFIC CONTROL FUNCTIONS

To meet the above objectives, the following two functions are a prerequisite for managing and controlling traffic in ATM networks : Connection Admission Control (CAC) and Usage Parameter Control (UPC).

7.2.1. Connection admission control

Connection Admission Control (CAC) represents the set of actions taken by the network at call set-up phase in order to accept or reject an ATM connection. A connection request for a given call is accepted only when sufficient resources are available to carry the new connection through the whole network at its requested Quality of Service (QoS) while maintaining the agreed QoS of already established connections in the network. During the connection establishment procedure (i.e. at call set-up phase) the following information, embedded in a traffic contract specification, has to be negotiated and agreed between "user" and "network" to enable CAC for making reliable connection acceptance/denial decisions :

- Specific limits on the traffic volume the network is expected to carry in terms of well-chosen traffic descriptors.

- A requested QoS class expressed in terms of for example, cell transfer delay, delay jitter, cell loss ratio and burst cell losses.

- A tolerance to accommodate cell delay variation introduced by for example the Terminal Equipment (TE) or the Customer's Premises Equipment (CPE), which may alter the negotiated limits of the expected traffic volume.

This information may be renegotiated during the lifetime of the connection at the request of the user. The network itself may limit the frequency of these renegotiations. CAC schemes are currently not standardized and are at the discretion of network operators.

7.2.2. Usage/network parameter control

Usage Parameter and Network Parameter Control (UPC/NPC) are performed at the User-Network Interface (UNI) and Network-Node Interface (NNI), respectively, and represent the set of actions taken by the network to monitor and control traffic on an ATM connection in terms of cell traffic volume and cell routing validity. This function is sometimes also called "police function". The main purpose is to enforce the compliance of every ATM connection to its negotiated traffic contract. Without a UPC/NPC function, a terminal equipment failure, excessive cell delay variation in for example the CPE or even traffic abuse could seriously affect the QoS committed to other already established connections.

An ideal UPC/NPC algorithm should exhibit the following main features :

- Capability of detecting any illegal traffic situation.

- Rapid response time to parameter violations.

- Simplicity of implementation.

7.3. TRAFFIC PARAMETER SPECIFICATION

7.3.1. Definitions

In order to guarantee a proper operation of both UPC/NPC and CAC functions, the intrinsic traffic characteristics of connections should first be adequately described by a set of standardized traffic parameters.

Traffic parameters

A traffic parameter is a specification of a particular traffic aspect. Traffic parameters may for example describe a quantitative aspect such as the average connection holding time, the peak cell rate, the mean cell rate, the average burst duration or a qualitative aspect such as the source type (e.g. telephone, video-phone).

ATM traffic descriptor

The ATM traffic descriptor is the generic list of traffic parameters, which can be used to capture the traffic characteristics of an ATM connection, e.g. the peak cell rate, the average cell rate, etc.

Source traffic descriptor

A source traffic descriptor is a set of traffic parameters belonging to the ATM traffic descriptor used during the connection set-up phase to specify the traffic characteristics of the connection requested by the source, e.g. the peak cell rate.

7.3.2. Characteristics of traffic parameters

It is widely accepted that any traffic parameter used in a source traffic descriptor should be :

- Simple and understandable in an unambiguous way to the user/terminal and to the network.
- Useful for CAC schemes in order to effectively meet network performance objectives.
- Enforceable by the UPC/NPC.

7.3.3. Statistical versus operational traffic specification

There exist two fundamentally opposite approaches for specifying traffic parameters, namely a statistical approach and an operational or so-called algorithmic approach.

Statistical approach

The statistical approach focuses on stochastic traffic parameters such as the average cell rate or average burst duration. It is a conventional approach in teletraffic theory due to the availability of methodologies for assessing performance characteristics of a wide range of queueing systems described with these parameters.

Unfortunately, statistical traffic parameters do not lend themselves easily to real time traffic compliance testing since they require a long observation time to detect with some confidence whether the negotiated average cell rate of a connection has been exceeded or not. Conversely, if the observation time is too short, then there exists a high probability that the connection is wrongly cataloged as non-compliant. On the other hand, a large observation interval reduces significantly the reaction time to detect a non-compliant situation. This leaves the door open for traffic abuse.

Operational approach

An operational approach defines the traffic parameters by means of a rule. It allows an unambiguous discrimination between conforming and non-conforming cells and is therefore referred to as a parameterized conformance-testing algorithm. The rule has been standardized in CCITT Recommendation I.371 and will be called here the Generic Cell Rate Algorithm.

7.3.4. Generic cell rate algorithm

Two equivalent versions for the Generic Cell Rate Algorithm (GCRA) are defined in CCITT Recommendation I.371, namely the Virtual Scheduling (VS) and continuous-state Leaky Bucket (LB) algorithm. For any sequence of cell arrival times, $\{t_a, a >= 1\}$ both algorithms determine the same cells to be conforming or non-conforming (see Fig. 7.1.).

The GCRA uses two real-valued parameters I and L, denoted as Increment and Limit, respectively, and a set of intermediate variables, and is described as GCRA (I, L).

At the arrival of a cell, the VS algorithm calculates the Theoretically predicted Arrival Time (TAT) of the cell assuming equally spaced cells (the distance between 2 consecutive cells is given by I) when the source is active. If the actual arrival time t_a of a cell is after TAT – L (L representing a certain tolerance value), then the cell is conforming, otherwise the cell arrived too early and is considered as non-conforming.

The continuous-state LB algorithm can be viewed as a finite-capacity bucket algorithm whose contents leak out at a continuous rate of 1 per time-unit and whose contents are increased by I for each conforming cell. If at a cell arrival the content of the bucket is less than L, then the cell is conforming, otherwise the cell is non-conforming. The capacity of the bucket is L + I.

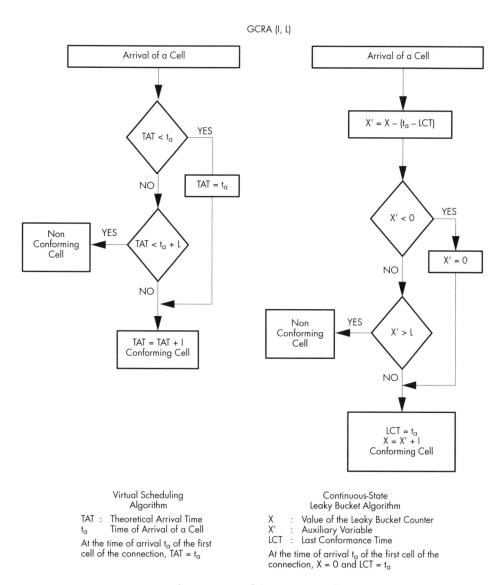

Fig. 7.1. – Equivalent Versions of the Generic Cell Rate Algorithm

The GCRA (I, L) is used to provide the formal definition of traffic conformance to the negotiated traffic parameters. Although traffic conformance is defined in terms of the GCRA, the network provider is, according to CCITT Recommendation I.371, not obliged to use this algorithm for UPC/NPC purposes. Rather, the network provider may use any UPC/NPC whose performance is consistent with the QoS objectives for the connection, and in particular provides transparency to compliant connections, the definition of which is given in Section 7.4.3.

7.4. TRAFFIC CONTRACT SPECIFICATION

The traffic contract negotiated during connection establishment consists of the connection traffic descriptor, the requested QoS class and the definition of a compliant connection. Each part of this contract will be briefly discussed later.

7.4.1. Connection traffic descriptor

The source traffic descriptor, together with its tolerance applicable at the UNI/NNI for any given ATM connection, define the connection traffic descriptor. The latter is declared by the user at connection set-up by means of for example signalling and comprises the mandatory peak cell rate and cell delay variation tolerance and optionally the sustainable cell rate with its associated burst tolerance. The definition of these parameters is given in the subsequent sections.

7.4.1.1. Peak cell rate

The Peak Cell Rate (PCR) traffic parameter for a connection is defined at the Physical Layer SAP (PHY-SAP) within an equivalent terminal representing the VPC/VCC in a reference model (Fig. 7.2.). Denoting a basic event as a request to send an ATM-PDU in the equivalent terminal, the Peak Cell Rate (R_p) of the ATM connection is defined as the inverse of the minimum interarrival time T between 2 consecutive basic events. T is denoted as the peak emission interval of the ATM connection.

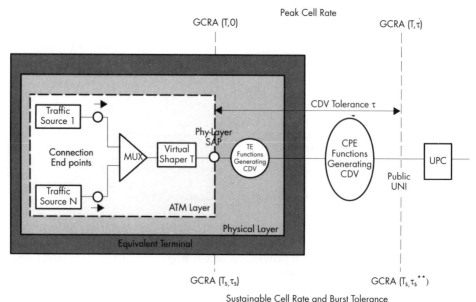

Fig. 7.2. – Reference Model

The PCR is a mandatory source traffic parameter and it applies to ATM connections supporting both Constant Bit Rate (CBR) and Variable Bit Rate (VBR) services. Due to a possible multiplexing process (MUX) before the PHY-SAP, a virtual shaping function was defined in the equivalent terminal to allow an unambiguous definition of the peak cell rate at the PHY-SAP.

7.4.1.2.   *Cell delay variation tolerance*

ATM Layer functions may alter the traffic characteristics of ATM connections by introducing Cell Delay Variation (CDV). When cells from 2 or more ATM connections are multiplexed (MUX), cells of a given ATM connection may be delayed when cells of another ATM connection are being inserted at the output of this multiplexer. Also Customer EQuipments (CEQ) may introduce CDV.

Similarly, some cells may be delayed when physical layer overhead or OAM cells are inserted. Therefore, some randomness affects the interarrival time between consecutive VPC/VCC cells as monitored by the GCRA at the UNI/NNI. This implies that UPC/NPC functions cannot solely rely on the PCR traffic parameter. In addition the degree of distortion of the interarrival time has to be defined and is called CDV tolerance, τ.

The CDV tolerance, τ, is defined in relation to the peak cell rate according to the algorithm GCRA(T, τ), where T is the inverse of R_p (the peak cell rate). The CDV tolerance allocated to a particular VPC/VCC at the UNI/NNI represents at this interface a quantitative measure of the VPC/VCC cell clumping phenomenon due to the slotted nature of the ATM, the physical layer overhead and the ATM layer functions. Consequently, τ is not a source traffic parameter.

When τ is greater than or equal to T − 1, the maximum number of cells B that may be passed at link rate (i.e. back-to-back) is given by :

$$B = \lfloor 1 + \tau / (T - 1) \rfloor \qquad For\ T > 1 \qquad (7.1.)$$

where $\lfloor x \rfloor$ stands for the largest integer smaller than x.

A user may explicitly or implicitly select a value for the CDV tolerance at the UNI/NNI for an ATM connection from amongst a set of values supported by the network.

7.4.1.3.   *Sustainable cell rate*

For ATM connections that support VBR services, the peak cell rate will provide an upper bound of the cell rate of the connection. However, in order to allow the network to allocate resources more efficiently, an additional traffic parameter such as the Sustainable Cell Rate (SCR) may be specified.

The SCR is an optional source traffic parameter; a user/terminal may choose to place an upper bound on the realized average cell rate of an ATM connection to a value below the peak cell rate. To be useful to the network provider, the SCR value must be less than the PCR value. For CBR connections, the user would not declare the SCR and would only negotiate the PCR.

The sustainable cell rate traffic parameter for a VPC/VCC, supporting VBR services, is defined at the PHY-SAP within the equivalent terminal of the reference model of Fig. 7.2. If a request to send an ATM-PDU in the equivalent terminal refers to a basic event, then the Sustainable Cell Rate (R_s) of the ATM connection is the inverse of a so-called average interarrival time T_s between two basic events. Consequently $R_s = 1/T_s$.

The sustainable cell rate descriptor is uniquely defined by the GCRA with 2 parameters, namely T_s and the burst tolerance τ_s, both specified at the PHY-SAP.

7.4.1.4. Burst tolerance

The burst tolerance τ_s is a source traffic parameter and reflects the "time scale" during which cell rate fluctuations are tolerated. It is defined in relation to the sustainable cell rate according to the algorithm GCRA(T_s, τ_s) and determines an upper bound on the length of a burst transmitted in compliance with the connection's peak cell rate.

The maximum number of cells which may pass the GCRA transparently at peak cell rate is given by the following formula :

$$MBS = | \, 1 + \tau_s \, / \, (T_s - T) \, | \qquad (7.2.)$$

where $| \, x \, |$ is the greatest integer less than or equal to x and MBS stands for Maximum Burst Size (see Fig. 7.3.).

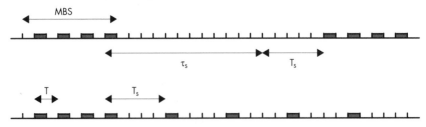

Fig. 7.3. – Relation between MBS , τ_s , T_s and T.

The maximum compliant burst size, MBS, does not imply that bursts of this size with arbitrary spacing between the bursts would be compliant. In order for a burst this large to be compliant, the cell stream needs to be idle long enough for the state of the GCRA(T_s, τ_s) to become zero (i.e. long enough for the continuous-state leaky bucket to become empty).

If a user chooses to specify a value for the SCR traffic parameter and wishes to emit compliant bursts at the peak rate, then the appropriate choice of T_s and τ_s depends on the minimum spacing between bursts ($T_s + \tau_s$ in Fig. 7.3.) as well as the burst size MBS.

To summarize, the connection traffic descriptor specifies the source traffic descriptors (peak cell rate, sustainable cell rate and the burst tolerance τ_s.) defined at the PHY-SAP within an equivalent terminal and the CDV tolerance τ specified at the UNI/NNI. The Burst tolerance τ_s accounts for the tolerance in relation to the SCR at the PHY-SAP while the CDV tolerance specified at the UNI/NNI is defined in relation to the peak cell rate by the GCRA (T, τ) rule. The burst tolerance τ_s** specified at the UNI/NNI takes the CDV tolerance τ into account and is also defined in relation to the sustainable cell rate by the GCRA (Ts, τ_s**) rule as shown in Fig. 7.2.

7.4.2. Requested quality of service class

The requested Quality of Service class, negotiated during connection establishment, specifies the required cell loss ratio, the cell transfer delay and delay jitter. Other performance parameters such as burst cell loss are for further study in CCITT.

7.4.3. Definition of a compliant connection

The CAC and UPC procedures, which are operator specific, should take into account the connection traffic descriptor and the requested QoS to operate efficiently. Once the connection has been accepted, the QoS requested is provided as long as the connection is compliant with the traffic contract.

A connection is cataloged as compliant as long as the proportion of non-conforming cells does not exceed a certain positive threshold, the value of which has to be specified in the traffic contract by the network operator. For non-compliant connections, the network need not to respect the contracted QOS, i.e. the network could release the connection in case of congestion. For compliant connections, the requested QOS has always to be supported by the network.

7.5. GRANULARITY OF TRAFFIC CONTRACT PARAMETERS

UPC/NPC functions cannot be requested to handle any specific parameter value. Due to hardware limitations, only a finite and discrete set of for example PCR, CDV tolerance τ, SCR and burst tolerance τ_s** values can actually be handled at the ATM layer.

The set of PCR values is referred to as the ATM peak cell rate granularity in CCITT Recommendation I.371 and needs to be standardized to allow for simple interworking. The choice between a linear scheme in terms of cells per second or in terms of peak emission interval (time unit) is still under discussion in CCITT.

The CDV tolerance τ can for instance be expressed as integer multiples of the cell emission time, being 2.73 μs at 155.52 Mbit/s.

It is natural that both PCR and SCR have an identical granularity. Since the user can specify any burst tolerance value corresponding to its declared sustainable cell rate, an integer multiple of the basic cell emission time would probably be too costly to implement. To reduce implementation complexity as much as possible in cases where the UPC has to monitor both PCR and SCR for different cell substreams within a single connection, one could envisage the standardization of a limited set of burst tolerance classes.

7.6. BOUNDS ON CELL DELAY VARIATION AND BURST TOLERANCES

When tolerances are introduced in the UPC/NPC functions, very different traffic patterns can be considered as compliant to the traffic contract and can pass transparently through the UPC/NPC. Since the network is committed to achieve the requested Quality of Service required by those connections which comply to their traffic contracts, a conservative network allocation scheme should be based on the most resource demanding traffic pattern among all compliant ones. This particular traffic pattern is often referred to as the worst case traffic pattern of the ON-OFF type, for which the maximum number of cells in the ON period is a function of T (T_s) and τ (τ_s) for a UPC monitoring respectively the peak cell rate and the sustainable cell rate (see formulae (7.1.) and (7.2.) of section 7.4.). The ON period for the PCR case is characterized by a clump of back-to-back cells at full link rate (see Fig. 7.4. and 7.5.) while, for the SCR case, it is described by a burst of consecutive cells emitted at peak cell rate.

This section illustrates the impact of the CDV tolerance τ on the amount of required ATM network resources to guarantee a predefined QoS for constant bit rate sources. The analysis is tentatively restricted to a homogeneous traffic environment considering a single contracted peak cell rate value for each ATM connection.

7.6.1. The simulation model

Each source is characterized by a recurrent cell interarrival time pattern, dictated by formula (7.1.), with the following parameters at the UNI :

T_{min} : Minimum cell interarrival time.

T_{max} : Maximum cell interarrival time.

T_{rec} : Period of the recurrent interarrival time pattern.

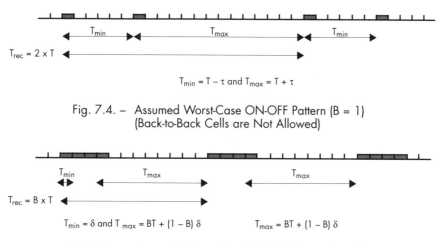

$$T_{min} = T - \tau \text{ and } T_{max} = T + \tau$$

Fig. 7.4. – Assumed Worst-Case ON-OFF Pattern (B = 1)
(Back-to-Back Cells are Not Allowed)

$$T_{min} = \delta \text{ and } T_{max} = BT + (1 - B) \delta \qquad T_{max} = BT + (1 - B) \delta$$

Fig. 7.5. – Assumed Worst-Case ON-OFF Pattern (B > 1)
(B Back-to-Back Cells are Allowed)

The identified type of deterministic ON-OFF sources is offered to a single stage multiplexer FIFO output queue of infinite capacity (Fig. 7.6.). A random phasing of the sources with respect to each other, uniformly distributed over T_{rec}, is assumed. In this way representative results for the buffer occupancy distribution can be derived from the aggregate superposition process.

As a function of the offered load, i.e. the number of connections N, the necessary buffer capacity K to guarantee in a statistical way a Cell Loss Ratio (CLR) of 10^{-10} is then estimated through simulation as a function of the CDV tolerance τ. The obtained reliable overflow probabilities are extrapolated by means of a least squares fit to an assumed geometric distribution in order to derive CLR values. An example of a simulation outcome is illustrated in Fig. 7.7. and represents the ensemble average of 50,000 simulated random phasings.

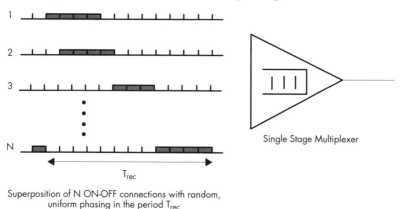

Superposition of N ON-OFF connections with random,
uniform phasing in the period T_{rec}

Single Stage Multiplexer

Fig. 7.6. – Single Stage Multiplexer Model

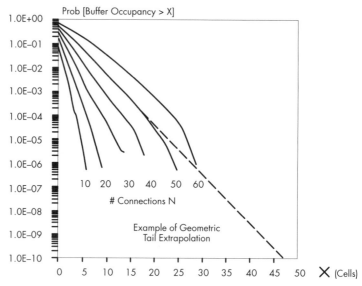

Fig. 7.7. – Example of Buffer Occupancy Tail Distributions

7.6.2. The reference model

A reference model is indispensable in order to assess the impact of the CDV tolerance τ on the resource allocation process of CBR sources. For reasons of robustness, a connection admission control algorithm for CBR connections should be independent of its actual location in the network, i.e. preferably a unique CAC function for CBR sources in any multiplexing stage. Yet, as a CBR connection is switched along consecutive ATM multiplexing stages, it naturally experiences CDV, primarily determined by the load and type of the perturbing background traffic. In order to capture this statistical phenomenon, a discrete-time Geo(N)/D/1 reference model is tentatively preferred above the self-evident N*D/D/1 queueing model for pure CBR sources (Roberts, 1992). The former reference model is itself upperbounded by the well-known M/D/1 queueing model for large enough values of N, being the number of multiplexed connections.

7.6.3. Some key results

For the sake of simplicity a single ATM connection Peak Cell Rate of 2 Mbit/s is selected, assuming the link rate to be exactly 150 Mbit/s. Consequently, the connection is characterized by an integer intercell arrival time T of exactly 75 cell units. From the chosen M/D/1 reference model, it can be verified that a buffer with a capacity K_{ref} of 54 ATM cells suffices to guarantee a CLR of 10^{-10} at a reference load arbitrarily fixed at 0.80 Erlang. This means that the CAC function only accepts a maximum of 60 "statistically jitterized" CBR connections of 2 Mbit/s.

For every selected CDV tolerance τ in the simulation model, a graph can be plotted of the extrapolated 10^{-10} quantile of the buffer occupancy tail distribution as a function of the number N of multiplexed ON-OFF connections. From these graphs, the maximum number of connections N_{max} that can be accepted on the link is then derived according to the reference buffer capacity K_{ref}. Finally, to illustrate the impact of the CDV tolerance τ on the resource allocation process for the 2 Mbit/s connections, the quantified N_{max} values are listed in Table 7.1. as a function of the CDV tolerance τ.

τ (δ unit)	B	N_{max} (No. of connections)	Load (Erlang)
25	1	60	0.80
50	1	60	0.80
75	2	60	0.80
150	3	42	0.56
225	4	33	0.44
300	5	27	0.36
375	6	22	0.29

Table 7.1. – Impact of the CDV Tolerance on the Link Load Efficiency for 2 Mbit/s Sources (T = 75 δ)

From Table 7.1., it is obvious that the larger the CDV tolerance τ, the fewer connections N can be accepted with respect to the reference buffer capacity for the chosen nominal load of 0.8 Erlang and a target CLR value of 10^{-10}. For instance, for the largest selected τ value of 375 cell time units, only one-third of the nominal 60 connections can be multiplexed, representing a reduction in link load efficiency of about 64 %. For the latter case, it is clear that much more bandwidth than the connection's PCR has to be allocated. This implies that CAC algorithms should not only rely on the PCR (or T) but also on the CDV tolerance τ value.

Similar simulation experiments can be carried out for the SCR and the burst tolerance τ_s in order to investigate the impact of both parameters on the achievable multiplexing gain in ATM networks. When the ATM network is equipped with rather small cell buffers, it is very unlikely that significant benefits are to be expected from the use of the SCR for link load efficiency purposes when large burst tolerance are imposed. Further study is required to investigate the relationships between all involved parameters.

The presented simulation results clearly demonstrate the beneficial outcome of keeping the CDV tolerance τ, as a function of the contracted PCR for CBR sources, within proper bounds for reasons of network efficiency. Indeed, this allows the network to efficiently transport the CBR connections through a CAC function solely based on the contracted PCR value.

7.6.4. Bounds for CDV tolerance

The CDV tolerance τ can be limited to a value derived from an appropriate reference model as a function of the contracted PCR. A tentative example for such a reference model could for instance be an M+D/D/1 FIFO queue. This model corresponds to the smallest ATM network composed of one multiplexing stage.

Without priorities, the CDV tolerance τ is highly constrained, the value of which is depicted in Table 7.2. as a function of the contracted PCR and the offered load to the reference model.

However, the potential existence of several VPCs/VCCs sharing the same transmission link could introduce a very high CDV, depending on the CPE implementation, possibly incompatible with a highly constraining CDV bound imposed at the UNI/NNI or by the UPC/NPC (due to hardware limitations).

T	0.50 E	0.60 E	0.70 E	0.80 E	0.90 E
2	–	7.84	13.40	23.47	52.60
3	9.08	13.44	20.21	33.29	71.89
4	11.33	16.03	23.52	38.16	81.51
5	12.62	17.56	25.50	41.07	87.28
6	13.46	18.56	26.81	43.01	91.13
7	14.06	19.28	27.74	44.39	93.87
8	14.50	19.82	28.44	45.43	95.92
9	14.85	20.23	28.98	46.23	97.52
10	15.13	20.56	29.42	46.87	98.81
12	15.54	21.06	30.07	47.84	100.73
14	15.83	21.41	30.53	48.53	102.10
16	16.05	21.68	30.88	49.04	103.13
18	16.21	21.88	31.15	49.44	103.93
20	16.33	22.05	31.36	49.76	104.57
>> 20 (M/D/1)	17.55	23.50	33.28	52.63	110.33

Table 7.2. – CDV Tolerance τ Values as a Function of the Peak Emission Interval T and the Offered Load to the M+D/D/1 Reference Model

Bounding the CDV is still necessary since the UPC/NPC has to be designed for an upperbound CDV which can cover all existing and future applications. This upperbound CDV can be derived from a model with Head of the Line (HoL) priorities since simulations studies have demonstrated that this model mimics quite closely the traffic behavior of classical LANs and other shared medium based ATM switches (DQDB, etc.) which are assumed to produce from time to time large bursts of clustered cells (Roberts, 1992). Some typical values are depicted in Table 7.3.

Load (Erlang)	τ (Cell time units)	τ (ms)
0.5	93	0.263
0.6	162	0.458
0.7	317	0.896
0.8	775	2.19
0.85	1433	4.05

Table 7.3. – CDV Tolerance τ Values as a Function of the Offered Load to the M+D/D/1 HoL Priority Reference Model

7.7. UPC/NPC PERFORMANCE METRICS

7.7.1. UPC location

Usage parameter control is performed on VCCs or VPCs at the point where the first VP or VC links are terminated within the network. Three possibilities can be identified as shown in Fig. 7.8.

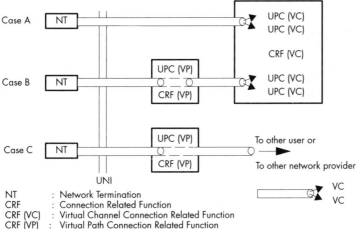

Fig. 7.8. – Location of the Usage Parameter Control Functions

- In case A the user is connected directly to the Virtual Channel Connection Related Function CRF(VC) and Usage Parameter Control is performed within the CRF(VC) on VCCs before the switching function is executed.
- When the user is connected directly to CRF(VC) via CRF(VP), as shown in case B, then the UPC is performed within the CRF(VP) on VPCs only and within the CRF(VC) on VCCs only.
- In case C the user is connected to a user or to another network provider via CRF(VP) the UPC is performed within the CRF(VP) on VPCs only. VCC usage parameter control will be done by another network provider whenever a CRF(VC) is present.

7.7.2. UPC/NPC actions

The UPC/NPC is intended to control the traffic offered by an ATM connection to ensure compliance with the negotiated traffic contract. The objective is to prevent a user from exceeding the traffic contract. At the cell level, actions of the UPC/NPC function may be :

(a) Cell passing.
(b) Cell tagging (network operator optional); cell tagging operates on $CLP = 0$ cells only by overwriting the CLP bit to 1.
(c) Cell discarding.

Cell passing is performed on cells which are identified by a UPC/NPC as acceptable. Cell tagging and cell discarding are performed on cells which are identified by a UPC/NPC as non-acceptable.

At connection level the UPC/NPC may optionally release the connection.

7.7.3. UPC performance metrics

Two metrics have so far been identified in CCITT for assessing the performance of UPC/NPC mechanisms. Methods for evaluating UPC/NPC performance and the need to standardize these methods are still for further study. The considered metrics are :

- Response time : the time to detect a given non-compliant situation on a connection under given reference conditions.
- Transparency : for the same set of reference conditions, the accuracy with which the UPC/NPC initiates appropriate control actions on a non-compliant connection and avoids inappropriate control actions on a compliant connection.

Inappropriate actions of the UPC/NPC on conforming cells of a compliant connection are part of the overall network performance degradation. Safety margins may be provisioned depending upon the UPC/NPC algorithm to limit the degradation introduced by the UPC/NPC.

7.8. ADDITIONAL CONTROL FUNCTIONS

On top of the two basic control functions, UPC/NPC and CAC, which can make use of information that passes across the UNI/NNI, the following ones may be used in appropriate combinations to support and complement the defined actions of UPC/NPC and CAC :

- *Priority Control* (PC) comes into play when users generate different priority traffic flows by using the Cell Loss Priority (CLP) bit. A network element may then selectively discard cells with low priority if necessary to protect as far as possible the network performance for cells with high priority.
- *Traffic Shaping* (TS) is defined as a mechanism that alters the traffic characteristics of a stream of cells on a VCC or a VPC to ensure that for example the traffic crossing the UNI is compliant to the User-Network traffic or to maximize in some parts of the ATM network bandwidth resource utilization.
- *Network Resource Management* (NRM) describes the provisions used to allocate network resources in order to separate traffic flows according to service characteristics.
- *Feedback Controls* (FC) are defined as the set of actions taken by the network and by the users to regulate the traffic submitted on ATM connections according to the state of network elements.

7.8.1. Priority control

When an ATM connection utilizes the CLP capability on user request, network resources are allocated to CLP = 0 (high priority) and CLP = 1 (low priority) traffic flows. By controlling CLP = 0 and CLP = 0 + 1 traffic flows, allocating adequate resources and suitably routing, a network operator may provide 2 requested QoS classes for CLP = 0 and CLP = 1 cell flows.

   If the tagging option is used by a network operator, CLP = 0 cells identified by the UPC/NPC function performed on CLP = 0 flow as non-conforming are converted to CLP = 1 cells and merged with the user-submitted CLP = 1 traffic flow before the CLP = 0 + 1 traffic flow enters the UPC/NPC mechanism. A cell identified as non-conforming by the UPC/NPC function performed on the aggregate CLP = 0 + 1 flow is discarded.

   When no additional network resources have been allocated for CLP = 1 traffic flow (either on user request or due to network provisioning), CLP = 0 cells identified by the UPC/NPC as non-conforming are discarded. In this case, tagging is not applicable.

Since cell sequence integrity is maintained on any ATM connection, the UPC/NPC including its optional tagging action must operate as a single server using First In First Out (FIFO) service discipline for each ATM connection.

When the CLP capability is used by an ATM connection and the CLP = 0 + 1 aggregate flow is not compliant to the traffic contract, the UPC/NPC function performed on the aggregate flow may discard CLP = 0 cells which were not considered in excess by the UPC/NPC function performed on the CLP = 0 cell stream.

7.8.2. Traffic shaping

Traffic shaping (TS) partially compensates for the effects of CDV on the peak cell rate of the ATM connection. Examples of traffic shaping mechanisms are respacing cells of individual ATM connections according to their peak cell rate or suitable service schemes.

When used in the source ATM endpoint, traffic shaping is a mechanism that attains desired characteristics for the stream of cells emitted into a VCC or a VPC. When used in an ATM switch, traffic shaping is a mechanism that alters the traffic characteristics of a stream of cells on a VCC or a VPC to achieve a desired modification of those traffic characteristics. Traffic shaping must maintain cell sequence integrity on an ATM connection.

Examples of traffic shaping are peak cell rate reduction, burst length limiting and reduction of CDV by suitably spacing cells over time.

Traffic shaping in CPE may be done to be in compliance with the traffic descriptor and associated parameter values that were negotiated with the network. Traffic shaping is an optional function. For example, an ATM endpoint may choose to shape to the negotiated peak cell rate for the aggregate cell stream of CLP = 0 and CLP = 1 cells and may choose not to shape to the negotiated peak cell rate for the CLP = 0 cell stream and instead to allow the network to mark as CLP = 1 the non-conforming CLP = 0 cells.

7.8.3. Network resource management

Virtual Paths are an important component of traffic control and resource management in the BISDN. They can be used to :

- Simplify CAC.
- Implement a form of priority control by segregating traffic types requiring different QoS.
- Efficiently distribute messages for the operation of particular traffic control schemes.
- Aggregate user-to-user services such that the UPC/NPC can be applied to the traffic aggregate.

By reserving capacity on VPCs, the processing required to establish individual VCCs is drastically reduced. Individual VCCs can be established by making simple connection admission decisions at nodes where VPCs are terminated. Strategies for the reservation of capacity on VPCs will be determined by the trade-off between increased capacity costs and reduced control costs. These strategies are left to operator's decision.

Combining common routing and priority control may be used by CAC for services requiring a number of VCCs with low differential delays and different cell loss ratios (e.g. multimedia services).

When statistical multiplexing of virtual channel links is applied by the network operator, virtual path connections may be used in order to separate traffic thereby preventing statistical multiplexing with other types of traffic. This requirement for separation implies that more than one virtual path connection may be necessary between network origination/destination pairs to carry a full range of QoS between them.

7.9. BIBLIOGRAPHY

ATM Forum, "Traffic Management Baseline text of the ATM UNI Specification", February 1993

Bellcore Technical Advisory "Broadband ISDN Switching System Generic Requirements", TA-NWT-001110, Issue 1, August 1992

Boyer P., Servel M., Guillemin F., "The Spacer-Controller : An Efficient UPC/NPC for ATM Networks", ISS '92, Symposium, Yokohama, October 1992

Boyer P., Guillemin F., Servel M., Coudreuse J., "Spacing Cells Protects and Enhances Utilization of ATM Network Links", IEEE Network Magazine, pp 38-49, September 1992

Brochin F., "A Cell Spacing Device for Congestion Control in ATM Networks", Performance Evaluation 16 (1992) 107-127, North Holland

Bruneel H., Kim B., "Discrete-time models for communication systems including ATM", Kluwer Academic Publishers, Boston 1993

CCITT Draft Recommendation I.371, "Traffic Control and Congestion Control in B-ISDN", Geneva, June 1992

CCITT SGXVIII/8, "Dimensioning CDV Parameter for UPC algorithms and limiting its effect on an ATM network", Document 2419, British Telecom, Geneva, Switzerland, January 18-29, 1993

Desmet E., "About the impact of the CDV tolerance on the allocation of network resources for Constant Bit Rate Connections", Contribution submitted to the ATM Forum, November 1992

Eckberg A., Doshi B., Zoccolillo R., " Controlling Congestion in B-ISDN/ATM : Issues and Strategies", IEEE Communications Magazine, pp 64-70, September 1991

Eckberg A., "B-ISDN/ATM Traffic and Congestion Control", IEEE Network Magazine, pp 28-37, September 1992

ETSI-NA5, "An Upper-bound for the Clumping Tolerance Parameter at the T_B interface", Technical Document TD65, France Telecom, Ostende, Belgium, November 1992

ETSI-NA5, "Granularity of ATM Connection Peak Rate", Technical Document TD63, France Telecom, Ostende, Belgium, November 1992

ETSI-NA5-TCR Working Group, Draft Specification on "Traffic Control and Congestion Control in B-ISDN", 1993

Guillemin F., Dupuis A., "A Basic Requirement for the Policing Function in ATM Networks", Computer Networks and ISDN Systems 24 (1992) 311-320, North Holland

Rathgeb E., "Modeling and Performance Comparison of Policing Mechanisms for ATM Networks", IEEE JSAC 9, No. 3, pp. 325-334, 1991

Roberts J., Guillemin F., "Jitter in ATM Networks and its Impact on Peak Rate Enforcement", Performance Evaluation 16 (1992) 35-48, North Holland

Roberts J., "COST 224 : Performance Evaluation and Design of Multiservice Networks", Commission of the European Communities – Information Technologies and Sciences, Luxembourg, 1992

Turner J., "Managing Bandwidth in ATM Networks with Bursty Traffic", IEEE Network Magazine, pp 50-58, September 1992

Wallmeier E., Worster T., "The Spacing Policer, An Algorithm for Efficient Peak Bit Rate Control in ATM Networks", ISS '92, Yokohama, October 1992

Yamanaka N., Sato Y., Sato K., "Traffic Shaping for VBR Traffic in ATM Networks", IEICE Transactions on Communications, Vol. E75-B, No. 10, October 1992

8

Introduction Strategies for ATM

8.1. INTRODUCTION

ATM represents a major step forward with respect to the telecommunication service offered, compared with the existing services. It does not only offer customers a large number of new services using higher bit rates, but offers them also the possibility to integrate its different services into one generic solution.

However, since most of today's installed terminals (TV, telephone, router, computer, ...) and telecommunication networks (LAN, PABX, ...) are not ATM based, a careful introduction plan must be worked out, to guarantee a smooth transition from the current situation to the final target solution, in which all terminals have a direct ATM interface, and where all services are transported via the ATM network.

To reach this final solution, ATM will be introduced in several places of the network, like the customer's network, the access network, the switching and trunk network. For each part of the network, the introduction strategy must be adapted to the specific functionalities of that part of the network.

I will therefore describe the way ATM can be introduced in these 3 parts of the network separately. The introduction phases of these 3 solutions can occur at a different moment in time for each specific part of the network. One can for instance start with the introduction of ATM in the private customer's network without an ATM access or switching network. In this case only local ATM high speed switching functionality is offered. Or, one can imagine the use of ATM only in the access network, where only the existing services of the access network are multiplexed on a single ATM access network. Terminals and the switching network remain unmodified. Or, thirdly, one can also imagine a public ATM switching system without private ATM systems, offering wide area broadband interconnectivity for all existing services.

It is however clear, that if the introduction phases of these 3 individual network elements can optimally be aligned in time, the interworking problems can be reduced, thereby reducing the cost and enhancing the chances for an early success of the broadband ATM solution.

I will now describe separately the introduction scenario for the 3 network elements mentioned : private networks, access network and switching network.

8.2. ATM IN THE PRIVATE NETWORK

In the private environment, the ever increasing power of workstations and servers, along with the introduction of multimedia to the desktop has generated an increase in bandwidth requirements for the transfer of information in the office, campus, etc. This increasing demand has stepwise put the existing LANs to its limitations in terms of capacity (bit rate, distance) and is one of the reasons for the success of hubs in the late 1980s. This evolution will continue, and will stepwise justify the introduction of ATM in the private environment.

8.2.1. The evolution of intelligent hubs

Today's intelligent hubs are direct descendants of the simple wiring hubs that first appeared in the mid-1980s. Wiring hubs were a major step forward for LAN technologies because shared medium LANs moved onto the backplane of the hub, rather than being distributed throughout a building on a cable plant. This hub approach allowed LANs to be deployed in star topologies with users plugged in on point-to-point links to the hub. In addition, it simplified the administration of the networks and it increased their reliability. Although the topology of the network is physically different, from a logical viewpoint, wiring hubs are still shared medium devices – traffic from all users is sent across the LAN backplane and hence to all user ports.

The administrative and reliability advantages of hubs lead to the rapid replacement of traditional LAN designs. Another benefit of hubs that became apparent was that the centralization of all networks in the hub also facilitated (and often mandated, due to the single point of failure) the incorporation of network management capabilities into the hub. Wiring hubs became intelligent hubs, supporting increasingly sophisticated network management capabilities. This in turn fueled the popularity of hubs and LANs, with the result that the single LAN backplanes of first generation hubs soon became saturated, and users began demanding greater bandwidth in their hubs.

The need for additional bandwidth lead to the generation of intelligent hubs (Fig. 8.1.).

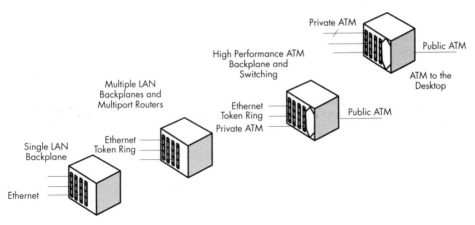

Fig. 8.1. – Evolution of Wiring Hubs

These intelligent hubs support multiple LAN segments of multiple LAN types (Ethernet, Token Ring and FDDI for instance) and provide bridge and routing functionality. Segmented backplanes allow network administrators to form communities of interest, grouping together users with common communication patterns onto their own segments, thereby reducing congestion for other users. These multiple segments are connected together through multiport routing and bridging hubs.

But, even this generation hubs suffer from the same fundamental limitations of LAN backplanes – all bandwidth is shared, so that even high speed internetworking modules must share bandwidth with user ports. The amount of bandwidth that any one user can use is still only a fraction of that of the LAN segment.

To extend further the capabilities of the hubs, 2 distinct approaches have been developed, both by adding ATM to the hub. One approach is to add a cell-based backplane to current hubs. Such systems, called ATM Hubs, incorporate a segmented LAN backplane for Ethernet, Token Rings, and FDDI, and a high speed (gigabit plus) cell-based bus.

The second approach for adding ATM to the hub uses an ATM gateway or ATM routing module – a module that performs the AAL function for the entire hub. This allows these hubs to interconnect with private or public ATM networks.

8.2.2. Initial application of ATM hubs

In a first step, only the very powerful systems (servers, powerful workstations), requiring high bandwidths, will be directly connected through an ATM interface to the ATM hub. The major part of the terminals will be connected through dedicated LAN interfaces. The ATM hub will support local switching and concentration. A dedicated LAN interface gives each user a "private or personal" network since it provides the equivalent of one user per network. Because Ethernet is the most widely deployed media today and associated with many high performance workstations, much of the demand for dedicated LAN support is driven by Ethernet users. A full ATM interface will only be used to support a small group of applications with very high bandwidth needs, such as powerful servers for multimedia applications, for which the high bandwidths are economically justifiable.

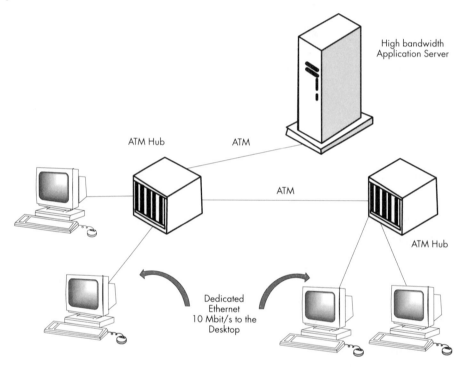

Fig. 8.2. – Dedicated LAN Interfaces and ATM UNI

As shown in Fig. 8.2., the workstations are directly connected to the ATM hubs via point-to-point Ethernet links. Only the powerful server is directly connected through an ATM private UNI interface. This way, ATM will gradually enter the customer premises network.

8.2.3. The use of ATM LANs

ATM hubs will support the installed base of existing LANS (Ethernet, Token Ring, ...), but will give every terminal the full capacity, by relying on the high switching capabilities of the hub (Fig. 8.3.). Multiple hubs (one per floor in the technical room) will be connected to each other via a router.

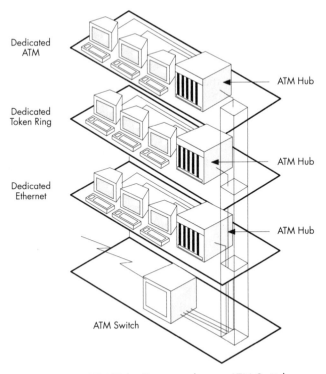

Fig. 8.3. – ATM Hubs Connected to an ATM Switch

The connection capabilities and performance of a router are limited, so that finally an ATM switch will be installed. This ATM switch can then provide full switching capabilities amongst the hubs, but it will also give direct access to powerful workstations and servers via an ATM interface. In addition this ATM switch will provide the necessary interfaces to the public ATM network.

In the coming years, the terminals will become more and more powerful, and also multimedia features will be provided to every terminal. This will create higher bandwidth requirements for every terminal, so that finally every terminal will have its ATM interface, just like today's PC all have their direct Ethernet interface.

8.3. ATM IN THE ACCESS NETWORK

Residential customers today are mainly interested in POTS (Plain Old Telephone Service) and TV distribution. Potentially, they may also require VOD (Video On Demand) services. POTS and TV distribution services are already nowadays offered by the existing copper networks (twisted pairs for POTS, coax CATV for TV). However, several operators have plans to start deployment of fiber in the loop (FITL). Most of them have already running experiments and trials (Tenzer, 1991).

However, a FITL solution which offers only POTS and TV distribution without any evolutionary capabilities to BISDN services is not defensible, since the huge investment to be put in the infrastructure, needs the capability to evolve to BISDN. Or, what is even more important, must give the operators the capabilities to generate additional revenues on top of these for POTS and CATV.

On the other hand, business customers today are frequently using a PABX, for voice, and routers and LANs for data. They are interested to get the different types of information across the wide area network. Especially, they are interested in transporting all this information over a shared access, since this may reduce its operational costs thanks to a better pooling of resources, less administration and support. It is also expected that they will install in the future an ATM LAN as described above and will thus need a BISDN public interface.

To guarantee a smooth evolution to ATM based BISDN, a local access architecture can be deployed, which is fully future safe and on the other hand is not more expensive than other comparable proposals which offer only the existing services (POTS, NISDN and TV distribution). Figure 8.4. illustrates the system approach : on one hand, it is FITL a system that is well suited for provision of today's <u>narrowband</u> (POTS, ISDN, frame relay, T1/E1) <u>and TV distribution services,</u> on the other hand, it is well suited for use as <u>BISDN local loop</u> to offer future BISDN services (SMDS/CBDS, frame relay, ATM, Video on Demand). SMDS is the service for high speed data interconnectivity defined by Bellcore, CBDS offers a comparable service and is standardized by ETSI.

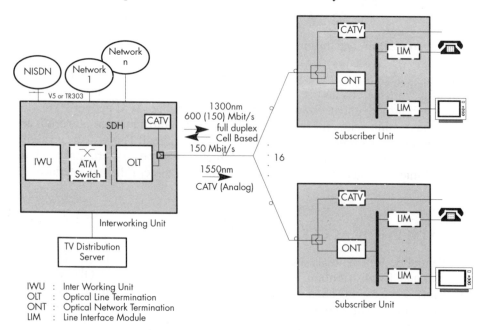

IWU : Inter Working Unit
OLT : Optical Line Termination
ONT : Optical Network Termination
LIM : Line Interface Module

Fig. 8.4. – ATM in the Access Network

The basic options selected for this access architecture are a cell based ATM transport over a PON (Passive Optical Network) topology, sharing the total bandwidth over multiple subscribers in the access network. Since the sytem combines ATM and PON technology in one solution, it will be referred to as APON (ATM PON).

8.3.1. FITL with PON technology

A PON technology based on passive optical splitters gives the lowest cost, both for current FITL as for future BISDN applications. A flexible sharing of the bandwidth resources between the connected subscribers and proper dimensioning guarantees sufficient bandwidth for future BISDN services. The privacy and security issues are coped with by encryption of the digital information.

8.3.2. High capacity point-to-multipoint transport system

All interactive services (from POTS, NISDN, frame relay to BISDN including VOD (Video on Demand), SMDS, CBDS,...) are transported in the 1.3 μm window in ATM cells. Upstream a useful bit rate of 150 Mbit/s is available (physical rate is 155 Mbit/s). Downstream a useful bit rate of 150 or 600 Mbit/s is available out of a physical rate of 155 or 622 Mbit/s. The selection of the bit rate (150 or 600 Mbit/s) can be based on the expected services. If only interactive services (including VOD) are envisaged, 150 Mbit/s downstream will be sufficient. If distributive services have also to be transported, an additional 450 Mbit/s (e.g. 100 channels at 4.5 Mbit/s video) can be added resulting in a 600 Mbit/s downstream channel.

A cell based transport system is used, since ATM provides a proper basis for multiplexing and for a multiple access scheme for the point-to-multipoint transport system. As was explained in Chapter 2, ATM is very flexible for multiplexing different service mixes as well as for different bandwidth requirements. This is also valid in the access network. The cell based format also turns out to be economical in terms of required buffer space, implementation complexity and hence cost. In addition compatibility with the future BISDN network is provided by using ATM cells. Sufficient bandwidth capacity is foreseen to cover the requirements for the expected BISDN services.

Within the system, existing services like POTS and NISDN are also transported over the ATM based transport system, hence this solution is not an overlay, but an integrated system. The subscriber units, installed at the customer premises, can be equipped with as many service adaptors (LIM or Line Interface Module on Fig. 8.4.), as required by the customer. One can imagine that the customer only starts with POTS, and later will add a LIM (plug-in module) for VOD.

In addition, it can be envisaged to transport the distributive services in the 1.55 μm window, using linear lasers and optical amplifiers to guarantee enough power to the receiving side. The TV channels are transported in an analog format.

8.3.2.1. *Transport system*

The transport system includes the following parts:

- OLT (Optical Line Termination) at the exchange side.
- Passive splitter (distributed or centralized) in the subscriber loop plant.
- ONT (Optical Network Termination) at the subscriber premises.

The ONT module is the most critical element for the APON system, since it will be installed at every customer (16 times), versus one OLT at the network side. Its cost will therefore greatly determine the overall cost of the system. Consequently, its concept must be as simple as possible and optimized with respect to power consumption, reliability, and cost.

(1) *Multiplexing / multiple access*

A cell based TDM/TDMA technique is used to support this access topology, assuring full duplex operation and multiple access to one fiber feeder (Fig. 8.5.).

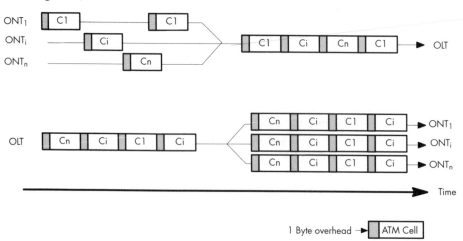

Fig. 8.5. – The TDM/TDMA Technique for the APON System

For both directions, ATM cells are encapsulated in APON packets. A small packet overhead is added to each ATM cell to provide synchronization and network transport related functions, e.g. ONT identification for the upstream multiple access protocol. Special care has been taken to minimize the length of the packet overhead in order to keep the network efficiency as high as possible with regard to ATM payload transport capacity. A single octet overhead per ATM cell has been proven to be sufficient to provide the required functionalities (Mestdagh, 1991).

This results in exactly the same overhead as SDH : 155.52 Mbit/s physical bit rates for 149.76 Mbit/s payload, or 4 times this value for 622 Mbit/s. Operation and Maintenance (O&M) functions are provided by means of PLOAM cells (Physical Layer O&M).

In the downstream direction, individual cells are identified by their VCI/VPI field, and addressing of the subscribers is based on this field. In the upstream direction, only one subscriber is allowed to transmit at a given time. This is determined by the OLT, which generates grants for the different ONTs. The grants are transported in the downstream overhead octets. Grants and upstream transmission are pipelined in such a way that in the upstream direction a continuous stream of cells is multiplexed on the fiber, separated by only a small guardband. This guardband is provided by the one byte overhead per ATM cel. In addition, this mechanism of "granting" every individual cell provides an implicit policing function.

(2) *Capacity*

The system is designed for a splitting factor of up to 16. The limiting factor is mainly the available bandwidth to be shared over the subscribers and the available optical power budget. It is proposed to share a capacity of 155 Mbit/s over up to 16 subscribers. For higher splitting factors, higher bit rates would be required, or less bandwidth would be available to every customer.

For the downstream direction, a bit rate of 155 Mbit/s or 622 Mbit/s has been selected. The 622 Mbit/s solution is required in order to provide sufficient bandwidth capacity for TV distribution services. The APON system provides an excellent platform for the implementation of Video-On-Demand services.

8.3.2.2.   *Enabling techniques*

To achieve a low cost, high performance and flexible transport system, the following techniques can be adopted.

(1) *Full duplex operation*

Full duplex operation on a single wavelength (i.e. upstream and downstream transmission at 1300 nm) has been selected for the following reasons:

- Single fiber access.
- No stringent requirements on wavelength stability (as would be required with WDM (Wavelength Division Multiplexing) in the same optical window).

- 100 % bandwidth available (compared to about 30 % for ping-pong operation).
- 1550 nm window is kept free for analog CATV or future extensions.

For full duplex operation, a power penalty has to be added to the optical power budget, in order to compensate for the light reflected backwards in the optical cable plant and a 3 dB coupler. Calculations, confirmed by experimental evidence (Mestdagh, 1991), showed that this power penalty is negligible if following conditions are met:

- Power splitter directivity > +50 dB.
- Connector and splice reflectivity < –45 dB.

The first condition is easily achieved with fused fiber or planar waveguide splitters.

The second condition restricts the type of connectors that can be used. SC (Subscriber Connector) or FC/APC (Angled-face Physical Contact) connectors currently provide the required specification. New low cost, low reflectivity connectors are becoming available (EC (European Connector) connector).

For environments where full duplex is not possible (e.g. high reflectivity cable plants) or not requested, the APON transport system can also support 2 fiber mode of operation (one fiber for upstream, one fiber for downstream). It could also support WDM (1300 nm for upstream, 1500 nm for downstream).

(2) *Synchronization*

Cells transmitted in the upstream directions are interleaved at the optical splitter. In order to reduce the overhead between consecutive cells as much as possible, and thus to achieve maximum bandwidth performance, a fast synchronization method has been developed, allowing recovery of the clock phase with a very short preamble (3 bits).

The uncertainty of the arrival of a cell from a given subscriber unit, is first reduced to +/– 1 bit by a ranging mechanism. (See further.)

Each upstream ATM cell is preceded by a 3 bit CPA (Clock Phase Alignment) pattern, i.e. 010. This pattern is sampled by n clock signals, with an offset of 360/n degrees. The center of the pattern is searched for, and the clock corresponding with this center is used to sample the data.

The instantaneous clock phase is integrated over time with previous measurements for the same subscriber unit, in order to avoid bit error multiplication, if the CPA pattern is corrupted.

(3) *Optical power equalization*

Due to the differences in fiber length and splitting factor, the optical power received from the different subscriber units is in general not equal. The maximum difference is less than 20 dB (1:2 splitter at short distance compared to 1:16 at maximum distance). Half of this power difference and laser output uncertainty is eliminated by levelling the laser output at the ONT side, while the remaining power difference and laser output uncertainty is handled by the limiting amplifier of the receiver in the OLT.

(4) *Non-interrupting ranging technique*

A two-step ranging technique can be used, which allows for hot insert of subscriber units, and does not generate excessive cell jitter (access jitter).

In a first step, coarse ranging is carried out to reduce the uncertainty on the delay to within +/– 1 cell. This coarse ranging is based on the transmission of a low power, low frequency correlation pattern, PSK modulated on a 155 MHz carrier, from ONT to OLT, at the request of the OLT during the initialization phase.

At the OLT side, this ranging signal is recovered by correlating the noisy input signal with the correlation pattern. The location of the autocorrelation peak is an indication for the delay and thus the distance of the ONT. An accuracy of +/– 1 cell is attained.

In a second step, a 2 cell period (to cover the uncertainty of +/– 1 cell) is reserved in the upstream direction, and a fine ranging pattern is introduced during this time period. The delay for this pattern to reach the OLT is counted, and gives a measure of the subscriber unit distance to within +/– 1 bit.

If no coarse ranging were to be used, a 36 cell period would need to be reserved in the upstream direction, which would lead to excessive cell jitter for the already active subscriber units. As a consequence, this would introduce extra delay and memory requirements for the system.

(5) *Access mechanism*

Due to the physical topology, it is difficult to develop a high performance connectionless access mechanism for a PON based local loop. The main problem is that communication between neighboring subscriber units is only possible via the OLT. Due to the propagation time, it takes at least 100 μs (10 km) to exchange access control information between neighboring subscriber units.

Therefore, a different and simple approach has been selected. By confining to peak bandwidth allocation, the access mechanism becomes a semi-static process, which can be centralized in the OLT. The (peak) bandwidth requirements of all subscriber units are known at the OLT side (communicated by the subscriber units at initialization time or call set-up time). Therefore, it is possible to implement a simple scheduler at the OLT side, which schedules grants to the subscriber units. The frequency of the grants is proportional to the bandwidth allocated to the subscriber units.

The grants are communicated to the subscriber units by inserting a TEA (Transmit Enable Address) in the downstream direction. When the TEA matches the physical address of a subscriber unit, the subscriber unit can transmit during the corresponding cell slot in the upstream direction. These TEA bits can easily be put in the one byte overhead of the APON system.

As the whole access mechanism is a semi-static process, it can be pipelined, relieving the speed requirements at both the ONT and the OLT side.

8.3.3. Modular equipment at the subscriber side

The evolutionary strategy of the system is largely based on the modular extensibility of the user equipment. For a FITL installation, this equipment will support for example POTS and analog CATV termination. For upgrading to BISDN, a Video-On-Demand and/or a PRA interface (E1/T1) for circuit emulation, an S_b termination or SMDS/CBDS termination board could be plugged in, without interrupting the operational services.

Data from different subscriber applications are adapted to the ATM format in the subscriber unit using the appropriate AAL. The resulting ATM cells are multiplexed into one ATM stream, and sent to the transport system. Conversely, ATM cells received from the transport system are demultiplexed according to their VPI/VCI and translated into the original format. Common functions such as powering, battery backup, operation and maintenance are also performed within the subscriber unit (Fig. 8.6.).

The key to the system is the modularity of this subscriber unit. It is based on a set of LIMs (Line Interface Modules), each implemented on individual PCBs, all with a common shared ATM bus. All service terminal adaptation functions (AAL) are provided on a per service and a per board basis.

LIMS can be imagined for current services, such as POTS, NISDN (AAL1) but also for future services, e.g. Video-On-Demand (VOD), including a video decoder (AAL2) for digital TV distribution based on MPEG, SMDS/CBDS termination (AAL3/4), S_b interface (no AAL), frame relay (AAL5), etc. These LIMs are plug-in compatible and different types can be exchanged.

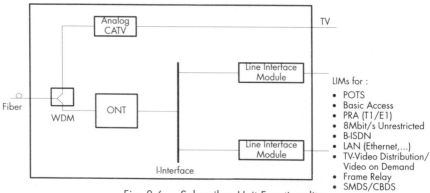

Fig. 8.6. – Subscriber Unit Functionality

For video-on-demand, a digital video decoder (based on MPEG, ...) can be plugged into this subscriber unit. The digital TV signal coming from the network will be converted to analog in the VOD LIM. It will then, in-house, be transported in an analog format to the TV set. The commands from the user to the TV set will, via a simple set-top box, be conveyed to the subscriber unit which will then transport it in ATM cells to the network. The network will then send the appropriate digital TV signal to the subscriber unit.

The equipment installed at the residential and business customers can be modularly upgraded when new BISDN services appear and when the customers need them. The equipment already installed at the CPE must not be replaced, but the new services will be offered by simply adding extra plug-in modules to the already installed equipment. At the Central Office, the equipment can easily be extended to give it access to the BISDN network or other specialized networks.

8.3.4. Expandable interworking unit at the central office

In its basic version, this interworking unit consists of an interface adaptor (including ATM/STM conversion) towards the PSTN over for example V5 or TR303. Note that such an interface adapter is required for every FITL system, even those only transporting PSTN services, since in PON solutions, the framing bits and multiplexing information have to be removed/inserted. With increasing demand, this IWU can be extended in functionality (VPI ATM cross-connect and switching functions) and size. Eventually, it will grow to a full size ATM exchange (Fig. 8.7.).

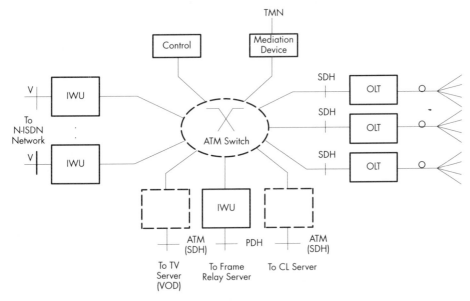

Fig. 8.7. – The APON Interworking Unit

The system is mainly oriented towards residential and small business subscribers. The bandwidth flexibility offered by the transport system makes it well suited for a mix of both types of subscribers, as is found in a lot of locations. It also allows a simple reconfiguration of bandwidth if required when a new customer is moving into an already served house, which has different bandwidth requirements compared to the previous user.

8.3.5. Evolution capabilities

The proposed approach provides an ideal evolution both with respect to the offered services and with respect to reuse of the installed equipment and cable plant.

(a) Services

Today's available services for the residential customers are POTS/ISDN for the interactive ones and TV distribution for the distributive ones. The proposed architecture will offer to those customers initially these POTS/NISDN and TV distributions services. To the business customers it will provide POTS, ISDN (BA and PRA (E1/T1)) and high speed data connectivity such as local area network interconnectivity often referred to as frame relay or SMDS/CBDS at a limited speed.

In the future, it is expected that BISDN based on ATM will bring to the residential customers services like videophone, digital video-on-demand and HDTV. To the business customer, it will bring videophone, video conference, frame relay and SMDS/CBDS at a higher speed. It is obvious that the ATM transport system can carry these current and future services in a straightforward manner.

(b) Cable plant and equipment

The equipment (Subscriber Unit) installed at the residential and business customers can be modularly upgraded when new BISDN services appear and when the customers need them. Evolution towards BISDN services is as simple as plugging in modules corresponding to the required services.

In addition, the in-house cabling at the customer can be fully reused. The TV set can continue to live with its analog interface. A small set-up box will provide the necessary interface for video-on-demand towards the subscriber unit. The control information from this set top box can easily be transported over the in-house installed coaxial cable towards the subscriber unit. This subscriber unit will then transport this control information towards the network, or interpret it locally if required.

8.4. ATM IN THE SWITCHING NETWORK

Today, large business users often construct their own virtual private network (VPN) using leased lines of a public operator. An ATM cross-connect network can offer these users a much higher flexibility in the use of the resources leased in the network.

Such ATM cross-connect network offers a number of advantages (Tokizawa, 1991) such as simplified multiplexing and cross-connecting paths with a variety of bandwidths, simplified multiplexing techniques and flexible bandwidth allocation.

These advantages are directly applicable to the business customer, since such a network (Fig. 8.8.) can offer to the user the following services :

- Semi-permanent virtual connections between the different subscriber units.
- These virtual connections are controlled by an operator based on a reservation scheme (e.g. peak bit rate allocation). The business customer can easily request at any moment in time a reorganization of its virtual private network. The information rate can be any value between 1 Kbit/s and 150 Mbit/s. If required, higher values can also be envisaged.
- Multiple virtual connections can be assigned to different destinations. These virtual connections can be point-to-point and point-to-multipoint.

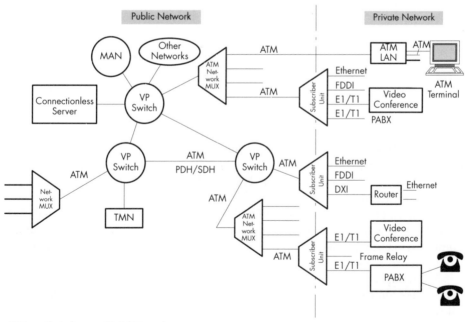

PDH : Plesiochronous Digital Hierarchy
SDH : Synchronous Digital Hierarchy
TMN : Telecommunication Management Network

Fig. 8.8. – ATM Cross-connect Network

Existing services and service interfaces are converted to ATM at the customer in the service multiplexer, also called the subscriber unit. As shown in Figure 8.9., the subscriber unit combines traffic from different local communication equipments such as LANs (Ethernet, FDDI, ...), PABXs (e.g. 2 Mbit/s PRA via circuit emulation), frame relay, B-Routers, ATM LANs, or video conference rooms. All traffic is converted into ATM cells at the customer's place and transported through the network to the correct destination.

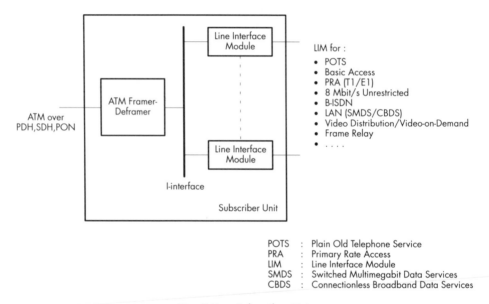

LIM for :
- POTS
- Basic Access
- PRA (T1/E1)
- 8 Mbit/s Unrestricted
- B-ISDN
- LAN (SMDS/CBDS)
- Video Distribution/Video-on-Demand
- Frame Relay
- . . . .

POTS	:	Plain Old Telephone Service
PRA	:	Primary Rate Access
LIM	:	Line Interface Module
SMDS	:	Switched Multimegabit Data Services
CBDS	:	Connectionless Broadband Data Services

Fig. 8.9. – Subscriber Unit

The ATM streams from different subscriber units (service multiplexer) are possibly combined in a network multiplexer, which can add/drop new virtual connections. This function can be compared to that of an ADM (Add-Drop Multiplexer) of SDH.

Finally, all the traffic is switched to the appropriate destination through the VP switch. This switch serves multiple virtual paths and/or multiple virtual channels combined in virtual paths. If required, a single data stream can be copied to multiple destinations.

The complete network is controlled by a network maintenance center (TMN). This center controls the allocation of virtual connections (VCI/VPI) and the related bit rate.

The transmission between the different entities of the network can be based on any physical layer, i.e. PDH, SDH or APON. Both in SDH (Synchronous Digital Hierarchy: G.709) and PDH (Plesiochronous Digital Hierarchy: G.703), the ATM cells are transported in the payload of the transmission capacity.

As is shown in Fig. 8.8., the main applications envisaged are the transportation of high speed data. However, for large customers, it can be interesting to use the same access line to get access to other networks such as ISDN, PSTN, PSPDN, etc. Therefore, also PABX and video conference interfaces are shown in the diagram.

With this solution, high speed data can easily be transported between endpoints. However, it requires that end-to-end semi-permanent connections are established, resulting in the allocation of resources which are not always fully occupied.

Therefore, another solution which overcomes some of the previously mentioned drawbacks is to connect a connectionless server to this backbone ATM cross-connect network. Such a server can for instance offer an SMDS/CBDS service.

Such a centralized server, called connectionless server in Fig. 8.8., receives all the data from the different subscriber units and decides on each packet to which destination it has to be sent.

Such a centralized connectionless server combines the functions which may otherwise be implemented in the subscriber units in a centralized place. This will make the subscriber units at the customer's premises less complex. The functions can be shared among multiple users. Such functions can for instance be :

- Routing : in the centralized approach, all packets are sent to the server, which makes the routing decision. In the VP network solution, the subscriber unit itself must decide on which virtual connection the packet has to be sent. The centralized approach may offer a faster reaction if rerouting is required due to overload or erroneous situations.
- Access class enforcement: this function will ensure that the information rate entering the network is limited to what was selected by the customer.
- Address screening: Both source and destination address screening are possible. This function allows closed user groups to be built.
- Group address expansion: this function allows the sending of information to multiple destinations.

As is also shown in Fig. 8.8., a MAN can also be connected to this ATM cross-connect network. Such a MAN can serve a specific metropolitan area and gather traffic to destinations outside that area. Since MAN and ATM standards are very close, interworking will be very straightforward, as was explained in Chapter 6.

The ATM cross-connect solution can easily evolve to fully on-demand ATM switching. Indeed, as soon as the standards for BISDN signalling are finalized, the control platforms of the ATM cross-connect can be upgraded to handle the full BISDN signalling, and ATM VC switch functionality can be added. At the business customer, the subscriber unit can be extended with an S_b interface, to which terminals with BISDN signalling can be connected.

8.5. CONCLUSION

As was shown in this chapter, ATM can be introduced step by step in different parts of the network. These introduction phases can be fully separated, but is is obvious that a coordinated effort in the 3 domains will increase the chances for success for BISDN. However, these chances are high, since firm indications are available today which confirm the simultaneous availability of products in the 3 domains of the telecommunications network.

8.6. BIBLIOGRAPHY

Borsotto J.L., Delisle D., "LAN Interconnection : An Early Application for ATM", ISS '92 Yokohoma, October 1992.

"Conceptual planning of a Pan European ATM nework", DBP, FTZ, September 1990

"Connectionless broadband data service", Draft ETS-ETSI, Karlsruhe, March 1991

De Prycker M., Paul J.L., Campos A., "Broadband national experiments in Belgium, France and Spain", Electrical Communication, Vol. 64, No. 2-3, 1990

De Prycker M., "Data Communications in an ATM network", Workshop on Fast Packet Switching, New York, September 1988

De Prycker M., "Impact of data communications on ATM", ICC '89, Boston, June 1989

"Eurescom Workplan", Doc. 17-19A, Heidelberg, March 1991

Fastrez M., De Prycker M., De Vleeschouwer A., Van Vyve J., Bousmar M., "A broadband ATM network with maximum integration of distribution and interactive services", Telecom Geneve 91, October 1991

"Generic system requirements in support of switched multimegabit data service", Bellcore TA-TSY-000772, October 1989

Inoue Y., Kawarasaki M., "Networking toward B-ISDN", NTT Review, Vol. 3, No. 3, May 1991

Mestdagh D. et al., "ATM local access over passive optical networks", Third IEEE Workshop on local optical networks", Tokyo, September 1991

Miki T. et al., "Japanese subscriber loop network and fiber optic loop development", IEEE Communications Magazine, March 1991

Miki T., "Migration strategies for Fiber to the Home", ICC '91, Denver, June 1991

Rowbotham T.R., "Local loop developments in the UK", IEEE Communications Magazine, March 1991

Sato K., Tokizawa I., "Flexible Asynchronous Transfer Mode Networks Utilizing Virtual Paths" ICC '90, San Diego, June 1990

Shumate P.W. et al., "Evolution of fiber in the residential loop plant", IEEE Communications Magazine, March 1991

Tenzer G., "The introduction of optical fiber in the subscriber loop in the telecommunication networks of DBP TELEKOM", IEEE Communications Magazine, March 1991

Tokizawa I., Kikuchi K., Sato K.,"Transmission Technologies for B-ISDN", NTT Review, Vol. 3, No. 3, May 1991

Van Landegem T., "Support of Connectionless Services in ATM", ICC' 91, Denver, June 1991

Walters S.M., Ahmed M., "Broadband Virtual Private Networks and their Evolution", ISS' 92, Yokohoma, October 1992.

Index

ELLIS HORWOOD SERIES IN COMPUTERS AND THEIR APPLICATIONS

Series Editor: IAN CHIVERS, Senior Analyst, The Computer Centre, King's College, London, and formerly Senior Programmer and Analyst, Imperial College of Science and Technology, University of London

Series continued from front of book

Michalewicz, Z.	**STATISTICAL AND SCIENTIFIC DATABASES**
Moseley, L.G., Sharp, J.A. & Salenieks, P.	**PASCAL IN PRACTICE**
Narayanan, A. & Sharkey, N.E.	**AN INTRODUCTION TO LISP**
Phillips, C. & Cornelius, B.J.	**COMPUTATIONAL NUMERICAL METHODS**
Rahtz, S.P.Q.	**INFORMATION TECHNOLOGY IN THE HUMANITIES**
Ramsden, E.	**MICROCOMPUTERS IN EDUCATION 2**
Rubin, T.	**USER INTERFACE DESIGN FOR COMPUTER SYSTEMS**
Rudd, A.S.	**PRACTICAL USAGE OF ISPF DIALOG MANAGER**
Rudd, A.S.	**PRACTICAL USAGE OF REXX**
Rudd, A.S.	**IMPLEMENTING PRACTICAL DB2 APPLICATIONS**
Rudd, A.S.	**IMPLEMENTING PRACTICAL DATABASE MANAGER APPLICATIONS**
Salomon, D.	**ASSEMBLERS AND LOADERS**
de Saram, H.	**PROGRAMMING IN MICRO-PROLOG**
Savic, D.	**OBJECT-ORIENTED PROGRAMMING WITH SMALLTALK/V**
Schofield, C.F.	**OPTIMIZING FORTRAN PROGRAMS**
Semmens, L. & Allen, P.	**Z FOR SOFTWARE ENGINEERS**
Sharp, J.A.	**DATA FLOW COMPUTING**
Sherif, M.A.	**DATABASE PROJECTS**
Smith, J.H.	**SGML AND RELATED STANDARDS: Document Description & Processing Languages**
Stein, R.	**REAL-TIME MULTICOMPUTER SOFTWARE SYSTEMS**
Teunissen, W.J. & van den Bos, J.	**3D INTERACTIVE COMPUTER GRAPHICS**
Tizzard, K.	**C FOR PROFESSIONAL PROGRAMMERS, 2nd Edition**
Tsuji, T.	**OPTIMIZING SCHEMES FOR STRUCTURED PROGRAMMING LANGUAGE PROCESSORS**
Whiddett, R.J.	**CONCURRENT PROGRAMMING FOR SOFTWARE ENGINEERS**
Whiddett, R.J., Berry, R.E., Blair, G.S., Hurley, P.N., Nicol, P.J. & Muir, S.J.	**UNIX**
Xu, Duan-Zheng	**COMPUTER ANALYSIS OF SEQUENTIAL MEDICAL TRIALS**
Zech, R.	**FORTH FOR THE PROFESSIONAL**

ELLIS HORWOOD SERIES IN COMPUTER COMMUNICATIONS AND NETWORKING

Series Editor: R.J. DEASINGTON, Principal Consultant, PA Consulting Group, Edinburgh, UK

Currie, W.S.	**LANS EXPLAINED**
Chiu, Dah Ming & Sudama, Ram	**NETWORK MONITORING EXPLAINED**
de Prycker, M.	**ASYNCHRONOUS TRANSFER MODE: Solution for Broadband ISDN, 2nd Edition**
Deasington, R.J.	**A PRACTICAL GUIDE TO COMPUTER COMMUNICATIONS AND NETWORKING, 2nd Edition**
Deasington, R.J.	**X.25 EXPLAINED, 2nd Edition**
Henshall, J.	**OPENING UP OSI: An Illustrated Introduction**
Henshall, J. & Shaw, S.	**OSI EXPLAINED, 2nd Edition**
Kauffels, F.-J.	**PRACTICAL LANS ANALYSED**
Kauffels, F.-J.	**PRACTICAL NETWORKS ANALYSED**
Kauffels, F.-J.	**UNDERSTANDING DATA COMMUNICATIONS**
Muftic, S.	**SECURITY MECHANISMS FOR COMPUTER NETWORKS**
Savikuya, B.	**PRINCIPLES OF PROTOCOL ENGINEERING & CONFORMANCE TESTING**